LEFT MARGINS

LEFT MARGINS

Cultural Studies and Composition Pedagogy

edited by
Karen Fitts and
Alan W. France

State University of New York Press

Donald Lazere's chapter, "Teaching the Conflicts about Wealth and Poverty," is a revised, expanded version of an earlier article, "Teaching the Political Conflicts: A Rhetorical Schema," *College Composition and Communication* 43 (1992), reprinted with permission of the National Council of Teachers of English. "Who Writes in a Cultural Studies Class? or, Where is the Pedagogy?" by Henry A. Giroux was printed as "Disturbing the Peace: Writing in the Cultural Studies Classroom" in *College Literature* 20.2 (June 1993). Mas'ud Zavarzadeh's "The Pedagogy of Pleasure 2: The Me-in-Crisis" appears in *College Literature* 21.3 (October 1994). We acknowledge the editor's kind permission to reprint.

Published by
State University of New York Press, Albany

For information, address the State University of New York Press, State University Plaza, Albany, NY 12246

Production by Christine Lynch
Marketing by Bernadette LaManna

Library of Congress Cataloging-in-Publication Data

Left margins : cultural studies and composition pedagogy / edited by
    Karen Fitts and Alan W. France.
        p. cm.
    Includes bibliographical references and index.
    ISBN 0-7914-2537-1. — ISBN 0-7914-2538-X (pbk.)
    1. English language—Composition and exercises—Study and
teaching. 2. English language—Rhetoric—Study and teaching.
3. Political correctness. 4. Language and culture. 5. Critical
pedagogy. I. Fitts, Karen, 1949– . II. France, Alan W.
PE1404.L44 1995
428'.007—dc20   94-32677
                                                         CIP

10 9 8 7 6 5 4 3 2 1

CONTENTS

PREFACE

Karen Fitts and Alan W. France ⸺⸺⸺⸺⸺⸺⸺

Left Margins began as a discussion of student evaluations. We found ourselves continually talking about student comments like "the class spent too much time on racist issues" and "there was too much about politics and not enough about writing." These comments echo recent criticism of (openly) "politicized pedagogy" from the right. Although we are convinced that there is no politically neutral or innocent way to teach (i.e., exert pedagogical authority), we realized we were failing to make manifest for many of our students the linkages between writing and cultural reproduction that recent theoretical work in rhetoric and composition has exposed. Analyzing student comments on evaluations, then (cf. Bauer), led us to formulate the problem as the general invisibility to students of the work of culture. Each semester, we have found ourselves plotting new pedagogical strategies to make students aware of the presence of ideology in their lives, to enable their reading and writing of powerful cultural texts, and to flag these texts as constructed, as not a part of the natural world, and therefore as susceptible to being reconstructed.[1] By inventing and refining writing assignments, we have worked to focus students' attention on culture as, in Fredric Jameson's words, "an objective mirage [or] . . . nimbus perceived by one group when it comes into contact with and observes another one" (33). Too often, this mirage or nimbus seems to them to be, plainly and simply, "the truth," or "nature," or "just the way things are."

In addition to tinkering with our own pedagogical strategies and tactics, we began to wonder how other teachers concerned with cultural politics conducted their classrooms. How does "progressive" writing instruction manifest itself at ground zero, in the pedagogical exchange between student-writer and composition teacher? How do other teachers teach students to engage important political issues

necessary to civic life in a democracy? Since openly political engagement offers excellent opportunities for teaching rhetoric and writing,
our conversation often turned to cultivating that moment of (sometimes profound) rhetorical conflict between the teacher's articulation
of an oppositional stance—an agenda that moves against the political
grain—and the student's resistance to it: how teachers prepare for
contention, generate it, receive it, and use it as a further teaching
occasion; how students respond to the teacher, each other, the texts,
and activities when asked to read culture critically.

In the spring of 1992, we began to circulate among colleagues at
professional conferences and in scholarly journals the following proposal:

> For a collection of essays tentatively entitled *Left Margins: Cultural
> Studies and Composition Pedagogy,* we are soliciting papers on practic-
> ing theoretically informed cultural criticism in the writing classroom.
> We're especially interested in exciting, "nuts-and-bolts"[2] strategies
> for teaching students to write critically about contemporary cultural
> media, thus developing awareness of their own ideological subjectiv-
> ity. Essays might move from theory to syllabus to assignment, ex-
> plaining what texts were used and in what way, how the pedagogy
> worked in practice, and how students responded. Our audience is
> primarily those who do the teaching of writing: GTA's, adjuncts, and
> younger regular faculty.

The proposal suggests a number of objectives that we shared as
editors and that should be made explicit. First and most obviously, we
wanted to offer a practical, pedagogical companion to recent volumes
theorizing oppositional possibilities, most notably Harkin and Schilb's
Contending with Words, Bullock and Trimbur's *The Politics of Writing
Instruction,* and Hurlbert and Blitz's *Composition and Resistance.* These
works have increased the sophistication of composition studies and
are highly suggestive to experienced writing teachers. However, we
imagined for the *Left Margins* project a voice more engaged with day-
to-day classroom exchanges. Our objective was to enrich the body of
theoretical work in composition studies by focusing on the *actualiza-
tion* of theory in practice—that is, by illuminating the shadowy nether
world where theory interacts with and informs real-world work: designing course syllabi and writing assignments, negotiating with students, and evaluating their work. We hope the collection will extend
the work begun by the second, more "hands-on," section of Berlin and
Vivion's *Cultural Studies in the English Classroom.*

We hope, therefore, that *Left Margins'* unique contribution will be
its close-up view of how teachers and students engage radical peda-

gogy (as Giroux uses that term). Because there already exist many fine articulations of theory about teaching writing, we asked contributors to focus on the classroom dialectic initiated by critical practice in confrontation with late-twentieth-century U.S. culture. We wanted to know, for example, how their assignments succeeded in light of their goals, which ones they regarded as less successful, and why. We asked them to show students dismissing their claims, or accepting them, or partially doing one or the other, and the instructor's responses to these developments. We requested that they consider why any one approach or sequence of approaches succeeded in breathing life into students' critical perspectives while others did not. How would they do things differently next time and why?

As a result, the essays in this volume are closely focused in on classroom exchange. Although the theories that undergird the pedagogy described here have generated intense debate (Hairston concisely documents rightists' objections), our contributors give scant attention in these pages to the swirl of contention outside their classrooms. They consistently highlight teacher-student interaction, rather than the larger dialectics of professional discourse. For discussions of the broader context in which contemporary classroom practices occur (particularly the notion of applying contemporary literary theory and cultural criticism to the teaching of composition), we refer readers to the many fine works that explore that terrain (see, for example, Easthope; Edsforth and Bennett; Ross; Giroux; and Grossberg, Nelson, and Treichler).

In addition to its focus on pedagogical practice, our call for papers reflected as well our persuasive intent: to make available compelling examples of writing instruction that facilitate political demystification and social change. Of course, placing the focus on *teaching* as a cultural practice is itself a political move; it reverses the invidious hierarchy that locates theory as an elite (read "masculine") intellectual prerogative and classroom practice as private (read "feminine") sphere bounded by, in Susan Miller's words, "the initiating care, pedagogic seduction, and practice for adulthood provided by nurses in bourgeois homes" (48). In other words, we hope to intervene in the tendency to reduce teaching to a set of "implications" that anyone can "apply" to the classroom or conference. Instead, we assume that pedagogies have theoretical implications with which our audience is already familiar, and that in this instance at least, we can reverse the polarity of the privileged theory/practice binary. Writing pedagogy steps forward as the social praxis of (too often empty or "unrealized") rhetorical theory and cultural criticism.

In the process of editing submissions to *Left Margins,* we became increasingly dissatisfied with limiting the project to the production of a political manifesto. The descriptions of and reflections on pedagogy we were reading demanded wider consideration than would be accorded to them in isolation from other perspectives. In an effort to contribute to contemporary debate on the politics of instruction, we set about creating a dialogue between our contributors and critics of oppositional pedagogy. It was at this point that Gary Tate and Gerald Graff agreed to critique the essays in parts 1 through 5. Later, the idea of counterresponses was suggested to us by an anonymous reviewer of the manuscript (who described the critiques as "shooting fish in a barrel").

With the addition of part 6, the comments and counterstatements, *Left Margins* fully realizes its title's implied dialectic: for only in their contention with a "center" (a status quo) do positions become more or less "left" (or for that matter "right"). In these pages, therefore, the central point of dispute in composition studies becomes overt: it is the containment or extension of "writing" as the subject of pedagogy.

Those who want to stabilize the meaning of writing conceive of it as individual expression or as individual control over discursive conventions. For them, the aims of writing instruction are unproblematic and inherently liberating: to facilitate the individual's growth as a self-conscious, reflective person and a useful, productive citizen. Because the composing process is focused on the individual, it is seen as apolitical. As a result, the knowledges deemed most appropriate to "composition" are those necessary for students to realize private objectives (although those private objectives may articulate political conviction). To require a critical approach or to stipulate a topic that students would find uninteresting or uncomfortable is, for those who defend a traditional view of composition, to introduce a political agenda into what is essentially a private and therefore primarily an apolitical engagement with language. (See Hairston, Stotsky, and especially Phelps, who argues explicitly for "A Constrained Vision of the Writing Classroom.")

In parts 1 through 5, contributors to this volume reject the "constrained" view of composition. Rather they seek to extend in some way the definition of writing to include its social and cultural context. "Writing" cannot be isolated from the communal work that it accomplishes and out of which it grows. This means that culture coauthors each text, rendering chimerical the claim that individuals freely choose meanings to encode in writing. The contentious quality of *Left Margins* represents this more basic dispute over what constitutes "writing," suggesting that the process of writing is itself a dialectical act, originating in, reformulating, and redirecting contradiction.

The subtitle of this collection, *Cultural Studies and Composition Theory*, implies a family relationship between these trans- or postdisciplinary fields of study. It reflects a search for writing pedagogy capable of challenging the "squeamishness about worldly matters of power [that] still infuses even leading scholarship in composition" (Schilb 179). For a number of our contributors, "cultural studies" is a rhetorical strategy for opening the classroom door to (post)Marxist criticism, invested as Gramscian "hegemony," Bourdieu's concept of education as reproduction of cultural capital, Althusserian interpellation of subjects by "IGAs," or Raymond Williams's "cultural materialism," among other elaborations of Marx and Engels (Brantlinger 85–101, Johnson, Murphy). As we intend the term in our subtitle, however, "cultural studies" signifies a wide range of critical practices from mainstream communication and media studies to a fairly rigorous historical materialism.

The emergence in American universities of cultural studies as a postdisciplinary model of inquiry suggests a way for composition, itself a post- (or at least trans-) disciplinary field, to address the absence of "culture" as an intellectual category in the culture of North America, and to dissolve at last the false dichotomy, as we see it, of process (or skill) and content (Trimbur, Schilb). There is no writing that is not an act of cultural articulation. Like most of the contributors to *Left Margins*, we reject the idea that language is a property of individual writers, who choose their beliefs and behaviors as voluntarily and as freely as they "choose their own words."

In the opening section, Henry Giroux "appropriates" pedagogy for cultural studies, arguing against "the general indifference by many theorists to the importance of pedagogy as a form of cultural practice" (4). But this appropriation cuts both ways: composition practitioners have in general avoided cultural studies' postdisciplinary insights into the discursive formation of composing subjects. It is this "[b]order writing . . . as a form of cultural production and pedagogical practice" (16) that will allow composition, as a critical educational practice, to appropriate cultural studies by finally resolving distinctions between form or process of writing and content. From another perspective, Alan Kennedy feels his way toward a middle ground between the political and the polemical. For him, writing belongs to "[t]he realms of production" (18). It is inherently political (in a way that reflection

is not) because the very act of producing communicable meaning requires that individual experience "occupy ... public space" (36).

The contributors to part 2, "Expropriating the Powers of Language,"
attempt in their pedagogy to refigure the relationship between written
discourse and material culture. Joseph C. Bodziock and Christopher
Ferry characterize themselves as "tricksters" uncovering the "culturally 'sacred' " (43), violating "the perceived order of things" (44) that
empower and marginalize, and enacting a frightening "culture-in-
progress." In her explorations of the half-lit graveyard of cultural
mythos, Colleen M. Tremonte recounts her invitation to students—in
conjunction with and sanctioned by classical stasis theory—to raise "a
fine din tumbling linguistic tombstones and profaning cultural icons"
(67). For Paul Gutjahr, housebuilding is the metaphor for teaching
how (or at least *that*) "ideas manifest themselves in material ways"
(70). Students explore "signifying systems ... by studying tangible
examples of material culture": home construction (70). Finally, Keith
D. Miller, Gerardo de los Santos, and Ondra Witherspoon show how
literate practices constrain social meanings by "de-producing" the overt
politics of Martin Luther King, Jr., and how pedagogy might recover the
rhetorical power and political immediacy or "reality" of the oral text.

Writers in part 3, "(Re)Writing Cultural Texts," narrate their
engagement of students in analyses of popular culture. Kathleen
Dixon examines with her students their responses to female and
male rap musicians; as they contemplate Queen Latifah's performance in light of acts staged by 2 Live Crew or Yo-Yo and Ice
Cube, the students learn to recognize discursive behaviors that
preserve gender inequities: repression, universalizing, and binary
thinking. Todd Sformo and Barbara Tudor take their students behind the television lineup on Monday evenings to assess the roles
of technology and commentator reportage in manipulating, rather
than merely facilitating (in an ideologically innocent way), viewers'
experience of televised football. Christopher Wise uses Paul Ruben's
Pee-Wee's Playhouse as the pre/text for students to interrogate the
"nature" of sexual identity and orientation. His objective is "to
undermine traditional gender-roles ... [and] to alert students to their
own ideological subjectivity ... as 'gendered' subjects" (129).

Authors in part 4, "Practicing Rhetorics," describe courses in which
content and practice are conflated. Rae Rosenthal combines feminist
issues in rhetoric with feminist pedagogy. Offering students an opportunity to become "bilingual" in masculine and feminine modes of
discourse not only makes them "more sophisticated writers" but also

engages students for a semester with a "thought provoking and . . . potentially reformative" topic (140). Peter J. Caulfield believes that "a more comprehensive and powerful conception of rhetoric . . . ought to fundamentally alter how we actually teach writing" (157–58), and so he blends rhetorical practice in his classes with instruction in the ways in which "language (and everything that might augment it, such as color, music, or graphics) functions rhetorically to shape . . . our views of reality" (170). Raymond A. Mazurek initiates students into academic discourse by teaching and modeling Paulo Freire's Brazilian literacy experiments; a central tenet of his classes is the paradox that "[u]niversities are conflictive sites of power which often underwrite the status quo, but they are also places where traditions of critical thought create space for . . . self-reflective analyses of power" (175). Donald Lazere fuses instruction in critical research methods with explicit information on a range of partisan political positions. His goal, "to broaden the ideological scope of students' critical thinking, reading, and writing capacities" (190), is informed by "the need to counteract the deemphasis of politics, the absence of systematic exposition of a full spectrum of ideologies, and the atomized discourses that fragment American culture and education" (190–91).

While the material objectives of change envisioned by contributors to part 5, "Teaching for Social Change," differ, each constructs her or his writing class as a step—no matter how preliminary—toward social justice and equality. For Adam Katz, writing is the means to "sustained critiques of the hegemony exercised throughout everyday life" (211). Through critique of the university as an authoritarian institution (the rhetorical analysis of university documents, for example) and of the interests it serves, Katz exposes the inherent conflict between the ideology of educational emancipation and the training of literate workers in a capitalist system of production. Mas'ud Zavarzadeh admonishes a student who has suffered a "personal crisis" to work toward critical understanding of the relationship between this affective *experience* and the social and historical causes of such crises. Only by a social(ist) transformation (democratizing ownership of productive wealth) can the individual-in-crisis be relieved. Richard, the subject of Mary Beth Hines's qualitative case study, shares the emancipatory objectives of Katz and Zavarzadeh. As Hines's ethnography makes clear, Richard's pedagogy has as its object the defamiliarization (and eventual rejection) of the "imaginary relations" of the individual for "the real conditions of existence" (in Althusser's terms). Through critical study of cultural products (like the *OED*),

Richard attempts to intervene in the social construction of dominant ideology. Bob Nowlan makes a case for dealing directly and openly with racism in the writing classroom. In response to his interlocutor (June), Nowlan argues against the liberal doctrine of gradual amelioration, advocating instead "contestation" of racist positions and critical examination of advantages racism confers on whites (including liberals). Finally, John C. Hawley considers what the legacy of the Society of Jesus might contribute to politically liberating writing instruction. Traditions of Jesuit education, he argues, authorize the practices demanded of multicultural and postcolonial worlds.

The dialectical turn of part 6 exposes the political conflict inherent in the cultural work of teaching composition: Gary Tate and Gerald Graff critique the work of contributors in parts 1 through 5; a number of those contributors then counter with critiques of Tate and Graff; we step in with an evaluation of the basic issue of the politics of writing instruction; and the volume concludes with an overall appraisal, Richard Ohmann's "Afterword."

Although it's always difficult to remember everyone who has participated in a work so collaborative as this, we would like to mention a few of those whose help was particularly timely. (As Huey Long is reported to have said in thanking contributors, "Those who gave in the primary get jobs; those who gave in the election get good government.") In ways that we can't easily articulate because they are so bound up with all of our thinking about rhetoric and writing instruction, Vivienne Anderson has helped shape this project. Henry Giroux and Richard Ohmann gave us early and invaluable encouragement. Others who offered helpful criticism and to whom we owe special thanks are the late James Berlin, Dale Bauer, Chris Weedon, James Sosnoski, David Downing, Bruce Herzberg, and Min-Zhan Lu. We're also greatly indebted to Gerald Graff and Gary Tate, whose critical responses made this volume genuinely dialectical. Priscilla Ross, our editor at SUNY Press, Don Lloyd, Elizabeth Larsen, and anonymous reviewers gave us provocative and insightful criticism, for which we're grateful. Karen Fitts thanks Loyola College in Maryland for generous financial support. And to the original contributors to *Left Margins*, we thank you not only for your patient cooperation but also, and especially, for teaching us new ways of working for social change.

PART I

Appropriating Pedagogy

1

Who Writes in a Cultural Studies Class? or, Where Is the Pedagogy?

Henry A. Giroux _____

It is becoming increasingly more difficult to assess what cultural studies is either as a political project or as a postdisciplinary practice.[1] For some theorists, it is precisely the emergence of cultural studies outside of the university and its articulation with various social movements such as feminism, rather than its academic location, that have helped to prevent it from being incorporated into the university as merely an additive to the established canon.[2] For others, cultural studies must be developed with regard not only to the changing nature and specificity of the problems and conflicts it addresses, but also to the legacy of its history as a preeminently political and oppositional practice.[3]

It is not my intention here to replay the debate regarding the real history of cultural studies, though this is an important issue. Instead, I want to analyze how certain features of the history of cultural studies might inform its present and future politics. More specifically, I want to focus on the importance of pedagogy as a central aspect of cultural studies and writing as a pedagogical practice. In doing so, I want to develop a notion of border writing as a form of cultural production forged among the shifting borderlands of a politics of representation, identity, and struggle. In part, I am concerned with a notion of cultural recovery in which the production of knowledge, subjectivity, and agency can be addressed as ethical, political, and pedagogical issues. In part, this suggests critically appropriating from cultural studies the insights it has accrued as it has moved historically from its narrow concerns with class and language to its more recent analysis of the politics of race, gender, and colonialism. This is not meant to suggest that the history of cultural studies needs to be laid out in great detail as some sort of foundational exegesis. On the contrary, cultural studies needs to be approached historically as a mix of founding moments, transformative challenges, and self-critical interrogations (Nelson 32). It is precisely the rupturing spirit informing elements of its postdisciplinary practice, social activism, and historical awareness that prompts my concern for the current lacunae in cultural studies regarding the theoretical and political importance of pedagogy as a founding moment in its legacy. At the same time, it is important to stress that the general indifference of many theorists to pedagogy as a form of cultural practice does an injustice to the politically charged legacy of cultural studies, one that points to the necessity for combining self-criticism with a commitment to transforming existing social and political problems.

Neither critical educators nor cultural studies theorists can ignore the relationship of pedagogy to cultural studies in the current historical juncture. Indeed, such indifference warrants a deep suspicion of the viability of the political project that informs such a view of cultural studies. Central to my analysis as well as to the politics of my own location as a teacher and cultural worker is the assumption that cultural studies must be grounded, in part, in a project that deepens and expands the possibilities for radical democracy both in the United States and abroad. Democracy in this sense is the discursive face and lived experiences of struggling to expand the conditions for social justice, freedom, and equality across all the major political and economic spheres that shape, position, and locate people in everyday life. It is within this project that I want to address the importance of writing and pedagogy as central elements of an insurgent cultural studies.

In what follows, I want to argue that while cultural studies represents an ensemble of diverse discourses, it is an important historical, political, and cultural formation that points to a number of issues that need to be addressed in pedagogical terms. I then want to provide a rationale for re-inserting the language of pedagogy and politics back into the discourse of cultural studies as part of a broader attempt to expand and deepen what I will call a pedagogy of cultural studies. Finally, I will explore how I take up the issue of pedagogy as a cultural practice through the use of writing in my class. In part, this section not only discusses border writing as a form of pedagogical practice, but also suggests a connection between some of the central themes of cultural studies and writing as a cultural practice.

Cultural Studies and the Absence of Pedagogy

It is generally argued that cultural studies is largely defined through its analysis of the interrelationship between culture and power, particularly with regard to the production, reception, and diverse use of texts. Texts in this case constitute a wide range of aural, visual, and printed signifiers. These are often taken up as part of a broader attempt to analyze how individual and social identities are mobilized, engaged, and transformed within circuits of power informed by issues of race, gender, class, ethnicity, and other social formations. All of these concerns point to the intellectual and institutional borders that police, contain, and engage meaning as a site of social struggle. Moreover, one of the emerging theoretical features of cultural studies is to refute the notion that the struggle over meaning is primarily about the struggle over language and textuality.[4] On the contrary, a number of cultural studies theorists have named terror and oppression, in concrete terms and have addressed how domination is manifested in a variety of sites, on a number of different levels, and how it can be understood in historical and relational terms through a variety of articulations and categories.[5] In fact, cultural studies draws its theoretical inspiration from feminism, postmodernism, postcolonialism, and a host of other areas. Lawrence Grossberg claims that cultural studies as a strategic practice performs two functions: first, it keeps alive the importance of political work in an "age of diminishing possibilities." That is, it radicalizes the notion of hope by politicizing rather than romanticizing it. Second, it refuses to immobilize a commitment to political work in the frozen theoretical winter of orthodoxy. By responding to the specificity of history it leaves open the political cartography that informs how it names both its own strategies and the "world of political struggle" (*We Gotta Get Out* 18). For Grossberg, the notion that cultural studies is unstable, open, and always contested becomes the basis for its rewriting as both the condition for ideological self-criticism and constructing social agents within rather than outside historical struggles. Grossberg writes:

> [C]ultural studies assumes that history—its shape, its seams, its outcomes—is never guaranteed. As a result, doing cultural studies takes work, including the kind of work deciding what cultural studies is, of making cultural studies over again and again. Cultural studies constructs itself as it faces new questions and takes up new positions. In that sense, doing cultural studies is always risky and never totally comfortable. It is fraught with inescapable tensions (as well as with

real pleasures). In the U.S., the rapid institutional success of cultural studies has made it all a bit too easy. Cultural studies has to be wary of anything that makes its work too easy, that erases the real battles, both theoretical and political, that have to be waged, that defines the answers before it even begins. (18–19)

I want to take Grossberg at his word and argue that cultural studies is still too rigidly tied to the modernist, academic disciplinary structures that it often criticizes. This is not to suggest that it does not adequately engage the issue of academic disciplines. In fact, this is one of its most salient characteristics.[6] What it fails to do is critically address a major prop of disciplinarity, which is the notion of pedagogy as an unproblematic vehicle for transmitting knowledge. Lost here is the attempt to understand pedagogy as a mode of cultural criticism for questioning the very conditions under which knowledge and identities are produced. Of course, theorists such as Larry Grossberg, Stanley Aronowitz, and others do engage the relationship between cultural studies and pedagogy, but they constitute a small minority.[7] The haunting issue here is, what is it about pedagogy that allows cultural studies theorists to ignore it?

One answer may lie in the refusal of cultural studies theorists either to take schooling seriously as a site of struggle or to probe how traditional pedagogy produces particular forms of subjectification, how it constructs students through a range of subject positions. Of course, within radical educational theory, there is a long history of developing critical discourses of the subject around pedagogical issues.[8]

Another reason cultural studies theorists have devoted little attention to pedagogy may be the disciplinary terrorism that leaves the marks of its legacy on all areas of the humanities and liberal arts. Pedagogy is often deemed unworthy of being taken up as a serious subject. Even popular culture has more credibility than pedagogy. This can be seen not only in the general absence of any discussion of pedagogy in cultural studies texts, but also in those studies in the humanities that have begun to engage pedagogical issues. Even in these works there is a willful refusal to acknowledge some of the important theoretical gains in pedagogy that have been made in the last twenty years.[9] Within this silence lurk the imperatives of a disciplinary policing, a refusal to cross academic borders, and a shoring up of the imperatives of originality, competitiveness, and elitism. Of course, composition studies, one of the few fields in the humanities that does take pedagogy seriously, occupies a status as disparaged as the field of education.[10] The legacy of academic elitism and professionalism still exercises a strong influence in the field of cultural studies, in spite of its alleged democratization of social knowledge.

Reclaiming Pedagogy

In making my case for the importance of pedagogy as a central aspect of cultural studies, I first want to analyze the role that pedagogy played in the early founding stages of the Birmingham Centre for Cultural Studies. I then want to define more specifically the central dimensions of pedagogy as a cultural practice. But before I address these two important moments of critical pedagogy as a form of cultural politics, I think it is important to stress that the concept of pedagogy must be used with respectful caution. Not only are there different versions of what constitutes critical pedagogy, but there is no generic definition that can be applied to the term. At the same time, there are important theoretical insights and practices that weave through various approaches to critical pedagogy. It is precisely these insights, which often define a common set of problems, that serve to delineate critical pedagogy as a set of conditions articulated within the context of a particular political project—a project that takes up these problems differently within the specificity of particular contexts. These problems include but are not limited to the relationships between knowledge and power, language and experience, ethics and authority, student agency and transformative politics, and teacher location and student formations.

This is precisely how Raymond Williams addressed the issue of pedagogy in his discussion of the emergence of cultural studies in Britain. For Williams, pedagogy offered the opportunity to link cultural practice with the development of radical cultural theories. Not only did pedagogy connect questions of form and content, it also introduced a sense of how teaching, learning, textual studies, and knowledge could be addressed as a political issue that foregrounded considerations of power and social agency. According to Williams, cultural studies in the 1930s and 1940s emerged directly from the pedagogical work that was going on in Adult Education. The specificity of the content and context of adult education provided cultural studies with a number of issues that were to direct its subsequent developments in Birmingham. These included the refusal to accept the limitations of established academic boundaries and power structures, the demand for linking literature to the life situations of the adult learners, and the call that schooling be empowering rather than merely humanizing. Williams is quite adamant in refuting "encyclopedia articles dating the birth of cultural studies from this or that book in the late 'fifties." He goes on to say that:

> the shift of perspective about the teaching of art and literature and their relation to history and to contemporary society began in Adult Education, it didn't happen anywhere else. It was when it was taken across by people with that experience to the Universities that it was suddenly recognized as a subject. It is in these and other similar ways that the contribution of the process itself to social change itself, and specifically to learning, has happened. ("Adult Education"; see also "Future" 151–62)

For Williams there is more at stake here than reclaiming the history of cultural studies. He is most adamant in making clear that the "deepest impulse [informing cultural studies] was the desire to make learning part of the process of social change itself" ("Future" 158). It is precisely this attempt to broaden the notion of the political by making it more pedagogical that reminds us of the importance of pedagogy as a cultural practice. In this context, pedagogy deepens and extends the study of culture and power by addressing not only how culture is shaped, produced, circulated, and transformed, but also how it is actually taken up by human beings within specific settings and circumstances. It becomes an act of cultural production, a form of "writing" in which the process by which power is inscribed on the body and implicated in the production of desire, knowledge, and values begins not with a particular claim to postdisciplinary knowledge but with real people articulating and rewriting their lived experiences within, rather than outside, history.

The importance of pedagogy to the content and context of cultural studies lies in the relevance it has for illuminating how knowledge and subjectivities are produced in a variety of sites including schools. Pedagogy, in this sense, offers an articulatory concept for understanding how power and knowledge configure in the production, reception, and transformation of subject positions, forms of ethical address, and "desired versions of a future human community" (Simon 15). By refuting the objectivity of knowledge and asserting the partiality of all forms of pedagogical authority, critical pedagogy initiates an inquiry into the relationship between cultural work, authority, and the securing of particular cultural practices, and as a mode of cultural politics takes as an object of study the relationship between the possibilities for social agency expressed in a range of human capacities and the social forms that often constrain or enable them.

The politics of critical pedagogy are radical but not doctrinaire. That is, critical pedagogy self-consciously operates from a perspective in which teaching and learning are committed to expanding rather than restricting the opportunities for students and others to be social, political, and economic agents. As agents, students and others need to learn how to take risks, to understand how power works differently as both a productive and dominating force, to be able to "read" the world from a variety of perspectives, and to be willing to think beyond the commonsense assumptions that govern everyday existence. Critical pedagogy engages experience in order to inquire into the conditions of its production, authorization, and effects. What is radical about the relationship between pedagogy and the issue of experience is that it addresses the inner workings of experience, how it functions to produce knowledge, and how it might be implicated in the construction of forms of subjectification. Politicizing the relationship between thought and experience points to a pedagogical practice in which cultural workers can offer "questions, analyses, visions and practical options that people can pursue in their attempts to participate in the determination of various aspects of their lives. . . . Required is a practice rooted in an ethical-political vision that attempts to take people beyond the world they already know but in a way that does not insist on a fixed set of altered meanings" (Simon 46–47).

Defined as an attempt to alter experience in the interest of expanding the possibilities for human agency and social justice, critical pedagogy makes visible the need for social relations that inform a number of considerations that cut across the diverse terrain of cultural studies.

Writing as a Pedagogical Practice

In what follows, I want to describe how I use writing as a pedagogical practice to transgress certain dominant assumptions about the meaning of schooling, the discourse of authority, the relationship between language and experience, and the role of social responsibility within the politics of my own location as a university teacher. Most of the classes I teach at Penn State University are graduate courses in education and cultural studies. The students who take my courses are mostly working-class males and females, generally between the ages of 25 and 60. Very few of the students are familiar with the theoretical discourses of cultural studies and critical pedagogy. In the past, I have tried to organize my courses around selected critical texts, combining introductory lectures with a seminar format in which students were asked to engage the texts actively by reading them oppositionally. Though this approach attempted to make the class more democratic, it failed to unsettle the kinds of social relations that characterize teacher-centered environments. The reasons are numerous and they include the following. First, many students felt intimidated by the language of theory. They often noted at some point in the class that the assigned texts were too difficult to read, they didn't understand their practical application to education, or they simply did not feel comfortable speaking through a discourse that seemed foreign to them. Second, many students have not problematized the ways in which traditional schooling has shaped their perceptions of power, learning, and identity. Many of the students in my classes believed that either their own voices did not count for much or that the only role for students in the class was to accept what was dispensed to them as knowledge rather than either raise questions about taking control over the conditions of the production of knowledge or engage the classroom texts critically in light of their own experiences, histories, and concerns. Thirdly, whenever class discussion did occur it was more often than not dominated by males, especially white males, in spite of the fact that women often constituted over 50 percent of my classes. Moreover, when students did speak they often looked at me rather than direct their remarks to other students. In this instance, they were positioning me as the authorizing agent for their discourse and for some feedback.

It became clear to me very quickly that in spite of my use of oppositional material and the seminar format of the class, I was reproducing a set of pedagogical relations that did not decenter authority, that, on the contrary, undermined my efforts both to provide students with the opportunity to speak in a safe space and to appropriate power in the class in order to deconstruct the texts and engage in collective self-criticism and a critique of the politics of my location as a teacher.

In the first semester of the 1992–1993 school year, I taught a new course called "Postcolonialism, Race, and Critical Pedagogy." In this course, I attempted to address some of the above problems by organizing a series of pedagogical practices around particular writing assignments that helped to create what can be called, to use Homi Bhabha's phrase, a "third space" in the classroom. But before I articulate the specifics of the pedagogical practices that I employed, I want to mention a specific tension that I had to address in the classroom and in my own teaching.

Like many teachers, academics, and other cultural workers, I felt that the most substantive aspect of my pedagogy centered on defining my own goals for education along with the politics of my own location as a teacher. For example, my overriding pedagogical project was rooted in an attempt at majority democratic education, that is, an education whose aim was to advance the ideological and lived relations necessary for students at least to interrogate the possibility of addressing schooling as a site of ongoing struggle over the "social and political task of transformation, resistance, and radical democratization" (Butler 13). This is a project that has continually driven my own politics and pedagogy regardless of the specific courses I have taught in the university. In looking back at this project, I have fewer reservations about its political importance than I do about the pedagogical practice of removing it from the actual social formations that shaped students' histories and lived experiences, which served to undo its most promising possibilities. In other words, by not paying more attention to what it meant to give students more control over the conditions of their own knowledge production, I reproduced the binarism of being politically enlightened in my theorizing and pedagogically wrong in my organization of concrete class relations. Overcoming this binarism was a major goal behind the reorganization of my pedagogy in the "Postcolonialism, Race, and Critical Pedagogy" class. Developing a series of reading and writing activities as the basis of the new course helped me to work through and resist the negative effects of my own authority as a teacher. In what follows, I want to spell out how I used border writing less as technical exercise in skill development than as a form of cultural production that more closely articulated the relationship between my political project as a progressive teacher and the underlying principles and practices that informed the organization and character of my class.

My use of writing assignments was closely linked to getting students to theorize their own experiences rather than articulate the meaning of other peoples' theories. The assignments were designed to get students to examine how representations signify and position students through the institutional and ideological authority they carry in the dominant culture. Moreover, the writing assignments were constructed so as to give students the opportunity to acknowledge their own emotional and affective investments in issues regarding race, colonialism, and the politics of representation. In addition, writing was used not merely as an ideological marker for locating specific biographical interests and forms of identification; it was also viewed as a rupturing practice, as an oppositional pedagogy in which one pushes against the grain of traditional history, disciplinary structures, dominant readings, and existing relations of power.

Raymond Williams has rightly pointed out the need for cultural workers to be attentive to the formations out of which specific projects arise. As part of an attempt not to reproduce the legacy of those pedagogical practices that positioned students as objects rather than as subjects of learning, I attempted to organize the writing assignments in my seminar around a number of structuring principles necessary for the success of my own political and pedagogical project. For instance, I introduced the course by talking about power in the classroom and how it was implicated in all aspects of classroom teaching, including the development of a syllabus, the organization of classroom relations, and the method of evaluation. I also made clear the rationale for the authority I exercised in the course and how that authority was intended to be used to expand rather than restrict the possibility for student agency. In part, I made the form and content of my authority as a teacher visible in order to problematize and debate the moral vision and social ethic I used to justify my organization of the syllabus and the pedagogical practices that informed my class.

In doing so, I relinquished all claims to objectivity, and I attempted to refute the traditional notion that teachers were disinterested, that knowledge was unproblematic, and that teaching was merely a methodology for transmitting information to students. I argued that the latter positions were often used to obscure the ideological and political interests that regulated dominant versions of schooling and the role that teachers play in actively regulating the production of knowledge and values. By presenting a view of schools as a site of conflict and contestation, I attempted to open a space for students to engage political, social, and cultural differences in ways that highlighted pedagogy as an oppositional rather than merely a dominating practice.

In addition, I stressed the need for social relations in the class that would give students the opportunity to produce and appropriate knowledge as part of an ongoing struggle to represent themselves in terms of their interests, lived experiences, and wider political concerns. Two issues derived from the more political and emancipatory theoretical insights of cultural studies guided my pedagogical concerns. First, I wanted to make clear that no pedagogical process could be located outside of the intellectual and affective investments I brought to the class. Hence, the politics of my own location had to be subjected to extensive critique and dialogue in the written assignment and class debates. Second, the class had to become a site where writing offered the opportunity to "engage rather than displace the voices of aggressive, theorizing subjects [students]."[11] I further suggested that some of the major elements structuring teacher-student relations in the class would be taken up around some of the following considerations: How do language and experience intersect? That is, how do different discourses shape, engage, and deconstruct the experiences and stories told by ourselves and others? Second, what conditions are necessary to develop a sense of political, moral, and social agency in the class? For example, what pedagogical practices might be necessary to promote collaborative work? To engage dominant and subordinate traditions critically? To get students to question the partiality of both their own knowledge and the knowledge presented by the teacher? Third, how might teacher authority be manifested without being inimical to the issue and practice of student freedom?

By making my own theoretical and pedagogical concerns visible at the beginning of the course, I attempt to be up front about the parameters of the course, especially in a school of education where students often believe that they will not have to read intellectually challenging work or that educational theory is mainly about learning methodologies. But there is more at stake here than exercising authority in the spirit of promoting rigorous intellectual work and providing a call for self-discipline. I also posit the goals and project of the course as an invitation for the students to rethink how they might want to take up and transform certain aspects of their own learning. For instance, in an effort not to remove all traces of their own socially constructed voices, I asked students to form groups after my introductory remarks in order to respond to the issues I raised. I was particularly interested in whether the principles and rationale I offered for the course were suitable to their own perception of the course. I also invited the students to suggest specific readings outside of the assigned texts that we might take up in the class.

Within an hour the students convened their respective groups and a debate took place over the shape and format of the class. It became instantly clear to me that the students also wanted the class to be participatory, critical, and attentive to immediate and global concerns regarding racial politics, and that they wanted both to provide their own list of readings for the course and to evaluate their own performance for a course grade. Gently exercising my own authority I mediated their concerns with three qualifications. First, I suggested that the course had to be organized around a series of writing assignments that reproduced the principles they had articulated in the discussion. Second, in order to relieve the immediate fear that students often express about writing in a class, I suggested that as a major precondition for discussing the student writing presented to the class it was imperative for all of us to create the conditions for a "safe space" for each other. This means that since students often feel that their identities are on trial when they either speak from their writing or share it with the rest of the class, it is imperative that each student be given every opportunity to speak, argue, take risks, and position him/herself without fear of intimidation, humiliation, or outright pedagogical terrorism from either the teacher or other students. In this case, issues of trust and respect for difference become paramount in structuring classroom relations. In addition, it was suggested that every attempt be made to use student writing as a pedagogical tool to present one's theoretical position, to promote class discussions, to engage other texts, and to work collaboratively with others. Third, while they would be given the opportunity to evaluate their own final projects, the projects should be organized around an attempt to integrate the theoretical discourses taken up in the class with an analysis of some aspect of popular culture. For example, an individual or a group might decide to write about how the legacy of colonialism frames much of the racial discourse in a film like *Grand Canyon*. Students might also want to mix media in compiling a critical commentary on racism in the university, town, or in the national media. They might also want to focus on popular magazines as a source of social knowledge, use ethnographic approaches to conducting oral histories, or construct their own video, etc.

As part of an attempt to pay close attention to the political and pedagogical dynamics that structured the class, three major writing assignments were used to organize how texts were to be taken up and rewritten as part of a larger attempt to register differences, analyze diverse arguments, and cross disciplinary borders.

The writing assignments were organized in the following ways. The initial three weeks of the course were developed around analyzing the reading material largely selected by the class. The readings were taken up through the thematics of "Orientalism, Difference, and Multiculturalism," "Postcolonialism, Race, and Feminism," and "Nationalism and the Politics of Speaking for Others." The class was divided into three groups. Each group was assigned the task of developing position paper(s) on the readings for one of the three themes. The papers would then be duplicated for the rest of the class and used as a basis for class discussion.

Each group worked collaboratively to produce a paper that was duplicated and read by the rest of the class the evening their respective reading assignment was due. The group assigned to present a paper for that class first talked about how they came to address a particular aspect of the assignment, how they worked out the collaborative process, and why they thought the issues they addressed were important to them in terms of their own experiences. For example, the first group developed a paper that was a transcript of a dialogue they collectively held in analyzing certain aspects of the readings on Orientalism and the politics of multiculturalism. The paper clearly demonstrated those issues over which individual members of the group disagreed, what concerns they shared, and what questions they wanted to take up with the rest of the class. It is important to note that students who did not present a group paper during any one class meeting had to prepare journal entries on the readings assigned, and in doing so worked from their own notes in responding to both the group paper and other questions that arose from the readings. Since the readings ranged from sources as diverse as Cornel West's "The New Politics of Difference" to Diane Ravitch's "Multiculturalism," there was a range of ideological positions to engage and make for a lively discussion.

But in discussing the papers the emphasis was not merely on taking up conflicting positions. Students had to insert themselves into the texts by taking a position on the readings, talking about the consequences of their positions in terms of how they addressed questions of race, freedom, justice, and so on. Moreover, the group constantly talked about how the university itself was implicated in reproducing some of the racial problems they discussed and how the racial problems in the school articulated with and mutually reinforced larger societal problems.

During the second part of the course, students paired up in groups of two and for the remainder of the course each group taught a particular text that was assigned for any one particular week. Books discussed ranged from *There Ain't No Black in the Union Jack* by Paul Gilroy to *Black Looks* by bell hooks and *Learning to Question* by Paulo Freire and Antonio Faundez. In this assignment, students had to "write" the book; that is, they had to present a paper that provided an exegesis, offer a critical reading of the text's major assumptions, and analyze the relevance of the text to their own experiences as future educators. Moreover, they could present the analysis in a variety of mixed formats but had to use a substantial portion of their time for dialogue with the rest of the class. The presentations were on the whole amazingly imaginative. Most students combined a short lecture with some other form of media to illustrate their analysis of the texts. Most prepared open questions to partly structure the debates, and in some cases provided the rest of the class with alternative or supplementary readings.

The third writing assignment was organized around a collaborative position paper based on applying some aspect of what they learned about race and pedagogy in the class to a particular problem in the wider university community. The activities undertaken ranged from an analysis of the textbooks used in the local secondary school to an interrogation of the racial sensitivity seminars conducted by some faculty in the university. In each case, the students had little trouble in applying some of the theoretical issues they addressed in the class to wider practical and pedagogical concerns.

The final writing project in the class engaged writing as a pedagogical practice by getting students not only to analyze popular texts that extend the range of what constitutes social knowledge but also to be self-reflective about their own engagement with the course and what its implications were for rethinking the ways in which power works through diverse regimes of representation, institutional structures, and the larger spaces of social power.

All of these writing assignments positioned students as cultural producers and enabled them to rewrite their own experiences and perceptions through an engagement with various texts, ideological positions, and theories. In all cases, there was an ongoing attempt to get the students to learn from each other, to decenter the power in the classroom, to challenge disciplinary borders, to create a borderland where new hybridized identities might emerge, to take up in a problematic way the relationship between language and experience, and to appropriate knowledge as part of a broader effort at self-definition and ethical responsibility. Border writing in this case became a type of hybridized, border literacy, a form of cultural production and pedagogical practice where otherness becomes comprehensible, collective memory rewrites the narratives of insurgent social movements, and students travel between diverse theoretical and cultural zones of difference, and, in doing so, generate a space where new intersections between identity and culture emerge. It is precisely in this space informed by the critical imperatives of cultural studies, the ongoing demands of a restless critical pedagogy, and faith in a project of possibility that teachers and students can rewrite, reaffirm, and struggle over the assumption that the goal of achieving a multicultural, multiracial democracy in the United States remains the critical issue of modern politics and life.

2

Politics, Writing, Writing Instruction, Public Space, and the English Language

Alan Kennedy _____

What follows, it will be clear, reflects my own disturbances about the politics of the academy and of writing teaching. I trace a path through several related issues in an attempt to find a way to teach writing as if writing were something that could be political in itself, without at the same time being forced to find myself committed to a pedagogy that merely indoctrinates students. I attempt to find a way to a writing that is responsibly political as opposed to being apolitical. I attempt, therefore, to find a way of talking about teaching writing that can be socially responsible without having to be found in allegiance with any specific political agenda. So, while I shall be somewhat at odds with a notion that writing should be taught from any political margin, left or right, I work toward a vision of teaching that furthers a progressive social understanding, and if that understanding is not on the margin in hoping to be closer to a center, it will probably be found to be somewhat to the left of a liberal center.

Much as I might wish for a more muscular definition of politics, I shall have to be satisfied with one I borrow from Roland Barthes's *Mythologies*. I can confess that it comes from perhaps the weakest part of that book: his attempt to find a language within language that is "other" than that language, when he talks of a really transitive kind of speech. He speculates about a wood-cutter "naming" the tree as he fells it and believes he has found some kind of ur–speech act, for "whatever the form of my sentence, I 'speak the tree,' I do not speak about it" (145).

As apparently naive as this might seem, it does perhaps have an idea at its heart (perhaps also somewhat naive) that has a certain durability: the idea that those of us involved in the process of making things have an advantage over those who merely consume. It remains open for further discussion, of course, whether Marx was right when he claimed that the working classes have an inherently historical point of view (and hence a historical advantage) because they see the emergence of commodities through labor and therefore are less likely to fetishize them. This seems, at any rate, to be Barthes's point:

> There is therefore one language which is not mythical, it is the language of man as a producer: wherever man speaks in order to transform reality and no longer to preserve it as an image, wherever he links his language to the making of things, meta-language is referred to a language object, and myth is impossible. (146)

What I have to say in the following pages will play on this sense of the political: that one is more in the realm of politics, and history, when one produces rather than merely reflects. The realms of production can be merely mechanical; the realm of reflection can be merely cerebral, abstract, idealist. The realm of reflection and production combined is the realm where we work, where we do the work of the world and so remain open to history. Reflective production is another way of saying writing.

My humanistic training was old-fashioned enough for me to have deeply identified with the enlightenment belief in the power of the written and spoken word to further political freedom. My exposure to the rhetorical theories of Kenneth Burke made me believe even more forcefully in the need for us to develop and define modes of public communication that could contribute to the purification of war, as he puts it—to the shifting of conflict from the battlefield to the field of symbolic contestation. But Burke shows us also that for "rhetoric" to be powerful, its power must also be available for bad causes. An understanding of the grammar of motives gives one information useful for exploiting the motives of others in rhetorical fashion for ends that can vary widely in their ethical goals. The word *good* in the expression *good writing* invokes a vague universal sense of virtue in what gets written, when at best it can probably only mean "useful in the context," relative.

It is easy to get the idea that the issue of politics and writing instruction has become trivial. This is so because it is also so easy to mark off the major moments of writing in which politics appears to be a significant issue. "Politics and the English Language" is one of those moments, and perhaps the only other one, perhaps not known to many common readers (as, perhaps, Orwell's essay is equally unknown to the common reader) is Richard Ohmann's collection called *The Politics of Letters*.[1] Orwell made the issue heroic, one could believe that something was really at stake when one used language this way or that. Even more, in the teaching of language, when the fate of democracy seemed to hang on how phrases were turned, teachers of English clearly could know and feel the power of their profession. And with that power they could experience too the sense of responsibility that often accompanies access of power. What makes Orwell no longer so handy a reference on the topic of politics and language is the more complex notion we must now have of language and the degree of control we have over it, or that it has over us: the issue of ideology. Orwell warned that it was possible for political evil to insert itself like a virus in our society, and our only possible prophylactic was the defense of good usage which necessarily accompanied clear thinking. And of course for much of public life he is right; saying things with clarity and having people stand behind what they say would be one way to get more responsibility and commitment in public life.

What we cannot guarantee, no more could Orwell, is that clear speaking will be politically acceptable or effective, or that obscure language is necessarily a guide to the politically dangerous. After all, one of the "apologies" one often hears for the stylistically challenging texts of postmodern/poststructural theory is that they challenge the hidden political assumptions and agendas of the naturalized language of common sense. I have myself been chastised by colleagues occasionally for showing too much faith in clarity as a virtue, thereby signaling my compromised position with respect to institutions of authority and ideological state apparatuses. One has to allow for the possibility that "difficult" language might be functioning overall to effect positive change in our political lives, and that occasionally the clearest of languages will be functioning according to an authoritarian subtext.

We seem to have moved from a time in which the political importance of language and teaching was part of the belief of every English teacher, and nevertheless "being political" was not part of the system of beliefs of the average English teacher. We have perhaps arrived at a time when the nature and degree of political commitment of the teacher of writing is a matter of public concern—at least insofar as the turmoil over "political correctness" is really an issue of interest to the general public and not merely something cooked up by a few academics and a temporarily topic-starved press. Every teacher, of course, will have a politics of some kind. Every teacher will, in one way or another, to one degree or another, expose her political beliefs to her students; perhaps in the hope of influencing the political attitudes of those students. We need to assume that "exposing" one's beliefs is different from "teaching" those beliefs. In either case, however, that of putting beliefs on the table on the one hand, and trying to teach them on the other, we find ourselves faced with the problem of "uptake," or misfires. If we merely warn our students that we hold certain beliefs, in favor of abortion or against it, students may "learn" to hold those beliefs themselves. Additionally, if we try to "teach" (or indoctrinate students with) our beliefs, we confront the same unpredictability of uptake. Our teaching may misfire. If the situation were really, ultimately, that relative, then one might well say: well then, let us teach our beliefs since the uptake is completely unpredictable. Let me plead empirical ignorance on the issue of uptake; perhaps one day it will be a measurable factor. For now, the responsible position would seem to be that which discriminates teaching beliefs from responsibly exposing them so as to warn students against any possible ideological bias one may have.

Put simply: teaching people to write only in the left margins would be an attempt to indoctrinate; it would put all the emphasis on the topic, the subject matter, on having and expressing the correct leftist beliefs. Student success would be measured, then, by the adequacy of the political statements they produced, and not by the quality of the writing they produced (actually, it could only be measured by the adequacy of the political positions they held outside of written or verbal protestations). The attempt to teach how to write in a specific way, left marginally, immediately calls up the topic/technique dichotomy and reduces writing instruction to an external technology. One really does not have to teach writing, if one is concerned primarily with the successful transmission of an idea or ideology. Of course, my own desire to find a way of teaching writing that is not of necessity bound to any one politics, and yet is not apolitical, takes the same risk.

Similar considerations hold true, obviously, for any attempt to teach in the right margins. Those who favor writing in the right margins have seized the headlines in recent times by pretending to be apolitical and accusing the left of political correctness. What they are really doing is asserting the importance, as they see it, of one set of political values over and against another opposing set.

So we need to consider the problems of teaching politics through writing, and to try to conceive of a rhetorical strategy and related writing pedagogy that does not insist on ideological compliance, that teaches students something fundamental about how to enter ongoing conversations (verbally or in writing), and that is not politically irrelevant or inert. A tall task, one requiring that we walk a few knife edges in careful deliberation. As cautiously as I approach these issues, it is only fair to repeat that I conclude by insisting that a pedagogy that develops political commitment in our students is to be preferred over one that does not; that a writing pedagogy that fosters liberal views is to be preferred over one that does not; that one needs to make some kind of commitment in one's curriculum, while realizing that students need to be considered as free agents whose success should not be measured by a scale of political correctness.

What Shape Is the Public Sphere?

Margin as a term has recently too been pushed into carrying a certain glamour, a certain romance. Literary deconstruction has reshaped the way we habitually look for places of importance. So if the center of public life is occupied and controlled by the dominant forces of the military-industrial or medical-pharmaceutical complex, then we have been instructed to look to the margins for possible moments of resistance against that hegemony.

The key word of the new politics of postmodernism seems to be *resistance*.[2] And it may well be also that it is around this word and its resonances that much of the controversy over political correctness could be found to circulate. By a route too complex and long to trace out here, one could reconstruct a view not too atypical of postmodernist thinking about issues of ideology. Briefly, it might look something like this: The social world is structured according to the dictates of the "dominant." The dominant is hegemonic; which means that we participate unwittingly in perpetuating our own condition of being dominated. Our language itself is part of the larger structures of representation of a society driven by the profit motive. Participating in the larger structures of exploitation, our own speech is complicit with a network of exploitation even when it is "we" who might be exploited.

There is no direct opposition that can be mounted to this subliminal hegemonic exploitation because it will not come out into the public sphere and be counted. Its very essence is to operate unseen; that is part of its strategy. Besides being dominant, hegemonic, and subliminal, it has already predefined the public sphere. Equally, there is no evasion possible; this exploitative language, permeating every-thing, cannot be found anywhere—at least it cannot be found in any one place. Faced with such a foe, one can only hope to outwit it, to trick it by deconstructive strategies of resistance.

Who could say what the origin of such a politics of resistance might be? Clearly it would be possible to trace some of such thinking (hypothetical as it is, and based mainly on my observations of col-leagues in the professions) to the politics of the sixties and the Viet-nam war. The American army in Vietnam verifies the mistake of trying to work in the open by means of direct opposition. The only successful strategy is the undermining one of guerrilla warfare. The political writer, successfully to resist, must reincarnate the Viet Cong in the deep undergrowth of complex analysis of cultural forms.

How to Resist Resistance?

Now if the place of our working is to be the jungle, and our strategy is to be that of resistance, we face a particular problem, especially as writers and teachers of writing. Just think of the difficulty Orwell would have with such a strategy. And think of the change in concep-tion of public and intellectual space that needs to be historically ac-counted for from his time to ours. Our dilemma can be exemplified if we ask the simple question: how to know when to resist our resis-tance?[3] Resistance is one of those glory words from a day that is be-hind us—one might think of the pained nostalgia of Frederic Henry in *A Farewell to Arms* for all of the possible meanings of the expression "in vain" that were obliterated by the realities of battle. Resistance is a romantic anachronism at the "center" of a public sphere that is no longer spherical. Like the French underground in the Second World War, resistance is heroic and dares not speak its name in public. Simone de Beauvoir's text *The Mandarins* points out the difficulties for resist-ers who have to learn to resist their resistance after the war. If we adopt a writing pedagogy premised on the existence of a hegemonic ideological state, then we will have to reify romance and creativity. We will have to tend towards practices that we will like to call "strate-gies," strategies in some battle we cannot quite name except to say that we fight in the name of some ultimate fairness.

If we over-emphasize resistance we will find it difficult to handle issues of membership. As Kenneth Burke points out in *A Rhetoric of Motives,* a public rhetoric, the very possibility of the existence of a shared public sphere, is premised on a concept of identification. If our primary principle is one of differentiation, with an underdeveloped notion of identification, then it is not clear that we can ever arrive at a concept of writing and teaching of writing that can be anything but fragmented and fragmenting.

Instead of resisting, one might choose to resist resistance on occasions in order to insist that one is a player in a public field where the rational selection of goals is still possible. Resisting resistance promises an evaluation of resistance as a contested matter rather than a given value in the face of a mythologized negative "dominant." Resisting resistance suggests a conflict of values—which has to be one of the meanings of "public sphere": openly enunciated values, in conflict, and a possibility of choosing between them. It promises a public debate about positions in conflict, where there might not be any absolute truth, since we are in the realm of conflicts of meanings as well as values.

Which is to say that critical reflection on the value of resistance begins to move us into the realm of what Burke calls the dialogic: a place where "positive" utterances are not the only ones in play. The realm of the dialogic is the realm of rhetoric, of dispute and writing—not writing now as a recording of knowledge, but of what Burke would think of as the attempt to bring about identifications.

What Are Some of the Ways in Which Writing is Political?

David Bromwich argues that our time has been dominated by "self-contained (mostly left-wing) culture of the academy and the static (and right-wing) political culture that dominates America today" (ix). He notes that he writes "as an admirer of neither culture." His claim is open to a wide range of criticism and perhaps he would qualify what he says by equivocating on the meaning of the term *culture*. So he might be willing to admit that it is arguable that universities are dominated by left-wing academics, and still want to maintain that there is an academic culture (or perhaps subculture) that has a visible role in universities. In spite of possible deficiencies, however, there is a utility in the distinction he draws. As he puts it, "politics is not education; the means makes a difference to the end." He doesn't state the converse, but seems to assume it holds as well that education is not politics. Bromwich would probably agree that one can gain an education by engaging in politics, and that educational institutions (and therefore the activities that they encompass) are not free of politics. And still his distinction between the two spheres clarifies the issue for us. It seems plausible to argue that left-wing intellectuals have been driven out of active politics by the dominance of the Right in politics; and equally plausible to argue that left-wing intellectuals have taken refuge in the academy as the political scene in their wider society has become increasingly hostile. The belief that ideas will change the world is a powerful incentive to academics, and is a powerful motivating factor for teachers who find that direct political action has become a closed route for them.

Bromwich says that he is engaging

> in an attack on the ideologists of the right and left who believe that culture subordinates the mind of the initiate; that it speaks in one voice, or in two exactly opposed voices. . . . These journalists, scholars, disciples, and institutionalists believe that the inheritance they are obliged to continue, or to bring to an end, does have a meaning as a whole and that, whether for purposes of revival or of destruction, it must be taught and learned in principle. (52)

What he could have put more simply is this: what students learn is not in a one-to-one relation with what they are taught (the "uptake" issue). Let me attempt to exemplify with an anecdote from my own experience. In recent discussions of curriculum change in my department it was proposed (by me) that the core of classes required of all of our English majors be changed. We have students majoring in five distinct and self-contained tracks: in professional writing, creative writing, technical writing, rhetoric, and literary and cultural studies. Each major has been required to take a common set of four classes (this has now been changed). One of the classes was in creative writing, and the other three were in literary and cultural studies. The new proposal, the one that is now in place, would have each majoring student take one class in rhetoric, one in creative writing, and one in the area of literary and cultural studies. The department has had about one hundred students majoring in professional and technical writing combined, and has never had more than about fifteen majors focusing exclusively on literary and cultural studies. My object is not to argue that this state of affairs is desirable or otherwise, but rather to focus on the argument that was produced against making a change.

Some of our professional writing students focus on learning how to do documentation for software developers. Some of them take classes in, do internships in, or find employment in the Software Engineering

Institute at Carnegie Mellon. SEI is an object of attack because it gets lots of funding from DARPA (Defense Advanced Research Project) and is rumored to have been deeply involved in developing software for Reagan's "Star Wars" initiative. One of my colleagues argued that we had a responsibility to educate these professional writing students in cultural studies classes so as to save them from a career (politically unacceptable) of assisting in killing people. Only by exposure to three classes in cultural studies could we hope to save them for humanity. Now, as one might expect, this argument was offensive to some others in the room, because of its assumption of the moral high ground for one kind of teaching over another. My point is not only that the argument did not win the day.

At a slightly later date I was invited to describe to the minister of science and technology from India what our department might do to train people in India to do adequate software documentation. I showed him a highly professional sample of documentation prepared by two undergraduate students in our department—it is just by the way that the minister invited me to spend a couple of weeks in India to try to work out some deeper collaboration between CMU and developers in India. What I learned subsequently was that the two students in question, the undergraduates whose software documentation project was so impressive, claimed that two of the classes they had taken in the cultural studies curriculum (including one we call "Discursive Practices") had been amongst the best they had taken in preparing them for their careers in professional/technical writing. So, far from being an inoculation against success in late capitalist America, classes founded on resisting the dominant ideology might well be keys to success in it. So much for any direct connection, or determination, between what teachers might take to be the political content of their classes and what gets taken up and put into practice by students. And whatever the truth of the matter about which cadre, right or left, dominates the "culture" of the academy of our polity, there is a lesson in the anecdote for professors who insist on the political nature of their teaching, or of their writing, and that is simply that while there might be connections between the two, politics is not education and education is not politics.

The range of what counts for political in the classroom is perhaps very wide, and in attempting to understand how writing and writing instruction might be thought to be political, we could cover a bewildering number of topics. I'll focus on one or two and then consider a more general question of a possible political quality that our instruction might have if it really wants to belong to and contribute to (the reconstitution of) the public sphere. The classes in cultural studies that were useful to our professional writing students seem to have been successful because they sensitized students to complex language issues that are dependent on social context—indeed, the complex problem of the relation of meaning to context, and the possible variances in different social constructions of meaning (depending differentially on race, class, and gender at least) is a central one that cultural studies can explore. One could argue plausibly that such sensitivity to the context dependency of social meanings is the main political contribution of instruction in writing and reading. Which is to say that if "interpretation," or reading, is possible then it should be teachable and it should be thought of in a subtle way as a transmissible "skill" that teachers of writing and cultural studies can teach. More on interpretation below.

If, however, we believe that merely giving students the appropriate topical reading list, or topics for composition exercises, is where we might find a political function for pedagogy, then I think we will be disappointed. My exemplary anecdote applies, I believe, to any possible arrangement of texts we might think of as having a determining and sensitizing effect on our "subjects," our students. Similarly, our explications of texts, even explications done under the rubric of deconstruction, or ideological analysis, or cultural critique of the Frankfurt School variety, can all be reduced to mere lecturing, posturing, hectoring, or pep-talk. Students will encounter our talking heads and our analyses, our interpretations and our politically motivated dissections with their own prejudices in place, and there is no guarantee that being exposed to a different set of beliefs will lead them to change theirs. Indeed, analysis (reflection) that merely points out the submerged political content of a text contains no principle that even theoretically suggests why student views should change on exposure to the analysis. When they see that a text has a submerged fascist context, for example, why should we feel that they will instinctively reject it rather than identify with it? Why do we think that our own expression of moral revulsion at the message will be echoed in their minds? Clearly a considerable number of people still find fascist propaganda convincing. A pedagogy based simply on a belief in the freedom to choose, and the force of showing and knowing, leaves too much out of consideration concerning human motivations. An enlightenment pedagogy tries to teach people to know something. It assumes, without being able to demonstrate the claim, that knowing makes a difference in what one does. It is a commonplace, however, for people who know one thing to do another.

A pedagogy of writing must claim to teach people how to do something. The unfortunate split in our educational theories between reflection and practice has tended to favor reflection over practice. The elite in universities are those who know, the researchers. Even now as the climate is changing somewhat, those who are researchers are often exempted from teaching, from mere application. Teachers of writing are still not thought to be anything more than mere practitioners of skills—at least one would have to conclude that after a moment's consideration of where the clout lies in university departments of English.

Writing as Training for Jobs

The enlightened approach to ideology has a complementary strategy in those who oppose training, or the development of writing skills appropriate to the market-place. Enlightened reading supposedly liberates because it shows us opportunities for resisting, while training in applied or professional writing enslaves one to the dominant ideology because its practices are supposedly purely adaptive to the irresistible processes of capitalism. In a recent issue of *Lingua Franca*, Patricia Kean bemoans what she takes to be significant current developments in humanities education, moving the great literary texts closer and closer to a pedagogy designed to breed accommodation to business America. Apparently there is a classroom somewhere in America where students are asked to treat texts like *Beowulf* as if they were advertising copy for business. They are asked to make it "sell," and the justification offered by the teacher in question is that such an approach develops skills appropriate for roles students will have to take later in life when they enter the workplace. Kean in general laments the emergence of what she denigrates as applied education and suggests that education as it emerges from the controversy over what is "politically correct" now finds itself having to contend with business and government over what will be allowed as "workplace correct" in the academy:

> As barriers between vocational and academic education fall, a curious hybrid called "applied learning" is emerging, stressing real-world pertinence for all subjects. But while applied learning seems likely to enhance math and science instruction, it strikes this English teacher as having a chilling effect on what is left of the liberal arts. And as schools reinvent themselves, change will inevitably work its way up

the academic ladder. For universities, applied education will certainly mean mounting pressures to come down and "get real"; for my professorial colleagues, it may also mean confronting class upon class of freshmen trained to write mean memos and deconstruct the densest of technical manuals, students who have earned their place in the halls of academe not by grades but by résumés. Prepare yourself, in other words, for a whole new generation trained to measure the liberal arts against yet another yardstick: workplace correctness. (22)

The suggestion that the liberal arts are continually being measured by inadequate yardsticks vaguely suggests that they somehow exceed measurement, and the appeal Kean makes several times to Cardinal Newman may indicate that she sees the liberal arts as having an ineffable spiritual essence, like God, beyond mere mortal measurement. And yet, somewhat contradictorily, Kean also seems to believe that real liberal education can be measured by "grades"—probably she means simply "excellence"—and that grades are somehow less commodified than resumés. What Kean's piece lacks is a clear statement of how the liberal arts are valuable and how they are to be valued. She merely sees them threatened by any concept of utility. Without such a statement it is not at all clear how the ineffable will be able to defend itself against the onslaught of the marketplace and applied education.

Why it should be so difficult for English profs to accommodate themselves to a real world idea of work and the workplace is a puzzling fact. Kean's lack of familiarity with what she fears shows in her (perhaps satirical?) expectation that students in the future will have to "deconstruct" technical manuals. At one moment she foresees students becoming technical robots producing resumés instead of grades, and at the next moment she sees them indulging in a futile, nonproductive, but highly sophisticated textual analysis of manuals.

Recently I have had occasion to be involved in discussions concerning the possibility of developing technical-manual writing expertise in Japanese universities. We were asked if it were possible to teach people simply, and merely, to write a manual (for whatever electronic device or product that needed simple language explanation for the customer). Our answer was no, it is not possible. People can be guided in the preparation of one particular manual for one particular device or situation, but such guidance does not amount to educating them to be able to analyze any future situations and design the manual appropriate to new situations. One-manual robots are just that, capable of producing one manual but not capable of generalizing what they know to new situations. In order to develop the ability to write a technical manual, one has to be trained in a broad range of rhetoric, rhetorical theory, cross-cultural rhetoric, communications theory, organizational theory, possibly discourse analysis, and of course the kind of training that leads to a sophisticated sense of how language works in multiple contexts—one of the applied benefits, as I suggested above, of liberal arts training, particularly in literary explication. Why people who can write manuals in widely differing situations should be looked down on because they have intelligence that can be applied escapes me. There is apparently a politics of the liberal arts, and of writing instruction, that cannot be fully explained in public, but which seems to hold that being able to use anything one has learned in the liberal arts in the public sphere is a violation of some central principle. It could well be that an examination of the ideology of the practices of English departments would lead us close to one of the contributing causes of the deformation of the public sphere in our culture.

Technological Determinism and Libertarianism

Of course, we are being regularly reminded that technology is reshaping our public space. Not many invoke Marshall McLuhan's name these days, but many believe that not only is the global village at hand, but that the technologies that have made it possible are essentially democratizing. The guru of high tech in India, Sam Pitroda, can plausibly argue that the new technology has a democratizing influence in India, or at least it is at the heart of potentially huge social changes. Pitroda apparently believes that it is the new technology that brought about many of the changes in Russia. He believes that television in villages in India makes it possible for villagers to begin to understand the broader political world they inhabit. And such understanding may well contribute to a more fully realized democratic condition in a society.

Jay Bolter captures some of the excitement of the new electronic communications technology in his book *Writing Space*. Bolter displays unease at the ideological nature of the individual, the logical, linear, authoritarian author. He seems to have been heavily influenced by Derrida, especially the work *Glas:*

> In a traditional essay, destined for publication, the writer speaks apparently in his or her own voice and is expected to take responsibility for a text that will go out to hundreds or thousands of readers under his or her name. Publishing is fundamentally serious and

permanent, and it is for this reason that plagiarism in science or scholarship is taken so seriously. A scholar or scientist cannot even retract his or her own previously published argument without embarrassment. By contrast, a dialogue speaks with more than one voice and therefore shares or postpones responsibility. (117)

Bolter goes on to argue that a "hypertext" document in a computer "is always a dialogue between the writer and his or her readers, and the reader has to share the responsibility for the outcome." He argues that Derrida's text *Glas* differs from classic texts in that "the network of relationships that normally remains hidden beneath the printed page has emerged and overwhelmed the orderly presentation we expect of a printed book." He adds that *Glas* "belongs in the electronic medium, where such relationships are perfectly at home. In computer writing any relationships between textual elements can float to the surface; the computer invites the writer to reveal the inner structure in the appearance and behavior of the text."

Now, a lot of issues get begged in those few short quotations. If the computer invites the writer to reveal an inner structure, does the writer have to respond? If any relationship in a computer text *can* float to the surface, does it? Just how does a dialogue, a computer text, share or postpone responsibility? Whose responsibility gets postponed? If the reader "has to share" in the outcome, is the reader's responsibility never postponed, but only that of the writer? If we have two participants in a dialogue and only one of them is guaranteed a postponement of responsibility, do we really have a dialogue? Doesn't any dialogue require precisely a number of people, at least two, taking full responsibility for what they say? And doesn't it require also that the participants in a dialogue accept as a ground rule their own corrigibility? That is, in a dialogue there has be to an assumed ground rule that some people's views will change, be discarded, amended, replaced. Even scientists, it really goes without saying, regard the discourse of science as a history of corrigibility.

Bolter argues that a networked culture works against the previous hierarchy of cultural privilege. It puts special interest groups together in a subpublic sphere, and implicitly suggests that there is no greater importance to any one node or interest group than to another. So discussions of popular mechanics are equal to discussions of opera. One can still ask, however, how true this is in public space, how true viewed from another angle. What if, for example, all of the people participating in the symphony discussion group had annual incomes of over $250,000 and those in the popular mechanics group incomes averaging only $25,000? In the world of the network, one can ignore the symphony group with impunity, even enjoy one's deliberate nonparticipation, and have a feeling of equality inside the net. But that feeling would have done nothing to change the relations of power in society at large. Those with higher incomes, supporting the symphony with cash donations and ticket purchases, would also be the people buying stocks on Wall Street, making donations to politicians' election campaigns, and bringing their monetary influence to bear on the shape of everyday existence. To argue that a new technology, whether horses, or wells in villages in India, or electronic networks, make a society more egalitarian by necessity, without bothering to ask first who owns the horses, or wells, or networks, seems naive. It is more likely that new technologies will reflect existing power relations than overturn them, and it is not at all clear that changes in cultural formations effect political changes. If politics is different from education, it may turn out to be the case that culture is different from politics, at least in some important aspects.

Political Places for Writing

What about the politics of writing, then? Bolter actually invokes the traditional *topoi* of classical rhetoric to argue that writing with a word processor makes a writer more conscious of the place she is in when writing. The outline function of a word processor brings the usually submerged structures to the surface. On the other hand, Bolter's discussion of network space and virtual reality make one begin to think that he somehow believes that there is a new realm of writing and communication that is beyond place, in a place where old structures are magically altered and new social arrangements occur. There is an atopical realm of writing that is being invoked by the new electronic rhetoricians.[4] If the usual places of writing have a particular public authority, if they represent public ground on which any writer might stand, then that authority must be challenged by any new public formation. Bolter finds the old authority in the printed book, the serious publication mentioned above. The book somehow, as a technology apart from any deliberate social/monetary relations, necessitates a respect for the authority of the author. The book bespeaks a one-to-one relationship, or so Bolter seems to suggest. The reader of a book is apparently not an interactive participant, not at least partly responsible for the construction of the meaning the book will have. Bolter's view of texts, that is to say, is very old-fashioned. Because of that he believes they will be replaced by not only a new medium but by a new set of authority (or nonauthority) relations. A section of his book called "The End of Authority" begins like this:

> As long as the printed book remains the primary medium of literature, traditional views of the author as authority and of literature as monument will remain convincing for most readers. The electronic medium, however, threatens to bring down the whole edifice at once. (153)

Why should it be assumed that electronic networks or electronic texts will not be defined as authoritative? Shouldn't one be suspicious of the apparent invisibility of authority? Bolter invokes the name of Shelley to suggest the way that Romantic poetry operated to lay down the law. What he has forgotten is that Shelley, with due irony, called poets the *unacknowledged* legislators of the world. Should we be more wary of an openly avowed authority that disavows its power in the public sphere (as Shelley's does), or of a public disavowal of authority in a medium that apparently has the mysterious cataclysmic power to bring down the whole edifice at once?

All one has to do to notice the authority of network discussion groups is to begin to doubt their egalitarian nature. One notices quickly the phenomenon of "flaming," which suggests that there is a lot of anger getting worked out in network discussions. And where there is anger there is often a difference of power or authority asserting itself. One can also notice that new participants in a network group are very uncertain whether they have the authority to comment. There are usually many silent readers of postings, some of whom will carefully and apologetically enter a discussion. Those who are already writing messages to a network group are assumed to have the authority to do so, and their power inhibits newcomers. As in any other medium or technology, those who know how to use it have more power. Those who know how to create "kill" files know how to edit out voices they don't want to hear. Those who know how to create new topic groups on the network have more influence over how discussions occur than do others. Again, in a special sense, (applied) knowledge is power.

More than that, however, the network costs money to maintain. Not everyone in the country participates. One can't imagine the poor of this country, with no computer access, believing that this technological revolution that has destroyed the authority of the book has in any way made them more equal participants in network discussion groups, or society at large. There is a public sphere which is shaped in a way to exclude them and their interests.

The previously hidden economic structure of the network is currently being brought to the surface, not really by a new technology but by a public debate about who owns technology. The Clinton/Gore administration, in a welcome recognition that infrastructures for moving information are as economically important as infrastructures for moving other kinds of goods and services, have been supportive of the development of the new information superhighway that will transcend and replace the current network. As soon as this new technology has become thinkable, a debate has developed over who should own, control, and develop it. Should it remain a government-controlled facility, or should the telecommunications giants take over? My point is that rhetorically and aesthetically shaped bunches of electrons are really commodities, and their passage through an apparently egalitarian network ought not to blind us to the continuing relations of wealth, power, and authority that dominate technological advances.

Towards a More General Political Sense

So, finally, we must briefly address the question again: is there some generalized quality of writing and writing instruction that can be thought to be political? What I have said so far might make the reader doubtful of there being any great reward for having read this far. Indeed, I could not now argue that writing instruction ought to espouse new technology, or any particular set of political views, or that it ought either to resist or identify with writing instruction as training for getting a job. Nevertheless I do think that there is a kind of writing instruction, and a related conception of writing, that could assist us in recovering a belief that we can reshape our public sphere. Indeed, I would regard that as the primary political responsibility of a writing pedagogy. If writing is seen as correct usage, if it is seen as the five paragraph theme (a predetermined form to be filled), if it is seen as the recorder of knowledge, if it is seen in any way other than as social agency, then writing cannot be political. Writing is the construction of the world we understand; writing is rhetorical; there are no fixed forms for writing that will work for every occasion, although there are rhetorical forms that have gained currency (as coin of the communications realm). Our writing instruction ought, then, to be grounded in rhetorical theory and it ought to be historical.

Let me take the historical aspect first. Near the beginning of this essay I invoked Orwell and Richard Ohmann as two of the major thinkers of our time about the politics of writing. I briefly discussed

Orwell but scanted Ohmann, a scanting I would now like to correct. I had students in a graduate seminar (students at the M.A. level, not doctoral students) read a number of the essays in Ohmann's *Politics of Letters*, and had them pay particular attention to "The Shaping of a Canon: U.S. Fiction, 1960–1975." Just as I would like to argue that writing is a social process, a matter of social agency, Ohmann argues that reading is a social process. He offers a historical account of the ways in which some books get to be bestsellers and move towards canonical status. The crux of his analysis can be caught briefly in the following passage:

> To summarize: a small group of book buyers formed a screen through which novels passed on their way to commercial success; a handful of agents and editors picked the novels that would compete for the notice of those buyers; and a tight network of advertisers and reviewers, organized around the *New York Times Book Review*, selected from these a few to be recognized as compelling, important, "talked-about." (73)

I asked the students if they thought Ohmann had a political bias. It may have been their naiveté speaking, but they said no. Indeed, it took some pains for me to point out the places in the book where Ohmann responsibly identifies his political beliefs. I asked them if, after having read the essay in question, their attitudes to the canon question had changed; in particular how would they react to a claim that a canon had some kind of transcendent universal quality? They all agreed that they now understood the canon very differently, and could see that canon formation was a matter of historical contingency.

Now, my point is not that having students read Ohmann is a good way to make them political. Rather, I'm interested in what makes Ohmann's writing political. The answer is that his writing is historical. And that suggests perhaps that one way of achieving a generalized responsible political aspect to writing instruction would be to have our writing instruction be historical, focus on the writing of history perhaps, at least on writing with a reflective historical sense on the alert. Which would at least mean that students could not think that their writing was merely self-expression. Now such instruction would be difficult to bring about at the freshman level. In the class of M.A. students, the writing task I gave them was to do a paper that was an example of cultural analysis, using either the method of Ohmann or of Roland Barthes (we read *Mythologies*). That writing task required them to become practicing agents of cultural analysis, and I believe that also required them to become "political." They had to go out "into the world" and study something. One visited local coffeehouses and wrote about the reemerging coffeehouse culture. Another wrote on call-in radio shows, and made contact with local stations to gather information. Another imitated Ohmann a little more closely and wrote about TV news coverage of the election results in November (election coverage is the topic of one of the essays in *Politics of Letters*). I gave them no political instructions, no ideology they had to adapt to. I asked them to observe social conditions, and reflect on them either in a historical manner (Ohmann), on in a demystifying semiotic manner (Barthes). If one of the greatest dangers to our political lives is mystification, and if the other (collaborating with it) is a lack of historical sense, then such a writing task, it seems to me, deserves to be called a political writing task.

What about the politics of freshman comp though? I have written (with some of my colleagues at CMU) about this topic elsewhere,[5] so I won't go into the issue at length or in detail. What my coauthors and I claim is that, as a matter of social (rhetorical) agency, writing instruction can properly concern itself with the related topics of argument and interpretation. We regard writing as similar to mapmaking when one is setting out on a journey as an explorer. We ask students to consult existing maps, or representations, of the territory they intend to explore. We then lead them into the practice of making their own maps, or written contributions.

The maps they consult are other written argumentative essays. They learn first how to summarize other arguments, and come to understand that a summary of somebody else's position is a theoretical appropriation of it. A summary is also a representation, just as the essay they summarize makes a representation. They learn how to analyze a range of argumentative contributions on a particular topic. They learn how to recognize the main points at issue that divide the community of contributors. They learn how to draw on their own experience, in narrative form, as a way of entering the community of discourse.

I believe students have an opportunity to learn something important about writing in such situations. First they can learn that writing is a way of joining a community of discourse. They might learn that they must attempt to understand what others are saying, and that their interpretations of what others say are precisely that: interpretations, maps, representations. They are not implicitly invited to learn that everything is relative, only that our community of understanding is subject to change depending on how issues are represented. They learn that it is possible to represent things from a different point of view, once they have identified themselves with the discourse community in question. In Burke's terms, identification and differentiation play complementary roles in constructing both the written text and webs of social interaction.

They learn that their argumentative contribution is not likely to be the final word. Understanding the history of a contested issue, and noticing that things change, implicitly places them in a position to recognize their own contributions as corrigible, as subject to further representation (and misrepresentation) by other explorers. They learn, further, that writing is a matter of occupying—taking—a position. They find that the writers they study do take positions, and that their contributions will be positional. They will be encouraged to recognize that their own views are positional, that they come equipped with histories and views, not all of which have been critically scrutinized. When asked to write from their own experience, they are taught to think of their personal narratives not as self-expression, but as "cases of," as publicly available examples of one or another kind of experience. They are taught, that is to say, to regard their subjectivities as rhetorical. If their experience has meaning, it has to have social meaning, and has to occupy some kind of accountable public space. They become practitioners of writing—a point that perhaps deserves some emphasis: their acquisition of writing abilities is presented not merely as a knowledge issue: they are positioned as practitioners who must be reflective. Insofar as a writing pedagogy is a matter of reflective practice, and not merely a matter of enlightened reflection, then I would maintain that it is already more political than any exercise of enlightened critique or politically motivated teaching.

Well, perhaps that is enough about what has been said already more fully elsewhere. My conclusion is that there is a possible world of responsible pedagogy that we could develop together, which would do two things at once. On the one hand it would teach writing, and we could make public our claim that we really do have something to teach in our classrooms, that we really do know something not only about assigning and correcting writing, but something about teaching it as well. On the other, we could make a responsible claim that our writing pedagogy is political, and politically responsible on two counts. First count: it does not at all attempt to indoctrinate students in any one political view—not a view appropriate to the left or right margins, nor even the center of the page (although as I have already indicated, it could be plausibly claimed that the strategy I outline here is a centrist liberal one). Second count: it is political because it deals with essential matters for the political life of our time: issues of position and the shape of the public sphere, if we are to have one at all.

PART II

Expropriating the Powers of Language

3

Teaching "Myth, Difference, and Popular Culture"

Joseph C. Bodziock and Christopher Ferry _____

Our story is about creation, about teaching and learning, about anger, frustration, and compromise. It is about two white, middle-income men trying to represent a world full of difference to a group of largely white, middle- and lower-income students. It is a story about institutional, pedagogical, and personal change—or at least the possibilities for such change. It is about a class as a "culture in progress." It is a story without an end. It is the story of "Myth, Difference, and Popular Culture."

Our story is riddled with ambiguity and inconsistency. We did not always know what we were doing, and our aims at the beginning were different from those at the end. We were (and are) quite self-consciously parts of the culture in progress, and we accept responsibility for the contradictions and disparities in our story. We are still trying to reconcile them.

When we arrived at Clarion University in the fall of 1991, we noticed an interesting phenomenon: when confronted with issues of difference—that is, issues of gender, race, and class—many of our students tended to "shut down." We were familiar with student resistance to the ideas we discussed, but these students were not resistant, exactly. In one class, for example, Chris asked the students if they thought they lived in a sexist culture. They said no. When he pointed out (using concrete examples) that most positions of power were held by men, they (including the women) responded indifferently, as if to say, "oh, *that.*" Both of us value student rebellion and resistance; these qualities are, we think, the ground from which emerges critical consciousness. We were unprepared, however, for Clarion students' passivity, and attributed it, at first, to what we perceived as their rural conservatism.

We've since reevaluated our assumption. As Ann Berthoff has so frequently reminded us, teachers should "begin with where they [students] are as language animals, endowed with the form-finding and form-creating powers of mind and language" (9), sage advice we had both forgotten. Clarion University is located in one of Pennsylvania's poorest counties. We have the third highest unemployment rate in the commonwealth; the coal and lumber industries have played out; aside from one or two factories and the university, there are no jobs here. Sixty-seven percent of our students come from this and the adjoining county. Their median family income is $18,000. Further, many of our students are the first in their families to attend college, and they're here, moreover, because there are no jobs; they have nothing else to do. Our pedagogical sensibilities, on the other hand, had been shaped in largely urban research universities—the University of Minnesota and SUNY at Albany—and we brought these sensibilities to bear on Clarion students in rather the way Paulo Freire describes people who "proclaim devotion to the cause of liberation" but who don't "enter into *communion* with the people," and who regard the people as "totally ignorant":

> The convert who approaches the people but feels alarm at each step they take, each doubt they express, and each suggestion they offer, and attempts to impose his "status," remains nostalgic towards his origins. (*Pedagogy* 47, Freire's emphasis)

Before we began to know our students, then, to understand their reality, they appeared to us to purvey and reproduce white, European, Christian, male, heterosexist values. Our reevaluation allowed us to see, however, that they were, as Paulo Freire might say, "submerged" in a powerful and oppressive society, resulting in a "culture of silence" (*Action* 11, 3). Feeling quite abashed, we began a more meticulous consideration of our students and discovered that, far from being the intellectual zombies we had allowed ourselves to see them as, who fused their synaptic functions when confronted with racism or sexism, many students were, as Jane Tompkins says, "walking field[s] of energy, teeming with agendas" (659). In other words, the diversity we sought to expose our students to was already present in our classes; we were simply confronting our students with issues of gender, race, and class—without really exploring their impact on the students' lives.

We needed a new approach, one that did more than merely raise issues, and so we developed an experimental, writing-intensive course, "Myth, Difference, and Popular Culture."

We decided that rather than simply posing issues of sexism, racism, and classism we needed to explore how these "isms" get made. Specifically, we wanted to study the ways in which cultures define and marginalize particular groups of people—based upon gender, race, and/or class, for example—as "different" and "other." We reasoned that the various "isms" seemed to form systems of belief, just as myths might be described as systems of belief, and that cultures created and articulated myths about particular groups of people in order to marginalize them. We wondered further if stereotypes might be more accurately described as myths. We wanted a course, then, that would not only help students describe those myths, but would allow us to try to understand with the students the process by which the myths were made, the ways in which myths determined how the culture-at-large perceived the character of and responded to marginalized groups, and the ways in which myths might be a means of claiming and maintaining power.

Why did we decide to focus on myths and mythmaking? First, we took as our rubric Eric Gould's concept of "mythicity": "the ontological status of myth as part of a general theory of human expression" (3). As we said earlier, stereotypes constellate into systems of belief similar to mythic systems. Moreover, our culture tends to diminish the importance of myths: mythographer William Doty argues that "[m]yth tends to be lumped together with religion or philosophy or the arts as a superfluous facet of culture that may be considered enjoyable but not particularly functional" (7). In other words, myths are there, and we may pay attention to them as interesting little stories, but nobody takes them very seriously. So also with sexism, racism, and classism: they exist and, in fact, pervade popular culture and consciousness, but few people, let alone people submerged in popular culture, recognize their power. In this connection, Doty writes:

> Mythic themes may be present in a less than foundational way, just as many other thematic materials may guide composition, but mythic narratives themselves are ultimately "special." They are not little but big stories, touching not just the everyday but sacred or specially marked topics that concern more than just the immediate situation. And myths generally concern themes that humans face over and over again, rather than problems that are relevant only to one person or one group or at one particular period of life. We have many myths

about sexuality as a basic human perplexity, for example, but few about masturbation or "how far to go" on a first date. (8)

We also figured that this approach would permit us to discuss the function of ideology in popular culture. Consider Henry Giroux's definition of ideology:

> Ideology . . . refers to the production, interpretation, and effectivity of meaning. It contains both a positive and negative moment, each of which is determined, in part, by the degree to which it promotes or distorts reflexive thought and action. As a distortion ideology becomes hegemonic; as an illumination it contains elements of reflexivity and the grounds of social action. (66–67)

For Gould, mythicity is "human expression"; for Doty, myths are stories with special meaning, "large stories," and these two concepts dovetail with Giroux's definition of ideology: myths are human expression, stories we tell to organize and give significance and meaning to experience. These stories may take the mundane, the seemingly obvious, and make it "sacred," important, "charged." Further, myths can be used to reify hegemony—think, for example, of Nazi Germany— or to incite social action: Martin Luther King and his journey to the "promised land."

What we perceived as a fundamental problem with our students, however, was that they were not very familiar with their big stories— or even that such big stories exist. One way we could account for that would be to point to the complexity and diversity of cultural representations that the students had to confront. The big stories themselves had become fragmented, and now the students faced a mass of numbing images and "texts," all of which encapsulated bits and pieces of the big stories. What we felt the students needed were the tools to reassemble those bits and pieces.

We could also suggest that our students were the heirs to the "culture of narcissism," as described by Christopher Lasch. For Lasch, the culture of narcissism saw a turning away from historicity and continuity, to create a place where transhistorical big stories were displaced by a set of self-indulgent small tales. One no longer felt compelled to locate and justify the self within a larger communal and cultural sphere; rather, one created an existential universe out of oneself and one's own, immediate personal needs:

> To live for the moment is the prevailing passion—to live for yourself, not for your predecessors or posterity. We are fast losing the sense of historical continuity, the sense of belonging to a succession of generations originating in the past and stretching into the future. (5)

Our students, then, were caught in a double bind. They not only had to contend with an explosion of cultural representations, but had to do so without being grounded in the culturally and atemporally mythic.

By the end of the term, we wanted our students to be able to look at the "vulgar" iconography of popular culture and recognize that it did indeed embody something culturally "sacred," if not particularly pleasant or desirable. What we first needed to do, however, was to get them to recognize—or at least begin to consider—what the "popular" in *pop culture* meant: that it touched a large segment of a culture, including the students. Our students liked to perceive themselves as being too aware—of the media, of pop culture, of their separateness from all that—to be submerged in pop culture. We intended to persuade them otherwise. We did not go gently into that troubling notion; we kicked them into it on the first day of class.

Joe's Story: Myth and Culture-in-Progress

On the morning of the first day our class was to meet, we were both nervous about that session. Neither of us had ever done anything like this before; neither of us had team taught or taught this particular topic as the governing theme of a course. Moreover, no one at Clarion had ever done anything like this before. We were not even sure what our students would expect. Would they see the word "Myth" and expect an academic version of *Dungeons and Dragons?* Would they see the phrase "Popular Culture" and anticipate earnest discussions of Guns 'n Roses (or, horrible to think, discussion of what was popular with the teachers? Writing papers analyzing musical patterns in *The Touch of Wayne Newton?*) In short, we both believed—full of ourselves as we were—that a great deal was at stake in this course, and the whole tone of the semester would somehow be set on this first day.

So, naturally, we walked into class wearing funny hats. Without explanation, without comment. While we initially had no clear notion about why we wanted to do this, as I look back I believe we decided to wear the hats to announce what we saw to be, in part, our roles as teachers in the class: trickster figures, liminal figures hazing the boundaries between order and chaos. By playing such roles we would, with luck and skill, compel our students to both recognize and examine their particular locus in culture. Perhaps by changing the boundary between order and chaos from a double-solid line to a dotted line, the students themselves—for two mornings a week—would enjoy liminality and more clearly understand the difference between order and chaos, and the function of both.

Let me clarify: we did not consciously set out to be trickster figures. We did not realize that the idea of the trickster had informed our approach until well after the term ended. Nor did we set out to create a class or classroom that was a free-for-all. But in first designing the course we were aware that myth embraced and gave form to an amoebic world, and that was good. For an insulated culture, myth can create homogeneity, and give a group of individuals a unified purpose and a common field of expectations. But should one culture exist in a heterogeneous system—one culture among many, much as the melting pot, or chef's salad, of America—myth can also rigidify and set boundaries that both embrace and exclude, as one group becomes defined in relation to and against another. Furthermore, myth in conjunction with socioeconomic power can give a particular group the ability not only to confirm the rightness of its power through mythmaking, but also the power to marginalize through mythmaking.

If this were true, then our students likely had come to us already long-immersed in popular culture, integrally linked not only to myth but to the process of mythmaking, and so well-accustomed to their own particular sense of order and to the boundaries which encompassed their known, comfortable worlds that they respond as if restrained by an invisible electronic fence: we're bounded by something, but we can't see it, so we must really be free. But as trickster figures we could perhaps tempt them to step outside and look at their world from without, rather than within.

So why the hats? Since when do hats represent chaos, except maybe in the world of Bartholomew Cubbins? Well, they don't represent chaos so much as a violation of the perceived proper order of things, at least in the setting of an academic institution. By wearing silly hats we had hoped to invite the students to consider the mythic structures of the culture within which they were most immersed at that moment: the academic institution.

What struck me as we walked into the classroom and began the class was how few of the students actually laughed; the best we could elicit was a snicker or a giggle. Why? I doubt if we could say that the students were jaded, since even at Clarion teachers were not in the habit of wearing strange headgear to class. There is, of course, the possibility that what we did was not all that funny.

Or perhaps our students found that they had to pose questions to themselves they would normally not pose in this setting. Since this was not how teachers were "supposed" to behave, at least on a collegiate level, did they (the students) suddenly need to question the intelligence, the sense, the judgment of the teachers? Perhaps they wondered whether the hats had anything to do with the class. Perhaps they were concerned that the "proper" balance of student-teacher dynamics would have been upset if they had laughed, or laughed too loudly. After all, the teachers may not have thought the hats were silly at all. In essence, what Chris and I may have learned immediately was that the students had been mythicized into believing what and how teachers were supposed to be, and how they were to interact with their teachers. How were we threatening that stability? We wanted to allow such questions to bubble to the surface and be asked, out loud.

To create a peculiar metaphor, the hats were only the tip of the iceberg. The hats gave us access to broader questions about the dynamics of classroom structures—ranging from the nature of student-teacher interaction, to the configuration of the classroom, to the design of the classroom, to the very materials that compose the classroom space. A perfect irony would have been to conduct such a discussion while all of us stayed in our places—students at their desks, the teachers commanding the front of the room. But if we were going to be true to the trickster roles we sensed for ourselves, then we wanted the students to consider the mythic structures of this culture from the outside.

So we moved them to the outside. Or tried to. We wondered out loud why students sat, and sat where they sat. We wondered out loud why teachers—or at least us—stood, and stood where we stood. The answers we received were non-answers: no one had tried any other way. Translation: this is just the way it is since, to use a favorite student phrase, the beginning of time. What our students had clearly not considered was whether these configurations had *meaning*. Were they accidents, or were they symbolic articulations of power roles and appropriate teacher-student interactions?

We tried to find out by asking everyone to stand and move around the room—to leave their seats and mingle, reconfigure themselves according to individual wants and needs. For several seconds the students simply looked at us with blank faces—pedagogical humor, does anyone really get it? But as it became apparent that we were quite serious, a few students stood up, then finally most (but not all) of the class. Some left the room to get a drink, some invaded our space at the front of the room, a few settled onto our desk, most simply chatted and wandered aimlessly (as did we). Soon, in our new configuration, we spoke about the meanings of the structures of the class. What does it mean to sit where you sit? Why do you sit at all? Why do you raise your hands before you speak? What is the nature of the imaginary line that separates the teacher's space from the student's space? Why can teachers move, but students can't? Why can teachers penetrate the students' space, but students rarely penetrate the teacher's space, unless called to the front of the room to perform some task? Why do so few teachers bother to penetrate the students' space, but instead stay behind the imaginary line and the not-so-imaginary desk?

At the time that this was happening we both were excited and energized. For that time it felt as if we were talking on the edge of a cliff, giddy with the risk we were taking. At any one point we were skirting the possibility of losing control for the rest of the term, for in asking our students to read the symbolic structures of the classroom, we were also asking them to frame us as symbolic structures, subject to the same act of reading. But what happened instead was a recognition, that the structures of a class confirm and reconfirm the powerful tautology of the myth of the nature of the relationship between teacher and student. In other words, the structures articulated symbolically the hierarchy operating within the classroom, the nature of that hierarchy, and the place and role of both student and teacher in this particular universe and in this particular culture. What the students came to recognize was that what lay behind their behaviors and configurations was myth.

And so for the rest of the term, we—both students and teachers—engaged in open, probing dialogue about myth, difference, and popular culture, and the students lived happily ever after with a clarity of vision the likes of which they had never known.

Not.

As the term progressed, and after the term ended, we came to realize how deeply ingrained those structures are—and so how powerful myth is. Upon reflection, we realized that the students left their seats and altered their relationship to classroom space only after we had given them permission to do so. And not all students did so. We also recognized that what happened had a purpose, a teacher-defined purpose. We realized that never again in the term did the students, of their own will, reconfigure themselves in the classroom. They sat, in their usual places. And they almost always raised their hands.

And we, the trickster figures, realized just how powerfully the mythic structures worked through us. For all of our "bad boy" posturing we largely taught the class from the front, standing usually behind the imaginary line, and recognizing those who raised their hands. When the term came to an end, we pulled out the calculator and calculated the final grades, based upon assignments we had selected.

So was what happened a failure? No. One of our recognitions—and here "our" means teachers and students—was that some structure, some order, was essential if any learning was to take place, and that some hierarchy needed to be in place if learning was to have any direction. One, I suppose, can insist that learning is its own justification, but unless an academic institution can isolate itself entirely from the culture outside of it, learning without direction can never be. But perhaps more significantly we all began to perceive with depth the power of myth, its all-pervasiveness, and how, without our being fully aware of it, we are at one and the same time the heirs to and progenitors of myth. We are immersed in, and part of, the mythmaking process.

Chris's Story: Racism, Exclusion, and Difference

When we said we would discuss racism most of the students no doubt thought that our focus would be on black/white relations in the United States, and in a sense they were correct. But we began this discussion by showing clips (including the opening fifteen minutes) of Lenni Riefenstahl's *Triumph of the Will*. We asked students to write about the images they had seen, particularly to how the director portrayed the German people and Hitler in relationship to them. How, we asked, could a group of people let this happen, let one man's maniacal vision control their own? We returned to our point about myths and the creation of order from chaos, but wondered what happens when this process (the creation of order from chaos) becomes an end in itself rather than the means to an end.

We thought, perhaps, that we would try to illustrate how a group of people could let this happen. The semester was nearly half over, and the class had started to gel. People were making connections between the theory we discussed, the texts we read, and their own lives. Our student-centered approach helped the students to see us as something other than traditional teachers, trusting us enough, for example, not to call us Dr. Ferry and Dr. Bodziock. The time had arrived to exploit this trust.

On a Tuesday morning, we brought donuts to class, and I began serving them to students with a flourish. As I moved among the class, Joe asked everyone wearing glasses to stand. Four students did. He told them to go to the front of the room, which they also did. He then took their donuts away and announced that these were people who wore glasses as a symbol of their physical imperfections, and that for the rest of the period, we would ignore them except to make myths about them. He told the seated students they were the "elect" and the "elite" and asked them to get into their groups. Both of us berated those standing.

At first, everyone was confused: why should we want to do such a thing, the class wanted to know, and why should we do it to these four? Why not, was our response. Look at yourselves; you're not wearing glasses; you don't have this particular physical imperfection; therefore they are different from you—from us—and we have decided to exile them. "Huh," seemed to be the response of the seated students as they munched their donuts and watched Joe and me pick through the exiled students' belongings at what had once been their desks. When one asked us to leave her things alone, I shouted at her to shut up and moved toward her trying to look as threatening as a five-foot-eight man can. Some seated students persisted in defending those up front. Joe told them to be quiet or they might have to join them in banishment. Everyone now seemed just scared enough to believe us, and the elect set about their task.

Or was it, finally, fear? The most disturbing thing about this exercise was the ease with which we pulled off. It strikes me that while the students were uncertain how to act in this particular experience of "class," they knew it was, after all, "class," a place where "bad" things never actually happen, where teachers usually act in students' best interests. These students trusted us enough to know (or was it to believe?) that the exercise was canned, that whenever we finished making whatever point we were trying to make, we would resume our normal course. And certainly they were correct: Joe and I bore the exiles no ill will. We chose glasses as a distinguishing factor on our way into the room because, while we wanted the selection to be arbitrary, we also wanted the outcasts to share a common feature and eyewear seemed pretty obvious. Nevertheless it was *so* easy; they were *so* compliant. How could a group of people let this happen? How indeed!

But this story does not end here. In fact, it has barely begun. The exiles tried to say a few things, but we all ignored them. The elect set about their task with gusto: since they can't see clearly anyway, they're probably stupid; yeah, only nerds and stupid people wear glasses. This continued for fifteen or twenty minutes, and then an extraordinary thing happened. The exiles talked among themselves briefly and

marched out of the room. Joe and I jeered them, told them good rid-
dance, and continued with the class. But shortly thereafter the door
opened and the four, minus their glasses, returned. (This was a truly
stunning moment, except that one student, who obviously couldn't
see very well, tripped loudly over the trash can. Oh well.) One of the
returnees, Jon, seemed to be the leader: the four went with him to the
teacher's desk where Jon announced that, since they had rid themselves of their glasses, they were now our "equals," no longer different. You're only passing, I said, and one of the elect added that the
glasses simply symbolized deeper imperfections and deficiencies that
remained intact. But Jon and his people did not back down. In fact,
they ignored both Joe and me and engaged their (former?) classmates.
It was extraordinary. For the next forty-five minutes Joe and I sat on
the radiator at the room's edge and listened while the students talked
about their experiences as exiles and elect in our culture-in-progress,
and as African-Americans, as women, as the kids who always got beat
up in high-school, in short what it felt like to be the objects of, the
victims of, and the perpetrators of the myths we had talked about all
semester.

For us as teachers, the truly remarkable thing was that it was as
if we were not there. It's not that we felt uninvited to join the conversation—or maybe we did. But this moment clearly belonged to the
students. They claimed power for themselves, and even as I write this,
I'm beginning to realize that I knew during those minutes what it felt
like to be excluded from a discussion. Yet that seems too negative a
way to express what I feel, since neither Joe nor I were excluded. It's
more that what the students said seemed so much more important,
significant, consequential, than anything we might have added. The
students responded so well to Jon and the others that a genuine conversation took place; no one felt compelled to raise a hand and nearly
everyone joined in.

Nevertheless, I remain troubled. In subsequent class meetings, we
all returned effortlessly to a more familiar mode of instruction, hands
once again raised for recognition. In "Pedagogy of the Distressed"
Jane Tompkins argues that we in the United States do not have the
"banking model" of education Freire describes: "We have class discussion, we have oral reports, we have student participation of various
kinds—students often choose their own paper topics, suggest additional readings, propose topics for discussion. As far as most of us are
concerned, the banking model is obsolete" (653–54). I wonder, though,
if the many good things Tompkins describes form a false front behind

which lurks the old banking model—or something far worse. I'm thrilled by the ease with which students embraced their own power as thinkers, learners, and active members of the culture-in-progress that was the "Myth, Difference, and Popular Culture" classroom. On the other hand, I'm terrified by the similar ease with which they gave it back up and assumed the familiar roles. I reached the point where I pleaded with students not to raise their hands when they had something to say. In fact, I made this plea on the last day of the semester. How could a group of people let this happen? How indeed!

Conclusions?

We could tell you about other interesting classes—for example, our discussion of images of women's and men's bodies, during which we examined copies of *Playboy* and *Playgirl*. We looked not only at the naked people and their body types, but at the magazines' composition as well. We determined that *Playboy*, with its mainstream advertisers, high production values, and (pardon the cliche) interesting articles was somehow respectable. *Playgirl*, in contrast, seemed tawdry. The issue we studied contained no mainstream ads and the ads it did have were for sex toys and services. Moreover, the articles dealt not necessarily with "women's issues" but with sex. The class decided (with no prompting from us) that the culture sanctioned men's sexuality and expression—*Playboy* was respectable—but frowned upon women's sexuality and expression—*Playgirl* was sleazy. (An interesting aside: the men in the class were threatened when the women looked at *Playgirl* but seemed to take it as their right to look at *Playboy*.) Or our discussion of *Rubyfruit Jungle*, homosexuality, and heterosexism that nearly turned into a brawl and made sworn enemies (so we are told) of two students. Frankly, though, we would rather forget that incident.

Was "Myth, Difference, and Popular Culture" a success? This was our dream course, almost like a child, and we are proud parents. We felt energized as teachers and as learners, and certainly our favorite place to be during the fall 1992 semester was 253 Carlson Hall on Tuesday and Thursday mornings at 9:30. We were exhilarated to watch students who an English department colleague called in a national publication "woefully provincial" take steps—albeit first and tentative steps—toward critical thinking and more circumspect visions of the world. The student evaluations were unusually positive. With the students' permission, here are some excerpts from their personal (versus official and confidential) evaluations. Christine writes that "this class and the teachers are the best experiences I have had at Clarion. I am a Senior; therefore that says a lot." Jennifer adds that "this class has changed my life, and I have been given an example of how to see and understand all different kinds of people and *relate* to them." Finally, Patrick writes that "often I have gone home from this class either angry, depressed, happy, but never without a haunting idea or wish that I could say something more." The students have spread the word to such an extent that the registrar and the department chair have been besieged with requests for seats. As things stand now, however, "Myth, Difference, and Popular Culture" will be an interesting aberration in the curriculum. On the practical level, the university's dismal budget situation ensures there will be no released time for team teaching. From a philosophical (or perhaps political) perspective, the course did not enjoy overwhelming support from the department. While the dean and some of our colleagues did, in fact, endorse our efforts, others were heard to call us "crackpots," or to say that the course was "crazy" (one professor asked Chris while he was talking with a group of students in the hall before class how "your goofy class is going"), or to suggest that we should devote our time to teaching "real" courses.

And so, this is our story. When the students come back to visit us (and they frequently do) they tell us that they still see each other and still talk about the class and the issues we raised. They tell us they are impatient with teachers who lecture and yearn to start debate. They tell us they will never read a text in quite the same way as before, whether the "text" be a book, an advertisement, a television show, or the world. They tell us their lives are changed.

But we wonder. We are back pretty much where we were before the fall 1992 semester, each teaching four courses, serving on committees, advising zillions of students, pushing for change in the department and institution, and trying to live our lives. It has been so easy for us to slip back into familiar ways. How easy will it be, we wonder, for these students, "changed" though they may be, to change back?

4

Gravedigging: Excavating Cultural Myths

Colleen M. Tremonte _____

grave: to dig, excavate; to carve or shape with a chisel;
an excavation for burial of a body; authoritative, weighty,
meriting serious consideration.

dig: to turn up, loosen or remove dirt; to bring to the
surface (unearth); to hollow out or form by removing
earth; to drive down so as to penetrate; to excavate.

"I am Professor ———, and I am a Marxist and a feminist." With these
words a former colleague of mine swiftly opens the first-year writing
seminar that she teaches. After about thirty painfully silent seconds,
she proceeds to ask, "What did you hear?" Following another awkward pause she answers her own question: "That I'm a commie and
a bitch!"[1]

I sometimes tell this story by way of opening the dialogue in the
writing classes I teach. Knowing the frankness of my words startles
some students, I carefully ask why they think I might have shared this
anecdote. Haltingly, and sometimes angrily, come the replies: "Because
you're really her!" "It's a not-so-subtle message." "You don't like feminists or communists." While students may not initially appreciate the
tactic, with this one exchange we have clearly established the classroom as a rhetorical and political space, and, with little prompting, are
engaged in a lively conversation on the power of language to create
identity. We have also opened Pandora's box and let loose the "vices"
of confrontation and conflict—confrontation and conflict I believe
necessary so that students are more likely to query their longstanding
ideals and values and less apt to escape into silent apathy. Such vices

prompt us to undertake the unseemly task of "gravedigging": a systematic questioning of cultural myths and mythmaking that makes visible the ways in which we use language to construct, confer and consume identity.

An ugly word that conjures visions of morbidity and degradation, an act which by its very nature suggests physical and spiritual violations, gravedigging provides an appropriate metaphor for locating, dislocating, and relocating the various posturings buried within cultural texts.[2] By giving a reader or writer license to "assault" the text, gravedigging empowers her to challenge how society composes and interprets the world through the word. It enables the student to critically examine how this process involves the decomposition and recomposition of rhetorics and ideologies which compete for supremacy in the intellectual marketplace. You might say this activity encourages the student to dig into the dead issues of the cultural past and retill them so that she may eventually reap her own intellectual harvest by creating a space for resistance.

Rooted in the *stasis* theory of classical rhetoric, gravedigging begins with acknowledgment and definition: considering if and why we are wary of the word, speculating on its power as metaphor, and negotiating boundaries for its meaning. For example, first-class brainstorming sessions typically elicit responses like these from student groups:

> Group 1 *gravedigging:* corpses, burials, funerals, decay, Shakespeare, archaeologists, graverobbers, Mark Twain, cemeteries, dirt, shamans.

> Group 2 *gravedigging:* hidden treasures, bones, skeletons, six-foot plots, mausoleums, tombstones.

> Group 3 *gravedigging:* decaying matter, relics, rituals, bones, termites, parasites, coffins.

Each group betrays a cursory familiarity with the term and its associative connotations (that the list includes Shakespeare and Mark Twain also illustrates an awareness of the English class context), and each accords the requisite tenor of moroseness. Curiously, however, none recognizes gravedigging as an action, as a verb—and none acknowledges the participatory complexion of the activity. So I proffer a definition of gravedigging as ritually or culturally *unclean* and *aggressive* work that leads to unexpected and potentially taboo discoveries, much as the physical act of opening or excavating a burial plot. Gravedigging thus defined gives us permission to exhume and examine everything connected with a body/text: the way we speak about it, the way we describe it, the way we understand it.

To couple an anecdote that invites political identification with a discussion of gravedigging does little to build professorial ethos, and students soon suspect that I am not simply some liberal feminist (in the past, one student walked out of the room, sought out a trusted faculty member, and asked if he should drop my class because he was male), but that I am weird. Unorthodox and unexpected, such disruptions do, nonetheless, lay the foundations for writing pedagogy as a practice of cultural criticism by forcing students to ponder the politics of education.

To counter student dis-ease we begin with our gravedigging by *philosophizing* on language and politics in the writing class, first speculating on the meanings of the terms and then excavating our findings by considering what skeletons or ghosts lurk behind each. In one instance, Cindy, a student in an "Individual and Community in American Society" course, philosophized:[3]

> Language seems an important part of a writing class since writing is a way of communicating. Throughout history language enabled people to learn about the universe and man [sic], to build trade and commerce, and to communicate. . . . [A]rt, literature, and even civilization depend upon language. . . .
>
> I don't think politics has much place in a writing class, though. Maybe in a government class, but even then, a position shouldn't be presented as the only or the right way. Right now people are talking about Perot and Clinton and Bush (because MSU might host a debate) and the issue of family values everywhere I go. Overall, I think this is a good thing, but I don't think our class should spend time analyzing people's politics—or talking about feminism—it doesn't fit into writing.

In the first paragraph, Cindy gives a generalized description about language, a litany duly learned in an earlier world history or social science class. Her buzz words—history, literature, art, civilization— betray mimicry, and her sentence patterns and use of third-person pronouns belie an understanding of language as objective discourse. In the next paragraph, she reveals a common aversion to politicizing the classroom, including notions that politics should only be studied in its "proper" context (a government or political science class) and that teachers should not be openly political. Yet Cindy cannot escape the political, and as her excavation collapses into freewriting about media coverage and family values, she reveals her own stance.

Later, writing in her journal, Cindy proceeded to cull through the *ghosts* that might have influenced her understandings:

The ghosts behind my understandings of language must be my teachers in grade school and high school. I mean, I don't remember exactly what they said about language, but everything we studied used words. *Jane Eyre* and *The Color Purple*, history and science, even American Politics. Other ghosts? My parents, maybe. But they didn't talk about language, both my mom and dad thought us kids needed to read more books. They didn't like . . . [and] seemed very concerned with us watching tv. . . .

Ghosts and politics? . . . Maybe mom has a few ghosts. I believe she thinks of herself as a failure or something. She has a college degree but decided against working fulltime to stay home with my brothers and me. I don't think she regrets her decision but she doesn't like the way the feminists attack her choice. But she doesn't like for my father to agree with her either . . . the only connection I see [between language and politics] is that we use words to communicate our feelings.

While Cindy's excavation of her written responses on *language* remains schooled and objective, that on *politics* is immediately and overtly personalized (especially when she speaks of her mother). In an attempt to explain her mother's positions, Cindy felt compelled to qualify her own judgment with conditional markers such as *perhaps, sometimes,* and *but*. This rhetorical strategy, along with her final apologia that "words [enable us] to communicate our feelings," betrays an active resistance to linking language, politics, and personal experience.

Again, such resistance is not particular to Cindy, as few first-year students believe it necessary to politicize their opinions. And admittedly, the lure of expressivism beckons brightly, calling us to acknowledge self-discovery through writing as sufficiently enlightening. After all, has not Cindy discovered something about herself and her identity which, in turn, might help her negotiate her understandings of the world?

One way to challenge such hesitancy, to politicize the social and the personal, is to link gravedigging with the stasis theory of classical rhetoric, a theory which many scholars have noted is dialogic in nature.[4] Though often associated with Aristotelian rhetoric and understood as a techne, stasis has been connected to the broader tradition of Greek sophistic rhetoric, hence reestablishing its epistemological possibilities (Carter 107). It is within this context that stasis engenders a pedagogy of resistance (see John T. Gage's "An Adequate Epistemology for Composition: Classical and Modern Perspectives" and Michael Carter's "*Stasis* and *Kairos:* Principles of Social Construction in Classical Rhetoric").

Historically, stasis enabled rhetors in the classical world to identify an area of disagreement, the point to be argued, and the issue on
which the case hinged by asking a set of questions that established the
nature of the issue as fact, definition, and quality (value and consequence): *an sit, quid sit, quale sit.* Because these questions are recur-
sive—as students work through the questions they often see how
subsequent answers qualify or contradict earlier ones—they initiate a
generative dialogue in which students learn to be increasingly more
critical in evaluating an issue or topic.[5] By first isolating the point of
impasse, the point at which conflicting ideas bring a discussion to a
standstill, stasis forces students to seek a resolution. In other words,
stasis not only helps students identify the issue at hand, it provides a
direction for action. And because stasis is situational—it responds with
arguments appropriate to the "circumstances" of the situation—students are able to move beyond initial problem-solving strategies toward dialectical exchange.[6]

Gravedigging via stasis enables students to contextualize their
investigations so as to examine how socially constructed and politically situated myths affect their personal lives.[7] Stasis enables students
to rechannel their frustrations with difficult investigations into more
productive questioning. This, subsequently, transforms adversarial
conflict, what Henry Giroux terms "self-destructive opposition," into
constructive resistance (109). Constructive resistance, in turn, creates
an impetus for both rhetorical action and social action.

After philosophizing, digging, and working with stasis, students
begin to realize that everything—*everything*—in our class will be tied
to language, culture, and inquiry, so our conversations turn toward
social constructions of identity/ies within popular discourse. Given
the rapid globalization and commoditization of media technologies,
films, television, and magazines offer some of the most immediate and
productive sites for gravedigging.[8] Such study does not merely isolate
or deconstruct ideologies within particular cultural forms—for instance,
revealing the intentional artificiality or Sleeping Beauty-ishness of the
film *Pretty Woman*—nor does it simply determine how readers organize texts according to their own experiences. It also recognizes that
popular culture forms provide individuals with a means of accommo-
dating, negotiating, and even resisting culturally "packaged" identity
(Giroux and Simon, *Popular Culture* 16).

To examine how popular texts construct and promote cultural
myths, gravedigging draws on specific, interdependent tasks, such as
searches and seizures and media tracking. Of course, the mere notion

of "myth" conjures a number of attending ghosts which need to be exorcised—the ghost of myth as a lie, the ghost of myth as a false-hood, the ghost of myth as an exaggerated story. Thus, again asking the stasis questions, we draft a *transformational* definition of the term *cultural myth,* a definition that we actively seek to change in the course of our investigations.[9] For instance, we might initially write that "a myth is a story usually told to explain some phenomenon and is usually a fiction" (a textbook definition) or that "a cultural myth is an untruth, a wive's tale repeated throughout time, which encourages people to act in the same ways" (a group effort).

Simple, direct, and (students think) boring. But wait! By purpose-fully locating a specific myth in a popular form, then questioning the implicit or unspoken assumptions behind it, we realize the myth as being generated in respect to a need and/or an expectation. No longer able to judge the "myth" as true or false, but as oppressive or liberatory, our definition might be transformed to read: "a cultural myth is a story that depicts the seemingly basic and agreed upon values and structures of a culture or civilization." This primes the site for stasis.

The search and seizure authorizes students to police a text and to arrest its deceptive intent, to gather evidence by which to indict the myth. For example, one search and seizure has students locate an advertisement that makes overt appeals to the myth of individualism or to the American dream. Nothing startling—nothing new. But the musty smell of wealth seeps into the atmosphere when we continue our excavation from a class perspective (that is, when we question whether the texts covertly assume a posture on class status) by apply-ing stasis.[10] In one instance, after determining the target audience, rhetorical appeals, and unspoken assumptions of her ad, a student confidently reported that the myth of individualism was "alive and well" and inspirational to today's working woman. Amy argued that her text, which featured a young, white, professional woman contem-plating buying a sports car, promoted self-reliance and independence, essential attributes of American individualism. And, more importantly, she felt the ad implied that in the nineties "women as well as men" could achieve this goal.

Excavating the site, Amy wrote in her journal:

> *The fact of class:* does it exist? Well, I guess so, though despite what the news shows I think most of Americans are middle class.

> *The definition of class:* an economic group or category to which you belong because of income and assets.

The value of class: Class enables one to move between groups; to acquire material goods; to gain status. It encourages people to work to better themselves and their families (all the programs I watch show this).

Often, having generalized similar findings, students begin to challenge the entire course direction, complaining about where "this class is going" and about the "frivolity" of the course content. Fearing they have been "cheated" of what is real and useful about learning through the search and seizure, they sometimes become hostile to a pedagogy that fails to transmit knowledge or deal with serious and real topics.

To answer this charge and to reiterate the argument for popular culture as a preferred site of study, we evaluate our initial search and seizure findings from an imposed perspective generated by stasiastic inquiry. In so doing, we engage the text on yet another level, practicing critical literacy (Giroux 231). For example, we might retill Amy's excavation by questioning her reliance on an unspoken concept of class. We asked why she classified most Americans as middle class, why she restricted her definition to monetary income, and what connection she saw between income and status. In responding, Amy first looked to ghosts and skeletons in her family background (shades of a single mother supporting her three daughters). She then considered the ad as it was influenced by or was influencing other students, all of whom were part of a consumer culture.

Eventually, stasis led us from an *apparent* inquiry of individualism to a *contextual* one of class, status, and capital, and then to a *substantive* one of individualism in a consumer society. Thus, while this task readily introduces students to the art of hasty generalization, it also forces them to move beyond superficial recognition of stereotyping, to press beyond aesthetic or formal evaluation to cultural critiquing. It demands that students dissect the rhetorical components of a socially constructed myth and then overturn the legitimacy of their own findings.[11] Stasis also enables students to challenge their idea of the *popular,* admitting the connection between knowledge, power, and pleasure.

The most provocative and troublesome search and seizures, those which bore into the very marrow of a first-year student's identity, into her personal values and concrete experiences, are those that assault the myths of family and gender. Students especially resent any claim that media-created images actually contribute to the construction of these myths. They trust instead that popular media play with existent social realities. But just as viewers have begun recognizing rhetorical ploys and emotional pitches or have begun appreciating the "PC"-ness of commercials, the media have exploded our expectations and erased ironic self-distancing.

Nike's "Just Do It" advertisement illustrates the point. When a male student first pronounced the ad promoted individualism and was "the perfect example of progress in our attitudes toward women in the 90s," few voiced disagreement. Contrary to a sexist beer advertisement that appealed to "the voyeur in all of us," Greg felt Nike "let women get in shape for themselves." Yet, when a young woman pointedly asked Greg what first attracted him to the ad, the dirt flew! The scene grew tense as students argued over the aesthetics of an athletic body: even if a woman thought she wanted "to look this way" for herself, a female student reasoned, too many "silent pressures" contributed to this desire, including those of men. "I like these ads," the young woman admitted, "they're great." But she also saw the larger myth as "not so healthy," "controlled," and "not concerned with black, working women like my mother."

Once she introduced her mother's experience against which to judge the ad, Latoya shifted the general excavation site toward one haunted with personal ghosts. However, the personal soon merged with the social and public—when asking the question of consequence, the class decided that Nike had excluded all working mothers who do not have the means to "Just Do It!" and, further, that the ad implied that women who do not "get in" or "stay in" shape are not successful. Hence, though Nike undercut the standard beauty myth by promoting self-interest in terms of health and accomplishment, had it dismantled a potentially repressive ideal? What were the politics of "just doing it?"

Since the search and seizure can easily be converted into a collaborative task, the risk of normalizing exists. Students become quite facile at negotiating answers and speaking in "one voice" not only so as to avoid interpersonal discomfort, but so as to resist conflict. Gravedigging through stasis undermines the unified front, however, by continually displacing the group's assessments. As such, gravedigging can be likened to social-epistemic rhetoric: questions of fact, definition, and consequence force the student to acknowledge the "dialectical interaction of the observer, the discourse community (social group) in which the observer is functioning, and the material conditions of existence" (Berlin 488). It disrupts the students' attempts at interpreting the material world, forcing students to reconcile conflicts between what they "believe" about cultural myths and their perceptions of images of popular discourse which depend upon these myths.

For example, group D began its search and seizure by sharing the following ideas on the myth of family:

> Gary: I believe we've come a long way in bringing equality between men and women although there is a long way to go. Especially if you consider less than 70 years ago women couldn't even vote. But I don't think women should feel forced to change traditional roles, such as motherhood. I think that some women think that they have to have a career and that hurts the family.

> Michelle: A family is a group of people that live together. Each member . . . has a certain basic role to fulfill. The parents provide and guide the children whose role it is [sic] to grow up . . . have kids, and assume parental roles. There is no contract or written agreement; these roles are implied by society.

> Grant: A family is a unit of people, usually relatives, responsible for each other's well-being and tied together by common values and beliefs; may be single-parent household, though two parents are better able to meet needs of growing children.

When responses such as these were reintroduced in the larger class forum, a number of students reported they were products of single-parent, female-headed households and families and were none the worse for it. Grant, now writing against the grain of the group's definition, then offered that the myth of the family discriminated against female "providers":

> There is a certain falsehood in today's society regarding the myth of the family. This falsehood deals with people's perceptions of the father figure as the inherent provider. Although people believe women can enter the workplace, they also believe women are inferior providers. . . .
>
> Deputy Sheriff Deborah H., my mother, is a perfect example of how this myth hurts women. Although she receives the same pay as other deputies, she works under the impression that she will never be promoted and that people don't believe she can provide a comfortable standard of living for me and herself. . . . When a man has a job and is the sole support of his family he is considered a provider in the workforce; but when a woman is the sole supporter that same job is considered a gift. . . .

Since Grant's response readily conflicted with his group's earlier ideas, they had to renegotiate earlier definitions to reflect an expanded perspective.

The group's efforts encountered yet another setback when they excavated a series of Banana Republic ads that depict a "chosen family," an attempt to overturn the dominant media image. Shot in black and white, the first ad features a rainbow coalition lying in a circle, clasping hands, napping; the second features three women slouching in an open convertible, arms draped about each other's shoulders, one woman kissing another's wrist; the third is an in-your-face front shot with the woman on the left and the man on the right both resting their heads upon the center Adonis's shoulders. In a haphazard yet calculated manner, the ad suggests familial relationships should not be restricted to blood relations and seeks to blur distinctions between heterosexuality, homosexuality, and bisexuality.

While none of the members disliked the visual effect of the ad, only Grant endorsed its message. During our mob conference the group expressed an empathy for treating friends as family—all had at least one close friend whom they thought of as a brother or sister. The tenor of our conversation changed, though, when we questioned these sentiments in light of their earlier responses: what "role" would the friend assume? would expectations or responsibilities differ for male friends and female friends? would sexual preference matter in any assumed role, such as parental? Student outrage at gay parenting so strongly possessed them that they often recanted earlier *liberal* or *progressive* stances. Whereas single parenting was acceptable, gay or lesbian parenting was not. Jason, who had earlier lauded his single mother for doing "a fine job of raising him," soon argued that "all children need positive, male role models." When confronted with inconsistencies in his attitudes and stances, Jason retreated and espoused empty platitudes.

Such retreats indicate the practical limits of gravedigging for many students, and the need for multiple excavation sites when studying popular culture. Thus, along with search and seizures, *media trackings* signal the aggressive nature of the dig: figuratively, they suggest pursuit and capture, hostility and violence; literally, they require keen observation and cunning. Working independently or collaboratively, students locate and critique a myth as advanced, refuted, or parodied within a television sitcom, soap opera, drama, or cartoon (or movie) that relies on a sustained and developed narrative. Again working with *stasis*, students name the myth that is established within the text over an extended period of time for an audience. They then define the parameters set forth by the visual and narrative contexts of the show and question the effects on the viewers: they isolate the manner in which the text constructs the myth, and then question the consequences of such for a popular audience.

Not surprisingly, most students follow shows such as *Roseanne, Beverly Hills 90210, Home Improvement, Fresh Prince of Bel Air,* and *The Simpsons.* Sondra, for example, chose to track *Home Improvement* because it is "a hot, new, hip hit." Already familiar with the characters, she watched five episodes in an attempt to critique the show's construction of family and gender. As did all students, Sondra had an opportunity to talk about her show both in and outside of class before writing a short analysis of her findings. Gravedigging via stasis, Sondra wrote:

> *Ghosts:* I was prepared to hate this show last year when I first started watching it—the commercials for it were so sexist. When my younger brother began watching it (it came on before Roseanne), so did I, and it was funny! Jill and Tim have a good marriage. And when there's a problem, Jill usually wins. So I thought—I was wrong.

> *Fact:* Yes there's a family—Jill, Tim, the boys, even Wilson and Al.

> *Definition:* White, predominantly male unit. A traditional unit, with traditional roles and responsibilities (Jill only got a parttime job this season).

> *Consequences:* Even though Jill seems to get the upper hand, Tim wins.

> After watching five episodes numerous times I've decided that Jill and Tim always end up happy. No matter what Tim does that is sexist, Jill tells him, he says he's sorry and all is forgiven but nothing changes. I know this is too easy. Yet I find myself still laughing. I'm sort of mad and a bit confused.

Sondra's anger and confusion illustrate how television "shows ingratiate themselves with viewers who, ironically, want to feel superior to TV yet keep watching it" (Ozersky 342). Up until this point in the semester she had been troubled with feeling guilty and privileged about her own white, middle-class background. Now she challenged not only media constructions of cultural myths, but her own complicity in their identity-invention.

To further illustrate how popular media promote hegemonic ideologies even when advancing "radical" stances, we also excavate a variety of genre films. One semester, for example, we worked with George Steven's *Shane* (1953), Spike Lee's *Do the Right Thing* (1989), and Lawrence Kasdan's *Grand Canyon* (1992).[12] We began with *Shane* because it offers a readily identifiable presentation of a classic American myth—the West—thus allowing us to articulate a common, historic understanding of "cultural myth." With few exceptions, however, students tired quickly of the film: some were bored by an exaggerated plot; others wearied of the cinematography (too technicolored—too much Joey); all complained about the lack of relevance of "myth" to their own lives. So, once again, we needed to contextualize our dig, to assess parallels of the myth in contemporary society, such as the political arena, and to critique the presentation of the myth from an imposed perspective of race, gender or class. Writing dialogue journals, students' comments ran as follows:

> Hi Kim, Hi Grant,
>
> Well, I'm pretty sick of stasis questions and *Shane!* I mean, the movie was so overdone—gunfights, cowboys, homesteaders, lots of land. The only thing that surprised me was the way the movie tried to make Shane's character more mysterious. Anyway, on to fact, definition and consequence. That this movie dealt with the myth of the West is pretty obvious. I define the West as a place of freedom and expansion, of codes of honor, of individualism (I'm thinking of Turner). The significant consequence of this myth to the movie is that *it is* the movie, plot and all. I guess maybe the myth . . . [lives] today, given Bush's actions in the Persian Gulf War. . . . This is pretty confusing. Well, that's all I can think to say. Bye! Marc

While Marc says he will apply stasis to the myth, he resists taking risks or exploring possibilities, and he neglects to comment on the one aspect of the film that "surprised" him—the portrayal of Shane as a mysterious character. Kim, in responding to Marc's letter, notices this but avoids commenting, choosing to focus on her own interest in the role of woman:

> Hi Grant, Hi Marc,
>
> Marc, I agree with you, *Shane* was a bit predictable, but I think that's the whole point. To see how the myth works. I also agree with you about the West being a place of freedom and honor, but I think it probably only worked (and maybe still does) for men. Maybe that's why Shane is made mysterious. . . . Did you notice the way women were treated in this movie? The myth completely shut out Marion [Joe's wife and little Joey's mother]. Now I know this 1953 movie was trying to be as faithful to the historic "old" West as possible, but PLEAZZZE!!!! After all, the film was pretty stylized. Besides, all Marion did was whine—she was more of a prop than a character. Normally, I wouldn't be troubled by this, but the same thing happens in *Quigley Down Under* and in *Unforgiven,* and I like those movies. What do you think?

Though Kim doesn't overtly apply the stasis questions, she does two things which point toward definition and consequence: (1) she agrees that the West was a place of honor and freedom, but (2) she questions what this definition means to women. We might reexamine these responses as a class by scrutinizing their own latent assumptions, so as to open additional spaces of inquiry in movie mythmaking—including those concerned with audience needs, expectations, and participation as consumers.

Since *Shane* risks breeding superficial empathy, we next viewed *Do The Right Thing*. While most students could easily talk about the film's stylized, formal composition, many hesitated to discuss whether or not the subtext of the narrative was racist (blacks discriminating against Asians). Fewer still acknowledged the sexist tint of the film itself (the presentation of Rosie Perez's character). Most students simply wanted to excavate and to indict the phrase *do the right thing*. Or as one male student, Jabaar, wrote:

> "Do the right thing" isn't an excuse for doing whatever you want to do but to do what's best for the community, the people around you (the phrase is self-explanatory). People know what right behavior and action are—they just don't always do it—like Mookie.

When I asked Jabaar if Sal [the pizzeria owner] and Mookie [Lee's character, a delivery person] would agree on the self-evident nature of the phrase, he replied, "Probably, they just wouldn't act the same way." Then, in an attempt to shift attention, Jabaar asked me, "How do you think they would define the phrase?" In the ensuing discussion, I speculated as to how Sal's understanding and values, though seemingly tied to family and honor, were also tied to being a property owner, while Mookie's values were tied to non-ownership.

We further jeopardized our findings by exploring the possible consequences of gender marginalization in the film and by questioning the audience's acceptance of it. We asked: can films looking at the problems of race be sexist? Is racism a greater problem than sexism? Our responses to Lee's treatment of women—some lauding it as believable and thus necessary, others naming it exploitation—pressed us into a classic stasis impasse or standstill. We were forced to define *racism* and *sexism* before interrogating and explaining the consequences of each both in the movie narrative and for the larger audience. Again, we tried not to erase our resistance but, rather, to structure it into critical opposition. Both conversations provided openings for interrogating problems of gender marginalization and the acquisition of material wealth. What did Mookie or Sal "own" that Rosie Perez's character did not have access to? What does the film narrative promote in respect to "ownership" and violence and women? How do viewers participate or not participate in this process of ownership through their (social) class positionings?

Once *Shane* and *Do the Right Thing* set our gravedigging in motion, we tracked the competing rhetorics of gender, class, and/or race in more mainstream films (i.e., blockbusters). After all, just because we can locate cultural myths constructed, promoted, and/or resisted within these select genres we can't be sure that students will recognize how popular films in general can extend cultural hegemony and domesticate oppositional pedagogies. As Gitlin points out, *film,* as a part of a larger cultural industry, "organizes entertainment into terms that are, as much as possible, compatible with the hegemonic discourse" (242).

To illustrate this dilemma, we concluded this particular media tracking with *Grand Canyon* (Ron Howard's *Parenthood* or Christopher Columbus's *Mrs. Doubtfire* would probably also work). Once again, students opposed excavating such a "normal" movie, and when the question of class was introduced, and the issue of whether or not the American dream advanced within the film (and without in the commercial arena) was predominantly a "white" one, students bristled. All pointed out that Kevin Kline's and Danny Glover's characters had essentially the same goals and held similar values; it was just that Kline's character had "strayed a bit." One student argued we should read the film as a parable, replete with traditional archetypes. Within a relatively short time, though, we turned to scrutinizing the consequences of select characters' personal ameliorations, of their apparent transcendence of racial clash and gender constrictions.

Our conversations were prompted, in part, by two women laughing out loud during the scene when Mary McDonnell's character, Claire, finds an abandoned baby in an alleyway. These women felt the character's fawning over the child and her insistence on "keeping it at home" rather than giving the child to the authorities were indicative of "a male fantasy." In class the next day, we discussed ways of turning this initial response into a more critical reading of the film. Discussions over the portrayal of women ultimately resulted in several perceptive journal entries which excavated the male-female relationships of all the major female characters. Such entries, having exhumed personal ghosts and communal impositions, also provided the groundwork for more formal writing assignments.

Though searches and seizures and media trackings are the cornerstones of our cultural gravedigging, they are not the only tasks we set ourselves. The generative dialogue finds students interviewing various people—academics, battered women, homeless—to determine how media forms have or have not influenced their perceptions of cultural myths, and how such perceptions afford power and recognition. This dialogue provides numerous writing possibilities, all of which answer the more general literacy "goals" demanded of the composition course while still advancing a liberatory pedagogy. For example, for her final writing assignment Cindy chose to write a scholarly editorial in which she criticized television's refashioning June Cleaver for the nineties (eighties) through Claire Huxtable, and calling for a new "myth of mother" more closely portraying the powerful women in her own life. And though students groan that "we're doing the same thing again," they no longer reject the constructive possibilities laden within their own resistance.

The dissonance that arises when we play in the graveyard with the mythmakers is a fine noise, one that challenges us to recognize how products of popular media culture both enable and disable identity discourse. If we let the graveyard just sit and moulder in silence, then any chance of our owning "meaning-making" stagnates and dies. We risk a limited understanding of knowledge as sacred relics passed on by tradition alone. By taking our revels to the graveyard, however, by raising a fine din tumbling linguistic tombstones and profaning cultural icons, we free ourselves from myths which may no longer meet our needs. We can still recognize what was once powerful about them, respect that former power, but we learn to participate in the multiple forms of cultural production.

5

Constructing Art&Facts:
The Art of Composition, the Facts of
(Material) Culture

Paul Gutjahr _____

Surveying the Land

We all have favorite movie scenes. One of mine is found in Claude Rains's 1933 film debut, *The Invisible Man*. I love the part in this movie where police enter a house carrying smoke machines in order to locate the invisible man by using smoke to reveal his form. Perhaps I like this scene because it so aptly represents what I attempt to do with my students in the classroom.

Giving form to the invisible stands as one of the cornerstones to my pedagogy. I have sometimes shown my classes this movie clip to paint a picture of how the invisible can exert an influence on our lives. Many such influences—unwritten codes of behavior and incentives to action—we have come to associate with slippery labels like *ideology* and *culture*. What I try to do with my students is help them think critically and creatively about some of the seemingly invisible influences operating in their lives. I push my students to look at the ordinary in order to put what they often take for granted into broader conceptual frameworks. By doing this, I want to make them more thoughtful about their world and their own actions.

My composition course picks up on this idea of the ordinary by focusing on the idea, process, and products of construction. By playing with the various meanings of the term *construction*, I strive to teach my students not only the practical aspects of constructing a good piece of writing, but I push them to think more critically about various cultural constructions—including those of gender, race, and class.

Although I choose not to talk at great length in my classes about cultural theory, certain theoretical approaches pervade my pedagogy. Primary among these is Raymond Williams's concept of "a sociology of culture" where idealist notions of culture such as writing do more than reflect the material world. Williams writes that " 'cultural practice' and 'cultural production' . . . are not simply derived from an otherwise con-stituted social order but are themselves major elements in its constitu-tion." He argues that idealist notions of culture partake of a dialectical relationship with the material world. Thus, cultural practices both de-scribe and prescribe the society of which they are a part (11–13).

Raymond Williams "sees culture as the *signifying system* through which necessarily (though among other means) a social order is com-municated, reproduced, experienced and explored" (13). Writing is only one signifying system which serves to construct a social order. I try to teach my students not only to understand the activity of writing as a signifying system, but I ask them to analyze other signifying systems as well. Ultimately, I use the concept of signifying systems, and the dialectical interplay between the ideal and material, to help my students explore how ideas have power through the ways they are represented and interpreted in the material world. Thus, I primarily focus on how ideas manifest themselves in material ways. My ap-proach to teaching composition centers on exploring signifying sys-tems (and the issues of subjectivity and ideological interpellation which surround them) by studying tangible examples of material culture. To this end, I have built my course around the concept of home construction.

Everyone has a home. Some may live in a house, others in apart-ments, still others in dormitories, but no student I have taught has been without a place they have called "home." In the midst of the ordinariness of living in a home, the cultural constructions which have influenced how that home was built, where its foundation was laid, how space within it is utilized, and how it is furnished are usually invisible and inconsequential concerns for my students when they enter my class. Like the police officers tracking Claude Rains in *The Invisible Man*, I strive to train my students in various techniques and strategies which will help them trace, identify, and ultimately capture the ideas which guide their lives.

In tracking and identifying these ideas, I push my students to take greater responsibility for their own actions. If they do not like what a specific advertisement says or what a certain word means, what are their options for meaningful opposition? How do they even decide what should be opposed or resisted and what should not? In my course, I may not provide the answers to difficult questions such as these, but I do strive to provide my students with better analytical skills with which to examine the complexity of their world and their place within that complexity. Such critical thinking I believe to be foundational to any meaningful and socially constructive action.

What follows is an overview of the basic organization of my composition course. I offer this outline with the hope that others might also be able to explore cultural constructions through the thoughtful examination of material artifacts.

The Building Contract

Although most students—and I would venture to guess a great many teachers—do not think about it, the first piece of writing a student will analyze and interpret in a given course is that course's syllabus. For this reason, I do not hand out a syllabus on the first day of class. I use the first class period to show slides of various buildings, and I ask my students to give me their impressions of what they see. From the outset, I wish to send the message that this class is about thinking, not only about meeting expectations or comparing this class's workload to that of their others.

I show a wide range of buildings from cathedrals to tepees, from office buildings to local dormitories, from strip malls to suburban homes. I ask students to tell each other as much as they can from just looking at these pictures. When do you think these buildings were built? What kind of people use these buildings? Are the makers different than the users? What evidence do they have for their conclusions? Is it in the construction materials? Design? Location? Thus, the first thing I do in my class is something I will repeatedly demand of my students, namely, to think critically about what they see.

On the second day, I still do not hand out a syllabus. I begin by asking them what they want to see built in this class. I ask them what they want to be able to do, or do better, when they leave my composition class at the end of the semester. Usually, at this point the students have little to say. They treat this as some little game they must put up with in order to satisfy a rather idiosyncratic teacher. Comments range from: "I want to be able to build myself a Porsche," to "Does this mean you don't have any idea yet what you are going to teach us." I have found such comments inevitable, but they also provide a great opening into a discussion about responsibility, cooperation, and participation in my classroom. I use such comments to underline the truth that this class will (quite literally in some instances) be what they make of it. From the outset, I use as many ways as I can imagine to communicate that education—and culture—is a cooperative, dynamic, dialectical process.

To help dispel the mood that I have no idea where this class is going, I next move to break the class into small groups. I ask these groups to create a list of writing assignments. Before they do this, however, I ask them to work on an objective of the class. I make them articulate what they want to see built in this class and why.

To add a certain amount of structure to this exercise, I give each group three handouts. The first of these is entitled "Services Available." This sheet is designed to help my students understand that my relationship with them is similar to that of a contractor and their client. The homebuilder may have a vision of what she or he wants a home to be like, but the contractor brings a certain realism to the building process by offering a list of what can and cannot be done when certain parameters such as location, available materials, building codes, and finances are considered. In this spirit, I tell my students that I can offer them certain services—I can help them construct certain learning experiences—but the nature of the class is necessarily limited by a number of factors, including university course requirements, class size, and my own abilities.

The other two handouts I give my students include a sheet of examples of writing assignments which have been constructed by my students in the past. This gives them ideas and a starting point for their own writing assignments[1] I also give them an annotated version of the course syllabus. This allows them to get a sense of what they are going to be reading and discussing.

In considering their own desires in conjunction with what services I am able and willing to provide for them, this exercise forces students to grapple with what they want to get out of this course, how that objective might be achieved, and why that objective is important in the first place. I repeatedly refer back to the ideas which come up in these discussions as the semester progresses. By making the students analyze and articulate what they want as a result of this class, the first step has been taken to making them more reflective about their own educational experience.

While students may not have a good idea of what they want out of this course and why at the beginning of these discussions, by the end of them they have been forced to confront a number of issues, such as why writing is a valuable skill and who considers it valuable. I find that a majority of students consider education as simply the means to a financial end (i.e., I am in school so that I can make a lot of money.) I press hard on this argument to at least raise what Cornel West has described as a moral or ethical dimension to education. Is money the only end of education? If not, can they articulate what the other ends might be? Here, students often say that they came to college because "it was the right next step," "to meet my future spouse," "I didn't make a decision to come to college, my parents made it for me," and "to party." All of these responses to the role of education open doors to wider discussions. No one leaves this class period without having been seriously confronted with the question of why they are in the classroom at all. This begins the process of what my students have come to call the "relentless why." Again and again, I demand that my students always be able to formulate and articulate some kind of answer to the question why.

For their homework for the next class, I ask each of these groups to meet together outside of class and compose a proposal for the kind of assignments and evaluation criteria they would like to see in this class and why. Aside from the "Services Available" handout, I give each group an outline of the syllabus we will cover in this class. With an idea of what reading assignments will be given, the groups can thus think about what kind of writing assignments they want to pursue.

Giving group assignments is an important strategy in my teaching. I am thoroughly convinced that students need to understand the impact of people working together to truly understand that cultural behaviors and artifacts are never constructed or interpreted in a vacuum. As these students return for the next class armed with their ideas for writing assignments and grading structures, we use the class period to construct a syllabus which includes the greatest intersection of my course skeleton, their goals, and the administration's demands. While students have not been able to create completely their own course, they have had the chance to clarify their expectations and get a clearer idea of what expectations I have for our time together.

Building Materials

After we have settled on the syllabus, we move forward to explore different kinds of construction. Ostensibly we have come together to learn how to construct pieces of writing. So, we begin with a discussion of what kind of building materials are used in writing. What are pieces of writing composed of?[2] This inevitably leads us to the topics of words.

In discussing words, we begin with the common and ordinary. We begin with an analysis of swear words. If there was ever a group of words which are familiar to students and deeply tied to cultural constructions, it is swear words.

At first, students are taken aback by a teacher who even wants to discuss a topic like swear words. One student wrote the following memorable, and representative, comment about the time we spent studying swear words: "I came to school to learn about the language used by Shakespeare, not truck drivers." Such a comment reveals what kind of work can be done to help students better understand that words carry a kind of cultural capital. A person's social or ethnic position can often be detected by the words they use.

I begin our study of words in general, and swear words in particular, by asking my students if they are even comfortable discussing "four-letter" words. Most of them are, but inevitably a few are not. I begin with the uncomfortable ones. Why are they not comfortable with it? What have they been taught about swear words? Why shouldn't people say them? Who made them bad words? What do the words mean? If I write the word *tarc* on the board, why isn't that a swear word? It has four letters. What are the criteria and who sets them up for making certain words taboo to speak?

Through this discussion, we are able to come into contact with the culturally constructed nature of words. I am not only interested, however, in how these words came to be distinguished as bad, but also how these words are used. Who uses them and why? I ask my students if they can remember when they began swearing. A surprisingly large number can. I ask them why they began to swear, and it is here that we begin to discuss the idea of resistance. For a student culture largely unfamiliar with protest, swearing is often one of the largest acts of resistance they can recall. One student wrote: "I began swearing because it was forbidden fruit. It was something adults did, and that adults did not want me to do." While the practice of swearing is often tied to issues of fitting into peer groups, this student echoes the sentiments of many in my classes who begin swearing as some sort of rebellious act.

A text I have found to be extremely helpful in introducing students to the cultural construction of words is the Bible. I find the Bible works well because most students have the impression that the Bible has never changed. It was written down once a long time ago and reads the same now as it did then. I begin by comparing an early edition of the King James Version of the Bible to Leicester Sawyer's 1858 revision of the Bible. Sawyer believed that words like *piss, suck, whore,* and *shit* were too undignified for the Bible, and he edited them out.[3] I then move on to using excerpts of the New Revised Standard Version of the Bible, which was first published in 1989. Here we look at the shift from *mankind* to *humankind* and *Sons of God* to *children of God.* This leads us into a natural extension of the discussion of swear or taboo words, namely words I have come to call "PC words." Words like *Indian, boy, African-American, differently abled, chairperson, chick,* and *queer* fit into this category. I ask my students why people are willing to fight over such words? What does it mean that some people can use these words and others cannot?

The discussions we have on swearing introduces the notion that words and their usage have power. People can be hired or fired because of the words they use. From love letters to death threats, resumes to initiation rituals, slang to sacred words, language is a critical component in all our social relations. I want my students to understand this. Words are incredibly important. They have meanings, which may be different in different settings, but these meanings make or break people, organizations, civilizations. Thus, I relentlessly push my students to be thoughtful about what they say and what they write.[4]

Words are the building blocks of communication and self-reflection. Knowing words, and how they can be used, allows one to travel in a wider variety of social and conceptual realms. My students leave this section of the course knowing that even the most common words— seemingly throwaway words like *damn*—are pregnant with many meanings and implications.

Designing a Place to Live

Once, we have set the groundwork for some of the cultural issues which surround words and their usage, I move the class more directly into issues of how material artifacts intersect with the ideas that influence a culture. I do this first through an examination of architectural floor plans.

To begin this examination, I ask students to draw the floor plan of a home where they have spent the largest part of their life before coming to college. Often, I will hand out a sample floor plan for students who have little or no idea what a floor plan actually is.

By having my students examine a familiar place, I again focus our discussions and writing assignments on discovering the extraordinary in the ordinary. I then give them a list of questions about this home that raise issues that surround how space was/is used within this home. For instance: Did everyone have their own room to sleep in? Who shared sleeping rooms and why? Did certain people have rooms which were primarily theirs, like the kitchen, playroom, or study? Where were the bathrooms located and was there a pecking order on who got to use them? Where did certain members of the family end up spending most of their time? Were there any forbidden zones in the house? Forbidden by whom and to whom? Did people who were not related to the family live in the home? If so, did they use the home's space differently than family members?

I have found these and similar questions to be a helpful way of introducing the issue of gender roles to my students in a nonthreatening way. In discussing how space was used in the home, an opening is created for how different family members had different roles in terms of the use of space. The idea of differing roles raises questions of distinctions and how those distinctions are made. This lets us begin a discussion on gender and power. How does a culture, as seen in a home, construct gender and power distribution?

It comes as no surprise that students have strong opinions when it comes to how they have seen space used within their homes. It is also not surprising that many of their responses can easily be sorted along gender lines. One student wrote:

> I spent the first eighteen years of my life seeing my mother trapped in the kitchen with just enough links in her chain to reach the washing and sewing machines. If a home is a castle, my mother was more a slave than a queen. I am NEVER going to learn how to cook or sew. Freedom means too much to me.

While most students do not use such strong language, there is always a pronounced sense that the home is a heavily gendered space. Women might be "trapped in the kitchen," but men are quick to point out that yard work is "the burden" they must bear. These divisions are not universal, but they are prevalent. They are also not new.

To create a larger context for this discussion of gender roles and the home, I give my students excerpts from Catharine Beecher's classic advice manual, *A Treatise on Domestic Economy*. Even though this book was first published in 1841, its discussion of the two-sphere ideology (men ruling outside the home, women ruling inside the home) offers categories to begin exploring gender roles in today's society. To add to the categories Beecher offers in her work, I use a variety of reading assignments, including sections on Dinah's kitchen in Harriet Beecher Stowe's *Uncle Tom's Cabin* and bell hooks's essay entitled "Homeplace: A Site of Resistance." Using these, we explore how space and its usage can reveal not only certain ideas present in a given culture, but resistance to those ideas as well.

I then move to more texts, both written and nonwritten, which give a variety of living situations. In each of these we again explore what the building's design and usage have to say about the culture which produces and uses the building. Here, I find it helps to use a wide range of media to ask questions of how form and function are tied to issues of behavior and influence.

I use texts such as Thoreau's *Walden* and "Civil Disobedience" to broaden the discussion on issues of home and resistance. I also often use excerpts from Rhys Isaac's *The Transformation of Virginia*, Dolores Hayden's *Redesigning the American Dream*, Alice Walker's *The Color Purple*, and Tracy Kidder's *House* to further our discussion of how spatial design and usage are part of larger cultural considerations. I ask my students to look closely at what the homes in these various excerpts say about their inhabitants, their builders, and their cultural contexts.

I have also had great success with analyzing role and gender construction through space usage in clips from TV shows and movies. An analysis of TV shows like *Father Knows Best, The Brady Bunch, Three's Company,* and *Home Improvement* allows students to see how space both describes and prescribes gender roles. Movie clips provide yet another, wider angle of analysis for the cultural constructions of power tied to material design. Finally, documentaries on different aspects of the American experience frequently have shots of homes. By showing clips from specials on the inner city, Indian reservations, and farming, I make students more aware of what housing has to say about our culture. I juxtapose such documentaries against clips from *Lifestyles of the Rich and Famous* and ask my students to begin to explore how issues of wealth intersect with issues of housing. This provides a nice point of transition into the next portion of the course.

Choosing a Place to Build

I next ask students if they could build a house or apartment anywhere in the United States, where they would choose to build it. I also ask them the ever present "why." Why would they choose this place? What do they value in the location? What are the issues central to choosing a place to live?

To this last question, depending on the kind of ethnic diversity I have in the classroom, I almost always get the same answer. As one student wrote "Money, money, money. These are the only three things influencing where a person lives." My students enter my class with the notion that anyone in the United States can live wherever they want if they simply have the money. Much of what I strive to do in this section of the course in complicate this notion that money is the single most important factor in choosing a place to live. This involves addressing the belief that anyone can be anything they want in this country if they simply try hard enough.[5] It is here that I introduce the topic of ethnicity and its importance in determining where people choose to live. Much of this discussion centers on how ethnicity and economics are inextricably tied together.

For this section of the course, I use Alex Kotlowitz's book, *There Are No Children Here,* to focus the discussion. It is primarily the story of an African-American family living in a inner-city housing project. I use this book for two reasons. First, the class has mostly read or viewed only segments from various works up until this point. Usually assignments have been chapter or article length. An entire book allows for a good, and usually welcomed, change of pace. Second, I have found that the narrative of a book provides students with a better feeling for the complexity of issues which surround finding a place to live. They are confronted with the story of an actual family and their situation. This more personal scenario makes students less eager to point to hypothetical situations which refute the facts that race and class have a definite bearing on where people may live in the United States.

Although we center our discussions around this book, I make sure that students have at least one writing assignment exploring another ethnic group in the United States and discuss the issue of how their ethnicity intersects with how and where they choose to live. This is usually the closest my students come to an actual research paper during the term, but it is a paper most find deeply rewarding. From Chinatowns to Indian Reservations, Hispanic barrios to religious utopian communities, students begin to realize that ethnicity has a great deal to do with where people live. One student summed it up when she wrote: "For the first time it came home to me that the emperor we call the American dream has no clothes. People cannot become whatever they want. Hard work is not equally rewarded. People cannot live wherever they want. I'm depressed."

Furnishing Your Home

The last three weeks of the course are spent discussing the hows and whys of American home furnishing. I use this study of home furnishings in two ways. First, it provides an opportunity to examine the constellation of issues involved in a study of material artifacts. Second, I use this section of the course to explore the role of materialism in American Culture. Home furnishings may be the beginning point of this section, but by the end, students have been challenged to think about the role of accumulation and excess in the United States.

Because I eventually want to challenge students on the role and inequity of material acquisition in various segments of American culture, I focus this section around the analysis of objects in their own living situation. I wish to foreground their own connection to the material practices of their culture. Whether they live in a sorority house or dormitory, I ask them to choose an object found in their current home. Using a list of questions, I ask my students to begin analyzing the object they have chosen. They explore questions like: What is the appearance of this object, does it have any ornamentation, what materials is it made out of, who manufactured it, who uses it, what are the trade practices surrounding it, does it serve a symbolic or practical purpose? Each student stays with the same object for all three weeks; this makes them look ever closer at both the object, its history, and its role in society.[6]

What I attempt to do in this section of the course is ask students to examine more closely their own habits of material consumption and how these habits fit into some of the larger cultural matrices of their society. For instance, one of my students chose a beer stein from his fraternity house as his object. As it turned out, this beer stein became a great example of how material artifacts manifest the ideas found in certain cultures. He wrote:

> We call it "The Sacred Stein." No one knows how much it cost, but it must have been a ton. It is made entirely out of silver with gold inlaid hunting scenes. . . . No one can drink out of it but full members, and then only on the night of new pledge initiation. No one is even allowed to touch the Stein on any other day of the year. (This goes for everything from house cleaning to putting up decorations for a party. The Stein is on sacred, untouchable ground.) . . . Drinking

from the Stein is a great honor and not to be taken lightly. The rest of the time, the Sacred Stein sits on the house's mantlepiece reminding all of us that we belong to something very special.

First, the beer stein had the practical function of a vessel to hold liquid. Second, it had a social function because it played a key role in the ritual initiation of new members to the fraternity house. Third, the mug had economic value because it was old, well-crafted, and made of extremely expensive material. Fourth, its connection to beer drinking led to issues of the role of alcohol consumption in the social and economic life of the fraternity. Lastly, this issue of beer and drinking led us into a discussion of how beer and brewing fit into the larger considerations of American society, including how beer companies advertised their products and the problems generated by alcoholism. Thus, the study of material artifacts becomes a fascinating way to underline the complexity of American culture and the students' complicity in that culture.

Issues of complicity easily lead to issues of responsibility, and it is on this topic that I end the course. Using essays like Thomas Havrilesky's "A Compassionate solution to the Distributional Conflict" and Wendell Berry's "What Are People For" and "Why I am not Going to Buy a Computer," I push my students to consider what role material acquisition plays in their own lives and what effect that acquisition has on others.

To get at this topic, I ask my class to work toward a definition of luxury and necessity in furnishing their own home. They are quick to intellectually agree that there is little which truly falls into the necessity category. We then explore the reasons behind why we feel it necessary to have various luxuries in our homes. Students are often resistant to my inquiries about luxuries in their life, so I assign them the task of making a list of the things in their home which they have not used in the last year, including clothing, sporting equipment, books, and so forth. They are usually astounded by the sheer volume of stuff they have not used in the last year. One student wrote: "I hated this assignment. It was impossible and time consuming. Way to make us all feel guilty!!" I press on the emotions this assignment evokes as yet another angle to explore questions of luxury and necessity. Where does the guilt come from? In what ways does material acquisition give us pleasure? I also ask how necessary are those items which they have not touched in the last year? Why do people keep objects around that they use infrequently? Why do we buy new items when old items might serve our purposes equally well?

What begins as a discussion on home furnishings ends as a discussion on how the role of material acquisition and possession fits into an understanding of our culture and our own lives. I push students to think about how consumption values appear in our society and what effects these values have. I then encourage my students to think about their own practices of buying objects and using them. What implications do their own buying practices have for the world around them?

Building a Future

Father Guido Sarducci, the comedian of *Saturday Night Live* fame, has a comedy routine where he offers his audience a college education for eighty dollars. He calls it the "Five Minute University." He states that for eighty dollars he will teach you everything you are going to remember from a college education five years after you graduate. Why pay all the money demanded by some institution of higher education when you are only going to remember a few things from that education anyway? For instance, Father Guido confidently states that all you will remember from your economic classes is: "supply and demand." All you will remember from your Spanish classes is: "Como Estas." To top it off, Father Guido Sarducci includes a rental gown, one graduation picture, and a diploma, all for the low price of eighty dollars.

I end my class by asking my students what they think they will remember from my course five years after they have graduated. I hope the answer to this question reaches far beyond the basic skills of writing on which we have worked. The design of this course is to make their ordinary world a little less ordinary. My hope is that our excursions in the familiar have defamiliarized their surroundings in ways which make them more reflective and more capable of critical thought in a world which is in desperate need of people who are able to think clearly and are willing to take responsibility for what they say.

If students leave my class with a greater sense of some of the cultural values which envelope and guide their lives, I am happy. If they are motivated to change some of the cultural values which perpetuate various forms of injustice and oppression, I am happier still. I do not simply want my students to have fond memories of my class five years down the road, I want them to have analytical skills which have changed, and continue to change, their lives.

Appendix
Successful Assignments Constructed in the Past

1) Conversation books—Conversation books are like journals, but they are purposely designed with the intent that the student is able to hold a conversation with their instructor. They not only bring up insights, but questions. Students copied this assignment from another class—some of the best assignments enter my classroom this way—because they had heard that it enabled students to have greater access to their professor. Students often choose to make this assignment optional since journals are by no means a beloved assignment at all.

2) Argument papers—Argument papers have two parts: first, the student must compose a question which is listed at the top of the first page; second, the student needs to make an argument which answers this question in the body of the paper. This assignment was designed by a group of students in order to help them better learn how to argue a point. The question is all-important here. Good questions lead to good arguments.

3) Personal projects—Personal projects involve both a written and oral component. Students designed this assignment to help them integrate what they were reading and studying in this course with their other interests. Thus, biology majors took some topic in the course and brought biology to bear upon it. Math majors did the same. A woman interested in travel did a project on the mobile home industry, while a water enthusiast presented research on houseboats. This assignment included a three-page written speech which would be given in front of the class and then discussed.

4) Reflection papers—Students designed these as a way of improving their proofreading skills, as well as helping them think about some of the reading assignments before we discussed them in class. At predetermined intervals during the semester, each student was responsible for turning in a one-page, double-spaced, typed page on the day's reading assignment. These papers would then often be used to begin the class discussion on that day's reading. The students turned in these papers at the end of class, and I would grade them not so much on content, but on grammar, spelling, and clarity of presentation.

5) Time travel—My students and I worked together to create this assignment. In a four- to five-page paper, students explore how two different historical periods might speak to each other. For instance, how would Thoreau respond to the architecture of Frank Lloyd Wright or the T.V. show *Lifestyles of the Rich and Famous.*

6

Recovering "I Have a Dream"

Keith D. Miller, Gerardo de los Santos,
and Ondra Witherspoon _____

In 1970, surveying the state of Soviet literary studies, Mikhail Bakhtin declared, "For a fairly long period of time we have devoted special attention to questions of the specific features of literature"—a practice that is "alien to the best traditions of our scholarship." Bakhtin explained, "In our enthusiasm for specification we have ignored questions of the interconnection and interdependence of various areas of culture. . . . " He added,

> . . . we have not taken into account that the most intense and productive life of culture takes place on the boundaries of its individual areas and not in places where these areas have become enclosed in their own specificity. (2)

Roughly twenty-five years after Bakhtin offered these observations, some American editors and teachers continue to ignore the "intense and productive life" occurring at cultural intersections and instead spotlight "specific features" of dehistoricized texts. Why does such an approach still obtain? Because it is deeply rooted in Euro-American thought and history. As Stephen Toulmin argues, the tendency to rip texts from their cultural and rhetorical situations springs from the advent of modernity itself, specifically from the dominating influence of René Descartes. Toulmin unmasks Descartes's search for "timeless" philosophical truth as an attempt to transcend European military and political chaos by exalting a thoroughly decontextualized rationality. The study of "specific features" of dehistoricized literature stubbornly persists because it is firmly tied to the entire Western project of modernity.

Providing an historical analysis similar to Toulmin's, John Trimbur criticizes textbook authors for promoting what he terms "essayist literacy and its goal of fully present meaning in a self-sufficient text" (74). Trimbur explains,

> The practice of schooled reading is a profoundly arhetorical one that takes the language of textbooks as transparent and suppresses the processes of their production and use. And what our students thereby learn from their reading is not only the "content" of textbooks. They also learn to invest their textbooks with the power of the wider adult culture and the authority of fact. (83–84)

Although Trimbur writes of authored textbooks, portions of his analysis also apply to literary anthologies edited for the classroom.

Many such collections include Martin Luther King, Jr.'s, famous 1963 speech, "I Have a Dream." For reasons offered by Toulmin and Trimbur—and for other reasons as well—textbook anthologists obscure the oratorical/rhetorical nature of "I Have a Dream." They (mis)present it as something strongly resembling a self-contained, Western literary essay. We attempt to recover the rhetorical splendor of "I Have a Dream" by coaxing students to question four decisions that anthologists make (two of which one of us has made): printing corrupt texts, stuffing King's mellifluous poetry into expository paragraphs, erasing his collaborative process of composing, and ignoring his political bridging of militancy and moderation. In Trimbur's terms, we attempt to *re*produce a text that anthologists have *de*produced.

Printing Corrupt Texts

The first (and most disturbing) editorial choice is to publish strikingly erroneous versions of "I Have a Dream." In a 1982 essay, "The Inaccuracies in the Reprinting of Martin Luther King's 'I Have a Dream' Speech," Haig Bosmajian details numerous anthologists' gross distortions of King's words. More than ten years after Bosmajian's essay appeared, many anthologists make the same mistakes that Bosmajian noted.

For example, in one of the crowning sentences of the speech, King declared,

> Let freedom ring from the curvaceous slopes of California![1]

Eleven current anthologies print the sentence as:

> Let freedom ring from the curvaceous peaks of California![2]

By changing "curvaceous slopes" to the oxymoronic, geographically impossible "curvaceous peaks," anthologists make King sound inept—or worse.

In his famous litany, King stated:

> I have a dream that one day even the state of Mississippi, a state sweltering with the heat of injustice, sweltering with the heat of oppression, will be transformed into an oasis of freedom and justice.[3]

Eleven of the same collections (and one additional one) publish the sentence as:

> I have a dream that one day even the state of Mississippi, a desert state sweltering with the heat of injustice and oppression, will be transformed into an oasis of freedom and justice.[4]

King's melodic lines make much more sense than does the corrupt substitution for the simple reason that humid Mississippi is not a desert state. Also, by altering King's phrases "sweltering with the heat of injustice, sweltering with the heat of oppression" into the briefer "sweltering with the heat of injustice and oppression," editors eliminate the intensifying effect King sought and achieved by repeating the metaphorical phrase "sweltering with the heat."

In another sentence of the litany, King explained:

> I have a dream that one day, down in Alabama with its vicious racists, with its governor having his lips dripping with the words of "interposition" and "nullification"—one day right there in Alabama—little black boys and black girls will join hands with little white boys and white girls as sisters and brothers.[5]

The same twelve anthologies misprint the line as:

> I have a dream that one day the state of Alabama, whose governor's lips are presently dripping with the words of interposition and nullification, will be transformed into a situation where little black boys and black girls will be able to join hands with little white boys and white girls and walk together as sisters and brothers.[6]

The mangled passage adds a verb in passive voice—"will be transformed"—with no agent in sight and an equally pointless nominalization—"situation." The bungled construction also omits King's charge that Alabama contains "vicious racists," a strong phrase signaling that the governor is not acting in a vacuum. Also erased is a phrase—"one day right there in Alabama"—that King repeated in the middle of the long sentence to prevent listeners from getting lost.

Other significant errors occur in the twelve textbook anthologies and in three others as well. Only six textbook anthologies that we examined include fully or virtually accurate representations.[7]

Corruptions also surface in works about King, including Stephen Oates's popular 1982 biography, which also has King mislabel Mississippi as "a desert state" (259–62). Joining two other anthologists, James Washington, editor of *A Testament of Hope*, the standard collection of King's works, inserts the following sentence into "I Have a Dream":

> This offense we share mounted to storm the battlements of injustice must be carried forth by a biracial army.[8]

King clearly failed to include these stilted words in "I Have a Dream," and we doubt that he ever uttered anything so awkward.

Any responsible reconstruction of "I Have a Dream" must be made from audio and audiovisual recordings made at the scene. The written copy that King held in his hands that day has been lost; even if it were available, the speech itself consists of what King said, not what he wrote. Because certain egregious errors appear over and over, it appears that a group of anthologists treat written reproductions of the speech as authoritative, no matter how botched they happen to be. If these editors were representing "I Have a Dream" as an oration, rather than an essay, they would certainly transcribe their texts directly from one of the widely available recordings.

Jamming Anaphoras into Paragraphs

Although some anthologists print linguistically accurate renditions of "I Have a Dream," like James Washington they consistently box the address into belletristic paragraphs (albeit occasionally featuring one-sentence paragraphs). This decision squashes rhythms, parallelisms, and other rich oral qualities. Paragraphs flatten his seven sets of anaphoras by failing to align the repeated, rhythmical words. For example, consider the usual format:

> I have a dream that this and this. I have a dream that this and that.
> I have a dream and so forth and so forth and so forth and so forth.
> I have a dream and so on and so on. . . .

As an alternative one easily could set each anaphora into Walt Whitman's form of long lines:

I have a dream . . . .
. . . .
I have a dream . . . .
. . . .
I have a dream . . . .

thereby emphasizing King's parallelisms instead of burying them. But editors rarely choose an alignment like this one.

Omitting Participants' Contributions

Again like Washington, anthologists without exception obscure King's process of collaborative composition by printing his words while excluding listener/participants' interjections (e.g., "Amen," "Tell it!"), many of which are clearly audible in tapes of "I Have a Dream."[9] Following his normal practice, King expected the crowd to punctuate his cadences and organized his rhythms accordingly. And, like folk preachers before him, he sometimes adjusted speeches on the spot in response to listeners' participation. In the case of "I Have a Dream," while he was speaking, gospel singer Mahalia Jackson, who was sitting behind him, shouted, "Tell 'em about the dream, Martin!" (Branch 882). Whether King heard her or not, he proceeded to do just that. Later he seemed to attribute the most famous passage of his oratory to the reactions of his listeners/collaborators:

> I started out reading the speech. . . . The audience response was wonderful that day, and all of a sudden this thing came to me that I have used. I'd used it many times before, that thing about "I have a dream," and I just felt that I wanted to use it here. I don't know why. I hadn't thought about it before the speech. (qtd. in Garrow 283)

Unlike the first two choices, the decision to ignore participants' interplay—the call-and-response dynamic of folk preaching—results not from editors' failure to recognize "I Have a Dream" as a speech, but from their refusal to identify it as African-American folk oratory. Eliminating interjections means creating the appearance of overly familiar, transparent, self-sufficient discourse.

Such elimination also obscures listeners' role in the long, collaborative process of composing King's oration, a process prompted by the electrical charge between pulpit and pew that inevitably occurred when King spoke to either African-American or racially mixed groups. In his sanctuary, the electricity ran both ways: like other black ministers, not only did he provoke vocal reactions, he also heeded them both immediately and later. Using congregations and conventions as sounding boards, he repeatedly tested material out loud, honing and replaying passages that received enthusiastic responses and dropping those that did not. His speeches and sermons typically served as drafts for future speeches and sermons.

King began rehearsing material for "I Have a Dream" in his first civil rights speech, "Address at Holt Street Baptist Church," which he gave in December 1955 at the initial rally of the Montgomery bus boycott. A double metaphor from "Address at Holt Street"—"long night of captivity" and "daybreak of freedom"—resurfaces in "I Have a Dream" as a "joyous daybreak to end the long night of . . . captivity." In the same speech he tested a metaphor from the Book of Amos ("justice rolls down like waters") that reappears in "I Have a Dream." He previewed many other tropes for "I Have a Dream" as well. In a 1957 sermon he recited metaphorical lines from the Book of Isaiah that climax the "I have a dream" litany ("Birth"). In 1962 he criticized the governor of Mississippi, whose lips were "dripping" with the word " 'interposition' " ("Who?"). By the time of "I Have a Dream," the lips of the governor of Alabama were dripping with the word " 'interposition.' " The metaphor worked just as well with either state.

King tested not only metaphors and Biblical citations, but also major themes, including the crucial argument that, in his words, "unearned suffering is redemptive"—an appeal that explained and justified the pain his followers experienced when facing billy clubs, police dogs, fire hoses, and jail. He made the argument throughout his career, using the phrase at least as early as 1957 ("Fragment") before incorporating it into his most renowned oration.

Earlier in 1963 he previewed the entire "I have a dream" passage in speeches given in Birmingham and Detroit (Garrow 283; Fairclough 155).

In a number of perorations, beginning at least as early as 1956, King projected a utopian future by quoting lyrics from "America" followed by a multisentence metaphor extending the last line of the patriotic anthem ("Let freedom ring") (see "Desegregation," "Annual Report," and "Facing.") He borrowed this entire conclusion from black pastor Archibald Carey's speech at the 1952 Republican National Convention. Like dozens of King's other perorations, the ending of "I Have a Dream" reflects his constant process of sifting and refining material.

King's composing process also reflected his aides' advice. According to Stephen Oates, on the night before the talk, Walter Fauntroy and King's other lieutenants urged him to exceed the eight-minute time limit granted to each speaker (256). Together with the response of the crowd, his assistants' counsel may have prompted him to exceed the designated eight minutes by adding the "I have a dream" and "Let freedom ring" segments to his prepared text.

The resplendent reception of the address encouraged King to embed its phrases, metaphors, and themes in future talks. Early in "I Have a Dream," he described Negroes as isolated "on a lonely island of poverty in the midst of a vast ocean of material prosperity." Over the next four years, as he watched Americans ignore the poor while pouring funds into a ghastly war in Vietnam, he grew increasingly radical. To define his change of mind, he played with, extended, and reiterated earlier metaphors:

> In 1963 . . . I tried to talk to the nation about a dream that I had had. . . . I watched that dream turn into a nightmare as I . . . saw black brothers and sisters perishing on a lonely island of poverty in the midst of a vast ocean of material prosperity. . . . I saw the dream turn into a nightmare as I watched the war in Vietnam escalating. . . . (Qtd. in Cone 213)

These metaphors linked the more radical King of 1967 to the more familiar King of 1963.

King also borrowed substantial portions of published sermons by Harry Emerson Fosdick and other ministers, which they had already rehearsed with both listeners and readers (Miller).

Clearly, although editors ignore King's listeners' responses, King himself sought their reactions. By preaching back, listeners told him what they wanted to hear and contributed to his ongoing process of composing.

Bridging Militance and Moderation

In their introductions to "I Have a Dream," editors generally define its meaning as self-contained by ignoring the political division between militance and moderation that King negotiated as he spoke. As Robert Hariman observes, even at the time of "I Have a Dream," King was "struggling against more radical speakers for continued control of his movement" (206). Tired of waiting for federal authorities to intervene decisively for civil rights, many activists had already grown skeptical of the federal government—a pessimism evident in the speech that their representative John Lewis had prepared to give at the March on Washington prior to "I Have a Dream." On the day of the March,

Table 6.1   Orientational Metaphors in "I Have a Dream"

UP Metaphors	DOWN Metaphors
high plane of dignity	dark and desolate
majestic heights of meeting	valley of segregation
physical force with soul force	quicksands of injustice
hew out of the mountain of despair	valley of despair
a stone of hope	
Let freedom ring from	
every mountainside	
prodigious hilltops of New Hampshire	
mighty mountains of New York	
heightening Alleghenies of Pennsylvania	
snow-capped Rockies of Colorado	
curvaceous slopes of California	
Stone Mountain of Georgia	
Lookout Mountain of Tennessee	
hill of Mississippi	

One could add to this list King's Biblical metaphors—"justice rolls down like waters" and "every valley shall be exalted, every hill and mountain shall be made low"—which are complex tropes of transformation as well as orientation.

having read Lewis's prepared text, officials from the Kennedy Administration pressured Lewis to censor himself. Archbishop Patrick O'Boyle, scheduled to give the invocation, threatened to walk off the platform unless Lewis softened his tone. Wanting to present a fictitious public image of civil rights solidarity, King and other March leaders urged Lewis to moderate his speech, in part by withdrawing his explicit refusal to support Kennedy's civil rights bill (Garrow 281–83; Branch 868–80).

The impulse to unite black and white radicals, liberals, and moderates under a single banner prompted not only King's advice to Lewis, but much of the strategy of "I Have a Dream." King expressed his militancy by leading boycotts, demonstrations, marches, and—especially—massive civil disobedience. Though his speeches explain his "street rhetoric," they also seem moderate, establishing him, in August Meier's phrase, as a "conservative militant." While King uses "I Have a Dream" to oppose his segregationist opponents, the speech

Table 6.2   Light and Dark Metaphors in "I Have a Dream"

LIGHT Metaphors	*DARK* Metaphors
great beacon light of hope	long night of captivity
joyous daybreak	dark and desolate
sunlit path of racial justice	valley of segregation
bright day of justice	

also serves, in Kenneth Burke's words, as a "bridging device" or "symbolic structure whereby one 'transcends' a conflict" (224).

King did so by following Burke's principle: "if the excommunicated would avoid the corner of negativism, he must recruit a group who steal the insignia of the orthodox" (223). King delivered "I Have a Dream" from what he called the "hallowed spot" of the Lincoln Memorial one hundred years following the Emancipation Proclamation. He brandished orthodox insignia by echoing well-known phrases from Lincoln, Jefferson, Amos, Isaiah, and "America"—words that help constitute our civil religion.

King also developed his "bridging device" to moderates by structuring "I Have a Dream" through three metaphorical systems—Up/Down, Light/Dark, and Temperature.[10] In the Up/Down system, anything low, such as a valley, must be bad, and something high, such as a mountain, is almost always good. In the Light/Dark system, light, of course, is positive, and darkness is negative. King builds "I Have a Dream" with sixteen Up/Down metaphors and six Light/Dark metaphors (see tables 6.1 and 6.2). While these two metaphorical systems might seem independent, they mesh seamlessly, as when King urges Americans metaphorically "to *rise* from the *dark* and desolate *valley* of segregation to the *sunlit* path of racial justice" (our emphasis). In the eight examples of the third metaphorical system—temperature— extremity, such as "sweltering heat," is invariably bad, and moderation, such as an "invigorating autumn," is almost always good (see table 6.3).

The Up/Down, Light/Dark, and Temperature tropes seem reassuringly "logical" and "natural." Everyone would rather climb high than low, see sunlight rather than clouds, and bask in a climate of seventy degrees. As George Lakoff and Mark Johnson explain, these metaphorical systems are deeply embedded in our everyday language. King chose these (and other) metaphors because their sheer, even clichéd familiarity (e.g., "sunlit path") made him seem far less

Table 6.3 Temperature Metaphors in "I Have a Dream"

Metaphors of *EXTREMITY*	Metaphors of *MODERATION*
flames of withering injustice	luxury of cooling off
sweltering summer of . . .	invigorating autumn of
discontent	freedom and equality
a state [Mississippi]	warm threshold which
sweltering with the heat	leads into the
of injustice,	palace of justice*
sweltering with the heat	oasis of freedom and
of oppression	justice

* It is difficult to tell whether King said "warm threshold" or "worn threshold."

radical and threatening, especially when combined with his pleas for nonviolence and genuflections to the Bible, Jefferson, and Lincoln.

Constructing the other side of his bridge, King voiced frustration and preached resistance, not simply through street rhetoric, but also within "I Have a Dream." He sketched the abject horrors of segregation against the backdrop of the grand promises made by the national founders. He celebrated the "marvelous new militancy which has engulfed the Negro community" and claimed that the "whirlwinds of revolt will continue to shake the foundations of our nation" until justice arrives. Because the promises of the Bible and the founders are secure, however, and because "unearned suffering is redemptive," that day, prophesied by the conservative militant, will certainly come.

The project of enshrining King's speech as a variation of a Western, belletristic essay is consistent with a longstanding but fruitless claim that King's ideas and language were inspired by prestigious Euro-American thinkers whom he studied in graduate school. Like John Ansbro and others who make this argument explicitly, anthologists obscure King's rhetorical practices and the most important sources of his intellectual and rhetorical prowess—his father and other preachers, both black and white (Miller).

Further, stripping off the rhetorical/African-American dimensions of the oration helps in the larger effort to monumentalize King as an icon of (often nonexistent) racial progress and harmony. Hariman argues that, in relation to "I Have a Dream," "we need to beware of the alternative inducement to substitute the satisfactions of the text for the labor of working in the world it supposedly describes" (213). Such substitution often occurs when Americans celebrate King's birthday while in virtually every American city spotless limousines glide past squadrons of the wretched and the homeless. While our politicians extol King, they simultaneously reject the vision that King expressed in a 1963 sermon: "We can use our vast resources of wealth to wipe poverty from the earth" (*Strength* 53).

In "I Have a Dream" King urged listeners, "Go back to Alabama. Go back to Mississippi. Go back to the slums and ghettoes of our Northern cities." While we admire his speech, most of us don't want to go to the Third World slums and ghettoes of our cities. We do not want to initiate or join the "whirlwind of revolt" that can shake our national foundations "until the bright day of justice emerges." We prefer to study a classic.

Paradoxically, if we rehistoricize and recontextualize this classic, perhaps we can learn to heed it. Before examining King's traffic across what Bakhtin calls "the intense and productive life of culture on the boundaries," teachers should ask why anthologies omit John Lewis's speech, both the censored and uncensored versions. They should wonder why anthologists ordinarily exclude both speeches by Malcolm X and his reaction to the March on Washington, which he ridiculed as the "Farce on Washington."

For that matter, teachers should ask why, except for "I Have a Dream," speeches and overtly political writing generally fail to materialize in English anthologies. Where are Tom Paine and Thomas Jefferson? Are their texts not worth studying as texts? What exempts "I Have a Dream" from the general policy of excluding overtly political discourse? Did King reinforce the moderate end of his bridge too strongly? Are we nostalgic for a day when civil disobedience could create the shock of the new? Or does "I Have a Dream" qualify as literary mainly because we have canonized King as well as his speech?

When presenting the address, we first play a tape for students. Then they read published texts. We play the tape again, asking them to read along to check for accuracy. We encourage them to examine not only linguistic corruptions, but other editorial decisions and the rhetorical assumptions underlying them.

We hand out Carey's "Let freedom ring" peroration, asking students to compare Carey's conclusion to that of "I Have a Dream."

After students analyze the cornucopia of schemes and tropes in "I Have a Dream," we wonder aloud whether the oration crosses a cultural boundary into poetry. Though it is rarely, if ever, viewed as poetry, we ask whether our poetry curricula exclude it merely because it does not conform to modernist conventions and instead resembles the more oral poetry of Homer or Whitman. Is it not a poem because editors package it into an essay? Or because, unlike most modernist verse, it is overtly political and fails to express twentieth-century alienation? Or because King reached a mass audience instead of the intellectual elite defined and nurtured by Ezra Pound and T. S. Eliot?

Following this discussion, we ask students to brainstorm methods of printing "I Have a Dream" and note their suggestions. On the following class day, we hand out another textual representation, which is linguistically accurate but arranged in an oddly jumbled way. In different sections of this text, we incorporate as many student suggestions as possible. For example, we alternately capitalize listener/participants' responses, underline them, and omit them. We set passages into standard paragraphs and others into Whitman's long lines. Still others we display in the stairstep lines that William Carlos Williams sometimes favored:

I have a dream
    and so forth . . .
        and so forth . . .

After discussing larger rhetorical and political issues, we ask students to edit (or, in Trimbur's term, *re*produce) the text themselves, using whatever fonts, italics, capitals, spacing, or other typography they deem appropriate. We tell them they might format certain segments (e.g., the anaphoras) one way and other passages another. Because King's crowd sometimes reacted in midsentence or midphrase, some of the interjections present an intriguing problem: how does one include them without visually interrupting King's lines? Then students write essays defending their arrangements.

Although students might defend the standard paragraph format, so far no one has done so. Some experiment with wild typography and spacing. Most struggle to include participants' interjections, but a few omit them entirely on the grounds that no pattern can include them without visually distracting the reader. One student made short lines from fairly brief phrases, lines roughly parallel to those that Langston Hughes developed to align his poetry according to blues rhythms.

The chief goal of this assignment is to expose a now sacred American text as culturally misrepresented, problematic, and yet-to-be-determined. So far, no one, least of all the three of us, has created a model text of "I Have a Dream" and resolved the textual issues that it raises. For that reason, students, although they are not professional editors, face an actual editorial problem—not a simulated one in which they seek to mimic someone else's solution.

Another goal is to help students, in Trimbur's words, "to unlearn the authority and autonomy they habitually ascribe to textbooks" by teaching them "to re-materialize the circumstances of text production" (85) for at least one text.

Because students can come to see "I Have a Dream" as a fluid, intertextual text-in-process, we can fantasize that the assignment may help them accept the fluidity and complexity of their own writing processes, which, we hope, also transgresses cultural boundaries while refusing any attempted escape from history and politics.

PART III
(Re)Writing Cultural Texts

PART II

7

Making and Taking Apart "Culture" in the (Writing) Classroom

Kathleen Dixon _____

Liberatory pedagogy, social constructionism, postmodernism—big words which theorists use, but what relation do they have to the university classroom?

Some social constructionists and liberatory pedagogues have conceived of the classroom as a relatively benign "community" (Bruffee; Stock and Robinson); others have seen it as a kind of rite of passage into a competitive academe that requires students to speak *its* language (Bartholomae). The only classroom communities that would count in this formulation would be those that moved students closer to "academic discourse." Recent composition theorizing moves away from or builds upon these influential conceptualizations of college-level pedagogy.

Although the class I will describe below was created before I read Harkin and Schilb's *Contending with Words: Composition and Rhetoric in a Post-Modern Age*, it shares its philosophical foundations with several of the essays in *Contending*. Many of the writers in this collection seem interested in changing the discursive practices of both students and academe. Susan Jarrett critiques both "expressivism" and the "community" classroom by pointing out that these student-centered classrooms will likely reproduce the inequities of the larger culture wherein certain individuals achieve hegemony over others. John Schilb is dismayed that "composition programs—and indeed, the academy in general—often regard [students] as would-be consumers of previously formulated wisdom" (187). Patricia Bizzell wants to "complicate our communal relations" (66).

How could all of these concerns be answered? I would like to reinvision the university classroom as a pocket of "cultures." Like the larger society out of which it comes, the classroom cultures—including the culture(s) of academe—are dominated by a liberal discourse which fools us into thinking that the multiple cultures are or ought to be one, and that liberty, equality, and fraternity for all are either firmly in place or ultimately achievable (through hard work, individual ingenuity, etc.). The course I will propose below regards the classroom as a laboratory for studying culture, and more specifically, for critiquing liberal discourse.

I call my course "Reading Popular Culture." This course could be, but is not necessarily, a composition course. Everyone at the university ought to teach students how to think better and as we (compositionists, Writing Across the Curriculum faculty) know that writing is a mode of learning—often the means and the result of thinking—most university classes could and should emphasize writing. Teaching assistants and other faculty associated with composition programs can take their places alongside all other university faculty as the intended audience for this piece. "Reading Popular Culture" is intended for first- or second-year college students.

A description of just the first few weeks of the course will illustrate the workings of the whole:

From the first day's handout:

> We will take a reader-response/spectator theory approach to "reading" popular culture—that's fancy talk for saying we will focus on *your* response to the magazines, music, and movies that we will jointly choose to interpret. Although the focus may be on the individual consumer (I dislike that word), we will nonetheless attempt to place our individual responses within a larger social framework. In other words, we will try to say something about the *cultural* nature of popular culture. My own speciality is gender studies, so you can expect me to import gender analyses into our discussions.
>
> Required texts will include:
>
> - *Reading Culture: Contexts for Critical Reading and Writing*
>   edited by Diana George and John Trimbur
> - two magazines (to be decided in class)
> - one or more photocopied articles
> - probably a dozen or more music albums
> - at least three music videos
> - at least two movies

... You will be part of a group that will present some piece of popular culture to the class, so you will be responsible for acquiring whatever your group decides upon, be that music, a video, etc. You will also need to buy a notebook for writing a journal. . . .

Your grade will be based upon (1) a 5 pp. paper, (2) a group report, (3) in-class writing, (4) your journal, (5) class participation.

The journal was a Berthoffian double-entry journal mostly focussed on readings in the George and Trimbur text. The first in-class writing was a description/narration of a "cultural experience." I saw this as the first step in understanding one's own experience as cultural. I was especially interested in specificity in these descriptions—a kind of ethnographic account. These are the instructions I gave to the students:

In 25 minutes, write a short paper (2–3 handwritten pages) on a popular culture experience—listening to a song, album, watching a TV show, etc. Be specific: *exactly* what are you listening to, viewing, etc.? Describe it a bit. Tell me where you are and what you are doing, who you are with (or are you alone) and why. What are the feelings associated with this experience? Is it a ritual or a one-time thing? Give me as full a sense as possible of this experience: specify, specify, specify. Finally, at the end, try to figure out what this experience means to you—why it is important enough in your life to claim your time.

These papers were a great success. It was a moving experience to learn what it was that mattered to the students, so much so that I gave only checks, plusses, and minuses for grades. I asked for permission to copy some papers and kept a couple for later use. The immediate use was to get students accustomed to describing experience specifically: we can only analyze culture when we know the specifics of how it is working. This would be the basis for the cultural critiques that I would later assign.

In the meantime, students set to work reading the first chapter in George and Trimbur, which was a case study of published responses to the 2 Live Crew obscenity controversy. We had a lively class discussion on the controversy itself, though not much specific attention was paid to the readings. Many of the rural white students in this North Dakota classroom had never or had rarely heard rap music. We considered whether we could even get hold of the 2 Live Crew video in question.

Also in the meantime, students had formed groups to choose popular culture artifacts to bring before the whole class. I noticed that some groups imported artists and artifacts I had suggested on the first day of class. One group, for example, decided that it wanted to make a class presentation on *Rolling Stone* magazine. The two music groups were enamored of male rock artists, as I had expected. However, I also noticed that some suggestions were dropped rather quickly. I had offered the possibility of listening to the rap artist Queen Latifah. One of the few black women in the class mentioned Queen Latifah to her group; the next time I visited the group, Queen Latifah was forgotten.

The stage was set for my improvisations. I had to get closer scrutiny on the texts. I also decided to reintroduce that which had dropped out of the discourse, namely female rap artists. So I asked the students to form groups to discuss only two of the George and Trimbur pieces, George Will's *Newsweek* diatribe against 2 Live Crew's lyrics, and Michelle Wallace's "When Black Feminism Faces the Music and the Music is Rap." I told them that I thought Wallace's piece was a much better example of a cultural critique, so would they compare the two to see how they differed? Many complained that Wallace was "biased" against male rappers (some seemed offended by the term *feminism*), but most of the class conceded that she had brought a greater knowledge of rap music to her piece than had George Will, who only quoted from one 2 Live Crew tune. They had stated one constituent of a cultural critique: a range of knowledge about the phenomenon being analyzed. I told them to write this down and file it away in their memories for later use.

I also drew their attention to a quotation from Wallace's piece in which she claims that popular culture "provides symbolic resolutions to life's contradictions" (26). We broke the quotation into two parts: what are "life's contradictions?" I asked. They were stumped, and so I offered an illustration: young inner-city black men understand from the dominant culture that to be a man means to earn money—the more money the bigger man he is. But let's say the best jobs a man can get are dead-end minimum-wage Burger King jobs; he is faced with a rather painful contradiction. "Are you saying that black men put down women because they don't feel like men?" The question burst forth from one of the older white men in class (there were no black men in this class). "I didn't say that," I retorted with a comical tone (and the class laughed), "but what do you think?" "Symbolic resolutions," I explained, were resolutions that occur not in real life, but in our imaginations.

I told the class about my observation of their group work, and I asked them why Queen Latifah might have dropped out of their discourse. "Because we don't know much about rap music"—and why not? I asked.

"Because we're from North Dakota"—but not everyone was a North Dakotan, and several students challenged those who actually said they didn't like rap when they had admitted so little exposure to the music. The class had noted the urban/rural cultural split, but the black-white split was dealt with a little more gingerly, and nobody mentioned that Queen Latifah might have dropped out of the discourse because she was a *female* rapper. So I acknowledged one of the many reasons why race, especially, was so hard to talk about: categorizing people somehow doesn't seem right. "Not all white people are the same; not all black people are the same. Not all women are the same; not all men are the same. We can notice this even in our classroom right now. Nonetheless, there might be some differences in our experiences that have to do with our race and gender." I pointed out that not only I but the "feminist" Michelle Wallace had mentioned Queen Latifah. "So since this class on its own would like to ignore Queen Latifah, I'll bring in a music video so we can watch her perform."

The performance was videotaped from a concert entitled "Sisters in the Name of Rap." Queen Latifah sang three songs, including "Ladies First." I asked the students to watch carefully, since their homework would be to describe the performance in great specificity on the left side of a spread in their journals; on the right side would be the customary subjective response. We looked at how Queen Latifah sang, moved, dressed; at how her back-up group acted; at how the audience responded. The night before I myself had experienced a rush watching the entire video tape of about a dozen female rappers. All of the artists and apparently all of the audience were black and quite definitely devotees of rap. I could feel the energy of the music and movements; I enjoyed the political and sexual content of the lyrics. It was exciting to see the intelligent and disciplined artistry of the singers and dancers, an image so at odds with the dominant culture's judgement of inner-city black culture (as George Will's piece had demonstrated). The audience was often visibly involved with the performances. But I thought I noticed that the black men were less involved with Queen Latifah's performance. Was it because she acted so queenly and deliberately addressed one of her songs to the women in the audience? Did I notice the differing reaction to Queen Latifah because I had seen the whole video? In discussion groups, some of the students objected to the practice of viewing only one rap artist. Ok, I said, and added the female rapper Yo-Yo to the line-up.

Some students complained that they could not understand the lyrics; others (especially men, I observed) seemed to lose interest in

Queen Latifah, but perked up when Yo-Yo and the male rapper Ice Cube (in a cameo appearance) came on stage, Yo-Yo singing "don't play with my yo-yo" and moving suggestively in synch with a male dancer (Ice Cube contributed a punctuating "Yo! Yo!" at regular intervals). Afterwards, I acknowledged the gender split that had been developing for some time and asked students to break up into same-sex small groups. When I asked the small groups to report to the whole class, the divisions became even clearer. Some male voices said: Queen Latifah isn't very talented, she dresses/acts like a man, she's arrogant; Yo-Yo looks/acts like a woman, she's sexy, people like Ice Cube better not because he's a man but because he's famous. Why are we only watching female rappers? Some female voices said: Queen Latifah doesn't look like a man, she just dresses conservatively; Queen Latifah has a message, but Yo-Yo's just selling sex. Other women challenged those last voices: why can't Yo-Yo dress and act the way she wants? Why does that mean she's a slut? I offered the possibility that Yo-Yo's "message" (the students' word) was that she wanted to be sexual, but on her own terms. I asked whether there was a contradiction involved in all this. Between her message and her actions? some women wondered aloud. Another thought that the contradiction was that, although Yo-Yo might want to be listened to, the men were not listening, only imagining having sex with her on *their* terms. But the contradiction was resolved by this popular culture experience, the same women said, since Yo-Yo was performing the whole thing on stage and not actually in the situation of negotiating sex with a man.

But then, the dam of male frustration finally broke. One man challenged me directly: why are we only watching female rappers? I repeated my reasoning, that I wanted to interject what the class seemed to want to forget. At some point during the ensuing dialogue, the young man began to agree with some of the women. Maybe it is the case that we judge men and women differently when it comes to sex. He was thinking aloud when he began comparing Yo-Yo's performance to that of a male pop singer: "When Michael Jackson grabs his balls—or whatever it is he's got down there. . . . " We all laughed. It was a startling, and to me, fascinating moment. I barely had time to think about it before another erupted. One of the men, in his own summary of the entire discussion, said, "They're both extreme, 2 Live Crew and Queen Latifah." This brought lots of male (and some female) nods. Another young man said, "Yeah, there's good and bad in both [male and female rap]."

Suddenly I knew what I wanted to do. It was time to talk theory.

I told them that a salient feature of the dominant culture in which we live is to repress ideas, and sometimes even the very existence of whole groups of people, which make the members of this dominant culture feel uncomfortable. I wrote "repression" on the board. The dominant culture erases the existence of these ideas or people by simply ignoring or forgetting them (as the music group did with the suggestion of studying Queen Latifah's work). "Watch for subjects that drop out of conversation in your small groups or in whole class discussions. That will be a clue to what might be being repressed by this class. And remember this term, *repression*. You've probably heard of Freud, who believed that we never truly forget anything—the repressed is merely stored away in our unconscious. It will surface in dreams and jokes, among other things.

"And speaking of jokes, what do you make of Todd's joke about Michael Jackson? Think back to what Todd was talking about when he made the joke." No one offered to recollect this for us, but the entire class was rapt, at this point. "Wasn't he changing his position, beginning to agree with some of the women in the class, in wondering if men and women really are judged differently with regard to their sexuality?" Their attention was unwavering. "And then suddenly, in pops a homosexual joke—or is that how you read it? That Michael Jackson lacks balls? That he isn't masculine enough?" Some nods around the room. Todd had left class early, as was his wont. "I wish Todd were here so that we could ask him, but let me make this interpretation: perhaps men make jokes about other men's masculinity when they fear they will lose their masculinity in the eyes of their male friends. In this classroom, where so many men today have made their positions clear, I could see where a man who was beginning to state a possibly feminist position might feel as though his masculinity were threatened. So that what many men might be repressing is the part of them that doesn't fit within a masculine image. Watch for this in your daily lives: when do men tell gay jokes or make fun of other men's masculinity?

"Now, as to this notion that 'there's good and bad in both.' Notice what this does to us as thinkers, as analyzers—for that's what a cultural critique is: analysis of culture. When you say 'there's good and bad in both,' you erase the differences between the two things, whatever those two things are. It makes it virtually impossible to analyze. Conversation and thinking stop when you say there's good and bad in both. No wonder you thought Michelle Wallace was 'biased!' She analyzed rap music and she came to the conclusion that male and female rap *were* different—and she preferred female rap because she thought it was less sexist.

"Some of you were using terms like 'objective' and 'biased' as you were reading the articles in your text, and some of your small groups last week were planning class presentations based upon a 'pro-and-con' approach. Where do these words and ideas come from?" They weren't quite following, so I filled in. "In my life, I remember pro-and-con debates in high school and on television newsmagazine programs, in newspapers and magazines. Does that sound right to you?" Some nods. "Now, I'm going to call this kind of thinking, the kind that is represented by 'good and bad in both' as 'binary thinking,' in which two terms (and only two terms) are supposedly in opposition to and in balance with each other, but really, when you look closely, there is often an imbalance. Think of the terms 'black' and 'white' and think of the history of race relations in this country. Think of 'male' and 'female' and of course—to borrow from Jim's actual phrase—'good' and 'bad': are all these exactly equal in terms of the way the dominant culture values them? The problem with this way of thinking is that it erases difference again, just like repression does. Instead of there being multiple points of view, there are only two. Instead of our looking complexly at whatever conflicts might arise among various cultures and subcultures, we are accustomed to looking simply at two points of view, and then, to act as though these two viewpoints are, or ought to be, equal." I wrote "binary thinking" on the board.

"Now, let's look at how Queen Latifah's performance can be seen as equally extreme as 2 Live Crew's. Ed, what is it about Queen Latifah's performance that seems extreme to you?"

Ed replied, "Well, she said 'ladies first.' "

"Ok, great. Let's look at that. 2 Live Crew talked about 'busting pussy' and Queen Latifah said 'ladies first.' How are these two equally extreme?" I made a chart on the board. "What would the female equivalent to the male 'busting pussy' be?" No one hazarded an answer; the silence itself was riveting. I wrote "busting dick" on the board—"actually, what I need to write is something that connotes castration, right?" North Dakotans are known to be reserved, churchgoing people; they were probably amazed that I would write these things on the board at all. "I don't mean to shock you by using these words," I said, "but they belong to popular culture and they come from members of this class. We have to face up to what they mean." I wrote "ladies first" on the board and wrote "men first" as its opposite.

"Obviously 'ladies first' is not the logical equivalent of 'busting pussy.' Why do you think that some of us perceived it that way?"

Debbie then made a brilliant observation. "We took 2 Live Crew as the standard and then saw Queen Latifah as the opposite."

I said, "Great. Now, pay careful attention to what acts as the standard against which you judge something else to be its opposite. Is it possible that the second thing might be entirely different from that standard? Remember how Queen Latifah addressed both men and women in her last song? Remember how she chided both men and women for the ways they behave towards one another?"

Finally, I chalked one more term on the board, "universalizing."

"One more way to erase differences between cultures and peoples is to use words that make it seem as though there is really only one culture—the dominant one. Take a look at the photocopy of the *Essence* interview with rap artists that Dave from the Black Cultural Center gave you. Notice on the last page how one of the male rappers speaks of 'we' and 'our' community and notice also that the female rappers' concerns never get mentioned during these statements about 'we' and 'our' community. Universalizing is something we all do, and it can be a good thing (just like the idea of a balanced opinion can be good) because it seems to bring us all together. But watch out for it. It is an especially tempting practice among members of dominant groups. I myself did it today when I was talking to members of a small group about why they may have had a hard time hearing Queen Latifah's lyrics: 'A lot of us white people aren't used to the vocabulary of rap culture. You know how you can hear stuff better when you're used to the language?' 'Oh, yeah,' said the Asian woman in the group, 'Like I can hear what my mom says when other people can't.' And then I felt profoundly embarrassed because I had acted like we were all white."

"White feminists spoke for 'all women' for some time, until they finally heard the objections of women of color. Notice that Michelle Wallace, a black woman, calls herself a feminist, but that Queen Latifah refuses that label, calling herself a 'commonsensist.' Not all women or men are alike; not all black or white women or men are alike."

I asked students to keep these terms in mind for the in-class cultural critique that I would soon ask them to write.

The cultural critique paper required students to write a critique of our class case study of rap—or female rap—whatever the writer of the critique thought our class had been doing for the past few weeks. I explained that critique means analysis. The critique was to have two

parts which could be separate or integrated. The first I called a "story"—
a description/narration something like the cultural experience paper,
which would represent some portion of what we had read, seen, and
talked about during these past weeks. The second part of the paper
was to be an analysis of the first part in which students could use the
theoretical terms I had introduced them to: *repression, universalizing,
binary thinking*—or words their classmates had used ("good and bad
in both"). I also offered them another term, *epiphany*, which referred to
the experience of getting a light bulb over one's head: a moment of
profound learning. Many of them seemed excited by this last idea.

The cultural critiques were not all successful papers by the standards that I had set (that the analyses be complex and coherent, for
instance), but they were all fascinating examples of thought-in-process.
I want to share four of them here, two from less conventionally successful papers, two that received an A or B. In each set, I chose one
from a man and one from a woman, since gender themes were salient
in so many of the papers. I read portions of these four papers aloud
to the class and used them as further teaching tools. They were in
some senses representative papers, both in terms of themes discussed
and approaches to the discussion. The first, for example, communicated a kind of anger that I saw in more than one young man's paper:

> The main focus of this paper is on rap. I was very excited at the
> beginning of the year knowing that we were going to study rap. We
> began by discussing 6 articles that were assigned to us in our text.
> The articles ranged from discussing Freedom of Speech, History of
> Rap, Feminists towards rap, Criticisms, and so on. We made entries
> in our journal discussing each of the articles and tabulating our
> opinions of those articles. Coming to class the next day, I was excited
> to discuss these articles and talk about what rap is all about. I left the
> class quite disappointed. Our focus of discussion was on 2 articles,
> one by George Will, a Conservative columnist and Michelle Wallace,
> a feminist. We basically discussed the negativity of rap and on the
> basis of what these two individuals thought. We ended the class with
> a fierce group discussion, with me against basically the rest of the
> females in the group. Once I get out of this class I just have to laugh
> at some of these people. They have no clue. I just wish there were
> some people in this class that understand what this music is about.
> There is only one other person in this class that I know of can tell you
> what rap is about (guy from Chicago). I guarantee you that not one
> other person in this class has heard 2 Live Crew music that talks
> *strictly* politics. They convey an important message, but people don't
> like to see people succeed who may offend them in a way, isn't that

what our contry is all about. As far as the 2 articles, the two groups (Conservative Republicans and Feminazis) opinions that are stated are as about as bad as you can get for a fariness element. Conservatives are not for freedom of speech and *some* feminists basically use no rational thinking. They are at the extreme-left side of the political spectrum, but yet they are denouncing this music on the basis that it offends women. Isn't that called freedom of speech? (A liberal concern) What are they doing analyzing this music for if it offends them, DON'T LISTEN TO IT!

The whole moral of this is: I think the way we are approaching this class is interesting. I think it is run well, but definately with a female approach, which is fine, it will do me good. I am an open-minded person and will listen to what others have to say, but I will be very pissed off, If I am continually interrupted while I am proving (stating) a point by other shallow individuals. I have an opinion and I hope others respect it and recognize it, they may disagree which is fine, but *I deserve to be heard.*

The entire class again was quiet. I read another paper, this one by a young female student:

It all began the day we first walked into popular culture class. We were told what was expected of us as individuals and as a whole. We were also informed that women and how they were treated in society was to become a major topic of this class. We were then informed that if we didn't like any thing we were expected to do, or if the males weren't willing to discuss the female topics, we have the option to drop.

I didn't drop and most of the others didn't either. From the very first day we've been learning, reading and talking about conflicts. Either it being music, gender, race, or even the way an article was written.

Looking back I came to the topic I'll attempt to grasp an idea from, this being how females are treated in our society.

In my opinion women are treated as second class citizens. We get paid less for the same work and are the butt of many jokes, when we say we feel this guys just say, "Well, I'm better trained, besides are you saying your better than me?"

I don't think that's fair. I think each and every one of us was created equally and we would all just like to be given the same respect.

I'm not saying its all males fault. I realize in our society men are considered to be the dominant race. I'd just like to know why. I realize they may be bigger and stronger in some cases, but that in my opinion doesn't necassarily mean better.

I'm in no means trying to male bash. I think there are many men out there who respect and also believe women are equal. However I believe there are just as many who only respect women for one thing.

I noticed in discussions that some males even though they may deny it, or maybe they never even realize because it's just second nature, talk as if we can't understand issues we discuss. Such as when someone was saying well it was ok for the guy to have his shirt off, but when the girl was dressed really skimppy for her show it was a different story. He said well I noticed her because of how she's dressed. That's not fair it's like saying a guy can do whatever he wants, but a female doing the same gets no respect.

I do believe everyone is equal male and female in every race and in any culture. I think we as a people need to sit down and decide what our values are and how we can make this a better world to live in.

But until we do this, men are the superior gender. Well at least they are in most men's minds!

analysis:

I tried to explain the roles males tend to take in society and how they perceive women.

In doing so I may have been a little harsh. I don't believe all men feel or act superior, but I feel men as a whole feel women are weak, and less powerful in many areas as they are.

I'm not one of those people who blame all men for my problems and shortcomings. I think we as women need to strive for change, but even so it may not help. It's hard when men have been raised to be dominant and superior in their minds.

I really have no solution for this problem. Its been here from the beginning of time and for as far as I can see, it will be here until the end.

I hoped that the students might hear, through my positioning of these papers, how the anger expressed by the men in the class might be affecting some of the women. I also told them that the second paper was moving to me, but that it seemed to be a general discussion of sexism, and that it needed more specificity regarding the conflicts in our classroom, and an analysis based upon that specific description. I told them that the first paper was also effective in expressing the anger of the writer, but less effective in making its author "heard" by me (the writer's last words were "I deserve to be heard") because he called me and other women in the class "feminazis"—among other things. I introduced to them the concept of self-reflexivity: reflecting upon one's feelings, thoughts, and actions in such a way as to critique oneself. "I wouldn't want this writer to pretend not to be angry," I said. "Besides being important for one's own personal well-being, strong emotions can also afford us insight into culture. I would ask this writer to think specifically about his anger. When, exactly, did he feel angry? What, exactly, did those other people say that set the anger off? Did he show his own anger at the time? How? Might he have said or done anything that could have made others angry? Who? Why? Are there any contradictions within or among cultural groups that would contribute to the anger felt by the writer and the other people in our class?"

The second set of papers, I told the students, were not only moving, but successful as cultural critiques. The first was written by a young man:

> One of the most interesting and stimulating exercises I have been involved in this class is the same-sex discussion groups. I'm not saying that I did not enjoy the class discussions or the other group discussions; it's just that this discussion group was more open and a little less stifling than the others.
>
> The discussion moved rapidly from one topic in race relations to another. It moved from the more specific subject of Queen Latifah to a broader subject, which was race relations in general.
>
> It started with Queen Latifah and there was a fair amount of agreement that she was not extreme like some had expressed in the class, and many were of the opinion that she was not all that entertaining.
>
> The conversation then moved on to other black artists, specifically Spike Lee. Several viewed him as extreme and felt that the movie "Boyz'n the Hood" gave a better portrayl of typical black hardships in the urban areas.
>
> The topics continued to evolve until the end, when we finished with a discussion on how the welfare system keeps blacks from achieving higher levels because it doesn't offer incentives and often goes to those who least deserve it.
>
> You may find it strange that our conversation transformed so rapidly, but the only way I can explain it is that it was the natural evolution of discussions compounded by our homogenius backgrounds that caused few disagreements.
>
> In this assignment, you asked us to discuss any epiphanies we had. Well, I feel during that discussion I had a major realization. An example pointed out was how many North Dakotans would treat a black with the utmost respect and dignity while treat[ing] an American Indian as drunk and a lazy bum. This "theory" made me think how true it was in many cases. The idea was so simple, anyone could of thought of it, but it was so obvious that it never occured to me. If anything came out of that discussion that will stay with me the rest of my life, it is that.

I repeated the line, "The idea was so simple, anyone could [have] thought of it, but it was so obvious that it never occured to me." I said that this was what a cultural critic needed to be able to do: to notice those simple-seeming, obvious things that usually go unnoticed. I said that was what cultural theory was good for, helping us to see what is ordinarily invisible to the people who are actually members of the culture being studied. I said I thought this writer understood that concept, and had become a cultural critic.

The next paper was impressive as well. It was written by a young woman:

> Once upon a time there was a class called 'Reading Popular Culture,' and it was full of very diffrent people who had very different ideas about most everything. For the first few weeks of school they studied rap music, with an emphasis on female artists. One day, the teacher, Ms. Dixon, brought a vidio of a performance by Queen Latifah to class. The students watched the tape, and most of them couldn't understand the lyrics. Nevertheless, many students were able to be highly critical of her message which, as I have said, most admitted to being unable to hear in the first place. Another time Ms. Dixon brought back her vidio and showed the class a female rapper called Yo-Yo. This resulted in a class discussion about contradictions in messages, which was never actually resolved. Then one day a man came to class and gave students a handout from *Essence* magazine, that threw some light on Queen Latifah's message and that of her contemporarys. The article was a transcript of a discussion between various rap artists. Finally, one day, Ms. Dixon stood up and talked to the class about a new word called "universalizing." She said that people need to be careful when they say words like "we" and "our" because they deminish diffrences among groups. She also said that students need to careful about saying that there is "good and bad in both" about any two things, because then students often dismiss the arguments and forget to analyse it. After that I went home and thought about what had transpired.
>
> The one feature that unites this class is that we are all registered for this course. Beyond that, we are all extremely diffrent individuals. We vary in age, sex, race, ethnic background, place of origin, intrests— everything. Yet, this group has a tendency, like many groups in our culture, to do a great deal of "we"ing. Sometimes "we" might mean the women in the class, or the men in the class, or the feminists, or the older-than-average students, or the greeks; or, as in the article from *Essence*, "we" might mean a specific race. Like the male rappers in this article who talked about "our community" and "our music," the "we" in this class tend to erase our diffrences by using this uni-

versalizing vernacular. I think this is part of the reason we come to so many points of conflict. Because we are so different, the "we" word makes people who don't feel a part of, or want to be a part of, that "we," extremely defensive. It is the same in American culture. Certain films, t.v. shows, music, etc. become popular culture because a majority of people enjoy them. That doesn't mean, however, that there are not differences among those people. Existing in the same space, under the same rule does not necessarily make Americans a unit, just like using the same medium (rap) does not make male and female artists a unit. I think that people, especially those in power, need to be very conscious of who they are talking about when they say "we" and "our." It's all very nice for people to have a group that they fit into and feel accepted in, but they (all people) need to be conscious of their differences because that way they will be more willing to speak up for what they feel is "good" or "bad" instead of saying that there is "both in everything." (THIS IS MY OPINION— that came about as a result of our class discussion about universalizing brought up in my story).

Something that really helped me think about the good/bad idea, was the last diologue in the rap article. One rapper said "Men and women need to work together," and another said, "Yo. That's the bottom line."—Well No Shit kidding huh? I really can't think of any groups that would disagree with that. Men and women are working together when women are completely subserviant—what kind of working together does he mean? We work together at all levels, but that doesn't mean we do so in a positive way. Further, by saying this, the subject of sexist, mysoginist lyrics was dropped. "We need to work together," he said. Well swell pal, but what about all these other things that were erased when you said that? What about the rappers that say things like, "Yo Bitches come up to the stage and say Ho"? What about 2 Live Crew? What about this sexism? And, yes women sometimes buy into this or do a reversal of this, but that's not good either, so what can we do about *that?* This kind of shoving things under the table is accepted in our culture (obviously, because that's where *Essence* closed the article), and in this class. If it wasn't that this group has someone to notice and point out when we do this, important issues would never be brought up again. I think this maybe happens because arguing is uncomfortable. People will stand up for their beliefs, but it seems like they have a tendency to do so more quietly than they did, say in the 1960's. So, it is important to remember that in this big mass of culture there are a great many individuals who are lost, not heard from—voiceless.

In the last essay in *Contending with Words,* James Sosnoski observes that we need a return to a "teacher-centered" classroom (208).

I wouldn't call my classroom teacher- or student-centered. It seemed to me as though we were pursuing subjects that were important to all of us, the students communicating in ways "natural" to them, and I in ways "natural" to me (as a member of a particular part of academe). The students provided me with insights into their culture(s), which inspired my improvisations. I believe as well that many of the students gained from my intervention in discussions and from my introduction of postmodernist theory which critiques liberal discourse. At the very least, some students learned how to use certain intellectual tools to formulate their heartfelt ideas. I myself gained great pride and confidence in this new generation of young people. If they can work this hard and think this well, change *can* come.

8

Monday Night Football: Entertainment or Indoctrination?

Todd Sformo and Barbara Tudor_____

A pedagogy which takes popular culture as an object of
study must recognize that all educational work is at root
contextual and conditional.
                    —*Henry A. Giroux and Roger I. Simon*

Professional football, along with baseball, is an all-American sport. To
the average fan, a distinctly American sport implies enthusiasm, teamwork, and, ultimately, despite signs to the contrary, the notion that
"it's not whether you win or lose, it's how you play the game." Many
Americans have assimilated, for the most part unconsciously,
Hollywood's "win one for the Gipper" view of football as a test of
personal fortitude and triumph in the face of inestimable odds. While
much of this is a fantasy, it sustains a multimillion dollar industry
which mythologizes a sport for corporate profit. Certainly, in the final
analysis, *Monday Night Football* is simply another commodity that is
for sale to the American public. As commodities, televised sports (and
popular culture in general) are appropriate texts for cultural interpretation, since students need to learn how these products encode the
beliefs and values of Americans. When used in the teaching of college
composition, for example, students not only will be improving their
writing, but they will also become conscious of their own ideologies
and those of the society in which they live. In fact, when students are
taught to think critically about cultural products such as *Monday Night
Football,* they are becoming culturally literate and insightful citizens.

Few undergraduate students perceive the multiple meanings underlying contemporary cultural products, nor do they realize their

own point of view in relation to this culture. For this reason, we had our class critically interpret a *Monday Night Football* game between the Los Angeles Raiders and the Kansas City Chiefs. Initially, the students resisted associating values, either positive or negative, with a cultural product such as football. By the end of the class, however, they were intrigued by the possibility of meaning encoded in a sports presentation.

In order to get the class to think critically about professional sports, we assigned Barbara S. Morris and Joel Nydahl's essay "Sports Spectacle as Drama: Image, Language and Technology" before attempting the in-class analysis of the *Monday Night* game. Morris and Nydahl discuss how technology and sport commentary work together to create a drama. Although this article does not address values and culture per se it can be used heuristically, teaching students how to isolate specific details of sports presentations for in-depth analysis.

The Pregame Show: Getting in the Mood

We introduced the in-class segment of the football exercise by having the class preview the *Monday Night* pregame montage with Hank Williams, Jr., singing the *Monday Night* theme. We had reasons for starting here rather than with the game itself. First, the students would be less intimidated by an assignment asking them to see values encoded in the pregame show than in the game itself. The pregame means less to the sports aficionado, since this segment is seen as marginal to the central event. Second, we felt that the overwhelming number of images would excite the students and set a pace and mood. The fast action and spliced-together clips might enable us to draw students out of their usual, passive TV posture. We introduced the interpretive process by noting specific details and surmising possible intentions for the pregame imagery, suggesting to the students that, as viewers, we receive imagery and information based on our particular cultural, social, and personal values. We hoped that, once they understood that the pregame show was not neutral, they would be more willing to "read" the images of the actual game.

Of course, this analytical approach did not occur immediately, but the class was more willing to interpret the pregame montage than the actual game. In the pregame segment Hank Williams, Jr., asks, "Are you ready for some football?" and computer-animated helmets butt heads on the field. The students felt that this imagery presented *Monday Night Football* as a tough, physical competition within a setting which made it fun, not frightening. Because of its humorous presentation, they did not believe that this imagery condoned violence nor male dominance.

At first, it was difficult for the students to reflect seriously on a cultural product which they consider entertainment. One student laughed at our viewing context (a freshman English class watching football at 8:00 A.M.), stating that the pregame presentation was a neutral introduction to the game, "just for the hype." Several students agreed with this response. In fact, they questioned why we would take a sporting event seriously and use it for classroom instruction, since they were accustomed to more traditional texts. "What's next?" was the general consensus. When we suggested that we might also critically interpret comic books or popular women's magazine articles, their reaction was mixed with apprehension and curiosity.

Another student felt that sports, especially the World Series, which was taking place at the time of this assignment, was "too sacred" to be analyzed. He said that analyzing sports, especially his beloved baseball, would "ruin the enjoyment" and, therefore, the purpose of the game. He felt that there must be boundaries set between intellectual activities and a more pleasurable realm of passive enjoyment.

Their resistance to interpreting sports presentations, or popular culture in general, reflects the idea that we (as instructors) are making more out of these subjects than there is. It was important, therefore, to clarify that we were not placing values on the actions of the players per se, but focusing on the presentation of the game, such as the commentator's remarks and the camera angles designated by the program director. The students had to be sure that we, as instructors, were not "messing with" the actions of the players, whom they felt would not understand our act of interpretation. One student stated, "they [the players] don't even know what we're doing, anyway," as if our analysis were unfair to the players.

In Class Protocol: Commentary and Technology Groups

In comparison to the actual game, the students understood the pregame dramatics as staged events that were created or constructed. By having students note the difference between the pregame montage and the "naturally" flowing "real thing" (i.e., the actual game), they began to differentiate between the various parts of a televised sports production, With this idea in mind, the live action of the game could now be further broken down into technology and commentary (categories borrowed from Morris and Nydahl), which helped the students focus on specific details. Based on these categories, we divided the class into two groups, commentary and technology, and handed out an in-class assignment for them to apply to *Monday Night Football*. To support their interpretation, they were instructed to rely on specific details rather than generalities.

The Commentary Group

The commentary group dealt with the interior and exterior reportage during the game. Interior reportage includes any interpretations given during the game, such as the opinions of the commentators. Exterior reportage includes any objective facts given, such as dates and statistics. The students recorded not only the exterior reportage but also (and more importantly) the commentators' diction, tone, jokes, and selection of historical facts. These, we felt, would provide further evidence of how cultural values crop up unexpectedly.

Morris and Nydahl contend that the "commentary by the announcers also plays its part in making the dramatic events [experienced through the TV] different from those experienced in the arena" (105). The students were asked to keep this point in mind. In order to distinguish the difference between a televised sports event and one experienced in the arena, we asked the students to consider the following questions: What kind of information do the commentators give? Why is it important for them to give us this information? How does this background influence our perception of the player(s) as well as the game as a whole?

To explain the assignment further, we gave the students an example from Morris and Nydahl, who believe that the commentators prompt the audience to notice particular skills on the part of the players. Morris and Nydahl discuss a commentator's use of the phrase "four corners defense" during a professional basketball game. According to the authors, this interpretive comment "establishes that the game has moved into a phase of action which will challenge each team's disciplined versatility anew" (106). In other words, the game is acknowledged as professional, with highly skilled players and all of the empowerment that professionalism implies. Thus, the game becomes more significant to the television viewer. Also, the commentator's use of the phrase "four corners defense" implies that the game has moved into a level of complexity which requires expert analysis. The viewer is also empowered as he or she is made privy to the commentator's expertise through the television medium.

One student resisted interpreting the commentary just prior to kick-off, explaining that the commentators' "talk" about the setting of the game has nothing to do with the sports' presentation: "It's just because the game is there." Again, his resistance and fear of overinterpreting "just what's there" is evident. Most of the students, however, noted that the commentators' language influenced their perception of the game even before it began. In one instance, the commentator began by calling the football game "a happening." For the students, this particular elaboration was an imperative to watch because something exciting was about to occur.

According to the class, excitement is intensified when the commentators note that the best two teams will meet, in the end, at the Super Bowl. Throughout the season, the audience is to anticipate the moment when one team will claim athletic and strategic superiority. One student felt that American sports presentations, such as the Super Bowl, are further sensationalized when the games are televised around the world. For this student, the broadcast of the Super Bowl worldwide is an indication of America's international influence. He argued that internationally televised sports "work so hard to bring excitement into the homes of Americans giving insight . . . providing statistics . . . [it is like a] drama unfolding on the field all over the world." Americans, the student surmised, are empowered as they view an American sports spectacle which they know is being transmitted around the world, as if the United States were staging an all-American Olympics with the citizens of other countries observing but not participating. There is the notion here that America possesses an exclusive commodity, an entertainment hegemony, which allows Americans to feel culturally superior to the rest of the world.

This same student went on to connect the international broadcast of American sports presentations with an attitude of political superiority. He was, however, disturbed by the warlike image of professional football, which contrasted to his understanding of the United States as an international peace keeper, not an aggressor. These two images, to him, seemed in conflict. Evident to this student was a discrepancy between the supposed foreign policy of the United States and the entertainment choice of its private citizens. His confusion was apparent when he paraphrased a question posed in the comic strip *Shoe:* "How [can] Americans sit at home watching football, perhaps the most violent spectator sport in the world, and fall asleep while fans of soccer go breaking and killing each other?" The question led the class into a discussion of whether or not Americans sanction institutional violence, as well as anarchic violence, as long as it does not threaten American social and political interests.

The class felt that the violence apparent in *Monday Night Football* is used for cathartic effect by many Americans. The *Monday Night* game, they concluded, is a safe venue for viewers to project their own frustrations and repressed hostility. Violence, according to the class, is one of the main selling points of televised football. The more aggressive or "intense" the action, the more marketable the game becomes as a commodity. Several students, lamenting the emphasis on violence, claimed that a negative aspect of the game is being emphasized by television producers in order to entice an audience into watching. These students seemed to believe that good sportsmanship and athletic acumen were the true essence of the game. According to this group, the television medium is corrupting an all-American sport and transforming the game into a product that is for sale to American consumers.

To other students, the commercial interruptions throughout *Monday Night Football* are further evidence that capitalism is infringing upon professional sports. One student, for example, stated that the commercials are "chang[ing] the face of sports forever." He resented "the consumer industry unveil[ing its] latest [products] during the game," for [the industry] knows that all the eyes of the nation will be watching." Several of his peers agreed, complaining that football was being adulterated. To these students, the true values inherent in football have nothing to do with selling a product. Including commercials during *Monday Night Football* misrepresents the positive values that they feel the game itself embodies. In fact, one student suggested that this corruption was being engineered by a minority of "greedy people" and did not perceive the sports presentation as part of an entertainment industry. Other students, however, in considering the constant barrage of commercials in relation to the game, discussed how televised sports, like Budweiser Beer or Pepsi, are also products that are "hyped" to make them more salable to the consumer.

While considering the ubiquity of hype, the class struggled to come to terms with whether or not the media actually creates sports heroes and mythologizes the game. One student, not sure whether he should trust the commentators' interpretation of the play or what he actually saw, wrote in his reading log: "Commentators in all sports enter into a game, seemingly to dictate the pace and interest of both adversaries." Yet, later, he also wrote,

> They do not dictate the pace of the event but do have some affect on it. When something happens that will work to the commentators' upper hand [they] will use it to stress a point. This will often happen and turn a not so great competitor... into a superstar. Often this is what is intended by those mike men.

The tone and diction of his opinion and the political connotations implied by words such as *upper hand* and *dictates* are important. For this student, the sports presentation is "biased"; it does not seem to be objective because the commentators enter into the "pace of the event." This, we felt, must be brought to the student's attention, since it not only indicates how the commentators construct the production but how the student projects his own values onto the presentation.

Like many of his peers, this student's understanding of commentary is tied to his notions of objectivity, which he related to the presidential campaign taking place during this assignment:

> If commentators are going to pick favorites and praise one team over the other, they shouldn't be there. That may be all right now in the [d]emocratic society Murphy Brown has created. HA!... The values one has been taught say that one is educated to form one's own non-biased opinion by one's self. This should be shaped by someone, but certainly not forced upon this nation's youth. I'm ashamed.

Again, this student's tone strongly suggests his belief in objective reporting. What he sees, as a viewer of sports presentations, is the loss of "sports [which] are supposed to be an American past time" into "some predetermined, overrated game." His passion for the natural and unpredictable carries a very telling political message. He feels that objectivity (i.e., objective reporting), which he values, is being subverted by people who care more about packaging entertainment than telling the "truth." On the other hand, of course, the student saw his own interpretation of the game as objective, unbiased, and correct.

Our aim was to have this student understand his use of, and the ideas embodied in, the word *objectivity.* We tried to point out that "knowledge," as R. W. Connell says, "is socially constructed, not that it is inherently subjective or non-objective" (124). This is not a small goal that can be dealt with effectively in one assignment, and it became a challenge throughout the semester. During the following weeks, we brought up the question of objectivity in relation to various contexts, including Sherry Ortner's essay, "Is

Female to Male as Nature is to Culture?" After reading the essay, the class discussed whether woman's procreative function made her naturally suited to the home and nurturing activities or if societal norms and social customs were responsible for woman's traditional role. The aforementioned student had firm beliefs regarding the appropriate roles of men and women, but when the discussion began, he did not connect his opinions to any particular ideology. As his peers explained their perspectives on gender, using life experiences to support their opinions, this student began relating his notions of gender to his middle-class upbringing and his continuing practice of fundamentalist Christianity. He began to understand that he was maintaining the value system that he had been taught as a child, which felt "right" for him, but his opinions were not objective. Our goal as educators was not to change the student's beliefs but to show him that his presumed impartiality was actually the result of social conditioning.

During the discussion of *Monday Night Football*, the issue of socially constructed beliefs was raised in regard to hero identification. A debate began in class about the "greatness" of particular football players. We suggested that the class establish a criteria for greatness by which to judge the players. Because nearly every student had different ideas about what makes a football hero and how to judge greatness, the class was unable to agree on a definition. Some students argued that toughness, the ability to take a lot of pain without flinching or losing ground, was the most important quality of a great football player. Other students suggested that a player's speed and finesse, lightness on his feet, and great hands (the ability to catch the most difficult pass), were the most significant qualities. One pupil, an older student and a military policeman in the U.S. Army, stated that physical strength and aggressiveness were indicative of greatness in the football arena. He admired defensemen who would "get in the face" of the opposing team. Initially, this student expressed his opinion confidently, as if his criteria were correct, period. Other students challenged him, however, explaining that "[his] ideas are not correct for every one," to which he eventually agreed. To clarify this point, many students shared some personal history, connecting their opinions with their life experiences. As the class debated such issues, explaining their reasoning in personal terms, it was clear that they were proceeding from different ideological positions. Class discussion was crucial, therefore, to their increasing awareness of how social factors construct beliefs.

The Technology Group

In the technology group's assignment sheet, we asked what possible cultural values may be encoded by the technological transformation. They were asked to note not only close-up shots but also how many different shots (and angles) are used. We asked the following questions: What cultural values may be associated with or signified by the use of different shots? Different angles? And why use close-ups at all? What is their function? What may a close-up encode, in terms of values? How does a close-up present an athlete differently than if you were viewing the player at the actual sporting event? How is slow motion different than "normal" vision on TV or in the stadium? How would you characterize slow motion?

According to Morris and Nydahl, the technology of multiple cameras and slow motion not only fill the "dead space" between the actions of the plays but reposition the observer both physically and temporally, allowing "us to be recipients of entirely new events outside of real time and space" (102). Technology's creation of "new events" was clearly evident to the students during the first series, from the kick-off to the first commercial.

The game began by focusing on the main offensive player, the quarterback, and on a defensive player. Their statistics and photographs were displayed as the players walked toward the line of scrimmage. The camera angles used to highlight these players were ground-level shots and close-ups. According to one student, this intensified adversarial relations, adding "extra excitement," although the game had just begun. Another student felt that technology, therefore, creates American sports heroes.

In the second play of the game, the camera presented a ground level close-up of Kansas City defensive player Neil Smith. The camera perspective was from ground level on the offensive side. This perspective seemed to place the viewer on the playing field with the athletes. The close focus and low angle reveal Smith to be an imposing figure. Smith turns his head from side to side, looking over the offensive line's positions and at the quarterback, while an offensive player comes into view. Because of the angle of the camera, the offensive player seems much smaller than Smith. Confrontation is established and intensified, and we, as viewers, are in the position of blocking this player. Before this play proceeded, another camera focused on the Los Angeles quarterback. Again, we, as viewers, were placed at his level on the field and lateral to him, his helmet taking up most of the TV screen. According to one student, the camera angles and changing viewpoints helped to produce "more competition."

Other students discussed the objectivity of the media in regard to penalties. Within the first series, Kansas City received the ball, and on the second down, a combination of slow-motion and instant replay revealed a potential face mask penalty; however, the referees either did not see the penalty or chose not to call it. During the live action, a camera was in aerial perspective; during slow-motion replay, on the other hand, a camera was positioned at ground level, allowing the viewers to see the running back's incredible twists and turns. From this vantage point, viewers could clearly see the penalty.

One student suggested that technology "[brought] out details that would otherwise be overlooked." For her, the slow motion and the instant replay suggested not the advantages of technology but, in her words, how an audience is "allow[ed] to see what [the director] wants them to see." She began to see the sports presentation as "manipulative" because particular shots have the potential of being or not being shown. This, she surmised, was a technique for making the production more exciting. Another student felt that "the use of slow motion is a contradiction to our fast-paced society." Technology, he stated, created a "paradox" between the pace of the "game itself" and its presentation. For him, the slow-motion camera now represented an issue worth exploring.

Comparing the actual game to the "images we've seen [of] sporting events [on TV]," another student stated: "Technology gives us opportunities to see things from various viewpoints and unexpected configurations. We experience this concept in all programs we watch as well as our everyday lifestyles." In other words, the images we see do not necessarily reveal the truth but actually portray what we think we should see. She was referring to the media's tendency to stereotype. Her reference to fashion makes this clear:

> On TV, we experience advertisements that convey images to us. At school, [we] discuss what the 'cool' things are to wear, and [we] get these ideas from TV ads or magazines.

For both of these students, therefore, the question becomes not only how the media "shows [the] importance" of certain events but also how "they make it."

The students now began to discuss Morris and Nydahl's statement about the zoom lens in relation to the idea of a constructed reality. According to Morris and Nydahl:

[Z]ooming in on, or pulling back from, . . . thus manipulat[es] our apparent relation to the subject . . . cutting immediately to a close-up or choosing to bring us gradually into apparent close proximity to the subject. In selecting images to be transmitted to the home viewer, then, the director, because of the available technology, has a seemingly infinite range of possible subjects to select from and has control of our point of view. (102)

One student observed that the number of camera monitors at the disposal of the director was like a control panel with which the director was able to manipulate the viewer's perspective. This comment seemed to demonize the director as if she or he were interfering with the viewer's "natural" experience.

Morris and Nydahl compare and contrast live sporting events to the advent of new technologies and its power to "change our experience of the drama inherent in a live event" (101). They state that "multiple cameras, special lenses and slow motion replays" (101) interrupt the continuous (live) action of the plays. As soon as the game begins, the cameras place viewers inside as well as outside the sporting facility, at ground level or high above the field in the blimp, viewing crowds or players warming up. Telephoto lenses also highlight players for us as if they were only a few feet away. For Morris and Nydahl, these multiple views and close-ups take the viewer out of the limited perspective of the spectator, what they designate as the "single vantage point in the stands" (102). Multiple perspectives refocus viewers' attention every few seconds. For our students, the notion that their attention (to a seemingly spontaneous event) was being refocused by a director allowed the game to take on a new, less natural perspective.

While we contrasted television viewing to attending an actual game, one student brought his economic position to our attention. When he attended a game, he "didn't have the money to pay for a box seat, so [he] got stuck up at the top with all the other financially unstable people." At the game he usually had to sit "so far away [that] by the end of the game [his] eyes hurt from [trying] to follow the play and [his] head hurt from [his] eyes hurting." Also, while at the game, he felt more susceptible to distraction because he was not secluded in a private box seat. Televised sports' presentations, for this student, became an economic equalizer. Through the TV, he could view the plays better than those who have the money to purchase the best seats. Pedagogically speaking, what stood out was this student's use of a spatial metaphor for economic status.

When we highlighted the student's metaphorical use of distance, not only could he begin to see possible interpretations of sports' presentations but he could also relate these to his own experience. This student could now "read" distance and point of view as part of the empowerment process through the TV screen. As Henry A. Giroux and Roger I. Simon state: "[T]he value of including popular culture in the development of a critical pedagogy is that it provides the opportunity to further our understanding of how students make investments in particular social forms and practices" (3).

Because of the multiple viewpoints available to the television audience, the students tended to feel that they were "closer" to the action and could therefore concentrate more closely on the game. Although the metaphor of distance may be too subtle for most students to realize, they did acknowledge a sense of empowerment from their position as viewers. However, they were angry when we noted the manipulation of images by the program director. The sheer number of perspectives, images, stills, and replays allows us to feel that we are in command, omnisciently viewing the whole. Leisurely and vicariously, we feel empowered by the director, who manages the number and kind of images we see while staying out of our view. And even when we may see the number of cameras, it does not appear to limit our experience, but gives us a more expansive vision. Prior to considering this manipulation, the students felt a sense of satisfaction, of control, which was satiating and fulfilling at a low cost to them. The group concluded that many viewers gaze passively at the TV screen without critically examining the presentation because of this sense of personal omnipotence that is created by technology.

Conclusion

To conclude the in-class assignment, the students were asked to write on the chalkboard the values, both positive and negative, that they now associated with *Monday Night Football.* One positive value they listed was teamwork, players cooperating with one another in order to achieve a common goal. Competition and the desire for victory were also seen by the class as positive, indicating how goal setting along with hard work and perseverance can pay off in American society. Although there was still a certain naivete to their assessment of positive values, the students were, perhaps for the first time, closely observing a cultural product and perceiving meaning in a sports program.

The commercialization of *Monday Night Football* was one of the negative aspects listed by the students. They believed that the commercial interruptions ruined the "purity" of the game, and they considered how consumerism dominates every facet of American life. At this point, the class did not hold the network solely responsible, but considered the viewer implicit in the process. Since the students were beginning to understand that values are created and shared by a community, they tried to define the *Monday Night Football* community. To do this, they turned to the values listed on the chalkboard. The list of negatives prompted them to visualize this community as a group in constant need of excitement, who expect women to cheer from the sidelines while men engage in the action, who condone violence (as long as it does not threaten them), and who are preoccupied with self-empowerment. While several students resisted this assessment, others considered it fair when considered in conjunction with the positive values previously discussed.

The goals of the in-class assignment were achieved by many students. They were able to perceive multiple—even contradictory—meanings underlying contemporary cultural products. Moreover, many students were beginning to understand their own social, political, economic, racial, and gender position as relevant to their beliefs. They were also considering their belief systems, those of their classmates, and those of the American middle class in relation to a cultural product such as *Monday Night Football.*

Now the students were prepared to tackle the out-of-class assignment: to critically interpret the sports presentation of their choice in a short (3–4 page) essay. We emphasized that we were not looking for one right or wrong response, but for students to support their interpretation with specific details and examples. Some of the sports written about included hockey, car racing, Olympic ice skating, snow boarding, boxing, and professional wrestling. Many of the essays were quite insightful. In the essay on professional wrestling, for example, the student was able to see past the hype and came to some perceptive conclusions. When considering the riotous response of the crowd to the cultural stereotypes presented in the wrestling ring, the student concluded that, despite the comic trappings, at some level the social caricatures represent the beliefs of the audience. He reported common patterns in audience response (an absolute distinction between good and evil, support for the underdog against a notorious villain, and concern for the damsel in distress), supporting his findings with specific examples. Reading this student's essay, we noted that professional wrestling appeared to be a contemporary form of the folktale, a means of sharing common beliefs. In our comments at the end of the student's essay, we asked what he thought these stereotypes indicate about American society.

For students to understand their own cultural context, they must be allowed to critically interpret texts which appear in their everyday lives. After this assignment, one student in particular said that English composition was finally becoming relevant to her everyday life. She felt the need to analyze the television programs she watched, the clothes she wore, the books she read, the people she associated with, even the major she had chosen to study in college. Decision making was becoming a more conscious process for her, as she contemplated her own beliefs and those of her community and nation.

9

Pee-Wee, Penley, and Pedagogy, or, Hands-On Feminism in The Writing Classroom

*Christopher Wise*_____

Issues of gender and human sexuality tend to provoke the most engaged student responses in the undergraduate classroom today, especially in settings that are neither urban nor ethnically diverse. Even college students with the most limited cultural experience and educational background can appreciate the urgency of contemporary academic inquiry into matters of gender. For Marxist pedagogues, the priority of the feminist agenda at present does not necessarily imply that issues of class are somehow less urgent than issues of gender, though it *does* imply that a remarkable opportunity presently exists to contribute towards an immediate and wide-ranging transformation of American society through exploiting the present confusion that exists about what is "appropriate" sexual behavior. This is especially true for "heterosexual-white-male" instructors of English (like myself), who are often perceived by students as having "the most to lose" in such debates. One successful writing assignment I have employed in attempting to undermine traditional gender-roles was inspired by the work of Constance Penley, especially her writings on Paul Rubens's now-defunct television series, *Pee-Wee's Playhouse*.

This assignment is primarily intended to alert students to their own ideological subjectivity, especially as "gendered" subjects, by analyzing Sigmund Freud's essay "Infantile Sexuality" and Penley's chapter "The Cabinet of Doctor Pee-Wee: Consumerism and Sexual Terror" from her *The Future of an Illusion* in relation to one or more episodes of Rubens's *Pee-Wee's Playhouse*. Besides incorporating critical insights from feminist, Marxist, and Freudian theory, this assignment also has the advantage of demonstrating to students the astonishingly complex process of interpretation itself that is involved in understanding something as "simple" as a popular children's television show. In the past two years, this composition exercise has proven to be successful in my writing classes at Mt. San Antonio Community College in Walnut, California, and at Central Oregon Community College in Bend, Oregon, where I presently teach.

Besides becoming better writers and more socially aware individuals, I also believe it is important that my students understand the historical background or foundation of what they are studying, or that they can ground their work within a larger historical context, especially the traditions of rhetoric and hermeneutics. Within these traditions, I insist that there exists a stable, coherent, and "objective" body of knowledge that human beings have made use of for centuries, and that we can continue to make use of today. I therefore make an effort to employ a variety of concepts and insights from these traditions whenever they are relevant, though mostly for pedagogical reasons rather than ideological ones.

By grounding composition courses in terms of classical rhetoric, referring often to the work of rhetoricians like Aristotle, Quintillian, and Vico, it has been my experience that one may obviate a wide variety of potential problems when making the transition to the more controversial or blatantly ideological aspects of the course. First, the "objective" and historical content of the course tends to legitimate the more radical pedagogy to follow (at least in the imagination of the student). A context of student respect for the instructor is also established, which the instructor can rely upon when introducing less palatable material.

For example, even the mere application of obscure Latinate terms from classical rhetoric and hermeneutics serves a sheer ritual value in mollifying students' reactionary fears about spending actual class time and taxpayers' dollars studying anything as "ridiculous" as *Pee-Wee's Playhouse*. More importantly, these terms may also be applied throughout the term while analyzing reading assignments as well as student essays. Once a student is able to both identify and give a name to common rhetorical fallacies (e.g., *post hoc*, *ad hominem*, and *non sequitur* arguments), she not only internalizes and thus masters these concepts for their own sake, but she also significantly develops her own reading and thinking skills. Secondly, the study of terminology from classical rhetoric serves a broadly heuristic function as well as critical one: for example, by memorizing terms like *pathos, ethos,* and *logos* (the three "legitimate" rhetorical appeals, according to Aristotle) helpful guidelines are thereby established towards the composition of student essays. A common vocabulary (or "grammar of rhetoric") may also be instituted between student and instructor to facillitate discussion throughout the course.

Finally, an instructor is forced to say very little in defending the "frivolity" of studying *Pee-Wee's Playhouse* given the rigorous context of the preceding material. In fact, after weeks of studying texts like Isocrates's *Against the Sophists,* Plato's *Phadreus,* and Aristotle's *Rhetoric,* students are often simply relieved to turn their attention to "less serious" matters. This relief is short-lived, however, once they discover the complexity of the material to follow.

Assuming the appropriate learning environment has been established, reading Freud's "Infantile Sexuality" will be considerably less shocking to many students, even those who will make no effort to disguise their initial repulsion. While almost all students will be familiar with Freud's basic oedipal thesis, few will be prepared for the frank carnality and astonishing detail of Freud's work on infantile sexuality. Additionally, Freud's essay will generate resentment from those students who feel cornered by the implication that their desires to preserve the "myth" of infantile asexuality may occur as a result of their own sexual repression, a common enough reaction to Freud's work. In any case, the reality is that most men and women, especially those in their late teens and early twenties, are not comfortable discussing human sexuality in an open forum; but it has been my experience that students will become more comfortable so long as the instructor is in full command of the discussion and is herself relaxed. Still, one must be sensitive to the obvious "weirdness" of the material, the "uncanny" nature of topics like masturbation, thumb-sucking, and bed-wetting. If Freud is correct, there are good reasons why it is difficult to broach such issues in the first place, and one should be careful not to ignore the very real psychological effects such insights may have upon one's students. For this reason, it is imperative that students be given a "way out," or real assurance that it is okay to dismiss Freud, even if it is obvious that they don't fully understand him. In one instance, a student informed me after our discussion of Freud that she felt "disoriented and muddle-headed." She approached my desk at the end of the period, and then she could not remember what she had originally wanted to ask.

Finally, I have encountered resistance from students who have learned in their "Introduction to Psychology" courses that the work of Freud is completely irrelevant and outdated for contemporary usage. In one case, this became a problem for me when a Psychology Department faculty member privately supported a student's views that Freud's work on infantile sexuality had been thoroughly discredited by contemporary American psychologists. Composition instructors teaching Freud might consider reviewing an "Introduction to Psychology" textbook in anticipation of such problems. My own solution in this particular case was to provide the student and faculty member with a lengthy reading list of contemporary psychoanalytic theorists like Jacques Lacan and numerous feminists like Penley. Although the student in question refused to accept any validity in Freud's views, she was able to see how her own essay had presented her textbook's view as "truth," whereas Freud's view had been presented as "theory"; in other words, she began to understand that she had offered in her paper yet another theory in opposition to Freud's, rather than providing the simple "facts" about infantile sexuality, as she had originally claimed.

The best way to present the essay by Freud is to focus on key terminology, making sure that each student develops a solid working vocabulary. This vocabulary will not only help students gain access to Freud's work, but it will also provide them with the appropriate critical framework for analyzing Penley's essay on Pee-Wee Herman. Terminology quizzes, group work, and lists on the chalkboard have all helped in clarifying these terms for my students. I also assign a formal summary (500–750 words) on Freud's "Infantile Sexuality," stressing that they may *not* insert their own critical views of the material in this essay. The summary must be as "objective" as possible, demonstrating their mastery of the major concepts discussed. As distasteful as they may find Freud's essay, they are informed that they will be evaluated for their ability to present his ideas in a fair and "straightforward" manner. In their second essay on either Freud or Penley, after they have "earned the right" to be critical, they may argue any position they choose, as long as they can persuasively support their views with solid textual evidence. Following submission of their summaries on Freud, two or three papers are selected to be copied and analyzed by the rest of the class. Often, it is during our discussion of student papers that Freud's theoretical concepts first become clear for many students, after having been summarized in a more palatable and concise manner—and by their fellow classmates.

As mentioned earlier, the goal of this assignment is to alert students to their own ideological and subjectivity, especially as "gendered" subjects. Hence, as valuable as Freud's work may be, it has obvious limitations in terms of reaching this ultimate goal. Most notably, many women students will rightly take offense at Freud's theory of penis envy, and this theory will inevitably form the topic of more than one student essay. However, it is not the student who has the perspicuity to take on Freud's sexism that one normally worries about in promoting awareness of gender formation; in fact, students interested in exploring such issues will largely be sympathetic with teacher advocacy of leftist and feminist goals.

After students read Penley's essay, "The Cabinet of Doctor Pee-Wee: Consumerism and Sexual Terror," and after they watch one or two episodes of *Pee-Wee's Playhouse*,[1] the concepts discussed earlier will take on a new meaning for them and will also become compelling to them in a way that no amount of ideological proselytizing could ever hope to achieve. More than once, I have heard students remark, "But you can apply these theories to *anything!*" And, when they realize that we are not really talking about Pee-Wee Herman, or about Sigmund Freud, but something much larger and much more significant, student resistance often gives way to admiration for what Penley has accomplished. Such admiration does not in itself constitute endorsement, but at this point any resentment at the "ridiculousness" of spending so much time and energy to understand *Pee-Wee's Playhouse* usually gives way to growing curiosity. It is now possible to approach the controversial question of how "appropriate" sexual desire is both channeled and created by far-ranging ideological forces in our society, which seem to most of us as inherent and as inevitable as nature itself.

In "The Cabinet of Dr. Pee-Wee," Penley argues that the unconscious subtext of *Pee-Wee's Playhouse* is a "fever pitch investigation of sexual identity" (142). In other words, children are both fascinated and terrified by Rubens's show because of its emphasis on the problem of gender formation, or because of its ambivalence on what constitutes appropriate sexual behavior in contemporary society. As nonexperienced individuals in consumer society, or as "subjects" who are not fully interpellated into the realm of the symbolic, children tend to be both more vulnerable and yet more wise than many adults who "*see*" but do not *register*" the actual content of Ruben's show (147, Penley's emphasis). Hence, Penley maintains that *Pee-Wee's Playhouse* poses the question of sexual relations and difference to an audience that is by definition receptive to any number of alternatives to contemporary patriarchical sexuality, especially heterosexual and bourgeois monogamy. To this end, Rubens borrows from camp and homosexual subculture, both of which are often sympathetic to issues of sexual (and racial) difference.

Thus, while Freud argued that repression itself was largely responsible for the myth of childhood asexuality, Penley sees much larger ideological forces at work within capitalist society's perpetuation of this myth. In other words, Penley differs from Freud in that she sees the deconstruction of this myth as an opportunity to examine the formation of gender roles in society. In the final paragraph of her essay, Penley asserts that "[i]t is almost as if the show [Pee-Wee's Playhouse] 'recognizes' that as long as infantile sexuality remains conceptually off-limits, it will be impossible to rethink sexual roles and sexed identities, masculine or otherwise" (162). By examining infantile sexuality in Pee-Wee's Playhouse, Penley then dramatically reveals the way in which patriarchical and capitalist society tends to insure the conditions of its own reproduction; more importantly, she demonstrates how those conditions may be both subverted and denied.

Assigned papers (1000–1250 words) focus on a single aspect of either Freud's or Penley's essay (see the Appendix for a list of paper topics). As with the summary, I also select two to three student papers to be copied and analyzed by the class at large; in this regard, it is important to select essays which are sympathetic with Penley's views, considering the potential impact of student advocacy of feminist goals (as opposed to teacher advocacy). If handled properly, it is quite possible to spend an entire month of class time on these assignments, significantly altering students' views about their own interpellation as "gendered" subjects, and never once deliberately clarify one's own ideological support of the represented views. My own response, when once asked what I thought about Penley's interpretation of Pee-Wee's Playhouse, was that I found a certain coherence and integrity in her argument, that her ideas seemed to me to "work" as theory, although I could imagine a competing theory about the show that might also work. In this way, students have the option to accept or reject the material for their own reasons, rather than simply taking my word for it. Obviously, however, most students also realize that I would not spend so much time and passion on Penley's essay if I were not convinced in the first place of its urgency.

Instructors should therefore avoid assuming a defensive posture in the face of student resistance to this assignment. For example, Penley is especially deft at illustrating the influence of camp and homosexual culture in *Pee-Wee's Playhouse,* and her argument that Rubens promotes a healthy tolerance of difference may prove even more controversial than Freud's suggestion that small children experience ordinary sexual desires. In Oregon, where I taught this assignment in winter 1993, an antihomosexual ballot measure (Ballot Measure 9), amending the state constitution to include descriptions of gays and lesbians as "abnormal" and "perverse," was only narrowly defeated during the October elections. For some students the wounds were still raw from the defeat at the polls, and performing a close reading of *Pee-Wee's Playhouse* was an extremely distasteful experience for them.

In one paper, a student complained that "the textual insinuation of both Freud and Penley seem to be pertaining to the homosexual lifestyle. . . . [Throughout Freud's] essay I got the impression that a homosexual lifestyle can be an acceptable way of life." Obviously, both Penley's essay and Rubens's show seemed even more offensive to him, insofar as they both tended to legitimate alternatives to heterosexual monogamy. His thesis then was that Penley's and Freud's ideas "only seem to pertain to mentally, physically, or sexually mixed-up people. . . . I cannot think of any reason for me to use information from Freud, Penley, or *Pee-Wee's Playhouse,* but the information was interesting and I was surprised that information was printed on infantile sexuality." This student went on to conclude that "[i]nfantile sexuality should be left to the psychologist to study and ponder." Given this particular student's avowed pro–Ballot Measure 9 stance, and his evident disdain for the topic, his relatively mild criticisms in his final paper seemed a victory of sorts, especially as they were among the most negative observations among a group of thirty-five students.

In another instance, student confusion about Penley's essay led to a near-comedy of misunderstanding. Though Penley's observations about gender-formation are crucial to her argument, many students seem to miss this point entirely, some even believing that Penley is a sort of moralist who wants to alert us to Rubens's "perversion." It is therefore necessary to carefully delineate for students the widely different reasons why Freud and Penley deconstruct this myth. One returning student, a woman in her mid fifties, was particularly disturbed by Penley's essay because she believed that Penley was too obsessed with human sexuality. To the amusement of the class, this student blurted out that Penley was "nothing more than a dirty-minded product of the sixties," and that *Pee-Wee's Playhouse* was "just a nice show for kids." Later, during a conference in my office, she bluntly refused to accept that Penley was not really interested in moral or ethical questions as such. This student's disavowal of Penley's essay seemed especially enigmatic, given her repeated claims to be a "radical feminist" from the early sixties to the present.

Despite these negative responses, other students commented outright, in their papers and in class discussions, that Penley's essay had changed their views on infantile sexuality and on homosexuality. One young woman even stated in class that she wished she had read Penley's essay before voting in the fall elections. Another young woman applauded the essay for "illustrat[ing] the suffocation of childhood expression by adults through the use of *Pee-Wee's Playhouse*." This student then concluded her essay by asserting that "[c]hildren need to be taken seriously for the emotional beings that they are. . . . [T]hey are sexual creatures and need to be treated as such." Similarly, a male student stated in his essay that "*Pee-Wee's Playhouse* is definitely the most sexually aware program ever to be in the Saturday morning lineup. Although some would argue that . . . children shouldn't view it, I feel it is a very important show."

However, the strongest response to this assignment came from a young man who rarely contributed to class discussion but who became fascinated with Penley's theorization of camp culture. This particular student worked weekends as a drummer in a heavy-metal rock band, and he seemed to have little in common with his fellow students. During a conference, he told me that he had always identified with the "freaks" while attending high school, and he did not really fit in anywhere now, except with other "freaks" and "metalheads" at the clubs where he played. He was interested in exploring camp culture because he felt a kinship with its marginality, or because it seemed a parallel subculture. Consequently, this student toured a number of gay bars and clubs in nearby Portland, where he interviewed people on videotape to ask what they thought "camp" meant. He also researched "camp" in libraries and finally wrote an essay that was later published in the campus newspaper.

Though challenging to teach, the essays of Freud and Penley proved to be rewarding in a variety of ways for both my students and myself. For my students, they received an introduction to the close reading of difficult texts, hence providing them with the necessary skills for survival within a college setting: namely, skills of textual analysis, interpretation, and criticism. Secondly, they were exposed to alternative views on human sexuality that contributed in many cases towards a new understanding of their own formation as gendered individuals in patriarchal society. Because this assignment also involved the analysis of a children's television show, students were also exposed to an entirely new approach to popular culture, demonstrating that critical thinking skills may be employed both inside and *outside* of the classroom.

For myself, through careful analysis of these texts, I became increasingly convinced of the validity of both Freud's and Penley's theses, as well as the greater implication that we must constantly re-examine and promote awareness of infantile sexuality as a means of dismantling the harmful gender stereotypes that are prevalent in American society.

Appendix

Potential Essay Topics on Constance Penley's "The Cabinet of Doctor Pee-Wee: Consumerism and Sexual Terror."

1. How does Penley use Freud's ideas about infantile sexuality in her essay? Do these ideas work in the context of *Pee-Wee's Playhouse?* Is Penley's essay convincing, or is she "reading into it" things that are not there? Be as specific as possible in your essay, citing textual evidence from either Freud's "Infantile Sexuality," Penley's essay, or the Pee-Wee Herman show. From the show "Monster in the Playhouse," pay careful attention to all of the following: the sphinx, the role of scissors, the word of the day, the monster, and the Penny cartoon.

2. Discuss Penley's employment of Freud's ideas about "the uncanny," especially as related to both animism and contemporary (American) consumer culture. Address the role of the various animated objects in Pee-Wee's playhouse. How does the theme of "the uncanny" relate to Penley's argument about the salesman and the children's television commercials which "frame" the show? Also examine Penley's discussion of Paul Rubens's disdain for marketing items from the show.

3. Define "camp" culture and its relation to *Pee-Wee's Playhouse.* How does the episode we viewed confirm or weaken Penley's discussion about "camp" in this show. Discuss the theme of tolerance for difference in *Pee-Wee's Playhouse.* How is Rubens's show influenced by gay culture?

4. Discuss gender formation in the context of *Pee-Wee's Playhouse.* How do the theoretical interests of Penley differ from those of Freud? For example, what do both authors have to say about the "myth" of childhood asexuality? Furthermore, for what differing reasons do both Penley and Freud want to do away with this "myth?" In this connection, discuss the theme of fear as presented in Pee-Wee's episode "Monster in the Playhouse" (consider Penley's subtitle, which emphasizes "sexual terror").

5. Apply the theories established by Freud and Penley to something else in popular culture, such as another children's television show, movies, sporting events, comic strips, and so on. Be sure to clearly explain your theoretical model before applying it.

PART IV
Practicing Rhetorics

10

Feminists in Action: How to Practice What We Teach

Rae Rosenthal _____

In the fall of 1989, I taught a composition class which completely bombed. The room was tense, the interchange unpleasant, and not all that surprisingly, the level of student writing did not improve significantly. In the years since then, I have wondered again and again about that class. Was it my decidedly feminist reading list? Was it my increasingly visible pregnancy? Was it the combination? Or was I simply "off" that semester? Gradually, what I have come to realize is that the failure of that course was rooted in my failure to connect, in any meaningful way, theory with practice. I was teaching, or trying to teach, feminist theory in a conventional, dictatorial, hierarchical classroom, and it just doesn't work. Clearly, as Dale Bauer suggests, "it is not enough to try to convince students to adopt feminism using a traditional teaching model of authority" ("Meanings" 8). In fact, I now see attempts to do so as the classic case of the round peg and the square hole. My failure then was that I did not know what I have learned forcibly since: you cannot just put your chairs in a circle and assume you have a feminist classroom.[1]

A composition class committed to feminist issues must be supported by a distinctly feminist pedagogy. Neither can survive without the other. And so in my most recent evolution, I am teaching a composition class which focuses, in terms of content, on feminist issues in rhetoric and which, in its pedagogical approach, is deliberately and openly feminist.

Feminist rhetoricians have, of late, had a great deal to say about writing and the teaching of writing. Indeed, feminist theory and rhetoric have become increasingly interconnected, and logically so—both fields are fundamentally concerned with issues of power and persuasion. During the course of the semester, my classes have read works by Pamela Annas, Joan Bolker, Helene Cixous, Elizabeth Flynn, Olivia Frey, Clara Juncker, and Jane Tompkins, amongst others; these women have in common their interest in rhetoric and feminist theory and their concern with the historical privileging of masculine discourse and the corresponding exclusion and devaluation of feminine modes of rhetoric. And as the class reads and becomes more educated about discourse communities and the effect of gender on these communities, I have noticed that students become more aware of their own language and more skilled in the manipulation of that language. Indeed, by the end of the semester, most students are able to differentiate between masculine and feminine discourse and to alternately adopt that which seems more appropriate to their subject and audience. Having thus become "bilingual," they are, as a result, more sophisticated writers and more knowledgeable about issues of writing.

I suspect that almost any composition issue would work well— postmodern theories of language, collaborative writing, technology and writing, standard versus nonstandard dialects, personal versus academic discourse, or a composite (I have also experimented with the latter two)—but I have found gender and writing to be the most thought provoking and most potentially reformative. Among the many benefits to having students read composition theory, regardless of focus, especially notable has been the resulting examination of their own writing which inevitably follows. By reading essays about writing, students begin to talk and think about writing—their own, their classmates', mine, and that of the authors whom they have been reading. I suspect that this is, in and of itself, a significant step towards improved student writing. But when assigned readings focus on feminist issues in rhetoric, students gain, additionally, insight into the interconnectedness of sex, power, and language and the ways in which those relations affect their own writing and their own lives.

In planning an introduction to this course, I kept in mind my earlier disaster and deliberately set out to establish a clear feminist pedagogy.[2] If we are going to be serious about a feminist classroom, which to my mind means both the acknowledgment and redistribution of power, to whatever extent possible within institutional constraints, then we must find ways to make that work for us and for our students. Surely, as Mary Rose O'Reilley points out, "the worst thing we can do is pretend we don't have power" (146). College professors pretending to be powerless over their students is undoubtedly a most sanctimonious, hypocritical trick, which students invariably sniff out at once. On the other hand, professorial efforts to openly give away power are also doomed; you cannot completely overturn the class-room structure when the larger institutional edifice remains looming overhead.[3] And, as many of us remember from our own educations, a dictatorial approach to teaching leads only to student passivity and recitation. Still, teachers are the major shareholders of power in the classroom, and as such, it seems to me that we had better think long and hard about what we intend to do with it. I see no advantage to feigning powerlessness, giving our power away, or clutching it pos-sessively; none of these will further our cause. We must be willing and able to come up with other alternatives, pedagogical practices which incorporate feminist values and feminist power into classroom tech-nique. One possibility is that we candidly identify the source of our power, clarify the way in which that power structure operates, and acknowledge the limitations of that power. And it is, I would argue, the limitations, the areas where our powers need not extend, which are most often disguised, but which can, paradoxically, be our greatest strength. In exploring the edges of that power, we can be most creative and energetic, most empowering of our students.

So as often as possible, I seek ways to minimize my own decision making in favor of student choice. On the first day of class, the stu-dents and I collectively make various decisions about the syllabus. Students choose the number of assigned essays (within the depart-mental requirements of six to ten, and no, students do not automati-cally vote for six); they decide how many of those essays will be research papers (again, assuming that the departmental requirement of one research paper must be fulfilled); and students decide how the grades for these essays will be weighed (evenly, or more heavily to-wards the end of the semester). Students also decide whether to "count" attendance and class participation in calculating final grades. Other possibilities abound.[4] I suspect, though, that the actual array of deci-sions matters less than the process itself, which amidst all this talk about empowerment of students, actually does give students some measure of control over their educational experience. If feminists are committed to the redistribution of power, then they must honor that commitment in their classrooms. According to Dana D. Nelson, dur-ing a conversation about women and power in which the majority of women were denouncing power as a source of corruption, Dale Spender asserted the contrary: " 'I want as much power as I can possibly get.

Share it with me mates' " (33). This strikes me as an excellent motto for the feminist classroom, one rooted in the realities of our educational system.

When initially selecting material for this course, I assumed that most, if not all, of my students would come to class with no knowledge of composition theory or of gender studies, so I decided to begin each semester by trying to establish some theoretical foundation. First, I introduce some of the basics of feminist terminology and theory. We briefly review the history of feminism, noting that its origins are as old as patriarchy and that twentieth-century America did not invent the "women's movement," despite all media myths to the contrary. I try to make clear the various feminist agendas, pointing out the range of positions within the ideological framework of feminism. I also hand out a definition sheet, based on Gerda Lerner's excellent glossary, which clarifies various terms useful in the feminist conversation: *gender, sex, feminism, sexism, patriarchy,* and *matriarchy.* (Often students will assert that we live in a matriarchal culture because their mothers control the home and hearth; it is useful for students to consider that in doing so, women are merely fulfilling their culturally determined gender role, which decrees that the home is the only acceptable sphere of female influence.)

Distinguishing between the biological given (sex) and the culturally created (gender) has proven especially useful. Clarifying these two terms eliminates a classroom problem that commonly occurs when discussing feminist issues: in any discussion of gender roles and domestic habits, for instance, at least one student is likely to exclaim, "but I know a male who does the laundry, or cooks dinner, or bathes the children," or "I know a female who does household repairs, fixes the car, or does yard work." Such arguments, I point out, would be meaningful only if gender were identical to sex, if gender could not be altered, if there were an innate, essential female/male being. Through these discussions, students gradually come to realize that because gender is culturally created and culturally determined, inevitably (and fortunately so) there are always exceptions; some of us have been more thoroughly indoctrinated than others. So the existence of a male who does the laundry or a female with her own tool box does not in any way contradict the prevalence of gender-determined stereotypes. And as long as these examples continue to be exceptions rather than the norm, then gender-prescribed roles still have us firmly within their grip. Correspondingly, a male who writes in a feminine mode about feminine topics does not in any way negate the existence of feminine writing or feminine topics; it merely indicates that this particular individual has had some success in resisting the gender lessons of our culture. Clarification of this issue is especially important in discussions of gender and writing, as it allows students to see that while writers cannot change their sex, they can change the extent to which their writing supports the gender-determined categories upon which our culture has been built. In this way, the seemingly simple task of defining *gender* and *sex* provides the basis for the entire semester, because distinguishing between the two brings to the forefront the most fundamental aspect of feminism—the possibility of change.

Following the definition of terms, we begin our reading of introductory material, starting with discussions of gender and its effect on children, speech, and classroom behavior. We read Gilligan, Lakoff, and Spender (Chodorow, Belenky, and Sadker would do just as well, among others), and following this brief introduction to basic feminist issues, we move directly to feminist rhetoric and Cixous. I like to begin with Cixous because her writing is the most innovative, the most obviously distinct from the prose my students have previously encountered. In selecting other articles, I try to choose those which strike me as most intriguing, most (not least) debatable, and least abstruse. (Other choices have previously included Annas, Bolker, readings from Caywood and Overing, Farrell, Flynn, Frey, Juncker, Lamb, Pigott, Tompkins, and Zawacki.) I suggest to students before they begin that they should attempt to read each article in its entirety and that rather than quit when they encounter an especially difficult passage, they should simply mark it and go on. We begin each day with a review of those passages which have proven difficult. And once the entire class feels comfortable with basic comprehension of the material under discussion for that day, we work in groups summarizing the argument and analyzing the strengths and weaknesses of the essay. Besides aiding in student comprehension, this procedure has a number of additional benefits: first, students learn to work and write collaboratively, an important feminist skill; second, they discover multiple possibilities for the construction of an argument, multiplicity being another important feminist value; and finally, and perhaps most usefully, they learn the difference between summarizing and analyzing, all without my having to employ any of the traditional pedagogical techniques such as lecturing, testing, or, worst of all, assigning exercises.

Through our readings, we gradually piece together definitions of masculine and feminine discourse, deciding collectively that masculine

writing tends to be (with heavy emphasis on the "tends") argumentative, factual, conclusive, and impersonal, whereas feminine writing
tends to be suggestive, intuitive, open-ended, and personal (see Cixous,
Farrell, Juncker, Rosenthal, Tompkins). It is important to keep in mind
that masculine does not necessarily translate to male, nor feminine to
female. The terms "male" and "female" writing are commonly used,
and I have used them in the past as well (see the title of my 1990
Focuses essay), but it seems to me more and more that such usage
encourages precisely the confusion which Lerner seeks to avoid, and
leads us directly into the essentialist trap. Male and female denote sex,
feminine and masculine denote gender, and as such they can be questioned, (con)tested, and altered.

All of this might sound, still, dangerously "essentialist," a loaded
and hotly disputed label. In response to the theoretical charge of essentialism, I try to explore, with the class, this site of feminist contention. We discuss the limitations inherent in theories of difference, the
so-called essentialist position, and we consider the danger of stabilizing through the study of gender differences that which is ever unstable and of further restraining that which has long been restrained.
On the other hand, though, we must consider, too, the importance of
commonality, of maintaining a sense of connection between all women,
a connection which the poststructuralist, antiessentialist position seems
to threaten in its insistence on indefiniteness. In the dialogue between
the cultural/radical feminists (read *essentialism*) and the poststructural
feminists (read *antiessentialism/constructivism*), there has been a good
deal of oppositional posturing. What has emerged for many feminists,
though, is a desire for what Ritchie terms "a 'both/and' perspective
that recognizes the complexity of women's identity" (255). For, as Alcoff
suggested early in the debate, "we can say at one and the same time
[despite the protestations of both camps to the contrary] that gender
is not natural, biological, universal, ahistorical, or essential and yet
still claim that gender is relevant because we are taking gender as a
position from which to act politically" (433). We cannot have feminism
without some concept, albeit preferably a broad, shifting, inclusive
concept, of "woman."

Accordingly, I try to keep in the forefront of the class this idea of
"woman" as both different and yet similar, as having certain common
experiences within a patriarchal environment, but recognizing at the
same time that those experiences can and do vary widely, as a result
of race, class, sexual orientation, and culture. In this way, I try to offer
a way out of the binary trap of essentialism or constructivism and to

offer in its place "a concept of women's identity that is neither fixed, powerless essence nor endlessly dissolving and invisible, but multiple and changing within a social, linguistic, and political context, and that has agency because of its reflective, self-analyzing power" (Ritchie describing de Lauretis 256). Through classroom discussions of these issues, I emphasize over and over again to my students that we are not examining masculine and feminine discourse in order to reinforce restrictive categories of essentialness, but rather in order to explore, expand, and experiment with those categories. (Readers further interested in the complexities of the essentialist debate should see Weedon, Fuss, Alcoff, hooks, Ritchie, and the 1988 special issue of *differences,* especially the influential lead article by Teresa de Lauretis.)

In reading the selected feminist rhetoricians, especially Cixous, Tompkins, and Zawacki, students are exposed, usually for the first time, to a different type of scholarly writing. These essays, they often notice, tend to be less combative, definitive, and formulaic and more anecdotal and questioning than is academic discourse generally. And in the intertextuality and self-referencing of many of these essays, there is a spirit of cooperation, a sense of building upon one another rather than in place of one another. Noticeably absent is the oftentimes embarrassing tone of aggression which frequently characterizes academic writing particularly in the reply sections in the back of our journals.[5]

After having examined for ourselves these discussions of masculine and feminine discourse, we begin to turn to our own writing. In class, we experiment daily with the ideas introduced by the feminist rhetoricians we have been reading. The emphasis, for each activity, is on multiplicity and exploration. After reading Joan Bolker's now famous "Teaching Griselda to Write," we identify the Griseldas in our class, those students of docility whose writing "aims to please all and offend none" (907); together, we try to move consciously towards and then away from that correct but lifeless tone which so often typifies the "good girl" essay. Following Joan Bolker's suggestions for the annihilation of Griselda, we seek to develop our own individualized, personal voices, a process through which we seek the dismantling of restrictive gender roles. In class, we practice by selecting a group topic, which we then explore through both masculine and feminine discourse, thereby simultaneously clarifying and questioning the influence of gender on voice. Following our discussion of Clara Juncker's essay, "Writing (with) Cixous," we experiment with a number of her suggestions, including class without speech (only written communication allowed), dialogue essays where students converse on paper about a topic of mutual interest, and exploratory papers which avoid closure.

For each graded essay, students select their own topic and a mode of discourse (masculine, feminine, or an androgynous blend) which they feel will work well for their topic. I have found that student selection of topics, rather than assigned topics, is crucial to the success of this course, and so paper topics is another pedagogical decision over which I have relinquished control. In addition to the advantages of further power redistribution, I think it is important for students to have the experience of independently searching for a topic, an experience which to my mind constitutes the most difficult aspect of writing, but one which must be surmounted. Students cannot though, be sent adrift without the proverbial life jacket, and I have experimented with a number of different "life jacket" techniques. For example, I used to see students individually in my office, asking them to bring to their conference a list of three potential topics, all of which interested them and about which they had some knowledge. Together, we would work through this list, selecting what appeared to be the topic most likely to generate an effective paper. As you can imagine, this was an exhausting task for me. (I slowly was forced to acknowledge that the first student received a good deal more from me than did the last.) This arrangement had the additional negative side effect of separating the group; collaboration, which I see as crucial to a feminist classroom, was lost during the most critical part of the writing process.

Recently, I have found what seems to be a much better system. Each student brings to class three possible topics; students then put their list on the board, and the class as a whole works through each student's list, offering suggestions and opinions as to which topic seems most fruitful. The benefits to this system are many: students get to consider a wide range of topics, students get to participate in and listen to a sustained discussion about the process of topic selection, and each student gets the benefit of a variety of opinions about his or her own topic. Also of great importance is that students gain skill in working, writing, and thinking together. And in addition (and of no less significance), I am far less exhausted because the burden of the discussion does not lie solely with me, and whatever useful comments I might make are available to the entire group rather than just to the individual student who happens to be sitting in my office first thing in the morning when I am still fresh.[6]

What has proven especially interesting, though, is the almost universal influence of gender on topic selection. I have found that once freed from assignment sheets and prescribed topics, students choose, with little exception, to write on subjects which readily fall into gender-determined categories. They tend to select topics (even the females who cling to typically academic/male voices) which our culture has deemed appropriate for their sex. Male students tend to write about sports, politics, cars, and physical experiences, a hiking trip for example. Female students tend to write about personal relationships, literature, and emotional experiences. The only topics which regularly cross gender boundaries are education, the environment, and music. This pattern, according to Linda H. Peterson, is not unusual; in a study of two composition classes, one at Yale and one at Utah State, Peterson discovered that the "topics that women students choose are almost always 'relational' " and that "In contrast, male writers more frequently choose topics that focus on the self, the self alone, the self as distinct from others" (173). In response to this gender gap, halfway through the semester I set aside a day to discuss gender patterns in student-generated topics, and invariably, the consistency of these patterns surprises students.

In one of my early classes, the students suggested, in light of this—to them—new and surprising information, that we experiment with "cross-dressing," that males write on a typically female topic in a feminine mode and that females try the reverse.[7] I have since used this assignment repeatedly, always with a good deal of success. By forcing themselves to write in the opposite gender mode, students learn a great deal about voice, tone, diction, and about their own writing style. This activity also encourages students to become more self-conscious about their writing and more stylistically innovative. Through the deliberate adoption of masculine discourse, students gain skill in the type of academic writing they will be so often called upon to write in the next few years. They gain, in this way, confidence in their ability to speak the language of the academy. In addition, through the reverse—the deliberate adoption of feminine discourse—students gain a wider perspective, a sense of the alternatives and possibilities beyond that standardized format. Also through this assignment, it is possible to reinforce one of the most basic premises of feminism—the long-standing feminist assertion that the personal is the political and the political is the personal. The historical devaluation of all that is personal, a devaluation which inevitably indicts all that is female because the two are so often conflated, has led to the academic exclusion of the personal in its discourse, its pedagogical practice, and its institutional values. By experimenting with writing in a deliberately feminine/personal mode, students experience, firsthand, the personal as a legitimate intellectual subject.

It becomes important, then, to validate the personal in classroom dialogue, as well. Once a number of female students have been heard from, describing the various ways in which they have experienced their femaleness, it is no longer possible to collapse all women into a single, universal, fixed identity. At the same time, students begin to recognize the common threads of oppression, the inherent political subtext of what has traditionally constituted the female experience. Personal knowledge thus becomes evidence of both the difference and sameness with which the class readings have been concerned. In this way, personal experience becomes acceptable as an appropriate learning tool in the classroom and is seen to work in conjunction with the theoretical material of this course. Once experience gains value as a legitimate means of knowing, students can gain skill in self-education; they can learn to theorize (not generalize) from their own stories. By merging the personal and the public, the overall quality of the learning process is enhanced; indeed, like bell hooks, "fundamentally I believe that combining the analytical and the experiential is a richer way of knowing" (181). The validation of personal experience in the classroom and in academic discourse thus provides yet another means for the further feminization of our educational system.

When students first begin self-selecting their topics, I encourage them to write about subjects with which they feel comfortable, even if those happen to fall into stereotypical gender categories. I have found that this introductory "comfort zone" enables students to begin to experiment and explore. But after perhaps two or three essays, I begin to encourage students to leave their comfort zone—to move beyond gender-determined topics. By having students generate their own topics and by confronting them with the inevitable gender gap in their own choices, they are forced to recognize the way in which they have been unwittingly coopted by the gender restrictions of our culture. It then becomes possible to move beyond cultural stereotypes of gender, to emphasize the feminist goal of choice for all.

Once having selected a topic, but before beginning to write, students meet in prearranged groups of three in order to discuss their topics and to solicit suggestions about various strategical matters: voice, organization, length, and so on. The inevitable questions about length are all handled in the group; in this way, students learn for themselves the way in which the choice of topic predetermines length. As a group, they decide for themselves when an issue has been explored thoroughly and when greater development is needed. Throughout the semester, these groups remain constant. I aim for groups which are balanced in terms of sex, ability, and outspokenness. By having the groups remain constant, I find that students develop a sustained rapport which ultimately enables them to get to work more quickly and to offer suggestions more readily. They also then have the additional benefit of prior knowledge; while working on any given paper, every student in the group has read and commented on all preceding papers. In this portfolio approach to peer-response groups, they have the advantage of the whole picture, as do I.

After having created a presentable working draft, students return to their peer-response groups, each with three copies for distribution. The system is set up so that the author of the draft under discussion has the responsibility to raise questions about his or her own paper; I suggest that students draw attention to the trouble spots in their essay and seek assistance, rather than defensively hide whatever weaknesses the draft may have. This way, peer editors are made to feel helpful rather than critical. I remind the groups repeatedly that comments such as "This is really great; I wouldn't change a thing" are useless and should not be tolerated. Students also know that if insurmountable problems arise within a group, changes can be made, but usually they work out their own differences. Student groups chart their own progress by regularly filling out evaluation forms which ask each student to comment on the effectiveness of the group and the value of his or her own contribution. Through this process, students become practiced and skilled at collaborative writing, and as a result, they produce better writing. They also gain, along the way, an appreciation of collaborative activity. And if collectivity and cooperation are, as I believe, central to all feminist activity, then students have begun to participate in and appreciate one of the most basic feminist principles.[8]

While overseeing these groups in class, I have often noticed peer editors pointing out those essays which were written exclusively in either the masculine or feminine mode, and in most instances, the editors have then been able to articulate the disadvantages resulting from that exclusivity of discourse. And a number of female students have been surprised to discover that they had been writing entirely in a masculine mode. Their academic indoctrination had been so complete, so thorough, that they had no individualized and/or feminized voice of their own; in their efforts to enter the academy, they had been writing flat, correct, and distinctly masculine prose—or in Joan Bolker's words, they had a Griselda complex, one which prevented them from recognizing alternative modes of discourse. Most often, too, these were the students who had been insisting that feminist issues are no longer relevant and that our culture is now thoroughly egalitarian. These students have now learned what many of us have had to face long ago: that patriarchy thrives upon invisibility and that the most oppressed are often the least aware of their own oppression.

In terms of student writing, by about midterm I generally begin to see evidence of change. Of course, this is the point in the semester when we usually begin to see change; our students' writing becomes sharper, stronger, and more correct. But with this course, other changes tend to occur as well. With a peculiar combination of hesitancy and determination, students begin to experiment; first, they usually select topics from the opposite gender mode and, then more daringly, they try to write in the opposite gender mode. For some, their first experiments are notably unsuccessful. The males who try to write about personal issues, who try to put something of themselves on paper, often sound, as the females quickly point out, like a Hallmark card. The females, on the other hand, often have difficulties of a different nature. Every semester, several remain trapped in a world of personal anecdotes, experience without context, and they find it uncomfortable to enter the formal world of academic discourse; others have so long been imitating masculine prose that self-expression feels foreign to them. Slowly though, most students begin to profit from their experiments, and with each essay, the results are more impressive. They steadily become more adept at identifying masculine and feminine prose and, in turn, at willfully creating masculine and feminine prose. They learn to switch, from one to the other, in a rather sophisticated display of "bilingualism." Most importantly though, they begin to think, talk, and wonder about writing.

Without fail, though, each semester, there are resistors: the students who sit, arms crossed, faces scowled, and eyes narrowed. They feel cheated because they did not get the class which they expected. In contemplating these students, I am reminded of a colleague of mine who commented, when he heard what goes on in my composition class, "It's as though the student signed up for composition and found himself in Football 101." I have always appreciated that comment, as it brought back to me with great clarity how many times I found myself in a "liberal" arts class which might more honestly have been titled "Football 101." In response to both my students and my colleague, I contend, along with Dale Bauer, that in these complaints, "I hear a suggestion . . . that feminism is not a discipline, that gender issues are based on perspectives unsuitable for the labor of the intellectual" ("The 'F' Word" 386). Such a suggestion stems from the historical devaluing of all that is feminine, and as such, should be resisted mightily, both within the classroom and out.

Despite what some of my students and colleagues might think, my goal within the classroom is not to convert each student; I aim rather to educate each student about writing, about discourse, about power, and about the distribution of that power. And I want them to see most vividly the connections between language and power and power and sex. I want them to understand too, the goals of feminism, whether they agree with those goals or not. Some might argue (as does Maxine Hairston) that I have no business teaching this class as a feminist—it's only a composition class. But no one ever told my college professors, or some of my colleagues for that matter, that they have no business teaching their courses, regardless of subject matter, as white male supremacists. I cannot teach this class, or any other, as anything but a feminist because that's what I am. I can no more leave it in the hall than I can my femaleness or my Jewishness. I am a package deal, as are we all. And we have only two choices: open acknowledgment of what we are, or pretense. The choice to me seems obvious, especially as the latter doesn't work.

I am still left, though, with those cross-armed, squinty-eyed students, and the troubling question of how best to "handle" them, as we too often say. I am reminded, peculiarly, of *Dallas*, a TV show which I still consider to be among the most revealing of all twentieth-century artifacts. In one memorable scene, when JR found himself in need of additional funds but unable to attain the assistance of either friends or family, Sue Ellen cleverly inquired, "Well if your friends won't help you, why not try your enemies?" Such thinking I have taken to be my motto for encounters with classroom resistance. Student opposition can be wonderfully useful if we can only learn to think of these students as a source of dialogue and contrast, rather than as the enemy.

Jane Tompkins, in her "current rules of thumb," suggests that we "Talk to the class about the class" ("Pedagogy" 659). I have found this to be exceptionally good advice (it seems so obvious, but then perhaps that's why it's so successful), and I incorporate such discussions into each daily class plan. The success of these conversations depends, though, upon the presence of real dialogue which encourages, even invites, all expressions, both those of support and of resistance. In order to create such an environment, students must become accustomed to hear themselves speak, which is why I plan for the first day of each semester an activity in which everyone participates; after having spoken once, students more readily speak again. I make it clear, too, from the beginning that as a writing workshop, the success of the group as a whole depends upon the willingness of all individuals to contribute. Students must also regularly hear ideas being challenged by both student and teacher. If we value only consensus, that is what we will hear, but if we truly value dialogue, then we must not only acknowledge, but listen and respond to all comments. I also state early on two overarching classroom rules: all comments are welcome; no rudeness is tolerated. Once an atmosphere of candidness and civility has been established, resistance to feminist content or pedagogy can be usefully explored. If we profess to be feminists, we must act accordingly, and as openness and dialogue are fundamental values of all feminist movement, they must be fundamental to our classrooms.

Interestingly, though, I have found that few, if any, students ever resist feminist pedagogy. Shared decision making, collaboration, and validation of the personal do not often find resistance in my classes. Feminist content and theory, on the other hand, often lead to student discomfort and dismay, and understandably so. Most of what our students have been led to view as natural and permanent is being openly redefined by the feminist classroom as socially constructed and transmutable. If I am going to engage in pedagogical approaches which I know will lead to student defamiliarization, then it is my responsibility to create an opportunity for the expression and exploration of the new location in which they find themselves. I try to encourage student questioning of such changes, and in turn, I feel free to question students about their resistance. In the end, we often still do not agree, but for the most part, we have gained enormous respect for and knowledge of one another, and, I suspect, some self-knowledge as well. Without resistance in such a class, much of this would be lost.

Another means of engaging with student resistance is to schedule midsemester teaching evaluations. Most colleges and universities now require that evaluation forms be completed at the end of the semester, but by then the course is over. I now have students complete course evaluations during the middle of the semester as well. It might be feared that such timing would not promote honesty, but I have found that if evaluations are presented as a vehicle for making suggestions, and if it is made clear that such suggestions are genuinely desired, then students are as honest at midsemester as they are during finals. These evaluation forms then provide a wonderful occasion for discussion of feminist pedagogy. But in order for this conversation to be inclusive, a sincere attempt must be made to solicit the opinions of the resistors. They need to be heard, and their dissatisfaction examined. I try, as Dale Bauer suggests, to work "from the notion that the classroom is a place to explore resistances and identifications, a place also to explore the ambiguous and often ambivalent space of values and ethics" ("The 'F' Word" 387). In such an environment, dialogue includes all voices, all participants, regardless of location.

One complaint commonly heard about the feminist classroom— why are politics being brought into this _____ (read *English, History, Philosophy,* etc.) class?—deserves especial attention. This line of questioning assumes that all other classrooms have no political agenda, and that the feminist classroom has violated the principle (I would say myth) of academic neutrality and objectivity. Students making such arguments have been led, mistakenly, to believe that any class in which there is no overt mention of politics therefore has no politics. They fail to see the way in which silence reinforces the status quo. They fail to see the way in which, for example, a literature course which reads only canonical writers and focuses on the history of traditional literary movements inherently endorses a conservative agenda. Because the politics of such a course are rarely articulated, and because such courses reflect the politics of the culture at large, a factor which contributes to their seeming innocuousness, students generally fail to question the agenda of such a course. They do not see that the traditional classroom is no more neutral or objective than the feminist class about which they are currently complaining. This is an important lesson for students, though, because if they are going to benefit from their educational experiences, then they must be given the means by which to read those experiences. They must become aware of the inevitability of a political agenda, and when that agenda has not been articulated clearly, as it should be, then they must be able to discern it for what it is. So I especially welcome questioning of my approach, as it allows me to introduce the concept of education as politics. And if they don't like the politics of my class, I remind them that at least they know what those politics are. I point out, too, that the classroom has been set up in such a way that students are not only allowed but encouraged to discuss, question, and resist the politics of the course.

In order to assist students in the assessment of classroom climate and politics, I provide a checklist which I suggest that they apply to all classes, mine included. The questions on the checklist include: Whose view of the world is being offered as truth in this class? Who are the generators of knowledge and what populations are being studied? Is this class chilly or comfortable for women, students of color, students of differing religions, sexual orientation, and other historically marginalized groups? Whose interests are being served by how the course is taught?[9] With this tool in hand, students can begin to interpret their own educational experiences, to recognize the inevitability of political orientation, and to appreciate the advantages of a direct pedagogical approach, one which makes clear from the very beginning the answers to the questions above.

At the end of the semester, two compelling questions remain: how do we define good teaching, and how do we define good writing? In answer to the latter, some students argue for the inherent superiority of either the masculine or feminine mode. A number of other students argue for androgyny; they feel that the best essays include personal input as well as an ability to generalize beyond the particular, that good writing should be factual and intuitive, expressive and argumentative. But at some point, this reasoning breaks down. Writing cannot be both conclusive and open-ended, combative and noncombative; choices must be made. As for myself, I find that after years of teaching writing, I am no longer able to offer a standard definition of good writing; more and more it seems to me that while there might be a number of ways to write poorly, there might be an even greater number of ways to write well. Defining good writing is, after all, much like defining good literature, a task which we have all learned is far more problematic than it once seemed. My new aim for my students then is a multiplicity of voices; I would like for them to be able to consciously select and shift their mode of discourse, moving freely from masculine to feminine and back again. Such command of their writing would surely lead the way to excellence.

As to the question of good teaching, the answer is equally complicated. Feminists need to find a way to incorporate both content and practice; the two cannot responsibly be separated. To do either without the other is to diminish our cause altogether, and leads, further, to the specter of legitimate student disillusion with a theory which fails to practice what it preaches. Ritchie argues, I think wisely, that "[s]uch a separation subverts one of the most important contributions of feminism: the model of a discipline that constantly connects intellectual activity—the study of literature, language, and ideas—to the history and experience of people's lives" (271). By avoiding that separation, by taking the risk of active feminist pedagogy, one furthers the possibility of change, which is, after all, the foremost purpose of all feminist movement.[10]

Through this new course, a great deal has been gained. I have found a new and invigorating approach to teaching composition. My students have found that by reading about writing, they in turn can become better writers. And by examining the influence of gender on writing and teaching, they also have become educated about the ways in which our culture is gender determined and the ways in which they have been brought into that culture. It is then their choice whether they acquiesce or resist, but at least they know that there is a choice to be made.

11

Teaching Rhetoric as a Way of Knowing

*Peter J. Caulfield*_____

Asserting that rhetoric is epistemic means, among other things, that the act of writing creates new knowledge, new insights. By now, most of those who think seriously about writing and about teaching writing believe this, whether or not they embrace completely the epistemic perspective of rhetoric.

Powerful as it is, though, the concept that writing enables new knowledge *for the writer* vastly oversimplifies the much more inclusive concept, "rhetoric is epistemic," and its logical (though most radical) extension, "epistemology is itself rhetorical" (Leff 82). Those of us who embrace both of these more inclusive statements understand them to mean something more than Knoblauch and Brannon's trenchant observation a decade ago: "Writing enables new knowledge because it involves precisely that active effort to state relationships which is at the heart of learning" (467–68). As accurate and important as that concept is, we understand the epistemic function of rhetoric to be something more comprehensive, something more like Berlin's explanation that "[k]nowledge is dialectical, the result of a relationship involving the interaction of opposing elements," which he asserts are "the very ones that make up the communications process: interlocutor, audience, reality, and language" (166). Marilyn Cooper adds that each of the elements in the communications process are influenced by "dynamic interlocking systems" which shape and are shaped by rhetorical acts: (1) the system of ideas, (2) the system of purposes, (3) the system of interpersonal relationships, (4) the system of cultural norms, and (5) the system of textual forms (367–70).

I have become convinced that a more comprehensive and powerful conception of rhetoric, as suggested by Berlin, Cooper, and others, ought to fundamentally alter how we actually teach writing and not just how we talk about rhetoric to one another. Through a discussion of a new introductory composition course I designed around an epistemic theory of rhetoric, I intend to show that to understand more accurately the role of rhetoric in shaping knowledge, we must begin to examine—and help our students learn to examine—a complex web of semiotic experiences. We, and our students, interact with these experiences, and through those interactions, often dialectical in nature, we continually reconfigure our perceptions of reality and of ourselves. And, of course, whenever we or our students attempt to write, we can only write out of a consciousness constructed from those experiences: "Consciousness takes shape and being in the material of signs" (Bakhtin 930).

I began with an exercise designed to push students to think more directly about who they are and how they came to believe what they believed. This exercise helped students begin to "bring to light" the sort of rough "epistemic self-portrait" suggested by Toulmin (qtd. in Scott 262–63). During the first week of class, I passed out a sheet I labelled the "Attitudes and Attributes List" (see figure 11.1). I asked the students in both sections—one Honors and one regular—of the course to subdivide the clearly arbitrary list into "me" and "not me" lists of their own. They then brainstormed for ten minutes to add other attributes or attitudes which might describe them. After this, I asked them to choose one or more items from this new list and to freewrite for about fifteen minutes, reflecting on how that/those aspect(s) of who they are might affect how they viewed the world. Following that, a few were read aloud or paraphrased, and we discussed the differing perspectives and where they came from and what they might imply. I felt that their active participation in these exercises was important in allowing them to at least *begin* to become aware of some of the forces, particularly rhetorical forces, which had shaped their beliefs and values to date. I then explained how all of our attitudes and attributes form a sort of epistemic lens through which we experience the world. Part of that world, of course, would include this particular class and all the rhetorical experiences it would involve, experiences which would include their own writing as well as the writing of their peers, which they would read and react to throughout the semester.

I had spent part of the previous summer plotting as many of those experiences as I could ahead of time. I chose a new text, Clegg's *Critical Reading and Writing Across the Disciplines*, primarily because several

Figure 11.1 Attributes and Attitudes List

17–21 yrs. old	dorm student
American	commuter
North Carolina native	tall
Caucasian	average height
African American	short
Asian	brown/black hair
Christian	blond
agnostic	thin
male	average weight
female	not-so-thin
working class	from excellent H.S.
middle class	from average H.S.
upper-middle class	from poor H.S.
rich	a good writer
an athelete	an avid reader
unathletic	a couch potato
a romantic	good student
a realist	average student
part of nuclear family	struggling student
conservative republican	high school graduate
moderate republican	assertive
liberal democrat	timid
heterosexual	politically aware
homosexual	apolitical

of its essays set up problematics I wanted my students to puzzle over, such as Herbert Muller's argument in "The Premises of Inquiry" on the inescapable bias of all historical writing. Also, I wanted to use a text because college textbooks obviously play an important role in creating new knowledge, and I wanted to prepare my students to experience them more critically. Yet to view rhetoric epistemically is to recognize the power of a very broad range of rhetoric to create new knowledge. In late-twentieth-century America, rhetoric appears in many guises. And just as students must learn to read college texts critically, so too must they learn to "read" the other rhetorical forms which continually influence who they are, what they believe, and what they value: "But the fact that much, probably most of our behavior is well fixed through complex reinforcements does not mean that we cannot become *focally aware* of these patterns and their consequences" (Scott 263, emphasis mine).

With that in mind, I set out to expose my students to a wide variety of rhetorical media, composing a syllabus which included various essays from the primary textbook; examples of television and radio rhetoric; a movie; a wider range of print rhetoric, some of which depended heavily on graphics; and guest lecturers.

As is typical of many universities, one stated purpose of this second course in our two-semester writing sequence is to teach students to write analytical essays on material, usually readings, from a number of disciplines. While retaining the focus on perceiving and writing critically, I broadened the scope of materials under consideration to include materials beyond the usual academic prose. Americans, for the most part passively and uncritically, take in information from television as well as textbooks, from talk shows as well as teachers. One's writing, by necessity, will reflect the impact on one's mind of all the sign systems of a culture. This course was designed to reflect and interrogate that reality.

As is also typical, this second-semester course is expected by the university community to prepare students to write critically on material from many disciplines. Thus, I divided the course into five units: (1) science, (2) history/politics/economics, (3) psychology/sociology/anthropology, (4) philosophy/theology/religion, and (5) the arts. A closer look at some aspects of two of the units, the second and third, may help illustrate something of my approach and how the course more fully explored and exploited the epistemic function of rhetoric.

The second unit began with the students reading the Muller essay on historical writing mentioned above. Although many found Muller difficult, most grasped his essential point concerning the inevitable bias in all historical writing, even though it challenged their faith in the accuracy of their understanding of the past, especially of America's past. In addition, Muller explains that like writers, readers also bring a bias to whatever history they encounter. One student, from the regular section of the course, wrote the following reaction to Muller in her journal before we had discussed the essay in class. I quote a rather large chunk of her response here because it represents the kind of reaction— that is, a discovery of new knowledge—I had hoped to illicit:

> This essay brings to light a very interesting perspective on the past
> I have ... learned growing up in grade school and junior high his-
> tory classes. These courses were taught to us as the absolute truth, a

collection of facts to memorize and understand. In "The Premises of Inquiry" I have begun to understand more fully the fact that the history we read about is based on factual events, but that these events were recorded by people who had a bias—like all of us do—to what events were most important, what people had the most influence or the best ideas, which types of government are the most desirable.

I was gratified to see those insights emerge in her journal, but she didn't stop there. She not only learned something about biases in historical writing, but about the limits of her own perspective:

I do not consider myself a prejudiced person, and yet I did not realize my own nationalistic prejudices until reading this piece. Anyways, in today's world I truly believed that Democracy and especially the United States was the best way and place to live. There is no doubt this is a bit self-righteous.

The fact that it is difficult to know precisely when this new knowledge emerged for her illustrates the problem with limiting epistemic rhetoric to the notion of *writing* to learn. Her learning, as Berlin, Cooper, and others have suggested, is the result of a complex interaction among her previous education, reading and annotating Muller's essay initially, and her own thinking and journal writing. Her previous conception of reality is now reconfigured as the result, in varying degrees, of all the pieces in that interaction. Having read and annotated Muller, explored his ideas informally in a journal, then discussed the essay in class, she and the other students could, and many did, incorporate his insights into their formal papers of various historical accounts.

In addition, the complexity of these interrelated, rhetorical experiences points to a need for a much more sophisticated notion of what it means to write, a notion which includes *all* of these activities—at a minimum—as part of the *process* which eventually yields a more or less completed essay.

As suggested above, I wanted to impress upon my students that textbooks are by no means the only rhetorical forces which shape our perceptions of reality, including history. Clearly, historical novels, movies, and perhaps especially, television programs help shade in our pictures of various historical eras and events. To illustrate that, I chose an example of television at its best, parts of two episodes of Ken Burns's acclaimed PBS series, *The Civil War*. After viewing those, various students commented in class and in their journals and papers on how the still photo of slaves and battle scenes, the panning of the camera, the music and other sound effects, and the various "voices" recounting their personal experiences during that era radically altered their understanding of the Civil War and the events which led up to it.

For each video presentation, including the Burns piece, I insisted the students view it *actively*—as they would read and annotate a written text—for two reasons. First, since I would be showing a number of videos during the semester, I didn't want them to view those sections of the course as a time to sit back and relax their attention. Secondly, my goal was to teach students to see each "text" under consideration (whether a documentary, an essay, or a movie) as, at some level, a consciously crafted piece with both overt and covert rhetorical messages. I wanted them to attend precisely to how that crafting worked or could work on their thoughts and feelings. To assist them, I provided handouts for each rhetorical form, including one for television/movies, detailing some of the director's options which they might note (see figure 11.2). Here I also introduced the notion of semiotics to help them to begin to try to "read" the "language" of television. I discussed the sometimes slippery relationship between signifiers and signifieds and explained that signifiers need not be limited to words. I reminded them, for example, how often music is used in film and television to signify, among other things, impending danger. I also encouraged the students to reflect on these audiovisual considerations in the formal analytical essays on the piece. Students took notes during each viewing, and, whenever possible, I placed copies of the video and audio tapes on reserve at the library so students could "reread" the "texts," just as they would be expected to reread a written work on which they intended to write.

In general I was pleased with the analytical essays students wrote on the Burns video. In the first place, the video engaged most of them on several levels. Their writing, as a result, often seemed more committed and less mechanical. The best papers, in addition, discussed not only the content of the historical account, but its technical, that is to say rhetorical, presentation, commenting on the effect of the still photographs, the panning of the camera, the music and other audio effects, and the voices of the actors on the overall impact of the rhetorical message(s) contained in the work. Some also brought in Muller's insights, discussing Burns's own biases in the selection of photographs, specific quotations, and so on.

For the politics portion of that unit, we read King's "Letter from Birmingham Jail," from the Clegg text. I decided to juxtapose that with James Baldwin's letter to his fourteen-year-old nephew, which forms the introductory portion of his *The Fire Next Time*. Interestingly,

Figure 11.2   Television/Movie Guidelines

Could include all the considerations of print—Plus:
Type of piece (e.g., ad, music video, drama, sit. com., news)
Length of piece (e.g., 30 sec., 30 min., an hour or more)
Historical context(s) (e.g., contemporary era, past era)
Number, identity and relation of speakers/actors/characters
Relative quality/skill of each speaker/actor
Message (overt and covert) of each speaker/character
Interactions among speakers/characters
Function of nonhuman "characters" (e.g., pets, whales, monsters)
Audio considerations (e.g., music, sound effects, natural sounds)
Visual considerations
    Visual *setting* (when and where, viewed broadly *and* narrowly)
        e.g., 1943, winter, nightfall, France, countryside,
        farmhouse, kitchen
    Significance of specific, relevant objects (e.g., a flag)
    Visual appearance of relevant people (speakers, characters)
    Use and effects of color(s)
    Camera use (e.g., angles, close ups, wide shorts, panning)
Arrangement and movement
    Within scene
    From scene to scene
    From segment to segment
    Still photos panned
Relationship among visual and audio factors
Structure of piece (varies from type to type *and* within types)
Apparent underlying assumptions of writer(s)/director/producer(s)

both appeared originally in the same year, 1963. This juxtaposition provided two somewhat different perspectives on race relations during that era.

To prevent students, particularly the white students, from simply dismissing the issues dealt with in Burns, Baldwin, and King as certainly sad or even tragic aspects of our past, but no longer particularly relevant, I also showed them something much more contemporary: a video of a Bill Moyers's panel discussion on the 1992 Los Angeles riots. The participants (rhetors) included "raptivist" Sister Souljah, as well as some older, more traditional male leaders from the African-American community and one white, female sociologist. I felt this

program would give students the opportunity to observe a clear example of an (at times) rather heated discussion of racial issues in
contemporary America. Also, having watched the Burns video and
read the King and Baldwin letters, students were pushed to reevaluate
their own initial reactions to the Los Angeles riots, seeing them now
through the lens of America's history of slavery and segregation, as
well as against the views of the panelists. In addition, Sister Souljah's
presence on the panel enabled them to see someone closer to most of
their own ages participating in the national dialogue on critical issues.

In that connection, I wanted my students to see all of the rhetorical forms we read, watched, and listened to as pieces of an ongoing
human "conversation" on enduring issues, a conversation I was inviting them to join: "Education is not a process of assimilating 'the truth'
but, as Rorty has put it, a process of learning to 'take a hand in what
is going on' by joining 'the conversation of mankind' " (Bruffee 647).
To that end, I put together another handout I titled "Race: Issues,
Events, and Voices in the Human Conversation" (See figure 11.3). After
tracing some connections among certain aspects of that conversation,
I drew their attention to the bottom of the handout where I had included their own essays and our class discussions to stress that they
were also a part of that crucial dialogue.

Since this was, first and foremost, a writing course, one of my
goals was to get my students to think in a radically different way
about their own, as well as their classmates', writing. I hoped they
would begin to view their writing as contributions to that ongoing
national dialogue, at the very least as contributions which might affect
the views of their peers in this class. One incident during a whole-
class, peer-critique session, in fact, illustrated that possibility beauti-
fully. A sixty-five-year-old white man happened to be a student in one
section of this course, and he read the draft of his paper on King's
letter to the class. His paper discussed what King's letter had taught
him and included his own powerful and moving memories of living
in the South in the thirties, forties, and fifties, and when he finished
reading, a number of students were clearly moved, some saying so
openly.

This incident illustrates one of the principal tenets of an epistemic
view of rhetoric, that the "contact of minds affects knowledge: and
that knowledge is not so much either objective or subjective, but is
instead, intersubjective, the result of a dialectic among subjective views"
(Berlin 165). The dialectic, of course, can occur between a reader and
a text, a viewer and a "text," and also between a writer and her own

Figure 11.3 Race: Issues, Events, and Voices in the Human Conversation

Economics
Slavery (1600s–1863)
The Civil War (1861–65)

Muller's "Premises
of Inquiry" (1952)

Baldwin's Letter to his nephew (1963)	King's "Letter From Birmingham Jail" (1963) Pearce's "Feminization of Ghetto Poverty" (1983)

Ken Burns's
The Civil War (1989)
L.A. Riots (Rebellion?)
(April 1992)
Moyers L.A. Riot Special

Sister Souljah and the youth to/for whom she speaks	The Older African American males and those to/for whom they speak

Our class discussions—Your essays

evolving text. Concerning the incident involving the older man above, for example, the other students in that class would later, by necessity, bring his insights to the ongoing dialectic with their own evolving drafts, at least unconsciously.

Various other experiences, both in class and in reading students' journals and essays, further reinforced for me the validity of that view of rhetoric and confirmed the importance of bringing that insight directly into our composition classrooms. One experience occurred during the next unit, psychology/sociology/anthropology, following the showing of another PBS program called *Color Adjustment,* a documentary by Marlin Riggs on the depiction of African Americans on television from its beginnings in the early 1950s up to the present. During the show, footage was presented and discussed, beginning with shows from the 1950s like *Amos and Andy* and *The Beulah Show* (which features an overweight, grinning caricature of a Black maid living with a White family), through *Julia* and *I Spy* from the 1960s, up to more contemporary programs like *The Cosby Show*.

I followed this up with an audio tape of a local National Public Radio show's group discussion of *Color Adjustment* ("Conversations"), which included three of our own faculty, some of whom were already known to a few of the students. The students seemed intrigued by both programs, and some, particularly the younger ones, were shocked by the caricatures of Blacks in the very early television shows. Also, *Color Adjustment* juxtaposed footage of more comfortable shows like *Julia*, which depicted Black/White harmony, with footage of dogs and fire hoses unleashed on Black civil rights workers during that same era.

A little later in the semester, a few white students from the Honors section mentioned to me that they had gone to the library and watched the show a second time together. These were all eighteen- and nineteen-year-olds, and one young woman wrote about that experience in her journal (Apparently they had seen the film *A Clockwork Orange* elsewhere, as it wasn't part of my course). I've changed only the names of the students in her response, wherein the new knowledge which emerges for her is quite evident:

> The group . . . first discussed . . . *A Clockwork Orange*. I had said how deeply the film had bothered me. Joey spoke of how the news clips in *Color Adjustment* bothered him more. To this, Teresa answered, "That's because this is real." And it *was* real. Too real. . . . I knew of wrongs against Blacks during this time and always condemned them. But I never personally hurt and grieved for everyone involved until I saw the Blacks being forced against walls by water hoses. I cannot imagine that. I thought *Color Adjustment* was beautifully made. It was so touching and real and shocking. It made me think and feel. I needed that on a subject I needed to understand better.

Robert Scott, in his "On Viewing Rhetoric as Epistemic: Ten Years Later," makes a point which this young woman's journal response illustrates:

> Thus far I have used the terms "knowing" and "understanding" as if they were interchangeable . . . [but] the nuances that seem to cling to "understanding" make me prefer it to ascribe to rhetoric as epistemic. By "knowing" we may stress a sense of from-the-outside-in. . . . By "understanding" we may stress the sense of from-the-inside out, taking understanding as a human and personal capacity to embrace what is outside the self, creating rather than finding meaning in the world. (262)

Viewing *Color Adjustment*, discussing it in class, viewing it again with friends, and then writing about it has enabled this student to get beyond the level of knowledge where she *"knew"* of wrongs against Blacks during this time" to a place where she now "personally hurt and grieved for everyone involved." She writes that "until she *saw"* (emphasis mine) the brutal treatment of nonviolent civil rights workers, that she knew "of the wrongs" done to Blacks in that era. However, seeing it twice (the second time with classmates, where it was discussed), "made" her "think and feel" on what seems to be a whole new level about the issues involved. She better *understands* it now, "from-the-inside-out" (emphasis mine). Though we cannot get inside the head of this student to learn precisely when and how each piece of her new understanding of racial injustice emerged, she gives us enough in her journal response to allow us to draw some inferences. Clearly, the images themselves were powerfully affecting. She says as much. Also, I think we can fairly assume that the conversation among the students, particularly the remark by Teresa, prodded her to think more deeply about the fact that these images, unlike those in *A Clockwork Orange*, were "real. Too real." Finally, we might logically infer that these thoughts and feelings remained inchoate until she clarified them through the active effort of writing about them in her journal. Clearly, as Scott points out, she is "creating rather than finding meaning in the world." Thus, to view rhetoric epistemically involves understanding that new knowledge emerges not simply through *"writing*-to-learn" but through the complex engagement of a critical mind with many rhetorical forces, including, but not limited to, one's own writing, both formal and informal.

By the same token, it is simplistic to assume that a writing course should focus solely on the students' own writing, as if that writing emanated from individual minds unaffected by the plethora of semiotic encounters writers experience both in preparation for, and in reaction to, that writing.

In the same unit, as a follow up or parallel assignment, I asked each of the students themselves to choose and bring to class three to five "images of women" from various print media. After the students brought in the "texts" they had selected, I broke them into groups of four or five (purposely selecting both males and females for each group wherever I could) and asked them to share and discuss their images, using another handout I provided (see figure 11.4). They brought in a wide range of images, mostly from mainstream advertising in magazines. This exercise produced lively discussions in both sections of the course. Following the small group work, someone from each group summarized the results of their discussions for the rest of the class, holding up the images as each was critiqued. As the discussion grew more heated, I was surprised yet gratified at the candor of several of the young women, many of whom were clearly angry at some of the depictions of women they and their classmates had discovered, discussed, and debated. Again, Scott: "To assent or dissent truly one must know intersubjectively. . . . To communicate and to agree or disagree is to know differently. Rhetoric aims at knowledge that is social and ethical; it has the potential of creating commitment" (Scott 259).

Later, several of the female students and one male chose to write their formal essays for this unit on this exercise, each focusing on and analyzing a few images in detail. One young woman, one of the weaker writers in the regular section of the course, worked very hard on this paper, revising it several times after repeatedly seeking my feedback as well as help from our Writing Center. Though the final draft still had some problems, it was much stronger than her earlier work, apparently because it became personally important to her, as the following insight suggests:

> Now that I know what viewing critically is, when I look at a magazine, I look at it in this way. I am sorry and pleased that I can do this now. I am sorry because I now see the offensive way in which women are depicted. But I am pleased because knowing this makes me feel more educated concerning how people might look at me and how I look at myself.

An interesting follow-up to this assignment may help suggest the effect this approach can have on the quality of students' writing. I was asked to do a presentation on this assignment in connection with Women's History Month, and I selected some of the students to read parts of their papers on this topic to the audience. After the presentation, a colleague from mass communications mentioned to me that she had tried a similar assignment with her students, with less positive results, and asked me how I had managed to get such sophisticated critical analyses from my students. One female student, who had struggled somewhat in her earlier papers, wrote an especially strong essay analyzing four ads. Her description of the second ad in her analysis should illustrate what impressed my colleague:

> Photo B caused me be to be more appreciative of the honesty in Lee's ad [for Lee's shorts]. The advertisement for Request Jeans does not display anything that even *resembles* denim. Again, there is the beautiful girl with blowing hair and sculpted eyebrows. The dominant focus, however, is not on the *entire* female and, obviously, not

Figure 11.4   Print Plus Graphics Guidelines

May include all the considerations of print alone

Plus:

Colors (or Black and White)
Typeface(s)
Arrangements of print and graphics on page(s)
Abstract design elements vis-à-vis text
Representational drawings vis-à-vis text
Photographs vis-à-vis text
Sidebars (emphasizing quotes)
Columns/graphs/charts vis-à-vis text
Texture/type/color/quality of paper
Inserts/tear outs, etc.
Graphic features' effects on balance of logical vs. emotional appeals

Some Special Considerations for "Images of Women"

Physical features of woman/women in image
(Consider a range of features represented, e.g., eyes, lips, hands, figure)

Clothing of woman/women in image
(Note overall clothing as well as details, e.g., rings, shoes)

Any props or other objects in image vis-à-vis people

Arrangement of male(s) and female(s) in image
(interaction or relationship suggested?)
　　　—female to male
　　　—female to female
　　　—male to male

Arrangement and relationship of words to figures in image

Overall message(s), if any, suggested by the image?

the jeans. The exposed cleavage of the model seems to be the eye-catching feature of this. . . . Dressed in calf-high, lace-up boots, striped hot pants, and a black bra, this voluptuous beauty sits high on the steering wheel of a tractor.

After providing more specific detail on the ad, she concludes:

The portrayal of women in the Lee and Request ads is completely unnatural. Ever since the image of the well endowed, young, tan, and skinny women has been labelled desirable, there has been an increase in plastic surgery, skin cancer, and eating disorders.

This overall description of the course, as well as the student quotations presented here, should demonstrate what I was attempting in the course and how several students responded. By the end of the semester, most of my students had come to a much broader understanding of how language (and everything that might augment it, such as color, music, or graphics) functions rhetorically to shape—and distort—our views of reality. A list of some of the topics the students chose for their final research papers further illustrates that more inclusive understanding quite clearly:

- The depiction of gays and lesbians in film
- The effects of television advertising on children
- Zora Neale Hurston's challenge to traditional women's roles in *Their Eyes Were Watching God*
- The controversy surrounding Martin Scorsese's *The Last Temptation of Christ*
- The social and political reasons for the resurgence in the popularity of country and western music
- An exploration of the renewed influence of the message of Malcolm X, considering clothing, the Spike Lee film, and rap music (this student quoted Sister Souljah and Ice T lyrics in the final paper)

In the late 1970s, in his review of the role of epistemic rhetoric in the literature of his discipline at that time, speech theorist Michael Leff wrote, "In general, contemporary theorists expand the scope of rhetoric well beyond the boundaries established by the classical authorities" (88). I suspect that a review of the *literature* of rhetoric and composition for the last decade or so might yield a similar conclusion. Yet I get no sense that a look at the classroom practices of most writing teachers would mirror that more inclusive awareness. Why might that matter?

A few years ago in North Carolina, where I teach, Jesse Helms and Harvey Gantt (an African-American) were locked in a very tight Senate race. Many were predicting that Gantt had a real shot at unseating Helms, a conservative institution in the Senate. At the tail end of the campaign, the Helms camp released a powerful political ad. The spot featured a pair of white, male hands holding a sheet of paper. The male voice-over said something like, "You were the best qualified for the job, but they had to give it to a minority candidate." The white hands then crumpled the piece of paper, presumably a rejection letter, and the disembodied voice urged listeners to vote for Jesse Helms.

If we can begin to teach our students to understand the full range of rhetorical media and the strategies each may employ, they will be in a better position to understand and evaluate political spots like this one for what they are. By contrast, students who remain unaware of current, as well as more traditional, rhetorical strategies and devices remain pawns, easily manipulated by cynical politicians, advertising agencies, movie makers, and even some college professors, who teach their own subjective perceptions of reality as unshakable dogma.

Having said that, I want to conclude by admitting that restructuring a writing course to reflect an epistemic theory of rhetoric is by no means a panacea for all the problems writing teachers face. Bringing epistemic theory into the classroom will not cause all students' writing to improve automatically and drastically. Differences in students' writing abilities will not magically disappear, and some will continue to approach the class half-heartedly, seeing it as just another academic exercise or, conversely, actively resisting the sociopolitical content of the course. All students will not suddenly become more open-minded and tolerant—though a seed for that attitude will have been planted. And finally, of course, the usual stacks of student journals and essays will still have to be read and evaluated in some way.

And yet, after having tried this approach, I remain more convinced than ever of its importance. Most of the students in those two sections of my writing course left with a clearer sense of how rhetoric, in many guises, has formed and will continue to shape their own attitudes about themselves, the world, and the other people in that world. Perhaps most importantly, they now have a better grasp of the power their own writing can have on others in the ongoing human conversation on crucial issues in our society. This awareness helps motivate them to put in the effort to make their writing as effective as possible.

This broader understanding of rhetoric is crucially important. As Scott writes, "Rhetoric may be the art of persuasion, that is, it may be seen from one angle as a practical capacity to find means to ends on specific occasions; but rhetoric must also be seen more broadly as a human potentiality to understand the human condition" (265). In my course, I pushed my students to see the power of rhetoric, especially their own writing, in both ways—as a practical skill certainly, but also as a philosophical tool, a way to better understand themselves, others, and the larger society. Now, somewhat more "focally aware," they can begin to explore more fully what they believe and why, and to take some measure of control over who they wish to become and the kind of world in which they wish to live.

One way to affect that world, of course, is to become a more skilled writer. As writing teachers, therefore, we cannot in good conscience ignore our responsibilities to help our students become more proficient writers. In that connection, in this particular course, I took pains to insure that I continued to give plenty of attention to the students' own writing: providing instruction in essay forms, discussing models of successful students papers, meeting with students individually to work on drafts, and scheduling class time for peer critiques of evolving drafts.

And yet, at the same time, I pushed these students to stop seeing their own writing in academic isolation. Instead, I urged them to begin to recognize the epistemic power of the swirl of rhetorical forces to which their own writing connected and out of which it grew.

12

Freirean Pedagogy, Cultural Studies, and the Initiation of Students to Academic Discourse

*Raymond A. Mazurek*_____

Cultural studies offers to teachers in the 1990s some of the same attractions that Freirean pedagogy offered in the 1960s and subsequent years: the hope of engaging students in critical reflection on generative issues that are simultaneously of great public significance and personal resonance. However, like Freirean pedagogy in North America, cultural studies is difficult to put into practice. Freirean pedagogy, itself a contested term, has often been identified with a nonauthoritarian approach that would empower students, validating their own voices, while furthering an implicit critique, gradually developed, of the cultural and political institutions that disempower them. However, as Donald Lazere has argued in a recent essay in *College English,* nonauthoritarian pedagogy has in North America succeeded especially well with students in elite universities who are "already socialized to the elaborated codes implicit in such methods" (17), and less well with upwardly mobile working-class students and others in non-elite colleges. Such students are often in need of initiation into the codes through which the university (and the white-collar institutions which employ university graduates) operates before they can comfortably engage in critique. A similar paradox is at work when we consider cultural studies and its relation to the non-elite students who make up the vast majority of those in college writing classes. Cultural studies can be alienating and abstract for students from families that lack "cultural capital," students who need work in basic strategies of writing and analysis and who are sometimes suspicious of the apparent "intrusion" of complex content areas into the writing courses which they believe that they desperately need. But I believe that it is precisely these students who have the most to gain from studying the sources of much of their own subjectivity in the mass media.

In recent years, I have experimented with both Freirean pedagogy and cultural studies in my composition classes, and I believe that cultural studies—particularly an analysis of the mass media—provides one of the best opportunities for furthering the original aims of Freirean approaches to composition. Within the mass media lie "generative themes," topics that embody central contradictions in contemporary ideology and whose exploration can lead to critical reflection and point to political empowerment. It is interesting to note that while Lazere advocates cultural studies—along with explicit instruction in the elaborated discourse of the academy and a deemphasis on nonauthoritarian methods such as the "open classroom"—as an alternative to the Left's emphasis on Freirean pedagogy in North America, he has not seemed to notice the close connection between the possibilities of media analysis (and the exploration of the social construction of subjectivity it implies) and the original Freirean project. Moreover, there is also another connection, for cultural studies is part of the complex, sometimes oppositional discourses of academic culture, and initiation of students (whose consciousness is often rooted in popular culture) into the contemporary academic styles of interpreting and writing about culture is in a sense a reapplication of the original Freirean project for overdeveloped societies in a postmodern age.

Recently, the project of initiating students into academic discourse has been critiqued as too narrow a focus for composition courses by scholars such as Patricia Bizzell, who was once a key advocate for the idea that the initiation of students to academic discourse might produce a sort of Freirean critical consciousness. Like Lazere, Bizzell points out that there is no *necessary* connection between academic discourse and critical consciousness. She also argues that "in the present political emergency . . . we should be trying to do something more than teach academic discourse, namely to help students acquire the language using abilities that will be of most use to them as citizens" ("Argument" 15). Bizzell wishes to distance herself from the notion of academic discourse as a neutral technique that will automatically lead to political insight regardless of content, and she argues against the idea that Freirean pedagogy, academic discourse, or indeed "*any* critical method could automatically lead to a left-oriented view of the socio-political world without any ideological arguments having to be made" (*Academic Discourse* 20–21). However, while I share these reservations, as well as her "dream of what democratic discourse might be" ("Argument" 15), I see a closer connection than Bizzell currently seems to between this dream and the academic sites and discourses that might foster it. Universities are conflictive sites of power which often underwrite the status quo, but they are also places where traditions of critical thought create space for arguments about values and self-reflective analyses of power. As one of my older students, who had just completed six years in the much more restrictive atmosphere of the U.S. Navy, recently put it, where else but in the university do people have so much time and freedom to pursue social questions in depth? While it would be, as Bizzell claims, a serious mistake to impose academic discourse "on all students at all costs with total disregard for whatever knowledge they might bring to school from other discourse communities" (*Academic Discourse* 27), the sophisticated literacy offered by academic discourses is nevertheless "highly advantageous . . . for effective opposition to the dominant culture in today's society" (Lazere 14), especially for many of the students at state universities. Moreover, cultural studies is itself an essentially academic discourse, however much it attempts to study the broader culture or contribute to the creation of a democratic culture by providing powerful tools for understanding society and producing critical discourses for various political ends.

Cultural studies offers a potential way out of the confusion that some of us have felt about the introduction of content and the role of politics in composition courses, a confusion that (at least in my own case) was sometimes increased by commitments to nonauthoritarian pedagogy. I offer the following discussion of my own experience as a potentially instructive example, for I believe that it contains many elements shared by others—at least by some of us on the institutional margins of the profession, who began our careers as (somewhat radical) literary scholars but who have accepted jobs with heavy commitments to composition.

For the first decade during which I worked as a full-time college teacher at several non-elite state universities, I kept my work in composition (the bulk of my teaching) compartmentalized and virtually segregated from my academic writing (on the ideological implications of literary texts), from my teaching of literature (where exploration of issues such as race, class, and gender played an important role), and from my political activism (chiefly anti-intervention work on Central

America during the Reagan presidency). Composition was a baffling, sometimes fulfilling world of daily labor, in which I had had little instruction but many years of practical experience. In Stephen North's terms, I was a "practitioner," proud of rolling up my sleeves and doing some of the hardest work in the department, perhaps fulfilling my blue-collar origins. I stole a good idea here and there (mostly from expressivists such as Peter Elbow and Ken Macrorie), but mostly just blundered along trying to improve students' writing and provide them with a little intellectual challenge. I included works such as Studs Terkel's *Working* and Frederick Douglass's *Narrative* in my writing courses to provide such a challenge, but presented them with an inductive approach that asked the students to write about the works before we had discussed them extensively in class, and I was usually hesitant about exploring my own controversial interpretations in detail. In argumentative papers and rhetorical analysis, we drifted into politics, but I felt somewhat self-conscious expressing my views (almost always far to the left of the students'). Strangely, this self-consciousness rarely intruded in literature classes, where it seemed perfectly natural to analyze the class conflicts underlying the literature of the 1930s or the causes of the Vietnam War. Since I thought of composition as "writing instruction" and "individual expression" rather than as a full-fledged field, my views seemed out of place in writing classes.

In 1989 I received tenure, and, freed from the necessity of churning out literary articles, I began to think more seriously about composition, its politics, and how I should teach it. I began rereading texts on radical pedagogy and English studies that I had had a cursory knowledge of before: Freire's *Pedagogy of the Oppressed*, Ira Shor's *Critical Teaching and Everyday Life*, and Richard Ohmann's *English in America* and *Politics of Letters*. I started revising my teaching of composition, gradually becoming reconvinced, as I had long suspected, that my previous hesitation about the "intrusion" of politics was also a politics, acquiescing to the trivialization of instruction in writing and rhetoric. Nevertheless, I was hesitant about the place of content (i.e., books) in composition courses. I believed that composition courses should provide the intellectual challenge of other introductory college courses, but "reading" had always seemed to confuse students, who wrote best about their own experience. My sense of the parameters of composition as a field was a muddled combination of current-traditionalism, linguistics, expressionism, and concern for audience. Working at a branch campus of a state university where there was little interest in composition studies as a research area and little reward for exploring new areas (there was pressure to publish, but that almost precluded spending research time outside one's traditional "field" while writing toward tenure), I felt that I had to invent composition as a field virtually on my own even though I had taught primarily composition, fulltime, for almost a decade, and although that decade was the 1980s, not the 1960s. I mention these details about my situation because I believe that the micropolitics of English departments—and the marginalization and isolation of those who teach composition—are vitally important to any analysis of the role of politics in a larger sense in composition studies. (Given this marginalization, it is no accident that the majority of teachers in composition classes have generally been women, and narratives such as Lynn Bloom's "Teaching College English as a Woman" offer vivid testimony to the consequences of the dual denigration of female scholars and the writing instruction they have typically provided. Some of the more extreme conditions that Bloom describes have improved. Yet composition as a field, and those who teach it (women and men), is *still* considered second-rate and invisible, like the students in the courses, and I suspect that this is more true at the non-Ph.D.-granting institutions, where the vast majority of practitioners and students labor, than at the research institutions, where the majority of composition scholars—who define the field—work.)

When I tried to apply Freirean pedagogy, it was in a way that reflected my uncertainty about the content of composition courses. Since expressionist theories dominated my thinking, that content seemed to lie somewhere in the students' own minds, and had to be invented out of their own experience. Expressionist composition theory was consistent with both my literary orientation and my radical politics. As Todd Gitlin has pointed out, the radical politics of participatory democracy, forged in Students for a Democratic Society and the Student Nonviolent Coordinating Committee in the 1960s but with a lasting influence on the Left, were dominated by a mystique of personal expression (163–66). In addition, the idea of rhetoric as personal expression has a consistent appeal to young students in contemporary society, though it is merely a starting point that needs to be worked through. Thus, the attraction of Freirean theory for me lay partly in its movement from personal expression to an awareness of the social, and the version of Freirean pedagogy I developed reflected my roots in expressionism (for a critique of expressionism, see Berlin, *Rhetoric and Reality* and "Rhetoric and Ideology," and Bauer).

Selecting for my first comprehensive "experiment" a sophomore writing course ("Writing in the Social Sciences") where many of the students were education majors, I introduced Freire as both a topic for discussion and a source of the pedagogy for the class, assigning the second chapter of *The Pedagogy of the Oppressed*, with its famous critique of the banking concept of education, and supplementary readings. I tried to guide the class through a reduplication of Freire's method (a word I use cautiously) as developed in his early literacy classes in Brazil: searching for generative themes, the issues in the class most urgently in need of critical reflection; codifying or representing those themes; and decoding or reflecting on them (for a discussion of this process, see Freire, "Education"; for discussions of Freirean pedagogy for North Americans, see Freire and Shor, as well as Tompkins.)

I began with an in-class writing, asking students what ideas and/ or experiences drew them to their major fields (almost all were in education or the social sciences), what issues they wished to explore at the university, and what goals they wished to attain after leaving college. After writing for forty minutes (half the period), I asked them to introduce themselves, saying as much or as little from their initial writings as they chose. On the second day, I returned the papers without comment, pointing out to them that I had *read* the essays and did not wish to critique them at this stage, and that reading their writing for content would always be more important to me than critiquing it, though I would do that also. I then asked them to circle the three words most resonant with meaning, for them, intellectually or emotionally, in their essays, to write briefly about why the words were resonant, and to suggest possible topics for the course's required long paper based on their reflection (the keywords exercise was derived from a somewhat different use of keywords in Freirean pedagogy by Finlay and Faith). In small groups, the students discussed why their words were resonant and tried to discover possible writing topics that grew out of the words, reporting their ideas to the class as a whole. For the first week, I tried to stay in the background as much as possible, as Ira Shor recommends when working with students who have known primarily teacher-centered classrooms.

In the second week, I introduced Freire's ideas, asked them to read the "banking education" section from *Pedagogy of the Oppressed*, and reproduced the class's complete list of resonant words and possible topics. I then gave an assignment, asking the students to find an article, picture, or (preferably) both that "represented" or codified some of the class's resonant words, and to briefly explain the relationship between the words and the "representation." It took a little time to clarify this: I was asking them to assume that significant intersubjective tendencies were revealed in the resonant words, and that these could lead us to issues worth exploring together. I was not asking them to continue to work with their own words to explore issues of personal interest, which was how many students wanted to interpret the assignment. Rather, I was suggesting that the class might uncover "generative themes" for exploration and decoding, in a way modelled roughly on Freire's Brazilian literacy experiments, which we had discussed in class. This naturally led to a discussion of ideological perspectives. I supplemented reading from Freire by assigning an interview with Frances Moore Lappe that had appeared in the *The Progressive,* suggesting that her definition of the political arts—"the exercise of judgment, listening, dialogues, reflection, evaluation, and the constructive expression of anger" (qtd. in Blanchard and Watrous 36)— paralleled Freire's. (Curiously, the more conservative students were much more hostile to Lappe's ideas than to Freire's. Perhaps he seemed more safely exotic; perhaps they felt safe with Freire's notion that the student's own voice was an important starting point for knowledge and could thus forgive him for his radicalism.) We also began an assignment on the political slant of an article in the news, and began reading a textbook, *Writing in the Social Sciences,* and I suggested that our own experiment with their resonant words modelled what social scientists tried to do. This suggestion was confusing to them, as most of the students were sophomores with little theoretical background in the social sciences, which they tended to define as fields designed to help other people.

The most common words the class (20 students, 18 of them women, all of them white) chose were *helping/help* (on 6 lists), *teaching/teaching methods* (6), *caring* (2), *communication* (2), *life, life/death* (2), *experience* (2), and *politics* (2). From their representations and explanations of the resonant words, I chose four to copy for class discussion. These I placed in a sequence, forming a sort of visual narrative, which I taped to the blackboard on the days when we discussed them. The first was a picture of Greg LeMond, the cycling champion, with a short write-up describing his struggle to achieve; the second was a picture of a homeless black man, sleeping in rags on the floor. (Also in the picture, but not showing up in my original xerox of it, was a young child with a teddy bear, curled up beside the man. Providing a better copy on the second day of discussion added to the controversy this picture generated.) The third showed parents, teachers, and police having a discussion in a school library as part of an education program in a local school, and the fourth was the widely circulated picture of triumphant Berliners on top of the Berlin wall. Each of these was accompanied by a short essay, discussing identification with self-achievement, the need to help the homeless, the need to deal with the problem of drugs, or the need to consider the worldwide impact of the changes in Eastern Europe.

Class discussion centered on the homeless issue, and on the relation between the first two representations. Debate and disagreement grew between those who looked at achievement as something that reflected the individual's efforts and worth and those who looked at social problems such as homelessness as the result of forces beyond individual control. Two writing assignments grew out of the discussion: first, a simple invitation to continue the discussion in an essay, and later, a second essay asking them to do so again, this time bringing in documented evidence that illuminated the discussion (most chose the more obvious news sources, but one student interviewed a homeless man). Not all students became engaged in the discussion, but some became very engaged. The most vocal student was a man in his twenties who was a political science major and ardent Reagan supporter; the most controversial paper referred to the class's resonant words to attack his position, saying:

> The reason that I was really shocked to hear the negative opinion about the homeless in class was because of the class we were in and the list of words that we gathered and said were important to us. Some of these words were: *helping, caring, society, communicating, teaching, learning, feelings, education, hope, influence,* and *life.* I think that anyone in our class who said that the homeless are lazy and just want to be that way, should take another look at our list of resonant words. All these words deal with helping people, but in our discussion, some people put the homeless down like a disease.

Another student, following a similar line of argument, wrote:

> One of the class's resonant words was *helping,* but how many are only interested in helping those on a similar social level as their own? Helping middle-class children carries more prestige than working in a shelter for the homeless.

One advantage of having begun with the generative words was that they provided a way of referring back to the contradictory ideas and feelings (the ideology and "structures of feeling," as Raymond Williams might say) with which the class began their exploration. To further class discussion and link it to our study of writing, I copied as many papers as possible, anonymously or with their names, as students permitted.

In our discussions, I repeatedly asked why the first two pictures generated so much more discussion than the others and why the identification of some students with the first picture was so strong. I encouraged them to consider the way social constructions (widely circulated images and ideas, the culture's resonant words) of achievement appealed to them in contrast to social representations of the Other. One student pointed to the resemblance of the LeMond picture to an advertisement; another wrote about all the help LeMond had received, in his supposedly individual achievement, from sports medicine, support crews, sponsors, and so on. I introduced my own interpretations of their ideas, summarizing what was happening in their discussions, suggesting that the culture had encouraged them to construct images of themselves as autonomous self-achievers and thus to blame those who did not achieve in a supposedly meritocratic society that worked to benefit the wealthy and disempower the poor. I also pointed out that in my own college years, the representations that evoked the least comment from them (especially the Berlin Wall with its image of revolution) would have provoked the most, and that if I had to name the story told by their representations, I would describe it as a narrative about the relation of public and private, self and other, about their own entrapment in public constructions of the private on the one hand and unrealized possibilities of social change on the other. But there was never consensus in the class, and my own remarks were (I think rightly) a bit to the side of what was happening. In ways that parallel the experience Tompkins describes, the class became its own audience for part of that semester to a degree I had not witnessed before, acknowledging and accomodating the positions of others and questioning their own, but remaining locked in ideological divisions they could not completely explain.

The second part of the semester, in which we worked on individual long papers, lacked the energy or engagement of the first, and I've never repeated this experiment in exactly the same way, for reasons similar to those Lazere gives in his critique of Freirean pedagogy. As Lazere suggests, Freirean pedagogy and other democratic learning methods have a positive value, yet in classes for non-elite students, "it must be kept in mind that these students are at a disadvantage compared to those at elite universities in their level of pertinent cultural literacy and familiarity with academic codes, so that compensatory time must be spent in these realms that unfortunately conflicts with the time available for Freirean pedagogy" (19). In my experiment, I included discussions of rhetorical principles and effective writing, especially in the last part of the course, but I came away feeling that more needed to be done to integrate rhetorical considerations more fully into the syllabus (which I intentionally invented as I went along, although students were aware of the major writing assignment from the beginning). This criticism is hardly an insurmountable one—it is always possible to include more or less explicit instruction on writing principles, and generating the desire to write for a real audience is far more difficult than providing a little structure when needed. However, too much energy (my own and the students') had gone into inventing the course and finding the themes to explore. Similar results might have been achieved had we discussed materials that had been previously chosen by the instructor. As it was, I selected the representations and their narrative arrangement anyway, and thus I implicitly suggested an interpretation of their ideological perspective from the beginning. Similarly, too much of the analysis of the representations as social constructions depended upon my analysis; it may have been more useful to read discussions of the social construction of self in advertising and to test those ideas against the students' own experience and resistance.

More recently, I have attempted to adopt a cultural studies approach to composition, influenced by the work of James Berlin, Diana George, John Trimbur, and others. However, it was my experience the second time that I attempted to use Freirean pedagogy, in the spring of 1991, that convinced me to use more structured approaches to cultural critique. That semester was dominated by the Gulf War, the occasion of a personal crisis for so many of us on all sides of the issue. Teaching two sections of "Writing in the Social Sciences" in January of 1991, I lacked the energy to go through the stages of exploring generative themes; I started the course in more or less the same way but ignored the resonant words and focused on finding topics for common exploration. One of the topics that emerged was the war, but there our discussion was frozen. Near the beginning of the semester, my picture and some of my remarks appeared on the front page of the local newspaper as part of the coverage of a Washington demonstration against the war; suddenly I was at the center of controversy and under suspicion, along with the rather strange Freirean ideas I had introduced but not fully developed. Neither of these two classes was as satisfactory as the first, though the section that finally selected the Gulf War as one of its common topics worked better than the class that steered away from it, probably because the section was able to more fully explore the issue and its hostility toward the instructor. In that class, however, dialogue did not have the free range that existed in the earlier semester. Students who were for the war allowed their names to appear on papers; other students expressed doubts but did not want papers copied; one young woman wrote strongly in opposition but insisted her paper be copied anonymously. Discussion on the topic was stifled, as only one person (the instructor) was really willing to voice opposition (and I, too, was feeling the pressure of the McCarthyite atmosphere in the community and the nation). Most students chose to write on something safer, and everyone, myself included, was relieved to get to the more traditional elements of the course, such as the long report on individually chosen topics.

The conditions that semester were probably unique, though they made apparent some of the problems of the pedagogy I had adopted. Inventing the content of the course through Freirean methods had proved to be a laborious process which I abandoned under pressure, and I was left with a set of controversial issues without a way of relating them to the deeply felt, often contradictory ideas and emotions which underlay the controversy. Probably there was no way to do this—no easy way—with a topic such as the Gulf War. But a further problem was the degree to which the pedagogy was implicit, and fell back into an expressivist mode, where we (teachers and students) expressed views on the Gulf War with no mediating ground. As Dale Bauer has noted in her discussion of the parallel problems of feminist pedagogy, expressivism, with its rigid separation of public and private, "reinforces, however indirectly, the dominant patriarchal model rather than challenges it" (390). A goal of feminist pedagogy, in contrast, "like Ira Shor's and Freire's, is to foreground dialogics in the classroom. This strategy uses one kind of mastery, feminist and dialogic in practice, against another, monologic and authoritarian" (387). In the minds of many of the students in my 1991 classroom, I had become the latter kind of monologic authority, especially for those in the section that did not choose to pursue the war as a topic for writing and thus did not have a chance to engage in the kind of negotiation of differences that Bauer advocates. A focus on texts which presented conflicting positions, and an exploration of rhetorical, academic, or cultural codes as ways of articulating and producing those positions, would have provided better ways of dealing with controversy. As it was, too much of the controversy and the pedagogy existed within the students and the instructor; too little in the analysis of texts and practices that had a material, intersubjective existence between them.

In "Writing and the Social Sciences," I now focus on contrasts between the presentation of the problem of literacy in popular media and in books such as Mike Rose's *Lives on the Boundary*, and on different styles of academic social science as represented by Rose's humanistic, ethnographic approach (which my students like) and more traditional empirical social science works such as William Julius Wilson's *The Truly Disadvantaged* (which my students find intimidating). The course attempts to introduce students to some of the different approaches to social issues produced within popular and academic discourses—knowledge which inexperienced students being initiated to those disciplines need. Students write rhetorical analyses of contrasting works, as well as critiques of the writer's ideas, before doing some independent research. However, it is very important that the works are selected for their exploration of "generative themes." For most of my students, the problem of literacy and their own difficulty initiating themselves to the alienating discourses of college is a central issue, for they have been portrayed (or "written") as insufficiently literate or capable by popular culture, by many of their teachers and professors, and by themselves; they have learned negative interpretations of themselves and of the academic discourse which they have rarely been invited to join. Issues of class, ethnicity, pedagogy, and power (the issues Rose and Wilson raise) are central to the way students have learned these perceptions of the university. They often perceive Rose's story as not unrelated to their own, and find Wilson more alien (in his race, for most of my students are white, but more significantly in his empirical and impersonal style), but both writers provide critical discourses which challenge their perceptions and beliefs.

The social-science writing course I have constructed is a formidable one, especially for sophomores who have had as little explicit instruction in writing on discourses other than personal experience as some of them have had in previous courses. It is a challenge to provide enough self-affirming exercises to mitigate the difficulty some of these students have with writing about and analyzing complex texts and relating these to their own lives. The political controversies of the course, however, are as much in the reading as in the instructor's and students' consciousness, and the social production of that consciousness through education and social class is itself the central issue. Curiously, the antagonism between the students and myself has been transformed from an opposition to my political views to an antagonism toward the difficulty of the course. Lazere notes a similar paradox, the "irony ... that when leftist teachers, including myself [Lazere], try to present students with

an honest account of the necessity—and difficulty—of critical education, students perceive *us* as the coercive authority figures, in contrast
to the permissive mainstream culture" (14).

A similar anatagonism often emerges in my freshmen writing
courses, which in recent years have usually focused either on the topic
of academic initiation and education (using Rose in ways similar to
those described above), on the mass media, or on both. Recently, I
have developed a freshmen writing course centered on the theme of
"Media, Self, and Culture," in which students move from (1) an essay
on their personal experiences and goals to essays which ask them (2)
to analyze the cultural meanings of advertisements, (3) to write a response to one of the essays on culture in the reader, and (4) to complete a longer paper on an issue presented in the news while also
taking account of the way the rhetoric of different news media influences the presentation of content. Because the assignments are
challenging for non-elite students, four summaries and exploratory
writings on the readings are also required (and graded, however lib-
erally, so these short assignments are taken seriously); there is also
ample time for revision of up to two essays and/or submission of a
fifth essay during the last three weeks of the semester, which are entirely devoted to workshop sessions. The readings (mostly from George
and Trimbur's *Reading Culture*) present interpretations of such topics
as rap music, advertising, the "baby bust" generation of the late 1980s,
and the news. Bill Moyers's 1989 PBS video series, *The Public Mind*,
provides an excellent video supplement. The sections on advertising
and generations, especially, provide some of the same insights into the
social construction of self and other as were attempted by my earlier
Freirean experiments, and the analysis of the news provides a rudi-
mentary analysis of the social construction of ideology.

Students often resist the ideas and insights in the reading, and I
find that it is difficult to provide sufficient time for reading, analysis,
writing, and critique on one topic before moving on to another. It is
never easy to give students' resistance enough time and room to be
recognized, heard, challenged, and redeveloped. But this problem exists
in every composition pedagogy based in critical thinking in the fullest
sense, recognizing that dialogue is, in Lappe's words, one of the "political arts." The cultural studies course I have developed has the
advantage of providing explicit instruction in rhetoric (the papers
include an expressive essay, an analysis, a response for a hostile audience, and an evaluation/research paper), time for revision and work
on basic literacy, recognition of the students' subjectivity, and analysis

of the social production of cultural meaning by powerful institutions which help construct that subjectivity. Thus, the course moves the project of critique away from the question of specific issues (though those get raised in the process) and toward the question of the social construction of consciousness (though some parts of that question, such as who constructs whose consciousness, and for what ends, remain highly controversial). Similarly, the responsibility for critique no longer resides exclusively within the teacher, but also in the theories and interpretations being examined, theories which are closely aligned with contemporary conceptions of rhetoric as a field. For study of the mass media is simultaneously the study of the most powerful means of persuasion in the culture and the most powerful source of ideas in the "public mind." If college rhetoric courses should focus on public discourse, as has been often suggested, then the study of mass media should be a key part of those courses, for the mass media (especially television) are at the center of the public discourse of late-twentieth-century culture; they are also the key sources of the *invention* of our students' ideas, which cannot be adequately explained by expressive theories.

Fears that cultural studies courses like my own might constitute the imposition of "political correctness" upon students are naive. Some of the best papers in the "Media, Self, and Culture" course have been written by women who became interested in the power of the mass media to construct negative gender stereotypes; other students have written strong essays developing their resistance to the idea that their values are shaped by the mass media. In her research paper, one of the best students in the class used ideas presented by the conservative columnist George Will (one of the required readings) to analyze what she perceived as the unfairly pro-choice slant in the coverage of abortion demonstrations, even though she clearly knew that my own sympathies lay elsewhere. Her paper was hardly unique in its presentation of ideas which directly opposed my own. While I can hardly claim to be as successful as I would like to be, I seek to create an atmosphere where students like her feel free to write against the grain of my own politics, as well as one where I feel free to critique her position. To try to foreclose the possibility of such a dialogue is to underestimate the resources of both students and teachers.

Cultural studies provides some resolution to the dilemmas radical teachers like myself sometimes experience regarding sharing their political viewpoints with students. For if the focus of the course is on "rhetoric" in the broadest sense—on the social processes and conflicts which produce ideas and discourses—rather than on specific issues perceived only as "content" to be written about, then the instructor's views do not seem as individual, odd, or intrusive. Heated controversies will still occur, between students and instructor and among students, but the rhetorical focus provides a mediating ground. Individual choices as to how much of one's thinking to reveal on issues are still complicated, unsettling choices, for students as well as teachers, choices that must be made in response to the urgencies and pressures of specific pedagogical moments.

13

Teaching the Conflicts about Wealth and Poverty

Donald Lazere _____

This article will apply the pedagogical approach developed in my anthology *American Media and Mass Culture: Left Perspectives* and my article "Teaching the Political Conflicts: A Rhetorical Schema" to a description of a writing course in argumentation, writing from sources, and the research paper, such as the second course in the freshman English sequence at my college. The particular application described here will be to generating a critical research paper on the pros and cons of the effects of the conservative economic policies hereafter called Reaganomics (for shorthand) on the rich, the poor, and the middle class in America.

In brief review of the theoretical grounding for this approach, I endorse the general concept of introducing political subject matter in writing courses that has occasioned much professional and public controversy in the last few years. But I also share the concern of critics that such courses can turn into an indoctrination to the instructor's particular ideology or, at best, into classes in political science rather than composition. This concern has certainly been warranted by the tendency of some leftist teachers and theorists to assume that all students and colleagues agree—or *should* agree—with their views, rather than formulating their approach in a manner that takes respectful account of opposing views. My own political leanings are toward democratic socialism, and I believe that college English courses have a responsibility to expose students to socialist viewpoints because those views are virtually excluded from all other realms of the American cognitive, rhetorical, semantic, and literary universe of discourse. I am firmly opposed, however, to instructors imposing socialist (or feminist, or Third-World, or gay) ideology on students as the one true faith—just as much as I am opposed to the present, generally unquestioned (and even unconscious) imposition of capitalist, white-male, heterosexual ideology that pervades American education and every other aspect of our culture.

I assert, then, that our primary aim should be to broaden the ideological scope of students' critical thinking, reading, and writing capacities so as to empower them to make their own autonomous judgments on opposing ideological positions in general and on specific issues. Part of my theoretical intention is to indicate ways in which partisan political positions—such as my own socialist views on economic matters or those on sexism and racism emphasized in comp courses elsewhere—can be introduced within a rhetorical schema that is acceptable to teachers and students of any reasoned political persuasion. In this way, I believe the left agenda of prompting students to question the subjectivity underlying socially constructed modes of thinking can be reconciled with the conservative agenda of objectivity and nonpartisanship. This approach obliges teachers to raise in class the question of their own partisan biases and how they can most honestly be dealt with in pedagogy and grading; I have found that students are immensely relieved at being able to discuss this taboo subject openly, to come to an open accord with the instructor about what guidelines are most fair, and to evaluate the instructor's fairness at the end of the course accordingly. Early in the class I explain that my own, publicly aired, views are democratic socialist, and that I will be exposing them to those views—not as "the truth" but as points of contrast with conservative and liberal views. Their task is to arrive at an understanding of the areas of disagreement among these viewpoints, to locate an equal number of sources on opposing sides, and to identify and evaluate the rhetoric distinctive to each source's viewpoint. My grading, then, is not based on whether the students' views agree with mine, but on how skillfully they have located and articulated opposing lines of argument and analyzed the rhetorical strengths and weaknesses of each source's arguments. I have found this to be an effective rule of thumb, and although it is impossible to avoid subjectivity in grading altogether, nearly all of my students have found this policy fair in principle and practice.

A second theoretical justification involves the need to counteract the deemphasis of politics, the absence of systematic exposition of a full spectrum of ideologies, and the atomized discourses that fragment

American culture and education and that result in a conservatism of inertia, in default of any articulated oppositional consciousness. At every level of education, we find the same avoidance of political controversy and absence of systematic exposure to a full spectrum of ideologies. The exposition of clearcut ideological viewpoints gets further blurred by the convention that teachers and textbooks are expected to be blandly neutral. Comprehensive political understanding is still further impeded by a departmentalized curriculum of unrelated courses, each jammed into a few hours a week for one semester or quarter, and each in turn broken up into discontinuous units corresponding to television's blips of information. Students and teachers alike are too hurried and overworked ever to gain a view of issues that goes beyond today's exam or exercise. Conservative critics of education claim the schools and colleges are threatened by teachers pushing left ideology, but many of those teachers are primarily attempting to combat the absence of *any* coherent exposition of ideas in the curriculum.

In the course described here I attempt to counteract the modular, politically sanitized structure of most such courses by focusing in depth for a full term on a single issue in current events—in this case Reaganomics—as mediated through the rhetoric of political speeches, news reporting and journals of opinion, or California ballot initiatives. Although the level of sources studied is that of popular political rhetoric and news media, not specialized social science scholarship, a major difficulty stems from most Cal Poly students' lack of knowledge about the rudiments of political economy—the kind of knowledge that should have been acquired in high school but usually isn't, because of teachers' avoidance of political controversy there.

Many students' initial reaction is bored resistance and protests that these subjects are too difficult and only of interest to political science majors. To bring these abstract issues down to a level they can relate to personally, I present at the beginning of the course (as a leftist viewpoint, to be evaluated against as many conservative sources as they can find) the hypothesis that their federal student grants may have been cut, their tuition raised, and the courses they need to graduate not funded due to a state budget crisis, in order for the California government to lower the taxes on Walter Annenberg's Palm Springs estate, or in order for the IRS to provide Bunker Hunt with additional millions with which to try to corner the world silver market. Many students are incredulous about this hypothesis, partly because the cultural conditioning of most at Cal Poly is conservative and they have never heard such a viewpoint before, partly because their cognitive capacities have been too restricted for them to follow a line of argument this complex. They have simply never made any connection between income in the private sector and the funding of education or other tax-supported public services, or else they have been indoctrinated with the most simplistic version of supply-side economics telling them that increased profits and low tax rates among the wealthy automatically trickle down to benefit everyone equally and provide increased tax revenues. Their faith in Reaganomic principles has been unshaken by the mushrooming national debt and the bankruptcy of state and local governments in the wake of Reaganite "tax reforms." Most do not even know the meaning of the term "progressive taxation," so they believe that flat-rate taxes and tax cuts are equitable because everyone pays or saves the same percentage and the rich pay the most in dollar amounts; they don't understand that under flat tax reductions the rich pay less relative to their after-tax savings and hence are constantly increasing the gap in wealth and power between them and those in lower income brackets. This is how Proposition 13, the regressive 1978 California property-tax-cut initiative, was sold to financially pressed middle-class homeowners by a realtors' lobby, with the consequence of immense savings for business property, landlords, and upper-bracket homeowners, while the middle class has gotten peanuts, rents have increased unabatedly—contrary to the backers' campaign promises—and both local and statewide public services, particularly education, have been decimated by tax-revenue shortfalls.

A ten-week English course is scarcely adequate to develop a coherent exposition of the elementary economic principles and multiplicity of possible ideological viewpoints involved in these issues, along with application to them of rhetorical analysis and exposure to research resources. With all the limitations in what can be covered on even this one topic throughout any such term, however, the experience at least has the value of demonstrating to students how much more complex political issues are than the way they are presented in campaign rhetoric, the mass media, and most other non-academic discourse; how narrow a range of ideology mainstream American discourse permits on such issues; and how that discourse works against any coherent system of analysis. I believe that this important lesson is what justifies such a course as one in writing and rhetoric, *not* political science, since the latter discipline typically stresses abstract theory or empirical approaches to particular cases to the neglect of the rhetorical principles needed for analysis of any particular case and for an understanding of the restrictions on American political discourse in general.

By way of remediating many students' near-vacuum of knowledge about political terminology and ideology, work on the term paper is preceded by four course units described more fully in "Teaching the Political Conflicts." The first, on political semantics, addresses the ambiguities of the public use of terms like *left wing, right wing, liberal, conservative, democracy, dictatorship, socialist,* and *capitalist* in the United States, and is accompanied by a glossary of such terms and charts presenting a national and worldwide spectrum of political positions, parties, and mass media from extreme right to extreme left. A key point here is that leftists and rightists differ even in how they define such terms, and that critical readers and writers need to be alert to the explicit or implicit definitions of them in any text and to how the selectivity of definitions reflects the author's ideology and controls the agenda of the argument. My own glossary attempts to make definitions that are acceptable to all sides, although I note that it is open to modification to counter my own possible biases. For purposes of leftist pedagogy, this unit serves to make students aware of what differentiates democratic socialism from liberal capitalism to its right and communism to its left (although, in a good example of semantic ambiguity, democratic socialism could be placed to the left of communism if *left* is defined in terms of authentic egalitarianism rather than of an extreme variety of socialism imposed by state force).

For the study of Reaganomics, the following section of the glossary is most pertinent:

CONSERVATIVES, LIBERALS, AND SOCIALISTS IN AMERICA

In the American context, conservatives (mostly Republicans, but many Democrats) are procapitalist. They believe the interests of business also serve the interests of labor, consumers, the environment, and the public in general—"What's good for General Motors is good for America." They believe that abuses by businesses can and should be best policed or regulated by business itself, and when conservatives control government, they usually appoint businesspeople to cabinet positions and regulatory agencies without perceiving any conflict of interest therein.

American liberals, usually Democrats, believe that the interests of business are frequently contrary to those of labor, consumers, the environment, and the public in general. So although they basically support capitalism, liberals think business abuses need to be policed by government regulatory agencies that are free from conflicts of interest, and that wealth should be limited.

American socialists, or radicals, believe even more strongly than liberals that the interests of business are contrary to the public interest. Under capitalism, wealthy business interests almost inevitably gain control over government through both the Republican and Democratic parties, foreign and military policy, the media, education, and so on, and use the power of employment to keep the workforce and electorate under their control. Socialists believe an economy based primarily on the profit motive is irrational and wasteful, leading to environmental destruction, dishonest business practices, and degradation of the value of work. (Democratic socialists also believe communist governments have simply implemented state-run bureaucracies imitating the worst aspects of capitalism.) They think liberal government reforms and attempts to regulate business are usually thwarted by the power of business lobbies, and that even sincere liberal reformers in government offices usually come from and represent the ethnocentric viewpoint of the upper classes. The socialist solution is to socialize at least the biggest national and international corporations, as well as the defense industry, to turn their management over to workers and operate them on a nonprofit basis, and to place much higher taxes on the rich, so as to reduce the power of wealthy corporations and individuals and to rechannel the proceeds toward filling public needs, providing full employment, and reducing work time.

The second preliminary unit addresses issues of ideological subjectivity and bias, through exposition of some of the common psychological blocks to perceiving bias in all of us—student writers, their research sources, and their teachers, including the present one. These blocks include culturally conditioned assumptions (which frequently emerge as hidden premises in arguments); closed-mindedness, prejudice, and stereotyping; authoritarianism, absolutism, and inability to recognize ambiguity, irony, and relativity of point of view; ethnocentrism and parochialism; inconsistency, double standard, or compartmentalization (Orwellian "doublethink"); rationalization, wishful thinking, and sentimentality. The practical aims here are alerting students to biases in themselves during the prewriting stage and in sources they analyze, as well as acquainting them with the way skillful writers use these terms as tools in argumentation.

The next unit addresses issues of partisanship, bias, and deception in argumentative rhetoric. In contrast to courses and textbooks that regard fallacious reasoning mainly in terms of impersonal, formal reasoning and unintentional fallacies, this approach emphasizes issues like political partisanship, conflicts of interest, sponsored research and journalism (e.g., that subsidized by corporate foundations and think tanks), special pleading, and other forms of propaganda and pure lying that have come to be known as public doublespeak. Furthermore, every ideology is predisposed toward its own distinct pattern of rhetoric that its conscious or unconscious partisans tend to follow on virtually any subject they are reading, writing, or speaking about. Critical readers need to learn to identify and understand the various ideologies explicit or implicit in all sources of information on controversial subjects. Having done so, they can then to a large extent anticipate what underlying assumptions, lines of argument, rhetorical strategies, logical fallacies, and modes of semantic slanting to watch for in any partisan source. This unit is accompanied by the following guide.

A SEMANTIC CALCULATOR FOR BIAS IN RHETORIC

1. What is the author's vantagepoint, in terms of social class, wealth, gender, ethnic group, political ideology, occupation, educational level, age, etc.? Is that vantagepoint apt to color her/his attitudes on the issue under discussion? Does she/he have anything personally to gain from the position she/he is arguing for, any conflicts of interest or other reasons for special pleading?

2. What organized financial, political, ethnic, or other interests are backing the advocated position? Who stands to profit financially, politically, or otherwise from it?

3. Once you have determined the author's vantagepoint and/or the special interests being favored, look for signs of ethnocentrism, rationalization of wishful thinking, sentimentality, and other blocks to clear thinking, as well as the rhetorical fallacy of stacking the deck with one-sidedness, selective vision, or a double standard.

4. Look for the following semantic patterns reflecting the biases in No. 3:

   a. Selectively or disproportionately playing up:
      (1) arguments and evidence favorable to one's own side, while playing down those favorable to the other;
      (2) the other side's power and wealth, while playing down one's own.

   b. Arbitrarily applying "clean" words (ones with positive connotations) to one's own side, and "dirty" words (ones with negative connotations) to the other.

   c. Assuming that the representatives of one's own side are trustworthy, truthful, and have no selfish motives, while assuming the opposite of the other side. Regarding misconduct on one's own side as an isolated exception to the rule, and misconduct on the other side as the rule.

   d. Arbitrarily giving credit to one's own side for positive political or economic events; placing blame on other side for negative events.

5. If you don't find strong signs of the above biases, that's a pretty good indication that the argument is a credible one. If there *is* a large amount of one-sided rhetoric and semantic bias, that's a pretty good sign that the writer is not a very credible source. However, finding signs of the above biases does not in itself prove that the writer's arguments are fallacious. Don't fall into the ad hominem ("to the man") fallacy—evading the issue by attacking the character of the writer or speaker without refuting the substance of the argument itself. What the writer says may or may not be factual, regardless of the semantic biases. The point is not to let yourself be swayed by words alone, especially when you are inclined to wishful thinking on one side of the subject yourself. When you find these biases in other writers, *or in yourself,* that is a sign that you need to be extra careful to check the facts out with a variety of other sources and to find out what the arguments are on the other side of the issue.

The final preliminary unit deals with locating and evaluating partisan sources. This is accompanied by lists of the most accessible leftist and rightist book publishers, research institutes and foundations, and periodicals, which students use to locate an equal number of sources on opposing sides of issues related to Reaganomics. A guide to evaluating such sources on any issue of controversy, titled "Predictable Patterns of Political Rhetoric," is included in "Teaching the Political Conflicts." The following portions of it are most pertinent to Reaganomics:

Leftists will play up:	*Rightists will play up:*
Conservative ethnocentrism, wishful thinking, and sentimentality rationalizing selfish interests of the middle and upper class and America abroad	Leftist "negative thinking," "sour grapes," anti-Americanism, and sentimentalizing of the lower classes and Third World rebellion
Right-wing bias in media and education	Left-wing bias in media and education
Rip-offs of taxpayers' money by the rich; luxury and waste in private industry and the military	Rip-offs of taxpayers' money by the poor; luxury and waste by government bureaucrats; selfish interests and inefficiency of labor, teachers, students, etc.

The point here is not to instill utter cynicism toward all sides but to encourage students, once they have become aware of the lines of argument they can expect on the left and right, to judge the quality of reasoning and evidence with which writers support their predictable positions.

After assimilating the material from these four units, students work collaboratively in locating sources and assembling a collective outline of specific arguments found in those sources. Their individual responsibility in the paper itself is to evaluate the strong and weak points in each source's evidence and reasoning, including their refutations of opposing arguments. Although I have emphasized leftist rebuttals to the conservative arguments most familiar to the majority from their family backgrounds and the prevailing attitudes of the Reagan-Bush era in which they have grown up, conservative students now have the chance to find all the counterrebuttals they can in conservative sources.

The following outline emerged from the last time I taught the course, in spring 1992. The preponderance of leftist arguments reflects the consensus even among most conservative students that although conservative sources present many initially appealing assertions, when it comes to both concrete support and rebuttal, their side is weaker. This consensus, repeated most times I have taught the course, and in a variety of term-paper topics, brings home to students through their own explorations that the mass appeal of conservative ideas lies mainly in simplistic, ethnocentric appeals and wishful thinking that do not stand up under extended, carefully researched analysis. The demonstrable superiority of leftist ideas on a level playing field of argumentation, free from the slant imposed by the ideological conditioning of a capitalist society, should give confidence to leftist teachers that the most authentic way to win converts is through the process of students' own free inquiry, not through teachers forcing on them leftist assumptions or lines of argument. Nevertheless, the fact that the leftist rebuttals are placed last in this model should not be taken to imply that this side has the last word logically or in a sequence of debate; it should be stressed to students that few arguments can be settled definitively, that counterrebuttals can almost always be found, and that, especially in statistically based arguments like those in (1n) and (2u), each side's statistics are likely to be selective and disputed by the other side.

A final note: this article was written shortly after President Clinton's election, and I haven't taught the course since. I envision teaching it again with the same approach and topic, but with the following adjustments. First, although Clinton's campaign rhetoric pretty closely followed the leftist lines of argument, students will now be able to evaluate how much Clintonomics in practice stays consistent or reverts toward Reaganomics. Second, throughout the Reagan and Bush years, differences receded between liberals and socialists on the beleaguered left. Under Clinton, those differences have become more salient again, as they did during Kennedy's presidency when the manifest limitations of Democratic Party liberalism within the confines of capitalism and American nationalism prompted the revived socialist viewpoint of the New Left. Therefore, it will become useful now to focus more in the leftist positions on differences between liberal and socialist arguments and sources.

The Rich, Poor, and Middle Class

1. The Conservative Position

The basic position of Presidents Reagan and Bush and their conservative supporters is that American government has been overloaded trying to provide for the public welfare in entitlement programs like education, Social Security, welfare, unemployment insurance, Medicare, and so on. Moreover, excessive taxation and bureaucratic government regulation of business (especially for environmental protection) have stifled the productive power of free enterprise. This overload on government has led to inflation, deficit spending, and dependency of beneficiaries of programs like welfare on "handouts." Therefore, if government spending on domestic programs is reduced and taxes cut by equal percentage rates across all income lines (with the largest savings going to wealthy individuals and corporations), private enterprise will be freed to function more effectively; it will be more efficient than government and the public sector of the economy in generating jobs, producing more tax revenue, and filling other public needs. The reason these beneficial Reaganomic policies haven't been fully effective is that they haven't been given an adequate chance to work, their full implementation having been blocked by Democrats in Congress and other leftist bureaucrats and special interest groups purely because of their partisan and selfish motives. Deficit spending has increased only because Democrats in Congress rejected every effort by Presidents Reagan and Bush to reduce the budget.

ADDITIONAL CONSERVATIVE ARGUMENTS:
    a. Budget cuts in the federal government under Presidents Reagan and Bush and in California since Proposition 13 have just trimmed the fat of unnecessary programs and administrative waste, leaving intact essential programs and the "safety net" of support for the truly needy.

b. Government spending in many areas such as education and welfare can be more properly and efficiently handled by states and localities than by the federal government; the funding burden should be shifted to them.

c. Much of the overload on government has resulted from selfish, excessive demands for "entitlements" from special interests like welfare recipients, minorities, the elderly, senior citizens, veterans, teachers, and students. These groups have become dependent on handouts and have lost their incentive to work.

d. Individual initiative, not government programs, is the best solution to social problems. Anyone in America can get a good job and be financially successful if they try hard enough. It is usually people's own fault if they are poor or unemployed. They should just try harder and be more virtuous.

e. Spending on national defense is an exception to the need for cutting government because increases in the eighties were necessary to defeat Russia in the arms race; maintaining strong defense is still necessary because of other potential threats to world peace.

f. The most effective way to reduce poverty and unemployment is to permit the rich to get richer—the trickle-down theory or "supply-side economics"—because their increased spending trickles down to benefit all other segments of society proportionately.

g. Wealthy individuals and corporate executives can be entrusted to use their increased benefits for the public welfare because in order to attain and maintain their position they have to be exceptionally intelligent, hard-working, honest, and civic-minded.

h. Most rich people have worked hard for their money and have risked their investments, so they shouldn't be penalized by high taxes and government regulations that stifle their incentive to work or to invest.

i. The rich are generous in sharing their wealth; the more money they are allowed to keep, the more they give to charities.

j. Wealth is compatible with religious, and especially Christian, morality. Many wealthy people like Bunker Hunt use their wealth to support religious organizations and causes.

k. Leftist criticisms of President Reagan or Bush and the rich often consist of "sour grapes" rationalizations by government bureaucrats, intellectuals, teachers, journalists, or public employees who are just unwilling or unable to make it themselves in the private sector and are jealous of those who do. These "bleeding hearts" sentimentalize the poor and exploit poverty to advance their own selfish interests.

l. Leftist teachers and other public employees' arguments may reflect ethnocentric bias, conflict of interest, or special pleading, since these sources benefit personally from higher taxation and the resulting increases in government spending. Likewise, arguments by leftist intellectuals may be self-interested, concealing their drive to replace the rich as the new ruling class.

m. In spite of all its faults, history has shown that capitalism or free enterprise is a more efficient and humane economic system than any form of socialism or mixed economy. Attempts to redistribute income don't work; confiscating wealth just kills the golden goose that creates prosperity and doesn't raise enough money to spread around adequately to fill the needs of the poor or the public.

n. Statistically based arguments: Empirical evidence that Reaganomics worked includes the facts that the 1980s saw a reduction in inflation and the longest period of steady growth in the American economy since World War II; millions of new jobs were created; the rich paid higher dollar amounts and an increased percentage of tax revenues; and total tax revenues increased.

2. The Leftist Position

Democracy in America is being destroyed and replaced by plutocracy—rule by and for the rich. Presidents Reagan and Bush (along with most other Republican and Democratic politicians, including presidents Kennedy and Clinton) are agents of plutocratic interests. Reaganomics policies have had the effect, intentionally or unintentionally, of entrenching plutocracy by making the rich richer, the poor poorer, and eliminating needed welfare programs and productive areas of public spending and employment. According to liberal, Keynesian theory, government spending serves to prime the pump when the economy slumps and to provide services the private sector fails to, while progressive taxation (progressively higher percentage as income or property value increases) serves to reduce the gap of wealth and power between the rich and the rest of the population. (Socialists criticize Keynesianism as a means of keeping the capitalist system from collapsing, as opposed to replacing it with socialism). The conservative line of argument against Keynesian economics is largely a propaganda program engineered by wealthy special interests to rationalize their own greed. In fact, Reagan and Bush consistently proposed budgets that were higher (mainly because of defense increases) than those passed by Congress, but their budget increases amounted to "Keynesian" socialism for the rich, free enterprise for the poor.

a. American cultural conditioning favors the rich by fostering common blocks to clear thinking, such as authoritarian awe and sentimentality toward the rich, the ethnocentrism and wishful thinking of middle-class people hoping to become rich, positively prejudiced stereotypes of the rich and negatively prejudiced ones of the working class and poor.

b. (1h) There is often little correlation between how hard people work or how much risk they take and how much money they make. Many of those who make the most money don't make it through work at all but through investments (often inherited) and speculation, while many of those who work the hardest and under the greatest risk (e.g., farmworkers, coalminers, police) make the least.

c. (1d) Conservative "try harder" arguments fail to recognize the basic inequities structured into a capitalist economy and the external economic forces—national and worldwide economic trends, inflation, recession, etc.—that often make individual effort futile. In a free-enterprise economy, there is no certainty of full employment or of a job being available for everyone who needs one. Furthermore, the minimum wage in America has lagged increasingly behind the cost of living; consequently, many people work full-time yet are still below the poverty level. If welfare is more attractive, it's not because welfare is too lavish but because the minimum wage is too low.

d. (1f) There is no conclusive evidence that the trickle-down theory has ever worked in practice or ever will. Much of what the rich get back in tax cuts is often invested not in job-producing enterprises but in personal luxuries, tax dodges, hedges against inflation, speculation, corporate takeovers resulting in monopolies and inflated prices for consumers and lost jobs for workers, or investments in foreign countries exploiting cheap labor there while taking jobs and money out of the United States.

e. (1c) In contrast to the private sector, where much money spent does not trickle down to the rest of society, virtually all money spent in the public sector "trickles up" back into the private sector. Spending on education, public health, welfare, and so on, is a good investment by society that pays off in higher productivity.

f. (1a) The private sector is just as wasteful and inefficient as the public sector, and the most waste in both occurs at the executive levels, where spending is administered (primarily in administrators' own interests). Thus, budget cuts resulting from laws like Proposition 13 have left governmental administrative "fat" intact while causing lay-offs of rank-and-file public employees and harmful cuts in essential services like education and law enforcement.

g. (1b) As a result of tax cuts like Proposition 13, state and local governments are even more hard pressed financially than the federal government, so conservative claims that funding responsibilities are better handled at the local level are simply rationalizations or passing the buck.

h. (1h) Those who can afford to pay the most taxes and who benefit most from a prosperous society—i.e., the rich—should be expected to pay the most. Lowering taxes for the rich (regressive taxation) widens the gap in wealth and ownership of income-producing holdings like stocks, bonds, real estate, and farms, and enables the rich to increase their power in all of the following ways:

i. The rich buy political influence with both the Republican and Democratic parties and government officials, causing legislation to be passed in their interest and against that of the middle class and poor, particularly in tax policies, such as regressive cuts in income, corporation, inheritance, and property taxes that in recent decades have sharply reduced the burden on the rich.

j. As a result of (h), the tax burden has shifted increasingly from the rich to the middle class; as a further result, the overtaxed middle class votes to support cuts in public services that harm themselves and society as a whole but that don't harm the rich because they don't depend on these services—services like education, Social Security, public health insurance, welfare, law enforcement, libraries, and public transportation. The middle class rationalizes these cuts by turning the poor, "big government," and public employees into scapegoats, blaming them instead of the rich for the financial squeeze on themselves.

k. The rich use the power of hiring and firing to force workers and students (as future workers) into compliance with pro-rich attitudes; because we have to cater to them to get or keep a job, we tend to fall into doublethink compartmentalized thinking to rationalize our servitude to them.

l. The rich are able to create a favorable public image of themselves through ownership or sponsorship of news and entertainment media, advertising, and public relations. They exert a large degree of control over education through positions as university trustees or school board members and through sponsoring research in both universities and private "think tanks" that supports their interests.

m. (1g) Many rich people and corporations get away with criminal or unethical activity that causes relatively little public indignation or opposition from law enforcement agencies, compared to lower-class criminals or "leeches." The middle class tends to have a double standard or selective vision in playing down misconduct by the rich and playing up that by the poor. How can we expect poor people to respect the law or act morally when those at the top of society set such a poor example?

n. (1c) It is often affluent conservative businesspeople who benefit most from the government subsidies that conservatives claim they oppose (compartmentalized thinking): subsidies to farmers (including for food stamps), to doctors and pharmaceutical manufacturers and sellers for Medicare, to bankers for student loans, to bondholders for government debts, and so on.

o. (1e) The biggest government subsidy of all is the defense industry, whose only customer is the government and whose spending on weapons that are only intended to be destroyed or replaced by more advanced ones is disastrous for the national economy. More and more of our national income has been eaten up on this wasteful spending that is the major cause of inflation and deficit spending and that has squeezed out spending on more productive domestic programs like education and welfare. During the Cold War, the military-industrial complex and its wealthy executives became the tail that wags the dog of defense policy in their own self-interest, artificially perpetuating tensions with Russia to bolster their profits and power (mirroring the military establishment in Russia that was similarly self-interested). The primary reason for the collapse of the Soviet Union was not the American arms buildup but the internal ineptitude of the ruling bureaucracy. Because conservatives sentimentalize the military, they tend to be blind to waste in military spending.

p. The rich influence foreign policy to protect their foreign investments, markets, and sources of natural resources and cheap labor. International competition for markets has frequently been the cause of wars throughout history.

q. The wealthy profit from wars conducted in their class interests and consuming weapons that they produce, but they and their children rarely risk their own lives fighting in those wars.

r. (1i) Rich people on the whole do not give a great amount to charity, relative to their income or net worth, and they benefit from what they give through tax deductions, trusteeships, and a favorable public image as philanthropists or supporters of religion.

s. (1j) Attempts to reconcile wealth with Christianity amount to hypocritical rationalizations, since they are completely contrary to the teachings of Jesus Christ.

t. (1m) Some semi-socialist countries (e.g., Denmark, Sweden) have surpassed America in per capita income, quality of life, and well-functioning democracy, while some capitalist countries (e.g., Chile, South Africa, El Salvador, the Philippines under Marcos) are pluto-cratic, right-wing dictatorships, and Americans' prosperity and freedom are paid for at the expense of poor people in those countries, which are in effect colonies of American corporations. In nineteenth- and early-twentieth-century America, unregulated free enterprise led to brutal exploitation of workers in low wages and unhealthy conditions, and to undemocratic extremes of wealth, poverty, and power; these conditions have been corrected as much as they have been mainly through the struggles to organize labor unions and to pass govern-ment regulations.

u. Statistically based arguments (1n): During the 1980s, the income of the richest 1 percent of Americans doubled, and the gap between the rich and poor became greater than at any time since the 1920s. The rich obviously are paying more in taxes because their *income* is greater in relation to everyone else's, thanks to Reaganomic subsidies, and their after-tax savings have increasingly outstripped everyone else's. Inflation has been reduced mainly through reduction of real income for the majority of workers. Economic growth in the eighties was slower than that in the seventies, and the jobs created were mostly low-wage ones. The main reason more people were working is that two or more people in the same households were forced to work in order to make the real income previously earned by one. Total tax revenue has been lower than it would have been under pre-Reagan progressive rates.

Conclusion

Many students at first feel bewildered in this course because the approach is so different from any English course they have taken, because the political terms and issues are alien to them, and because they have been sheltered from explicit expositions of right and left viewpoints. The initial misgivings, especially among conservatives, can be overcome day by day with good-humored, unintimidating class-room exchanges and a growing sense of communal involvement. As the course goes on and the students acquire the terminology and method, their confidence and commitment grow. The discovery that they are able to locate, organize, and evaluate source material in a scholarly way is exciting for most, and the collaborative search for and discussion of opposing viewpoints among them becomes a game-like challenge. As many have indicated on anonymous evaluations, the course has helped them overcome their sense of powerlessness in the face of sophisticated data and arguments in print, and has made them feel like independent-thinking adults instead of compliant children as most of their courses do. In spite of the anxieties I undergo at the beginning of each term, the payoff that makes it worthwhile for me comes as I see most of the students grow, far beyond my expectations, in intellectual and emotional maturity by the end.

PART V
Teaching for Social Change

14

Pedagogy, Resistance, and Critique in the Composition Class

Adam Katz _____

The dominant discourse among theorists and practitioners of critical pedagogy is currently that of "radical democracy." Radical democracy, following the work of Ernesto Laclau and Chantal Mouffe, abstracts social theory and social change from class exploitation and class struggle and situates it in a field of multiple sites of antagonism involving domination and subordination which are interrelated in contingent and indeterminate ways. Democratic politics in this case involves attempting to support the subordinate side in these various antagonisms, thereby undermining domination: presumably, enough reversals of this kind will add up to a democratic, or at least more democratic society. Within this postmodern framework, any attempt to single out any particular site of antagonism (for example, private property) as being of structural importance would only produce a totalizing and totalitarian "grand narrative."

A pedagogy committed to radical democracy is therefore interested in empowering pluralized identities and including excluded voices. As Henry Giroux writes, "[b]y refusing to create a hierarchy of struggles, it becomes possible for critical educators to take up notions of political community in which particularity, voice and difference provide the foundation for democracy" (209). If democracy is grounded in the particularity of different voices rather than in collective control over the means of production, then the inclusion of ever more voices within the public sphere represents that many steps towards a genuinely democratic polity. To quote Giroux again: "By viewing schooling as a form of cultural politics, radical educators can bring the concepts of culture, voice, and difference together to create a borderland where multiple subjectivities and identities exist as a part of a pedagogical practice that provides the potential to expand the politics of democratic community and solidarity" (206).

The notion that "democracy" is already "in" the "people," in their inherent diversity and plurality, and simply needs to be released from attempts to restrain its emergence through the proliferation of democratic sites and practices, is of course the dominant view of democracy in American culture. From Jefferson's conception of democracy as grounded in the small property owner, through de Touqeville's idealization of the New England town meeting, to Dewey's view of democracy as grounded in the enlightened and critical individual citizen, democracy in America has been viewed as a quality internal to the people, rather than a result of property structures and institutional forms. As Ben Agger puts it, "[t]he New England town meeting is our own equivalent of the Paris Commune and we must respect the difference lest we doom ourselves to irrelevance" (219). If democracy is the result of the proliferation of already democratic local sites and subjects, then it can be separated from systemic material confrontations between opposing social forces grounded in a totalizing social structure.

However, American history provides us with another version of democracy, with a radically opposed content. What I have in mind is the maroons established by escaped slaves. The maroons were materially connected to struggles against oppression—in addition to providing a haven for runaway slaves, the maroons provided bases from which guerilla operations could be carried out against slave-owning society. In addition, while the maroons were characterized by an extraordinary degree of continuity (maroons existed throughout the entire period of slavery, and individual maroons sometimes lasted for decades), hence constituting a legitimate "tradition" (and an American one at that), their function was not to embody an internalized democratic "ethos" but rather to engage in incessant struggle against the dominant culture; they had no meaning outside of this struggle. Finally, they represented the need to "abstract" such struggle from the terms and institutions of the dominant culture, involving a recognition that those institutions were not simply reversible given a "critical mass" of democratic subjects or communities.

I do not mean to posit the maroon as a "model" for social struggles today; it is no less historically specific and contradictory than the New

England town meeting to which I have contrasted it (but no more so, either). My purpose is to illustrate the exclusions exercised by the (liberal) theories of democracy supported by Giroux, Agger, and others, and to lay the groundwork for a theory of oppositional pedagogy based upon the following principles: first, abstraction (not abstention) from the dominant culture; second, material confrontation with the ruling class and its institutions within that structure. This means, with regard to teaching within the capitalist university, at least the following: students cannot be regarded as possessing a "good" democratic kernel which needs to be released from external restraints and permitted to flourish, nor as free and rational subjects who can simply "choose" from among a variety of intellectual options (I refer here to Gerald Graff's proposal that we "teach the conflicts"—which simply "canonizes" those conflicts in a relation of equivalence); rather, they must be understood as contradictory sites constituted by the enormous investment of the dominant culture in producing "authoritarian individuals," that is, by their resistance to "democracy" in the sense of any social and material forces which advance democracy in a consistent way. The point, then, is not to "expand" democracy (as if it already existed and there just wasn't enough of it) by producing more democratic subjects, but rather to give pedagogical representations to the results of past and present conflicts which already situate the students as agents of the dominant culture.

In this case, it is necessary to "expropriate" the ideological strategies available to students and which are reproduced by the proponents of "radical democracy." The most important of these strategies is what I would call "liberalization," in which students learn, with the aid of the liberal institutions of higher learning which expose them to the occasional radical teacher, to camouflage, modify, or suppress the more obviously problematic aspects of the American political imaginary which constitutes them, and to become agents of a sophisticated "hegemony" rather than of a "cruder force" in which one identifies directly with the cultural supports of order. The expropriation of this strategy entails a systematic demonstration of its complicity with the forces of order—in fact, its unintelligiblity and lack of actuality without this complicity and dependency. This type of pedagogy can open a space not for a more ethical discourse, but for sustained critiques of the hegemony exercised throughout everyday life, including the conservative/liberal and mainstream/extreme binaries required for that hegemony. In this essay I will outline some strategies by which such a pedagogy can be established.

Institutional Critique

The classroom space must be constructed with reference to a consistent institutional critique which sees the contradictions of the university (in particular that between its claims to provide emancipation through knowledge and its actual subordination to the needs of the ruling class) as internal to and constitutive of the classroom itself. This can be done by situating the class in relation to the explicit goals of the university and the department in which one works, as well as the structure of the conventional composition class. This might involve bringing in university documents, departmental memos, popular composition textbooks, assignments from other classrooms, and subjecting them to rigorous readings in the classroom. The university produces knowledges and subjects, and it does so with the use of social resources: what types of subjects and knowledges should it produce (how should those resources be used), what would it mean for such decisions to be made in a public forum and democratic manner, and what transformations would this require? In order to support the stated goals of the university, does one have to be opposed to the actually existing university?

In my own classes, I have brought in memos discussing such topics as curricular reform, merit pay raises, and directives for the instructors; I have encouraged students to account for the differences between my own class and those which their friends are taking; and I have spoken with them about the kind of evaluations I have received, both from students and from the department. This type of practice enables the teacher to demystify the institution by giving political readings of activities which are normally veiled behind claims of confidentiality, professionalism, and so on; it also makes it possible to give much more concrete representations to more general critiques by pointing out the direct ways in which seemingly banal and commonplace activities have profound effects upon the kind of education students will be able to receive.

Furthermore, by removing composition textbooks from their apparent connection to an abstract "mind" which simply wants to present "ideas" and placing them in their material connections with the kinds of writing that helps to reproduce the institution, the teacher is provided with powerful resources with which to critique the structure of the "mainstream" forms of writing that the conventional writing class seeks to train students to perform. So, for example, when the writing program I was working in decided to implement a merit-based pay raise, and some other teachers and myself "nominated" ourselves collectively for the reason that our teaching enables students to understand the mechanism of control represented by such devices, I brought the relevant documents into class. I was able to point out to students the kinds of writing which the dominant institution necessarily excludes by producing specific kinds of subjects with specific kinds of characteristics (individual teachers who "deserve" more money for their "excellent" teaching) while obscuring relevant questions such as "Excellent according to what criteria and in whose judgment?" The subjects and actions that can be articulated in sentences written in such a context must abstract individuals from their social context and situate them as "entrepreneurial" subjects of capitalist culture. The department, in fact, found our "nomination" unintelligible, since it didn't fit into this framework—the director asked us if we would be willing to accept the award individually if all of us didn't receive it (something which the terms of our letter implicitly excluded).

This enabled me to raise questions regarding the kinds of writing which would be unintelligible on the terms set by the rhetoric proposed by conventional composition courses. I was able to support my claim that while such rhetoric is presented as a "universal" form of clear and effective communication, it is in fact the kind of "communication" which those aspiring to middle-management positions in late capitalist institutions must master in order to manage contradictions and reify practices and agents on behalf of the ruling class.

The Classroom as Public Space

It is essential that the instructor make strong arguments from the beginning on behalf of understanding the classroom as a public space. By this I mean a space which is interested less in providing "skills" for individuals or "personal expression" (finding one's "voice") than in the positions represented by subjects and the consequences for which they are accountable in terms of their relation to the so-called general interest and contesting conceptions of that interest. Such arguments can be situated in relation to institutional critiques by counterposing the "economic" goals of the university (providing "skills") to its putative public responsibility to produce knowledges needed by a democratic social order. What kind of university would we have to struggle for in order to subordinate its economic function to its "public" or "democratic" function?

The establishment of the "publicness" of the classroom takes away from the students one of the central strategies by which they defend the ideological assumptions of the existing order—that, after all, it's only "my opinion," with which one is free to agree or disagree. By separating ideological positions from the private individuality of whomever happens to represent them at a given moment, it becomes possible to inquire into their determinations and consequences. The point here is not to "silence" students by "condemning" their "opinions," but to enable them to see their "opinions" as historical and social products (and not as their own private property), which can be critiqued and transformed. Also, this practice makes it possible to posit the classroom as a rigorously circumscribed public space, as a strong critique of the dominant or mainstream public space which does not meet such standards and in fact regularly employs the very "personalizing" demagogic tactics which one can critique in class.

This can be done with some of the following measures. First, the specific questions and issues discussed in class should be rigorously delimited and defined. The focus must be upon the opposing positions, and the arguments supporting such positions, which circulate within culture at large with regard to specific sites of contestation: what are the consequences of following through the "logic" of one argument as opposed to another? This does not mean that students are not "allowed" to raise apparently irrelevant questions, but that students must learn to argue for the relevance of such questions in relation to the questions and arguments which have situated the class discussion (and, of course, the instructor can help enable students to do so). Second, the relations between positions occupied by students in the class must by interrogated carefully: what kinds of conflicts and differences take shape, and why; what sorts of challenges compel apparently liberal or even radical students to form "blocs" with the more conservative students against whom they are usually concerned to define themselves; and so on. Third, the history of students' writing and speaking must be charted and explained, and the connections between seemingly discrete "opinions" investigated. Again, the point here is not that students should not be "allowed" to hold a given position throughout the course, or, conversely, to make dramatic or seemingly improbable changes in their positions. Rather, it means that students should be enabled to account for these transformations, to inquire into the connections between positions taken, in social, ideological, and subjective terms. (Such a class does not want to "exclude" the subjective but to offer readings of the subjective in terms of its public and ideological construction.)

Conceptual Ordering of the Class

To the extent possible (I recognize here that many departments, seeking to suppress theoretical and ideological classrooms, make this difficult or next to impossible), the classroom should be organized not thematically but conceptually. The teacher should attempt to construct the class in terms of a series of concepts which are also sites of ideological and political contestation. A "thematic" organization of the class will, for example, spend several weeks on "American democracy" by reading a variety of texts offering different and opposing views of that "topic." (Typically: "conservative," "liberal," and "radical" texts, which in the end balance out to a comfortable "middle ground.") A conceptual organization inquires critically into the concept of democracy in order to uncover the social contestations of opposing collectivities which it articulates and, in its dominant versions, seeks to suppress—it thereby reads various instances of "democratic" arguments and assumptions as different ways of engaging these contestations and advancing one set of interests or another, interests which construct the students themselves and the arguments they make.

A practice of ideology critique, one which produces concepts through a reading of the contradictions and "disproportionalities" of texts representing the dominant ideology, is necessary for this strategy. Sustained readings, drawing on and critiquing the students' own responses, of texts dealing with "current affairs" such as the Los Angeles riots or the Gulf War can demonstrate that such texts are engaged in struggles which not only take positions "for" or "against" particular policies, but over which meanings of terms such as "democracy," "peace," and "order" are going to become the dominant ones. In addition, student papers should be inserted into such contestations: the type of writing that is based upon what I call the "consensus model," in which the purpose of writing is to conceal and reconcile contradictions and opposition ("we all need to come together as a nation"), also needs to be expropriated from the students. Only in this way can the student's own positioning in relation to the dominant ideology be investigated for the student. Students should be shown how they are recruited into such struggles as foot soldiers or perhaps low-grade officers of the dominant culture, often regardless of whether they might be "against" the Gulf War or "sympathetic" to the "rioters" in Los Angeles. The classroom itself needs to be read not as a place of "free" inquiry into "ideas," but as a site in which these very conflicts are concentrated—where the dominant culture wishes to see them managed in a relatively freer environment than exists elsewhere, but where they can in fact be exacerbated and clarified.

Students' Resistance

The resistance of students to a pedagogy which posits them as agents of "preservative," "reformative," and "transformative" practices rather than as free and rational individuals (or as students seeking a good grade and an upgrading of their skills) should be made intrinsic to the workings of the classroom itself. Questions such as "Will I have to know this to write my paper (or get a good grade)?" or "What does this have to do with writing?" should not be taken merely as instances of the student's conservatism or philistinism. Rather, the teacher should understand that such questions reflect a problematization of the student's understanding of what "belongs" in a writing class (or any class for that matter), and hence are directly connected to an implicit crisis in legitimacy and authority which can be made extremely productive for the purposes of the class.

The students' resistance can be used to inquire into all of the interests and ideologies bound up in their everyday lives, as well as the relation between these interests and ideologies and their placement within the institution of the academy (which in turn prepare them for their insertion into other institutions). The students want the "public" skills which will enable them to enhance their "private" existence (they want to be "liberalized" in order to be more effective subjects within the corporate liberal order). The teacher, in this account, is to be an agent of this "liberalization." However, there is a contradiction here in that the students can't really know in advance precisely what this process should look like, what is "acceptable" and what is "illegitimate." The authority that the instructor must be granted to determine such limits, and the contradiction between this authority and its use by the oppositional pedagogue to undermine the interests it is supposed to serve, along with the contradictions intrinsic to liberalism which is reflected in this "anomaly," is what produces the crisis of legitimacy for the student.

These contradictions must be given representation in the class so that they can be explored, explained, and clarified. What are the limits of "freedom" (academic and otherwise), and why? Why, at a particular moment, do the free subjects the students wish to see themselves as become determined opponents of freedom? When must democracy be saved from democratizing practices, or rationality from a consistent insistence that reasons be given for practices? There is no better way to teach the lessons implicit in these questions than by examining them in circumstances when the student's own vital interest is at stake, when their opportunity for "free inquiry" seems to interfere with their transcript or their sense of "themselves."

In conclusion, I would like to relate a "paradox" which I have posed to my students and which has proven useful in raising a whole set of interrelated questions. In connection with discussions of categories such as "democracy," "work," or "responsibility," I "suddenly" ask students what is the normal working time for individuals in our society? Predictably, the answers returned are: eight hours a day, forty hours a week, fifty weeks a year. I then ask them why this particular amount? After what is usually a prolonged period of confused silence, students invariably offer a series of circular responses, which could easily have been taken out of the texts of the "classical" political economy critiqued by Marx: because that is the "standard," because that's what people need to work in order to "make a living," and so on. After pointing out to them that these "answers" simply rephrase the question, I put the question itself in different terms: I "remind" them that the average work week a century ago was approximately sixty hours, that is, about one-third higher than it is now. How great have been the technological advances over the last one hundred years; that is, are "we" more than 33 percent more productive now than "we" were then? Even taking into account increases in consumption, students can easily be shown that there is a massive disparity here.

I then make the question more concrete. I point out that just the last twenty years have seen greater increases in productivity than any equivalent period in history. Yet Americans, on the average, work longer hours now than they did twenty years ago while their standard of living has declined. Again, why? Why don't productivity increases translate into less working time and easier lives? Why does there seem to be no necessary connection between technological capacities, consumption levels, and work time?

Furthermore, why do these questions seem so strange and even unintelligible to them? What could be of greater interest to people than understanding why they will be doing what they will be doing for the greater portion of their lives? If there are students in the class who are studying economics or sociology one can ask them if such questions are raised, as one would assume they should be, in those disciplines. If there are no such students in the class, the teacher can point out that if they asked such questions in classes on economics, sociology, or anything else, most likely their professors would be as stunned as they are.

The students' sudden recognition of the complete absence in their education of questions concerned with what is arguably the central issue of social existence in the modern world can go a long way towards undermining the seeming naturalness and obviousness of that education. Is it possible that the purpose of their education is as much to produce individuals who will not recognize the "reality" of such questions as to actually "teach" them anything? Is the kind of writing they expect to master in this very course perhaps designed to make such questions invisible, and if so how? How can we reassess such "mainstream" writing and thinking in this context? And what would a type of writing interested in placing such questions on the public agenda look like, what would criteria regarding its quality be, and how would it be evaluated by the dominant culture?

All the texts of the dominant culture can then be reread within this framework, including the texts circulating through the students—how, for example, do discourses on "personal responsibility" ("everyone should take care of themselves") reproduce the (ideo)logic which excludes such questions? What are we to make of a "democratic" culture which cannot even raise such questions, much less answer them? The instructor can, of course, provide the "correct" answers to these questions, explaining that capitalist society produces for profit and not for need; that it requires a workforce dependent upon capital and not upon its own collective productive capacities, and so on. However, it seems to me most important that first of all these questions be pushed to their limits, and used to clarify and account for social contradictions, delegitimate the dominant ideologies, and direct attention towards producing critical readings of texts and practices.

In this way, students can be given a mode of evaluation based upon social needs and possibilities, rather than upon immediate "realities." That is, they have a standard of evaluation which is "outside" of (produced by an analytical abstraction from) the dominant culture, and yet which focuses attention not on some "better" or "ideal" future but upon the concrete ways in which existing social relations, institutions, and ideologies suppress and exclude these needs and possibilities, and can and should be contested on this basis—first of all, by writing, teaching, and thinking differently, by becoming a different kind of student.

15

The Pedagogy of Pleasure 2:
The Me-in-Crisis

Mas'ud Zavarzadeh _____

... and you have requested that I "comment" on your "text." I have, of course, commented on your "final paper" or rather, the *one-page* paper you have turned in for your final paper. But, I assume that by "comment" you mean my commenting on your accompanying "letter" in which you provide the narrative of a "crisis" in your subject relations that has effectively made it impossible for you to write the required third paper (a ten- to twelve-page paper dealing with six different texts from the course reading list). It is this narrative, I take it, that you wish me to address.

However, increasingly I have found that making such comments—which often go beyond the immediate issues raised in the course to deal with larger theoretical/social issues—is largely seen as irrelevant by the majority of students. Instead they seem more interested in protecting their right to "feel" *in-crisis* (as the most authentic response to their own contradictory relations to the relations of production) than in pursuing a disciplined understanding of the historical conditions

---

Editors' note: While the context of Mas'ud Zavarzadeh's essay is a paper (un)written for a theory class, the underlying issue is one of central importance to composition pedagogy: the privileging of the bourgeois subject (the "self" with its "authentic voice") as a discursive oracle transcending material culture. Expressivist rhetoric in composition studies (see Berlin, "Rhetoric and Ideology") is just the local manifestation of a global bourgeois humanism. Expressivism subverts critique of material sources of the student's "self" (the demands of late capitalist production and reproduction) by focusing entirely on the individual's *experience*—the affect and *effect* of the dominant culture. Instead, as Zavarzadeh suggests, self-knowledge must be historical; it must interrogate the *cause* of subjective experience.

of such crises. I have, therefore, stopped making such comments because students tend to use their various local narratives to effectively
shield themselves from the reach of any critique.

My decision to no longer initiate comments/critiques (beyond the
specific issues of a course) is intimately related to the prevailing social
practices . . . for instance, to point to one specific subject formation: the
historical emergence of the "cynical subject" in the moment of *pragmatism*. Recently a student who had presented him/herself as a politically interested and committed person, devoted to social change, to
transformative pedagogy, etc., etc. . . . gave me at the end of the semester—in a most cynical act—as his/her final paper a paper which
was more or less identical with the one she/he had turned in for
another class. The question for me became: How do you engage such
a cynical subject? It was quite clear that "critique" was irrelevant to
the cynical . . . the only way to engage him/her was therefore to provide her/him with a speculum: to "reflect" his/her opportunistic
narratives and pragmatic practices; let her/him repeat these narratives without any critique; let them spin on and on . . . maybe they will
be exhausted by their sheer repetition and by the stubbornness of
history, which is cruelly uninterpretable by such mock explanations.
The cynical subject cannot understand critique because he/she is
"pragmatic" . . . it seems as if the only way to "deal" with such a subject
is by "humoring" her/him . . . by accepting his/her narratives of crisis
at face value . . . by affirming her/him . . . indeed . . . by being affirmative, mimetic, and, following the code of the pedagogy of pleasure,
"supportive" and non-critique-al . . . that is to say *pragmatic*. . . .

Although, as I said, I no longer initiate "comments" (beyond the
ones that I write on the papers/assignments, as I have done on the
end comments attached to your own one-page paper), I still respond
to the requests of those who actively seek such "comments"—perhaps
as an act of resistance to cynical subjectivity. My response, in other
words, is a resistance to the prevailing cynicism which is engulfing
pedagogical practices at this moment of the postmodern. Soon, I may
find this useless as well. I have not yet. Therefore, in response to your
request, I have "commented" on your text.

I hope it is clear by now why I started with these remarks: whatever I say here is said in a specific historical context . . . I cannot "comment" on your text as if I have not already been a listener to the
narratives and practices of cynical subjects . . . I "comment" by/through
mediations . . . I "comment" with the history of these narratives around
me, which is part of my history as a pedagogue here. My discourses

are, in short, limited, and I want you to know that. . . . Taking this history into account (as well as the history of my comments/lectures/ discourses in class), I assume that in requesting my comments you were not asking me to offer "affirmative" comments (in the expected manner of bourgeois pedagogy, which regards critique-al comments to be unsupportive attacks and accusations . . . you know the stories). . . . I do not have affirmative comments . . . I cannot affirm existing things/practices (except, of course, in a parody that might exhaust the existing by infinite reflections: *yes, speculum*), for affirmation of the existing does not lead to social transformation . . . but (fortunately?) "affirmation peddling" is a popular practice here, and I am sure what you miss in my "comments" you can easily find elsewhere. . . .

I write these comments therefore very reluctantly . . . reluctantly for the reasons I have already mentioned and also because, as a pedagogue, I am not learning anything new from them—this is just another repetition . . . another rehearsal. . . . I am also reluctant because (as your text clearly shows) you are so thoroughly situated in your narratives of the subject-in-crisis that, I suspect, as you read these comments, your main interest will be to show how "wrong" they are in understanding you . . . how they do not explain *you, your own very different crisis.* . . . But I am not writing with the claim of being right about your-very-own-difference . . . I am writing to locate this difference in some broader frame of historical understanding and to show that it is, after all, not so much a "difference" as it is a "difference-effect" produced to protect the privileges of the bourgeois subject to feel *in-crisis* (whenever it encounters its contradictory practices and the pseudo-explanations for those contradictions) . . . and to hint at what makes such recurring crises so necessary. Of course, I write in the "hope" (that idealist residue without which no pedagogue can act) of providing frames of new understanding aimed at changing what is, in effect, a very reactionary form of self-explanation: a detour for self-affirmation—you-as-you-are, *in-crisis.* . . .

I am deeply disappointed that after a whole semester of intensive reading, discussing, and critiquing (not to mention the hours I spent reading and commenting on your first two papers), you have not written an essay engaging knowledges productive for social change but have chosen instead to repeat some of the most familiar clichés about subjectivity so popular at the present time among a group of students here. These students—who regard themselves to be "progressive"—deploy these banalities of bourgeois self-fashioning almost as a matter of routine in order to shield themselves from a rigorous critique of their situationality in history and their (nonreading and anti-intellectual) practices. I believe commitment to radical social change is, above all, a commitment to an untiring reading, thinking, and writing—seeking, in short, knowledges which might provide a theoretical and reliable guide for action (what Marx calls "science"). However, instead of such rigorous conceptual practices, they have concluded—like all members of their (middle, upper) class—that it is more urgent for them to probe their "experiences": after all to have "experience" (rather than abstract concepts/science) is a more readily recognizable mark of social concern. In fact, in some narratives of nonreading, "progressiveness" is deployed as a justification for nonreading. The progressive declares himself/herself opposed to a set of books he/she is to read, a course she/he is taking, an idea . . . and then concludes: because he/she is opposed to this book/idea . . . (an act which, it is implied, affirms her/his radicalism), he/she is not going to engage it. . . . This provides the cynical subject with an ideological alibi through which she/he is able to avoid the intellectual labor necessary in the production of rigorous knowledge and to substitute for it an other narrative of "I." . . . As Marx has taught, radicalism is characterized by rigorous intellectual work, by producing scientific knowledge, not by spinning anecdotes, narratives, and tales of self-affirmation (through performed crises) in the name of "progressiveness." There is nothing radical about *ignorance*. . . . It is the most reactionary stance one can possible take . . . it is the fetishization of the irrational. . . .

Experiential activism (which is ultimately a reformist mode of dealing with the social) thrives on such anti-intellectual and experiential (localizing) practices. Instead of reading, writing, and thinking in order to provide transformative (scientific) explanations and to help develop guidelines for praxis, such experientialists incessantly "talk" about what they call "subjectivity." In their discourses, "subjectivity" is deployed in a parodic and cynical manner since all it actually signifies is what is understood as "individualism," by which they mean, in practice, *"me"* . . . *"me*-here-and-now*" experiencing* the fullness of the tangible and the plenitude of the concrete . . . and, of course, nothing is more concrete than me-in-*crisis:* me-with-difference: me-with-my-glorious-distinction-from-others. . . . This reactionary move is fully supported and protected by various forms of experiential activism, whether they are modes of feminism, (post)modernism, anticolonialism . . . Green-ism. . . . They all have one, and only one, ideological function in the regime of wage-labor and capital: to commodify "difference" . . . which is finally the difference of the *experience* of the subject-in-crisis . . . a crisis whose main political outcome is to mystify the historicity and class-founded nature of subjectivity. . . .

In your text there are strong echoes of this popular mode of "talking" (i.e., non-knowing, anti-intellectual experientialism) about subjectivity with all its reactionary and counterrevolutionary consequences. Your discourse mimics the themes of *me-in-crisis* (in which "I" am authentically *experiencing* the real) and thus commodifies *experiential* "difference" . . . that is, focuses on the me. These reactionary discourses have found it beneficial to confuse an objective, scientific, rigorous historical inquiry into "subjectivity" (the construction of knowledges of the subject-in-history which could lead to change) with chatting about "individuality"—that is to say, the "experiences" of me-in-crisis (which is a pernicious form of naturalizing the dominant forms of knowing in order to keep the dominant dominating).

The goal of such a reactionary and anti-intellectual move is to substitute "experience" for "concept," "me" for "history," the "singular" for the "collective." . . . This is a move which is consistently legitimated and supported in the dominant academy. Instead of, for instance, theorizing *power* and thus producing historical knowledges about its formations and operation with an aim toward changing it, this shift from concept to experience simply declares that it is more important to "talk" about the "experience" of *power* (in the daily life of the "individual") and thus particularize it. Theorizing power in a rigorous and historically objective manner is regarded by anti-intellectual activist discourses to be abstract and remote, but me-in-the-process-of-experiencing (power) is thought to be the "real" thing. By subscribing to such a position, this reactionary activism (whose discourses saturate your text) participates in the classic idealist privileging of the *effects* of social practices, thereby blurring their *causes:* whereas "effects" are *experienced,* causes have to be *known* through *concepts.* (Remember Marx: "In the analysis of economic forms [i.e., producing knowledges of social practices], moreover, neither microscope nor chemical reagents are of use. The force of *abstraction* must replace both" [90; my emphasis].) Your text is exemplary in this respect: you continually foreground the effect (crisis) rather than the "cause." When you do attempt to provide a "cause," you offer what is basically a pseudo-cause—it is actually more an act of "blaming"— that is, another "experience" (they did it to me by forcing me to have "bad" habits)—than an analysis. It is a move which simply postpones scientific and objective inquiry into the real causes that you avoid. . . . You may wish to put more pressure on your own contradictory social practices which are located in the space of "talking" (experiencing) rather than "reading" (knowing).

I am using these two terms, "talking" and "reading" (as I have already hinted in my references to Marx), as two opposing structures of knowledge. By "talking," I mean the practice of "relating" to the social through pleasure/immediate feelings/experience. By "reading," I mean conceptuality/history/abstraction—science. For experientialists, it is more "real" to "experience" *crisis* than to know the conditions that lead to such a *crisis*. Some feminist theories have, in fact, acquired their authority by substituting *experience* for *conceptuality*, thus setting in motion diverse forms of anti-intellectualism which are celebrated as a mark of the distance of the authentic woman-subject-in-crisis from the authority of abstract masculinity. . . . Reading, thinking, writing, and the production of transformative concepts are, therefore, systematically discouraged in these discourses . . . instead an endless self-narration, anecdotes, autobiographical accounts . . . of the experience of power-by-the-subject-of-femininity (i.e., the "effect" of power, not its "causes") are foregrounded as marks of the authenticity of the subject in its "real"ity . . . this is, of course, the "real"ity of ideology, and its self-evidence is the "natural"ness effect of the ideological.

"Talking," I might add, is the privileged strategy of what I will call the "pedagogy of pleasure," while *"writing"* is the major conceptual means of intervention in the "pedagogy of critique." Let me explain.

When pedagogy violates the all-too-familiar code of "learning is fun" or "knowledge is neutral" (as I am doing in this letter), and instead proposes that education is an interventionary act for social change, it is automatically branded strict and authoritarian. This belief is based on the assumptions of a mode of teaching that I marked as the "pedagogy of pleasure." In the pedagogy of pleasure, the subject of knowledge is assumed to be a "unique," "independent," and "sovereign" person, who reads according to his/her individual imagination, experience, vision and originality, and all pedagogy has to do is to help her/him "discover" these "natural" and "given" qualities in himself/herself more fully. In other words, the purpose of liberal education is to make the student a "singular" well-rounded, free person. However, what is regarded as the "freedom" of the individual subject is not "natural" but is an ideology effect: the dominant ideology posits the individual as free in order that he/she may freely consent to the ruling relations of production which, through the social division of labor, produce and maintain (economic) inequality. The pedagogy of critique, in contrast to the pedagogy of pleasure, works not to enhance the pleasure of learning and the "freedom" of the individual but to produce knowledges that are effective in transforming the existing society into a society of genuine (economic and not simply discursive) equality. The focus of such a pedagogy is therefore on "collectivity," not "individuality"; on "knowledge," not "pleasure"; on "critique," not "experience"; on "social emancipation," not "private freedom" . . . its goal, in short, is to transform the culturally produced, reified consciousness which prevents the subject of pedagogy from realizing other social and political possibilities. Pedagogy is part of class struggle.

This, among other things, means that the subject of knowledge/ student in the pedagogy of critique is regarded to be a socially constructed subject and not a "naturally" given free individual (as traditionalist humanists assume) or a subject produced by the libidinal force of ahistorical desires (as poststructuralists propose). The pedagogy of critique argues that what is regarded to be the free self or differential subject in the pedagogy of pleasure is in fact an imaginary identity produced by the dominant ideology. It is part of the operation of ideology to place people in positions where they think of themselves as self-constituting and free so that they "freely" conclude that the way things *are* is how they *ought* to be and thus preserve the status quo. The pedagogy of critique seeks to make the student aware (through ideology critique) of the working of ideology and to place him in the position of a critical (not pleasureful) reader of texts—one who can then recognize (by producing historical knowledge of the social totality) the different ways social relations are organized in order to act on them. The pedagogy of critique is, *of course,* also an act of pleasure: the pleasure of emancipation from established views and of participation in the construction of a new world free from class, gender, and race exploitation.

In your text you (unconsciously?) identify the project of pedagogy with the pedagogy of pleasure. Consequently, rather than engaging concepts and producing transformative knowledges, what you actually "talk" about, when you began to talk about something you call "pedagogy," is an account of your own *experience* in a pedagogical situation . . . me-in-crisis-in-the-classroom. . . . This is not a theoretical account of pedagogy, this is autobiography and, like all autobiographies, it acquires its authority by positing the subject of experience as the object of knowledge. The goal of such autobiographical accounts *(me-in-crisis-in-the-classroom)* is to justify the *me* in its present form, immunize it from history, and say, in effect, this is not *my* pedagogy, I want *another* form of learning . . . concluding that there are other forms of pedagogy. *This* pedagogy is producing *crisis* in me . . . I cannot write . . . I need *affirmation* of *me-in-crisis.* . . . You repeat all these *topoi* of the subject-in-crisis . . . as if any of this was a new revelation. . . . Pedagogy (and the shift in the topic of your paper from abstract knowledge to the experience of knowledge in the name of pedagogy is quite telling here) is a structure of abstract concepts, not simply a memoir of *me-in-crisis-in-the-classroom* (as you seem to think) . . . it is this substitution of memoir for knowledge that eventually trivializes radical pedagogy (as a critique-al science of knowing) and reduces it to a mere game of "changing the furniture in the classroom" in order to make the *experience* of power (in the classroom) more democratic, more tolerable—in short, invisible—for the bourgeois subject. . . .

These series of substitutions (experience/concept: talking/reading: letter/formal paper) are the "common sense" of the pedagogy of pleasure. They are among the most popular pedagogical practices because they are so necessary for the naturalization of existing social relations. They are the most effective form of resistance to concepts. Conceptual knowledge (revolutionary science) is the knowledge of social totality. Experience is the ultimate form of feeling locality and individuality. "Crisis" in the discourses of bourgeois subjectivity is the site for the manifestation of self in its most "authentic" local moment. Such shifts—from *concept* to *experience,* from *knowing* to *crisis* (ignorance)—give the person an ideological alibi to evade confronting the historical and socioeconomic structures of the subject in history and instead produce anecdotes of the "experience" of the subject-in-crisis. . . .

You share the assumptions of the reactionary discourses on subjectivity that "crisis" makes all practices impossible—thus one who is in crisis cannot write a formal paper (cannot produce historical/conceptual knowledge). However, she/he can easily compose a "letter" narrating his/her crisis. To be *in-crisis,* you seem to say, one suddenly discovers one's difference; a difference that puts an end to all activities such as conceptualizing/writing/knowing . . . in these moments one can only *experience* . . . but if you read (as I do) the letters of the subjects-in-crisis that I get every semester around the time final papers are due, you realize how all these *differences* are similar, and how they are, in their predictable similarities, even stereotypical. These differences are all versions of *sameness* . . . they are all alike, which, among other things, means they are constructed to fulfill certain ideological effects . . . above all, as I said, the effect of the priority and firstness of *experience* and an attack on the concept (knowledge of totality) . . . they are, in short, a particular historical form of keeping the existing social relations intact, and their current particular manifestation is a form of bourgeois anti-intellectualism that you see among the students I referred to. The irony, however, is that these reactionary discourses are put forth as authentic, activist, and progressive practices. This is the formation of what I have called the *"cynical* subject": the subject who puts itself forth as "radical" but deploys the discourses of activism/radicalism only to achieve pragmatic goals (*"pragmatic"*: successful within the existing frames and structures), the subject who knows what he/she is acting on is a convenient belief (not the truth), but she/he acts on it as if he/she did not know that the convenient belief is the effect of ideology (and thus an alienated reality; a nontruth) . . . she/he knows and yet does it anyway . . . this is what Sloterdijk and, following him, Zizek, call "enlightened false consciousness": "one knows the false-hood very well, one is well aware of a particular interest hidden behind an ideological universality, but still one does not renounce it" (29).

But only when *crisis* is staged for the benefit of *me* does it lead to the erasure of praxis. *Crisis*, as a historical process—the eruptions of social contradictions—produces new possibilities . . . it is always inaugurating novel modes of engagement with the social. Crisis, as historical process, is always enabling . . . it is the necessary precondition of revolutionary transformations . . . but such an oppositional understanding of crisis is not legitimate in the pedagogy of pleasure since it foregrounds contradictions and forces a resolution of contradictions—not by narrating them ("talking"), but by praxis, by recognizing that *crisis* is always the mark of an "excess" that cannot be solved/absorbed within the existing frames of class relations, by recognizing (in the case of all these subjects-in-crisis performances) that one's subjectivity is, after all, *not* one's own . . . this is, of course, the last thing that the subject-in-crisis wishes to do . . . such a recognition re-situates the subject and annuls all its protective narratives . . . it brings back the *concept* . . . knowledge-as-social, as-historical.

The letter you have sent me (with some changes here and there) is identical to other letters I have received on the subject-in-crisis. If I had the time to put into my computer and mix the most recent letter I have received of a subject-in-crisis with your own, I am not sure you would be able to tell the difference between the two. This similarity does not mean that what you say is not *real* . . . it means that the *reality* of what you say is the reality of ideology and you should resist it and not make it the basis of your (non)praxis as you have done in this instance. Had you encountered the crisis as the effect of the historicity of your subjectivity and not as the naturality of your being-as-such you could have deployed it to re-understand the contradictions that have brought it about rather than indulge in the pseudo-explanations (blame games), anecdotes, autobiographical meditations—that are the luxury of the leisured class—etc., etc. You could, for instance, have re-understood your social practices to explain the *crisis*, not use the *crisis* to explain *you* (away) and thus erase your historicity, the absence of autonomy in your subjectivity. After all, the most ideologically important role that crisis plays in such moments is that it implies the autonomy of the subject: crisis, in bourgeois theory, is seen as the fisure that testifies to the everlasting gap between the self and history.

But you need to deploy the *crisis* in order to mystify the social "causes" of the actions of the subject (-in-crisis). You seem to say, for instance, that you are in such crisis that you sit in front of your computer without being able to write the paper. The reason for being unable to write the paper is a rather simple social (non)practice of yours: you do not *read* . . . you have not read the books which were the focus of our discussions and critique during the semester. You, in other words, have not labored to acquire the knowledges which are necessary for writing the paper—knowledges which are the enabling conditions for praxis. This is such a simple re-understanding of crisis as the effect of your social practices (and not as their cause) that the dominant frames of intelligibility inhibit even uttering it. The ruling academy has privileged the pedagogy of pleasure to such an extent that a materialist explanation such as the one I have hinted at looks quite out of place, looks, in fact, quite "crude."

Why have you not read the books? Because the social practice of reading, the intellectual labor involved in producing concepts . . . is disruptive of the pleasures of "talking." Reading/writing/thinking require discipline—the *other* of pleasure . . . *pleasure* is the last privilege that the white middle class person would give up; it is the mark of its autonomy; the *excessive* (i.e., the crisis-y). . . . By the way, why is it that all the letters I receive on the crisis of subjectivity are from white (upper-) middle-class students? I have never encountered a person of color who allowed herself/himself the luxury of being *in-crisis* . . . these luxuries are all part of the class privileges of the white (upper) middle class; something you may wish to think about. . . .

I am, of course, not denying the relevance of the subject . . . what I am opposing is the use of the subject (especially the subject-in-crisis) as an alibi for reducing the *subject* to a *me* and then deploying *me* as the limit text: nobody can critique *me* because unless you are *me* (which you obviously are not) how could you even know what *me* means . . . etc., etc. I am, however, aware how difficult such a shift in explaining the subject is and how unpopular advocating it is in the moment of the (post)modern. The pedagogue who refuses to found her/his practices on the notion of the subject-of-knowledge as an autonomous origin of reality-as-experience or who even enunciates his/her refusal and argues for the pedagogy of critique is quickly turned into the "other" of humanity itself. Such a pedagogue is the monster, the master, the totalitarian, the dogmatic . . . you know the epithets. . . .

These comments, as I have already hinted, will be read by the pedagogues of pleasure (of the humanist right as well as the poststructuralist center) as hostile, unhelpful, and, above all, as "crude." I understand pedagogy in a rather "crude" way: as an intervention in the dominant subtleties of bourgeois pedagogy. It is too late in the century, and there are too many urgencies to be anything but "crude." . . . Fortunately (?) there is no dearth of "subtle" pedagogies around . . . pedagogies that have "complex," "nuanced," and "flexible" discourses on the *subject-in-crisis* and affiliated matters. "Crude" pedagogy is a post-subtle inquiry into how knowledges are produced and disseminated as the effect of the social contradictions of historical societies that deploy the subject-as-*trager* in order to "change" the world. This is the limit question: what is the function of pedagogy in the late twentieth century? To change the world or to give pleasure to the subject. Please do not be subtle; do not say: Both! Let us be unsubtle and start "with taking sides" (Marx, *Early Writings* 208) . . . let us forget "both" and begin the task of a transformative pedagogy. . . .

16

Contested Terms, Competing Practices: Language Education and Social Change

Mary Beth Hines_____

> Whatever "the real" is, it is discursive.
> —Patti Lather, *Getting Smart*

As a former composition instructor and current teacher educator, I struggle to enable students to connect our classroom discussions and activities with larger movements for social justice. But frequently I envision the pedagogical and the political as mutually exclusive spheres, as a discussion of inequities supplementing, rather than transforming, classroom inquiry. Hoping to better understand how discursive practices could be linked to social change, I, a middle-class Anglo feminist researcher, became a nonparticipant observer in an undergraduate literature classroom taught by Richard, a Marxist instructor with strong feminist commitments who believed that teaching and language practices were always already implicated in issues of social justice.

Resonating with the larger social order, Richard's classroom practices evinced a complex relationship to the oppositional and the institutional, for Richard's teaching practices were characterized by efforts, as he said, to "expose" students to "alternative ways of seeing" without "imposing" his particular perspectives on students. But conscious of the contradictions of working within and against the institution which employed him to teach "literature," he invited students to write and discuss ads, media, cartoons, and other texts. These efforts culminated in the production of "academic discourse" which reflected his rejection of "normal" reading and writing practices and contributed to efforts to create a more equitable world. Richard articulated a pedagogical approach that not only enabled but reflected his commitments to equality, questioning power relations while acknowledging his own privilege as an Anglo middle-class male college instructor. In this chapter I hope to pinpoint the effective strategies Richard developed to promote ideological critique, those Bennett describes as mechanisms of "defamiliarization" or tactics designed to distance individuals from the dominant ideologies in order to "see" their workings (*Formalism* 21). In so doing, I hope to enable teachers to link language education to cultural critique. Because the obligation to work for social change required, in Richard's view, an interrogation and transformation of key pedagogical concepts, we will begin with his beliefs before tracing their manifestations in discursive practices.

The "Free Market" vs. "Alternative Ways of Seeing" the Classroom

An Englishman specializing in nineteenth-century colonialism and landscapes of imperialism, Richard had taught this literature course four times prior to this semester. In a series of interviews throughout the semester, Richard described himself as an oppositional instructor whose ultimate aim was not to "simply" or "freely" discuss and write about literature, not to make the individual a better reader and writer. His ambition was "to disturb," to challenge the dominant powers in our society:

> Students have been taught to see the world in the way that newspapers, their parents, the schools, and church represent. They have a certain way of seeing that they are told is a natural, commonsense way of seeing. Underlying that there are certain assumptions. What I want the students to do . . . is to question those assumptions.

In order to expedite that analysis Richard practiced ideological critique in the classroom, borrowing many concepts from Althusser, who says that ideology is a representation of "the imaginary relation of individuals to the real conditions of existence" (162). Individuals perceive their relations to the mode of production, in our case capitalism, through the lens offered by the dominant ideology, one which typically occludes the exploitation required to maintain the forces and relations of production. It is then an "imaginary relation," as Althusser says. As such, it does not "correspond to reality" (162), so it can be contrasted to "the real conditions of existence."

Richard hoped to introduce students to these concepts by juxtaposing the "advertised world" with the "real world," as he said. Central to this ideological critique was a focus on the constructed nature of language and texts. He explained,

> The main thing I want to stress is that we ourselves, as readers, as people, and the text are social constructs. . . . If it's a social construction, then who constructed it, what's it doing, and what are the elements going into this construction?

In other words, certain practices may appear to be universal and timeless or "normal" but actually represent the "interests" of a dominant power. As an oppositional instructor, Richard hopes to dislodge assumptions about the "natural," exposing the power relations which give rise to and perpetuate such beliefs.

Richard asserted that ideological critique was a first step toward changing the conditions of oppression in the world:

> Ideally I would like students to look at the society they are living in and at capitalism and say, "Ah, this is a system that is exploiting me or other people." I really don't feel students will go that far. So I see myself as creating a debate, giving them an alternative view so that they can choose.

Because students, as with most people, "misrecognize," as Althusser says, the ideologies which exploit them (183), they do not perceive the collusion of textual and social practices in perpetuating conditions of oppression. So Richard, adamantly committed to social change, understands his role to be that of "creating a debate."

Offering a pedagogical corollary of the challenge to "the dominant view," Richard refused "traditional" teaching practices that likewise failed to embrace the standpoints of the oppressed:

> I think the way that most people see the classroom is as kind of like a free market. You can throw things out, ideas will be circulated freely, and stuents will have a free voicing of their ideas. Then the best ideas, the best products, will win out. I just do not subscribe to that because it ignores that there are dominant ways of seeing. There is an ideology which is dominant.

Proliferating largely unchecked, masquerading under the guise of "free voicing," the dominant ideology flourishes—until the critical citizen challenges it, Richard argues, echoing Althusser. Because those ostensibly "free" discussions then typically issue from a single ideological position—that sanctioned by the dominant group in society— they are not, ultimately, "free." Such a view departs from the common valorization of "voice" and "free" expression which prevails in the liberal humanist pedagogical and composition theory literature, as neomarxist educators point out (see Aronowitz and Giroux; Giroux).

In promoting challenges to the normal, Richard made explicit his own responses to texts and social issues in discussion, conceding that he did have "a particular ideology and a particular agenda, and that's okay." Unlike mainstream teachers who refused to acknowledge the "interested" nature of all discourse, Richard felt that this move was superior if only because it was "more honest with his students." He made explicit what was often left unspoken: that all teachers have agendas; even those who claim to be unbiased have, in fact, an agenda of neutrality which by default reinforces the status quo.

While he worked to "undermine hierarchy" in the larger social order, Richard performed as "definitely an authority" in the classroom. This contradiction was necessary to "get students" to discuss issues that they would not discuss otherwise," he asserted. As an oppositional teacher, he considered himself not a more expert reader or writer but a more experienced subversive. His authority emanated from his "greater access to oppositional discourses."

And although Richard acknowledged a goal to challenge the status quo, he nonetheless stressed the importance of respecting the beliefs of his students who were equally committed to maintaining it. Convinced there were "no wrong answers," just answers which were steeped to varying degrees in "the dominant view," he developed pedagogical strategies to "connect" with students who supported the status quo:

> I think the best way of doing it is to take everyone's comments as legitimate, which they are. And then discuss those comments and try to show where they are coming from. What are their effects? What is their history? If you make clear that those ideas are not their own, that they have been given those, then sometimes the students are willing to let go of those ideas. Okay, it's nothing to do with me; it's not my problem, not my fault, you know; I was given it by my church, my parents, my society.

Here Richard outlines a tactic which defuses confrontation by concentrating on the social construction of individuals. If immersion in dominant ideologies is a "given," then the teacher or other students can point to the pull of the dominant ideologies, rather than to the failures of individuals, when talking about commitments to those entrenched and "received" views.

It was because Richard enabled students to understand the "interested" nature of beliefs and practices that his classroom was more "student-centered" than those mainstream classrooms which claimed this term, he asserted. Believing that he had his students' ultimate best interests at heart when he exposed the ways in which they and others were exploited, Richard reconfigured "student-centered" learning to reflect the dynamics of power relations, claiming the classroom as a sphere in which students learned to challenge and to change those practices which exploited them.

Yet in crafting a "student-centered process" approach which made available sources of exploitation, his discourse carried persuasive overtones:

> I have to "sell" ideas they are not familiar with. So I don't feel I can just throw out ideas and have a "free" discussion, just kind of "pick up" on things, because they're trained to see things in a certain way that I want to disrupt. I have to work very hard to persuade them to see through to my way of seeing.

Prodding students into ideological critique, Richard believes that students can distance themselves from the mechanisms of hegemonic ideologies. But part of that "process" involves persuading students to accept the new information he presents—creating a tension between "exposing" students to different perspectives and "imposing" on them his own commitments to social justice, between respecting their positions and changing them: "They can bring up anything, but the way they talk about it is what I'm structuring."

In order to galvanize this critique, Richard stressed priorities that mirrored those of many post-Althusserian and post-marxist theorists (e.g., Barrett; Bennett, *Outside;* Hartsock) who analyze the synergistic effects of gender, race, and cultural inequities on class struggle. We might expect, because Richard was a Marxist, that class would be the initial and exclusive focus of analysis; however, as a conscientious teacher, Richard tapped his students' prior understanding and experience. Consequently, he initiated students into this "reading formation" (Bennett, "Texts" 3) through a consideration of gender oppression rather than class struggle. Class was "invisible" to his typically middle-class students just as, in this predominately Anglo institution and state, most students "didn't have a personal relationship to issues of race." Despite his focus on feminist issues, Richard declined to be called a feminist or a Marxist-feminist, viewing male participation in feminist struggles as a form of patriarchal cooptation.

We can locate in Richard's remarks emergent tensions and contradictions, signalling the ways in which Marxism and mainstream pedagogical priorities alternately dovetailed and diverged. Because students came to his class blind to those "alternative ways of seeing," Richard felt compelled to perform as the "authority" or "critic" in the classroom. While he claimed a "student-centered" approach, he felt equally obligated to dictate the terms of students' "best" interests by legislating texts, writing topics, and issues for discussion. Likewise, he had to "sell" the less familiar standpoints of the oppressed, hoping to persuade and not "impose" his own commitments to those subjugated by ostensibly "natural" beliefs and practices. Yet, as the next section reveals, these strategies were necessary to enable students to engage in ideological critique.

To Beat: "As in to Beat One's Wife": Demythologizing the "Innocence" of Language

We can see the ways in which the classroom became a site for ideological struggle in a discussion which followed an investigation of the images of women in advertising. Tracing Richard's interventions, we can analyze how he negotiated that fine line between imposing and exposing, noting the effects of his tactics on students. On the heels of a discussion of misogyny in media, Richard assigned an excerpt from *Out of Focus* (Davies, Dickey, and Stratford). The editors interrogate a seemingly "innocent" definition found in the *Oxford English Dictionary*, which I provide here because of its importance to the subsequent discussion:

> Its definition of the verb "to beat" is truly unbelievable (or is it) in these supposedly enlightened days: "to beat—to strike repeatedly, as in to beat one's wife." Not only does this show the presumed sex of the reader (at least one half of the population does not have a wife), but it also clearly demonstrates that beating "one's" woman is an acceptable way for men to behave. Would it not otherwise have been struck from the "thinking man's bible?" (98)

Greg, an outspoken critic of Richard's ideas, initiated class discussion by citing this passage, reiterating themes he recorded in his journal:

> On page 98 talking about wife beating, "not only does that show the presumed sex of the reader, but it clearly demonstrates that beating one's wife is an acceptable way for men to behave." I can't draw that conclusion from what's found in the dictionary.

While Greg questions the relations between language and cultural practice, Richard attempts to "sell" Greg the view that the "commonplace" and "definitive meaning of the word" is complicitous with the perpetuation of wife beating:

> Why would they put that in the dictionary? It makes it very commonplace. As in beating one's wife. Like it happens all the time, right? And the dictionary is supposed to be the definitive meaning of the word.

In short, Richard seeks to expose how, through its function as a dictionary example, the term is "naturalized," as Marxists say, or made to seem legitimate.

Later, he encouraged Greg and others to understand that a "mental" concept, such as a seemingly innocent example in a dictionary, resonated in "real" world effects. He asked his students to situate their conversation amidst "the facts":

> You put this in the context of women's violence, of battery, wife abuse as a leading health threat and you can add statistics which are horrendous, but one in four women have been raped in their lives. So you say, "how come our culture allows this to happen, and how does the culture play into this?" Half of all the rape cases don't even go to court.

Here Richard links the circulation of beliefs and values to social practices, those which are both "damaging to women's health" and yet "commonplace," as he emphasizes. He then follows up the "facts" with probing questions:

> Why does it happen? It's domestic violence. That means beating one's wife. They have shelters all over every city for women who leave their husbands from beating. Why does that happen?

What were the effects of his interventions on students? While some "bought" his critique, others registered disagreement, reinforcing Richard's belief that counterhegemonic consensus was a utopian ideal:

> John: The author sends subtle unconscious messages which shape our attitudes.
>
> Jack: But a dictionary isn't the place where you make comments.

But students moved beyond the dictionary, "widening the debate" to cultural critique, as Richard had hoped, interrogating the roles that cultural artifacts played in reinforcing and contradicting "the messages being sold to us" by that dictionary:

> Tammy: When you're little you don't hear them say to a little girl, "You're not supposed to hit little boys." But it comes to that; little boys aren't

supposed to hit girls, but they play with GI Joes and stuff. So the whole thing is that they get those messages when they're little, from basketball players or cartoon characters, who are mostly male. A kid is too little to say, "Yeah, but that's not the way real life is." That's the point of the cartoon character. It is directed toward little kids, and that's the way life goes on.

Jim: When we look in the dictionary, what you see is what you believe. That's what you're taught. I think that what they're trying to say in this one quote is that something like that in there almost condones it. Like it's okay. Like a message if you're male it's something that is done or is okay to be done. It's tied in with a definition. It's just a message. But it's there.

Stressing the lessons "directed towards little kids," Tammy and Jim suggest the power of the dominant group to coerce citizens into its beliefs and practices, what Althusser describes as "interpellation," a process whereby the dominant ideology "hails" people to think and behave in particular ways (173).

Richard also prompted students to investigate how the ideological overlapped with the economic and political spheres as well. It was Richard's question, "Why don't women hit men over the head with weapons?" and a student's corollary, "Well, there are shelters, and why don't women just leave?" which triggered such analysis. Jim commented,

The point I was going to make is that most women are trapped financially. They've got five kids; the guy comes back and beats the wife. What are her choices? If she leaves, she has to pick up the kids. They go with her. She wouldn't leave them with him because he's violent. How does she survive? For rich people, the woman may become accustomed to a certain lifestyle. He beats her. I think a lot of times violence like that is carried over from one generation to another. The male sees that in his father, some violence against his mother, but he gets away with it. The kid sees the results. They stay together. They make up. Everything's okay. It carries on.

Accentuating the multiple messages issued through ideology by means of the media and the culture, messages reinforced by economic conditions, Jim stresses the interaction of capital and patriarchy structuring a woman's "choices" of response to domestic violence. Because the father "gets away" with violence against the mother, Jim argues that the legal system works in conjunction with this misogynistic ideology to subordinate women.

As a result of these interactions, Greg issued a partial retraction:

> I sort of find it degrading women, but some people do beat their wives, and it does explain the word *beat*. Striking repeatedly. But as I see it, they're putting the word *beat* in a certain context, and I don't think they should have used it. But at the same time I don't necessarily think it is a statement that it's okay to beat your wife.

Here Greg acknowledges that the inclusion of the example of wife beating is suspect, although he still believes that the dictionary is reporting, rather than instantiating, misogyny. He is, it might be argued, responding to the "alternative views" but refusing the indictment of society which Richard proposed. Providing an index to Richard's ability to "expose" the standpoints of the oppressed without "imposing" his beliefs on students, Greg's comments offer a counterpoint to Richard's views.

Noting that the women were silent, Richard asked for a woman to respond to this issue. Linda offered a rejoinder to Greg:

> By being in the dictionary it's something that people look at every day; they are stating that it's commonplace. You open a dictionary every day. If you read "beating one's wife," it may seem that that's what happens.

Several students offered new understandings of the ways in which they were implicated in these issues. Linda confided,

> But, see, reading it as I did, I felt like, geez, they're yelling at me and I didn't do anything. Yeah, I read those magazines, and I felt guilty from the exploitation too. I knew you said in the beginning that it was a really angry article, but I felt it was directed at society as a whole. I could see how men would feel, but even reading it as a female I felt guilt too.

Linda reveals the contradictory positions of women in a patriarchal society, serving alternately as challengers to and transmitters of patriarchy. Recognizing how she is responsible for reinforcing her own oppression, she expresses a "guilt" about that role.

And Jack, wrestling with the implications of this "new" information about gender and media, struggled to comprehend how best to demonstrate his commitment:

> I think they have a valid point; I can see the point. But my question is, How are we supposed to respond to the knowledge that we have? How are we supposed to change ourselves and our attitudes? How do we go about doing that?

Richard, sensitive to the burgeoning commitments that often accompanied a newfound awareness of exploitation, responded also:

> ... I don't think there are any ready made solutions. But I think the biggest step is to be aware of this stuff. . . . The next step is to tend to your own ways of seeing and to tell other people to change their ways of seeing.

Here Richard uses this occasion to shift students away from blame and toward productive action, nudging students toward a greater awareness of and challenge to oppressive "ways of seeing" and behaving in the world.

In this section we have witnessed Richard's strategies and their effects on student discussion. Students reinforced, refined, and challenged Greg's "normal" view of the dictionary, just as they likewise aligned with and contested Richard's "alternative" assertions. This multiplicity attested to Richard's ability to negotiate between "exposing" students to "alternative ways of seeing" and "imposing" his own views on students, tensions which coursed through written communication, as we will see.

The Role of Writing in Ideological Critique

Consistent with his role in discussion, Richard viewed himself as "selling" counterhegemonic positions. For instance, in response to the reading and discussion of *Out of Focus*, Jim wrote:

> In this piece while I agreed with some of what was being said, I felt these were extremist views. Of course, the authors would say that this is a typical response since I am male and all my life I've seen women subjugated in this matter. As with the Chapter Three piece, the authors paint a picture of a grand scheme of males to dominate women and keep them in their place by making them sex objects. From a purely argumentative viewpoint I offer this question: If the way men treat women is so abnormal, why has it been that way since the beginning of time? I don't have any answers, but it's definitely something to think about.

Particularly compelling in Jim's remarks is the voice, one marked by engagement and struggle with the issues on the table. While he doesn't "buy" the position of the writers, he acknowledges his own collusion in women's oppression. Furthermore, he doesn't understand (yet) the constructed nature of the history of women's oppression—in other words, why it's "been that way since the beginning of time."

Richard's comments on Jim's journal provided a scaffolding to prompt ideological critique:

> Jim, this is an interesting question. May I suggest two ways to this question: (1) Destroying the planet we live on is also abnormal and began centuries ago—why do we do it? It has a great deal to do with profit, making money. (2) What potentially lies behind the question is: Since it happened since the beginning of time—which, there is proof, it hasn't—isn't it therefore natural? Both sort of play into an expectation to do nothing even though we are faced with terrifying statistics of violence against women and blatant job discrimination. (Why does that happen? Does it have to do with the way men see women?) One has to ask what lies behind and what are the effects of violence, GI Joe, Barbie dolls, pornography, idealized models in the media, infinite beauty aids, dieting, etc., etc.

I have recorded the entire response because it glosses several recurrent themes and pedagogical strategies characteristic of Richard's approach. Richard opens his remarks with an analogy, hoping to connect with the student through a perhaps more familiar (and less threatening) experience: the ever-present tendencies toward destruction of the planet. This analogy, then, emerges out of Richard's dual commitments—to teach students about issues of social justice and to connect with their ultimate "best" interests. In exposing how practices which recur over time are not necessarily "natural" or "normal," Richard hopes to sensitize this student to gender justice, underscoring the historical nature of ostensibly ahistorical practices. Finally, in suggesting links between "ways of seeing" and economic policies of "blatant job discrimination," Richard encourages students to understand how representations contribute to oppressive social practices.

Several weeks after this discussion Richard invited students to write "formal" papers about this and other topics. He viewed the papers as the "culminating" events in the course, the "most gratifying" of his experiences in the classroom because they offered a gauge of his students' burgeoning abilities to expose and challenge the dominant ideologies. Keenly aware of the potential for sabotage by students who wrote for the teacher-as-examiner, he nevertheless "structured" the options for ideological critique, arguing that even the ubiquitous teacher-pleaser was nevertheless required to think about social change:

1. Choose an ad which you think one of the short stories we have read is concerned with, i.e., the story criticizes, refers to, or reinforces similar images and messages.

2. John Berger states that *"men act and women appear."*
   a) Relate this to a short story we have discussed.
   b) Discuss one or two themes from the article on women and the media from *Out of Focus* and how these themes are reflected and/or reinforced by a short story that we have read.
3. We have seen how people can be manipulated by language; how a certain word or description can control a person's life and way of seeing the world. Consider, for example: witch, mother, wife, foreigner, innocence (in relation to women), husband, progress. Discuss in relation to one or more of the stories how a character is controlled by (or tries to resist) a label and any numerous related connotations (other social codes).

Richard's prompts offered students an occasion to extend ideological critique by linking "social messages" to language, ads, and texts.

Perhaps because students were discussing war poems when the invitation was issued, most students wrote about ideologies of war in response to the last prompt. It was ironically Greg, the outspoken critic of Richard's "ways of seeing," who wrote the paper which received the highest grade in the class. Citing Baez's "Where Have All the Flowers Gone?" a popular anti–Vietnam War song, as an epigraph, Greg proceeded to investigate war "messages":

> Yes, indeed, when will we ever learn? Twenty years ago, when the Vietnam War was at its height, the draft in full force, and student deferments (my shield from the war until then) had just been canceled; I waited for my number to come up. All of the pressures that come into play when one is about to be called to fight for one's country were upon me. Just as Albert Lichtenstein, in his poem, "Leaving for the Front," knew that he was going to die, I knew that I would be drafted into war, if not to die then surely injured or emotionally scarred for life. But where Lichtenstein felt "There's nothing wrong with me," in that he was "glad to leave" I felt there was something wrong with me; I was not glad to leave. Why should I go to a strange land of rice paddies and jungles, to fight for people I don't even know or really even care about? Why should I believe in the so called "Domino Theory" and the need to stop the Communists now before they can creep closer to our shores? I started to examine my options. I could resist the draft, burn my card, and end up in jail—maybe safer than Nam. The conscientious objector angle was a possibility. I even thought about fleeing to Canada. Unlike Town, the soldier in Wilfred Owen's poem, "Disabled," who "asked to join" and then "wonders why" in a retrospective manner only after dismemberment, I was not asking and certainly wondering why, before hand in a prospective manner. I felt guilty. Guilty for even

thinking of not going and guilty for pondering the alternatives. What were the forces that made me feel this guilt and feel there was something wrong with me? I believe these are the same forces that keep the links between flowers, young girls, young men, soldiers, and graveyards intact.

Greg's paper suggested that the Vietnam pro-war ideology "hailed" him and other men by calling them "heroes," although the ideology worked against the best interests of those who returned in a casket or a wheelchair. Greg's paper provided a powerful critique of the pro-war ideologies, rendering his own experience as a subject within and then against this ideology. He explored how those war ideologies became articulated in institutions, social practices, and cultural artifacts of World War I society, as well as his own, ending his analysis with a critique of racism in the military.

Yet it was because Greg had been, on the one hand, the most outspoken critic of Richard's counterhegemonic views and, on the other, the most articulate writer of ideological critique that Greg brokered a complex and contradictory relationship to the dominant indeologies. Locating and rejecting the mechanisms for perpetuating the dominant views of war and race but accepting, to some degree, those for women, he disclosed himself as a "split" subject working within and against systems of domination.

Moreover, his relationship with the "dominant" authority in the classroom, the teacher, appeared to evoke contradiction. While he vociferously countered Richard's assertions in discussion, he reinforced Richard's counterhegemonic stances in this paper. When I asked Greg in an interview to explain this contradiction, he said he worried about the "impressionable" undergraduates who might unwittingly comply with Richard's politics, so he felt compelled to challenge Richard's views in discussions, offering alternatives to the alternative views. He did not worry about pleasing Richard in the paper or in the class because he did not believe Richard would penalize those who disagreed with him. Greg suggested again the tenuous line between "imposing" and "exposing" the teacher's views on students.

Towards "Pedagogically Correct" Opposition

Throughout this chapter we have seen the ways in which Richard refigured pedagogical principles, extending student understandings of ideology through discussion and writing. While his "control" of discussion and writing topics contradicted mainstream notions of "student-centered" learning and expressivist process approaches to composition, and the focus on "selling" ideas stood in counterpoint to his Marxist orientation, Richard felt morally obligated to "structure" student learning and thinking because students would not "freely" think about the ways in which oppression was naturalized.

While some may argue that any "control" of classroom discourse reinstates oppression, Richard's interventions were inherently necessary because they provoked the defamiliarization required to initiate students into ideological critique. They also provided the scaffolding needed to achieve more complex analyses. Yet, as the interaction with Greg suggested, Richard's explicit "structuring" of the discourse made him vulnerable to charges of "imposing" his views on those "impressionable" undergraduates as he zealously sought to "expose" and "sell" his own beliefs. It may be that this tension underscores the importance of what feminists call "self-subversive self-reflection"—an interrogation of practices by challenging the assumptions on which they rest. For teachers this might take the form of constructing a pedagogical framework and then questioning its very foundations.

While Richard did not self-consciously assess his approach, it was Greg who revealed its importance:

> He got me thinking about things I probably wouldn't have thought about, like with the advertisements. . . . I can guarantee that I wouldn't have seen it before.

Greg acknowledges Richard's influence, yet his ongoing critique of Richard's interventions suggests more questions than answers: How do tactics for subverting power relations inadvertently reinforce them if perceived by students as "imposing?" How might pedagogical strategies simultaneously enable and mirror resistance to domination? How are we to gauge the "effectiveness" of such pedagogical strategies, those designed to enact and produce a more just world?

These are the questions which issue from my experience in Richard's class, questions which resist an easy closure to this chapter or to our collective work in the classroom. Hoping to learn from Richard how to negotiate those many competing and often contradictory impulses which he so artfully managed, I have attempted in this chapter to reconcile my own agenda for language education with my commitments to social justice. It is this ongoing and dynamic struggle, to examine the complexities of claiming the classroom as a site for social change, that Richard at once challenged even as he enabled. We are, as Richard so effectively demonstrated, always already implicated in these issues.

17

Teaching Against Racism in the Radical College Composition Classroom: A Reply to a Student

Bob Nowlan _____

Dear Mr. Nowlan:

I am writing you this because I am very disturbed by some of the things that are going on in this class. You have urged us to ask our teachers to explain their objectives in teaching as they do—to account for what ends they seek to advance and what interests they seek to serve—so I ask you to answer this question in relation to what you are doing in teaching this class as you are. This question has a particular urgency for me because of my personal situation: I am married to a Black man and have a beautiful Black daughter. We often, and especially my husband and child, are victims of vicious kinds of abuse from racist people. It all makes me so angry that I would like to explode! I cannot talk about racism all that easily without just feeling enraged and wanting to vent all of that rage on the bigots. In this class many students have said very racist things, and not only have they got away with it, but it seems to me that this class has worked to draw these kinds of statements out of them. I know from what you say in arguing for your own position that you are not racist and in fact actively opposed to racism, but I cannot understand why you are teaching in this way, why you don't just tell these bigots off. You should tell them that their comments are simply unacceptable and will not be tolerated and that they cannot make these in class—or in their papers. You should lecture to us about what is racism and how it is wrong, and demand that students show they have understood and accepted that this is true.

I was not at our last class but I was glad I was not because I heard afterward that one student made very bigoted kinds of remarks and was allowed to argue for this position—and to insult James Baldwin and Black culture for a considerably length of time. This, to me, is totally unacceptable. I feel like if this is to continue that I will not be able to come to class at all. If I do, I don't know what I will say because I just cannot accept having to deal with these kinds of arguments.

I like the fact that this class is unlike other English classes I have taken and is not what I expected composition to be like. I like the fact that we are talking about serious social problems and that we are learning how to argue and critique. Yet, I think this could be improved if you changed how you are teaching this class, and if you prevented our discussions from degenerating into hostile exchanges involving outrageous positions. I really hope you will do something about this right away; it will make it a lot easier for me to learn, in comfort, and I am sure the same is true of others like myself in our class.

June

Dear June:

Thank you very much for your note. I think you raise very important issues which I want to take very seriously. I am going to respond at some length because of this, and I invite you to arrange a time to meet with me later and discuss what I am about to write.

First, I would like to take some time to address a point which might seem only indirectly related to what you have asked me, and yet which will, I think, provide me the basis from which to answer your questions. I would like to begin, that is, with an explanation of how I conceive of racism. I think this is very important because again and again in our class discussions and in texts written by students in and out of class I have encountered the same—I think very much inadequate—interpretation of racism and what needs to be done about it. Racism is usually discussed as a problem of *psychology:* as the manifestation of hatred and fear. Racism is seen, in other words, as almost entirely a matter of racist *attitudes.* This, in turn, is understood, by and large, to be the result of "ignorance," and the solution is, just as often, seen to be simply more and better "education." "People" are "racists," according to this position, because they "ignorantly" hate and fear people of a different skin-color, and this can be changed by teaching people, from an early age, that we are all "human beings," all "equal," and should be related to as "individuals," regardless of the color of our skin. According to this narrative, "we" "all" must "come together," setting aside our "prejudices," and "opening our minds" to "acceptance" and "toleration" of those who are "different" from ourselves, recognizing and understanding the fact that, despite these differences, we all are "ultimately" "equal" and have "equal right" to be and do as we "want" and "choose." If "we" can change our "attitudes" in this way, seemingly through mere exercise of "will," we will be able "gradually" to eliminate racism altogether, especially as we will be steadily better able to teach our "children and grandchildren" that it is wrong to judge—and especially to hate or fear—anyone simply on the basis of the color of his or her skin.

I have been teaching so as to contest this position, and to show its complicity with positions conventionally marked as "racist." As your letter points out, in our class we have seen superficially "antiracist" positions very quickly degenerate into virulently "racist" positions, once exposed to the pressure of a critique that forces people to struggle to develop consistent arguments and, in particular, to develop arguments that do not maintain a contradiction between a professed commitment to an ideal of "racial harmony" and a commitment, at the same time, to support of concrete policies and practices which work to prevent any real movement towards the realization of anything even approaching such a utopia.

Racist attitudes are ultimately the product of racist practices. These practices are in turn ultimately the product of a racist *social system* (a system of social *relations* and social *institutions* designed to facilitate, regulate, and govern these relations). Racist attitudes act back upon the forces which gave rise to them and the conditions which made them possible: in other words, the expression and communication of these attitudes work to legitimate racist practices. The reproduction and maintenance of these practices in turn contributes to the reproduction and maintenance of the racist social system. Racist attitudes do not merely express ignorance, or stupidity, or even mere fear and hatred—they instead indicate complicity and responsibility, and, even more than this, *interest* and *need*. Racism is not an aberration; it is *necessary* to the effective functioning of *business as usual* in our society.

Racism is pervasive and powerful in the United States today; in order to fight to eliminate it, we must start with a clear recognition of this fact. The vast majority of the White population in America maintains a significant stake in the perpetuation of racism. Whites cannot be let off the hook when they assume they are antiracist simply because they do not overtly fear or hate Black people—or because they do not communicate this fear and hatred in the rare, few places where they are *artificially prevented* from doing so. The most problematic racist attitudes in the United States today are *not* those that come from the minority of Whites who *overtly* express bigoted feelings towards Blacks, but rather those which come from the majority of Whites who refuse to recognize that they are relatively privileged versus Blacks in direct relation to the relative disprivileging of Blacks within a social system which denies Black people, on account of their "Blackness," equality with Whites in terms of right of access and opportunity to exercise the resources, powers, and capacities of this society.

Every day, all of the time, in even their most seemingly private and personal of practices, White people take up (and claim as their right and as their own) positions of privilege over and at the expense of Blacks. Blacks will continue to be denied the same rights and opportunities as Whites as long as Whites continue simply to take up and claim as their (natural) "right" and their (inalienable) "own" what their privilege of being White enables them to have. As long as Whites merely accept the benefits of their privilege, then they are denying Blacks right of access and opportunity to exercise the same kinds of resources, powers, and capacities—and to the same extent and to the same degree—that Whites *unfairly* enjoy, that Whites enjoy through the *exploitative expropriation* of the results of the productive activity of Black men and women.

Whites have to be *shown* that this is true: they have to be shown that they are benefitting from the perpetuation of racism even when they maintain no deliberate, overt hostility to Black people. Whites have to be shown that they *are* racist not only if and when they express hateful thoughts about or towards Black people, but also insofar as they simply accept their position of privilege and do not work actively to undermine the conditions by which their Whiteness alone entitles them to benefits which Blacks are denied on account of their Blackness. As long as this situation continues, Whites are benefitting at the expense of Blacks: they are unfairly receiving more than they give and Blacks are unfairly giving more than they receive in their respective contributions to the production and reproduction in the wealth of "our" society. And the question of whose society is this is key here—who ultimately owns and who effectively controls what "we" *collectively* produce, in our work together, with each other, as part of this social totality?

The only logical way to justify the continuation of this inequality between Blacks and Whites, once it is exposed for what it is, is to resort to overtly bigoted theories about some kind of natural and eternal, inevitable and unalterable difference in the "character" or "capacity" of Black versus White people. As we have seen in class, arguments that Blacks have the opportunity to "overcome racism" if they are willing to work to do this always lead to the logical conclusion that Blacks must be, as a race, either too stupid to recognize that this is possible, too lazy to do what is necessary to realize this possibility, or too perversely inclined to enjoy deprivation and subjugation (and, therefore, "crazy"). This again presupposes that there is something about melanin which creates very complex kinds of behavioral characteristics, and as we have discussed in class this is not only questionable as biology, but also reactionary as ideology.

I believe that it is necessary to *force* White people into the position where they *have* to try to put together an argument in support of their continuing unfairly to receive the privileges they unfairly do as a result of racism. This means that it is necessary to *show* Whites that the only way they can make such an argument, in a logically consistent manner, is to drop their supposed moral commitment to equality between Black and White along with their easy, sentimental profession of support for that great day when all people will be treated as one and no one will be judged on the basis of his or her skin color. If Whites want to justify continuing to reap the benefits of racism, Whites cannot at the same time suggest that all people *are*, or "should be," treated as equal—given the fact that these benefits would disappear if conditions between Whites and Black were made truly equal. To overcome racism, Whites will have to give up the privileges they gain as a result of racism—and unless they work to enable this to happen they are, in effect, supporting the continuation of racism, and are thus, in effect, racists.

White people have to be shown that the *consequences* of their *everyday* actions (and inactions) contradict the antiracist values they profess to support, and that therefore they really do not actually support these values at all—they pay them lip service, but do not support them in reality, and, in fact, in actual practice support the opposite. This is why it is necessary to show White people that they cannot consistently argue that they are in favor of ending racism while simultaneously arguing that affirmative action gives Blacks and other "minorities" unfair privileges over Whites, that Black English is not a language but rather an "ignorant" and "inferior" "slang" "dialect," and that Black people in poor urban centers are responsible themselves for the problems of poverty, violence, and despair they face in their lives. White people cannot consistently argue that they are opposed to racism and seek its end while simultaneously contending that Blacks must do the bulk of the work to overcome these problems themselves.

If Whites contend that racism is "simply," "largely," or "ultimately" a problem for Black people and other people of color, and one which Black people and other people of color "bear the burden" of responsibility for solving "themselves," it must be made impossible for these same Whites to pretend that they actually do, at the same time, support equality between Blacks and Whites. If affirmative action is undermined and ended, if Black English is dismissed and denigrated, and if Blacks are forced to bear the principal burden of having to fight against poverty, violence, and despair in their own communities, it will only serve to increase already existing inequalities, and, therefore, those who oppose affirmative action, who dismiss Black English, and who blame Blacks for Black poverty and crime are actually supporting not only the continuation of but also the increase in inequality between Black and White. It is very important to show White people that the positions they support and the practices they follow *contradict* the values they profess to support—and, therefore, they are actually supporting, *in practice,* a very different set of values than those they claim to support.

It may be tempting, artificially and temporarily, simply to silence racist attitudes in the space of a classroom taught by an antiracist White teacher, and yet to do so is not to *confront* and *contest* racism but rather to *avoid* and *evade* it. Racism will not be ended by pretending that we are all already opposed to it, or that it is better not talked about—and talked about as it really is. Simply to ban the expression of racist speech in a classroom and to move quickly to talk about "other issues" which only *seem* not to be connected with issues of race and racism does nothing more than create, at best, a very small refuge from the racist reality that remains overwhelmingly powerful and pervasive all around us. Racism is *not* simply a moral failing; it is a sign and symptom of a deeply political crisis, and it should be confronted and contested as such. This means bringing racist attitudes and beliefs out into the open and pressing the contradictions and the problems and limitations of these positions as far and as hard as possible. For racism to be eliminated, Whites will have to be *made* willing to fight actively against racism—and to suffer the consequences when they choose actively to break with what racist privilege allows them. This means that the majority of the White population must be shown that they, members of the White working class, maintain a potentially far greater interest in fighting against and overcoming racism than the interest they maintain in benefitting from its perpetuation: racism divides the working class against itself and thereby conquers its resistance to capitalist exploitation of labor, thus supporting the interest of maximizing capitalist profits. Racism even enables capitalist superprofits through the superexploitation of the relatively devalued labor of people of color, who receive substantially less than Whites do for comparable effort in comparable kinds of productive activity, thus leaving even more profit for capital. As long as racism divides the working class against itself and effectively conquers its resistance to capital, this enables the exploitation and alienation of the productive activity of both White and Black working-class men and women to continue—and to continue largely unchallenged and virtually unrecognized. As long as White working-class men and women can be bought off with (racist) privileges that set them a rank above Black working-class men and women, the exploitation and alienation of both White and Black working-class men and women and the injustices, the degradations, and the abuses that this allows will only continue—and only increase.

Liberals teach racism as a matter of bad moral attitudes—and liberals also teach as if these attitudes are only extrinsically and not intrinsically connected to practices, institutions, and relations. Liberals think it is enough to request—or occasionally demand—that racist attitudes and beliefs not be communicated for racism to go away. Radicals believe, on the contrary, that racism has got to be brought out into the open, made to show itself for what it truly is, in order for it to be fought all the way to the end. Radicals believe that this is a war, and that a war requires a *strategic* response: the goal must be to disrupt the possibility that racist positions and practices can be pursued unconsciously or unproblematically by those who do not know that their positions and practices are racist—when their positions and practices *do*, in effect, serve to maintain and reproduce racism. Racist positions must be attacked from within—and as such shown to be inconsistent, incoherent, and contradictory—as well as from outside, where they are shown what they are really based upon and what they really lead towards. Racist positions (and arguments) must be shown to be racist, and this takes careful, deliberate, patient, precise, and methodical work—and is not easily accomplished all at once, at one time, in one place, and by any one person.

The particular racist remarks to which you refer, those advanced by Jim in response to James Baldwin's article ("If Black English Is Not a Language, Then Tell Me, What Is?"), represent positions that are very commonly held and frequently expressed by many White people, and by many White people who maintain much greater power than Jim—and most often those who express these kinds of views do *not* see holding and expressing these views to be racist at all. This is why these positions need to be taken seriously and seriously engaged—not simply dismissed or evaded. To pretend they represent an anomaly, an aberration, a mere singular or disconnected instance of ignorance, hatred, and fear, is to fail to do justice to the depth of the problem. Jim's position on this question *is* the dominant position in our society today, and it is shared by most government officials, business executives, and media journalists.

The students—and the teacher—in this class (and in all classes, for that matter) do not express merely their own individual opinions, but rather represent social positions, positions which they share with many others in many other times and places, positions which occupy a much larger and more significant space than that of one individual's head. When students and teacher speak for and from these positions they speak as representatives of ends and interests much larger than their own immediately and consciously personal set of concerns. Expression of positions in this class is the expression, by representatives, of positions that occupy a much greater power and significance outside of and beyond this class. The struggle is against these positions and not simply against the particular individuals who merely happen to give voice to these positions at a particular place and time; these individuals need to be contested as *representatives* and not simply as individuals.

Serious contestation of racist positions is not a matter of simply cutting off or telling those who voice attitudes which emanate from and support racist practices and relations that they cannot speak. The goal is not to eliminate the visibility of racism from one classroom, but rather to contribute to the struggle to eliminate it in the whole society. Racism cannot be overcome by refusing to confront it; it must be overcome by struggling past one's mere hatred for it, as totally justifiable as that hatred is, to commit oneself to doing the only thing one who really hates it should do—fight it and not flee it.

If contestation in the space of a classroom is to be effective, those such as yourself, who hold oppositional views, *must* speak out—and as strongly as possible. Antiracists do not occupy the dominant position in this racist society, so it is an illusion for antiracists to wait for an antiracist authority to act to suppress racism in a rare space where this seems like a possibility. We should be demanding not that I, as teacher of this class, prevent racist remarks from being expressed in class discussion, but rather that we work through *contestation* in discussion towards making it impossible for as many people in this class as possible, and everyone with whom these people maintain significant relations, to participate any more unconsciously, uncritically, and unproblematically in racist practices within racist relations as part of racist institutions. Teachers who use their authority to silence contestation when a despicable position is articulated as part of the contestation do not make the best contribution they can to intervening in the reproduction and maintenance of the despicable position *beyond the classroom*. The goal should be, instead, to *critique* the position. And (other) students should not wait for the teacher to do this. What happens with and to and in classes depends as much upon what the students in the class do and do not do as what the teacher does and does not do. If antiracist student voices remain silent, then the antiracist position in class contestation is seriously weakened. Whenever *you* do not speak up in such places, you are not representing the interests to which you profess commitment. Rage, however, is not enough in and of itself to disrupt, subvert, or transform much of anything; White people are by and large so privileged that they can simply retreat and withdraw from that which does not *compel* them, but only *assaults* them. The goal is to make White people, at least some, at least a few, at least one, feel genuinely compelled to rethink their relationship to— and yes responsibility for and complicity in—the reproduction and maintenance of racism today, and to do this *beyond the scope of what merely has to be done within the space of classroom discussion or the writing of papers to meet the requirements of a single course.*

I look forward to discussing these issues further with you, and thank you once again, very much, for your letter.

Bob Nowlan

18

A *Ratio Studiorum* for the Postcolonialist's Classroom

John C. Hawley, S.J. ─────────────────────────

George Ganss, several decades ago, offered a fine analysis of the early educational philosophy that helped shape Jesuit schools throughout Europe and in much of the rest of the world in the sixteenth and seventeenth centuries. Since then, the vagaries of time have forced significant changes in that philosophy, as noted by Charles Bailey with regard to eighteenth-century France, and Rolando Bonachea and William O'Brien with regard to twentieth-century America.

In this essay I would like to take a brief look at one contemporary Jesuit's approach—my own—to a class in English composition, and offer an explanation of its methodology, a statement of its goals, and an indication of the dialectic it elicits from students. Entitled "Imagination versus The Law," it may seem a far cry from the emulation and *eloquentia* that formed a cornerstone of Jesuit educational methodology, but the goals it seeks, while not quite the same as those of the Renaissance Society of Jesus, *are* the goals of the contemporary Order. Walter Ong, as noted a scholar of the Renaissance as anyone, has argued that:

> We [Jesuit educators] are called on to cultivate and to communicate to our more mature students an attitude which sees literature not as simply a refuge or solace but as a part of our unfinished world, where the unknown is faced. . . . This point of view demands certain reservations in our attitudes toward Renaissance humanism . . . [otherwise] literature becomes a means of escape to the golden days of youth and intellectual irresponsibility. . . . The scholar who finds the twentieth century less comprehensible than the sixteenth century understands very little of the sixteenth. (83–84)

There are those today who have benefited from a humanistic education and who have, perhaps, incorrectly identified "understanding" as
a sufficient goal of "Jesuit" education. If that has historically been true
in the case of various Jesuit schools, it was not the intention of Ignatius
of Loyola, founder of the Society of Jesus. He saw education as a tool
for social change, not merely as an opportunity for a value-free and
objective exposure to Truth. Rooted in a religious understanding of the
world that demanded a confrontation between good and evil, his
schools had a *political* aim: awakening students to their Christian responsibilities, honing their individual talents, and bringing about a
commitment to put those talents at the service of the Church—a fal-
lible and often corrupt instrument that was nonetheless the best hope
in a world of cynicism, gullibility, and pride. Education, much like the
religious retreat described in his *Spiritual Exercises*, was to bring about
a *metanoia*, a change of heart, in students.

Historian Robert Quick points out that "for more than one hundred years nearly all the foremost men throughout Christendom, both
among the clergy and laity, had received the Jesuit training, and in
most cases retained for life an attachment to their old masters" (34).
Yet Quick goes on to observe that "the Jesuits fixed a course of study
which, as they frankly recognized, could not be made interesting. So
they endeavoured to secure accuracy by constant repetition" (57). This
ambivalence in response to the Jesuit approach has been typical. As
another historian has noted, "Descartes, Pascal, Voltaire, and Diderot,
to cite only some of their more prominent critics, charged the Jesuitic
didactic methods with rhetorical emptiness and moral laxism through
casuistry and duplicity. . . . Yet it is a sign of their pervasive influence
that even some of their most illustrious and articulate critics were
educated at their schools" (Scaglione 53).

If a good many students went on to serve the institutional Church,
the prominence of those who used their skills to counter its political
influence is also important to recognize: it is an equally important
product of the Jesuit method—one not especially appreciated at the
time, but one gradually seen by many in the Order itself as a benefit
to the larger world. It is still a point of controversy, but, viewed from
a theological point of view, the "creation" of a Voltaire by institutionally committed priests can be imagined as God writing straight with
crooked lines.

Very briefly, the methodology was as follows: The University was
entered at about the age of ten. Humane letters were begun in the
Faculty of Languages, especially in Latin and Greek; two years were

devoted to grammar, and two to rhetoric, poetry, and history. At the age of fourteen the pupil began the study of Philosophy, and after three years the degree of Bachelor of Arts was conferred; after six more months, the Master of Arts. At the age of seventeen, the study of Theology was begun, or Law, or Medicine. Following these four years, those who desired the degree of Doctor of Theology undertook two more years of acts and exercises (Ganss 45). The *Ratio studiorum* that organized this course was published in 1599, and was revised in 1616 and 1832. This was lock-step education, and would be eschewed by most Jesuit educators today.

What would be embraced, on the other hand, would be the point of the discipline. From the beginning, the ethical component of this *Ratio*, its possibilities for shaping the moral life of the student, was emphasized. Scaglione summarizes the intention:

> What the Jesuits did amounted to using the rhetorical approach, as Quintilian, perhaps their primary source of inspiration, would have wanted it, for the purpose of *Bildung* rather than sheer instruction, formation of the mind and personal character rather than erudition, following what could be referred to as Montaigne's rather than Rabelais' idea of education. They applied this method with an original emphasis on the psychological arrangement of doctrine and exercise, graduated and progressively ordered—a *methodus* which was akin to Ramus's desideratum and was unavailable before, and which was original but not unique, since it was shared by the Brethren and Sturm, as well as by the French town colleges. (57)

The world has changed a great deal since the Counter Reformation, and those changes have shaped not only the context for Jesuit education but the goals themselves—and not only for advocates of the Jesuit system. If early Jesuits partially rejected humanism because they considered it an insufficient goal, similar limitations of humanism are now openly discussed even by its advocates. Its implicit equation between the white European male and the best of all possible worlds is now criticized as a hegemonic imposition of Western European culture. But this, of course, was far from the criticism brought against humanism by the early Jesuits, whose dedication to the Church (criticized by Quick [55] and Scaglione [51]) reinforced significant aspects of the hegemony. An ancillary criticism aimed at these latter-day missionaries, therefore, would today demand a recognition by Jesuit educators that "the Church" that they see themselves called upon to serve cannot be identified with the European model that dominated Ignatius's imagination.

There are elements of the Jesuit tradition, clearly, that have benefited from the criticisms of such alumni as Voltaire and Diderot. Robert
Quick's criticism of what he takes to have been typically Jesuit educational philosophy is precisely the area where many of these changes
have taken place in the twentieth century. "I have said," he writes,

> that the object which the Jesuits proposed in their teaching was not
> the highest object. They did not aim at developing *all* the faculties of
> their pupils, but mainly the receptive and reproductive faculties. When
> the young man had acquired a thorough mastery of the Latin lan-
> guage for all purposes, when he was well versed in the theological
> and philosophical opinions of his preceptors, when he was skillful in
> dispute, and could make a brilliant display from the resources of a
> well-stored memory, he had reached the highest point to which the
> Jesuits sought to lead him. Originality and independence of mind,
> love of truth for its own sake, the power of reflecting, and of forming
> correct judgments were not merely neglected—they were suppressed
> in the Jesuits' system. (50–51)

This sort of objection is fine, as far as it goes; but a return to the radical
intentions at the heart of Ignatius's movement to reform society would
today demand far more than independent *reflection:* it would demand
action. Of immediate concern for those who may today be working in
schools with a historical connection to the Jesuit system of education
would be Quick's tendentious conclusion: "The Jesuit schools . . . still
exist, but they did their great work in other centuries; and I therefore
prefer to speak of them as things of the past" (34–35). To the extent
that they have lost contact with the urgency that motivated the early
educators, and to the extent that their philosophy has fallen away
from a clearly political intention, they have, perhaps, lost their calling
to "great work." To the extent that they endure the criticism that they
are becoming overly committed to "using" education to change their
students, they are, in fact, following in their great tradition. Teaching
students to love knowledge for its own sake is a fine and worthy goal,
but showing them its connection to their social responsibilities is more
desperately important in today's world.

What is called for in today's classroom is an increasing use of the
student's and the teacher's imagination. New paradigms are demanded;
flexibility in the face of change is an important skill that cannot be
memorized or cleverly summarized for national examinations, and yet
it must somehow be learned. In the face of the multicultural classroom
that increasingly becomes the order of the day; stepping into the shoes
of someone who will never be like "us" is crucial. It is for this reason

that I ask students, on the first day of class and occasionally throughout the semester, to consider Plato's cave. Ignoring the complexities of Plato's argument, we use his story to examine the idea that each of us has a specific, acquired "structure of perception," by which I mean, on the one hand, the cognitive schema through which we inevitably filter reality, and, on the other, the cultural text that interprets those aspects of reality that may "get through." Students are asked to consider that the notion of reality to which any one of us is chained is, in fact, limited, a mere shadow flickering on the distant wall of our comfortably familiar prisons. The importance of the concept, as I see it, becomes clear to students only when they are personally challenged by someone unlike themselves, and that is what my course hopes to bring about.

"Imagination versus The Law" is one option available to students at Santa Clara University to fulfill the third of three required writing courses. Each option available to them has a different theme, and they are therefore somewhat self-selective in choosing this particular course. It meets for an hour three times each week for ten weeks. During the term they read five books and write four five-page papers. They rewrite the first three, after individual conferences with the teacher. Full-period essay examinations follow each book, but the course has no final examination.

One might say that the course is based upon Henry Giroux's definition of pedagogy as "a configuration of textual, verbal, and visual practices that seek to engage the processes through which people understand themselves and the ways in which they engage others and their environment" (3). Class time, while sometimes devoted to the mechanics of writing, is also given over to films, videotapes, guest speakers, and discussion. The readings, films, and other materials draw from many disciplines: English, psychology, sociology, history, ethnic studies, and so on. What they demonstrate is that there are different rules that determine for each individual and for each society what is real, what is visible, what is allowable, what it means to be a fully developed and valuable human being. None of the materials seems to agree on these fundamental issues, and students are immediately and persistently presented with this conundrum. Most find it all quite fascinating, but some become openly hostile to the implied relativism.

The paper topics are assigned, and the first—"What Is a Hero"— seems simple enough, even trite. A surprising number of students begin with the sort of answer one might expect in elementary school: sports personalities, military personnel. A good number are stymied by the question, having apparently long ago given up on the notion of heroism. A significant number discuss the idealistic superstars, the Mother Teresas of the world; and a few single out a member of their family or an individual they have personally encountered. The purpose of the topic is to broach the question and to allow it to be taken seriously, to open a window on what it may mean *to stand out* from the expectations of those around us.

In the individual conferences that precede a rewriting of the first draft, some students clearly resent the topic as a throwback to high school themes like "What I Did on My Summer Vacation." When it becomes clear to them that I expect them to address the topic seriously, many seem confused, frustrated, annoyed that they don't have a handle on the "correct" answer to a question they would prefer to evade. Heroism, by definition, implies a responsibility that is more than most of us are willint to accept, and this implied inadequacy makes this the most difficult of the topics.

The students in my class are predominantly white, middle to upper-middle class, relatively wealthy, overwhelmingly Christian and principally Roman Catholic, and for the most part Californian. They are very intelligent and have a record of achievement and the promise of success by American standards. If the vibrancy of the volunteer organizations on campus are any indication, these are also generous people. But it must also be said that they seem passive, intent on good grades rather than the pursuit of ideas, relatively secure that the world be in better shape if everyone were American.

What is important, in terms of this course, is that they find opportunities to explain to themselves, in some limited degree, the source and possibly questionable value of this partial view on reality. This can be quite uncomfortable for some students, and I prefer that the initial papers provide a private opportunity for expressing their advocacy for a particular worldview. By the time we engage in class discussions, a bit later on, most people are "ready" and anxious to take a position in relation to the philosophy motivating the book, film, or guest speaker.

Subsequent paper topics demand some reflection on the increasing clash of cultures that graduates will encounter: "What are the prospects for the interplay between cultural imperialism and the global village?" "Can structures of perception be changed, and should they be?" "Define the contest between, and dual necessity for, all that we mean by imagination and all that we may mean by 'the Law.' " The basic difficulty many students face in these essays is this matter of definition; it is a task some of them protest against, since it seems to presuppose a relativizing view of such verities as common sense (generally defined as remarkably close to one's own viewpoint). Such discomfort is acknowledged, but the assignment nonetheless proceeds. The topics are designed to draw on the expertise students may be acquiring in other courses, and they respond in depth and with varying degrees of sophistication. During subsequent conferencing, I help students pursue their line of argumentation and frequently suggest that various individuals speak to each other and share their research.

In class, meanwhile, students are viewing Joseph Campbell's multipart series on world mythology, a series with installments like "The Hero's Adventure," "Sacrifice and Bliss," and "Masks of Eternity." For Catholics, for many other Christians, and perhaps for believers of other faiths, as well, the ex-Catholic Campbell can be quite upsetting. Once again, the question boils down to how much "relativizing" an individual student's structure of perception can tolerate without suffering some dents. Why do so many of the world's religions share so many tropes in common? Why does that faith's cultic ritual strike me as so much more bizarre than my own? And how can Campbell, so knowledgeable and so apparently serene, calmly announce that he does not believe in a personal God? Do I? What values expressed by these various foreign people appeal to me, and what do I find repellent? Why?

Guest speakers in class raise similar questions for many of the students. The husband of one of the department's secretaries was an internee at Manzanar; he addressed the class on that experience—without bitterness, but with a clearly puzzling effect on some of the more proudly patriotic students. The president and vice-president of the school's recently formed gay and lesbian support organization spoke for an hour, and their disarming and un-self-conscious manner defused what might have been a silent and fearful class period. While some otherwise garrulous students clammed up, others were heard from for the first time, and on a topic that is still a hot potato on Catholic campuses. A returning student of about thirty years of age, a published Chicana poet, read her poems for the class; it was the first time most students had heard an actual poet read, and the depth of conviction behind the words changed forever, I think, their notion of poetry's relevance to the world around them. Another returning student, one who had worked in Nepal, brought in pictures and stories of her experiences in a land far away from the wealth of Palo Alto, the town in which she had grown up. Again, her enthusiasm for the "wisdom" of the Nepalese became infectious. When we read from the Native American novelist, Scott Momaday, another faculty member who had worked with him came in and filled us in on what he was "really" like.

Some will object that this is all a bit colonial—Master Harold looking in on the "others" and then returning to the comfort of the big house. This is an easy and over-used criticism, and, in my view, it would be wrong if it were to obscure the startling effects that a raising of curtains can have in the minds of intelligent and well-meaning people. If we cannot have faith in these effects, then we must not hold out much hope for education in general. In itself, this may not be enough to change the world, but I share Ignatius's original insight into the importance of helping shape the mental framework of those individuals who are most likely to assume positions of power in a society that is still divided into the miserable and the wealthy. Alerting students to the conditions that maintain "their" "big house" can drive some to a paranoid and cynical selfishness, but the arguments that arise in class would indicate that students do not easily accept this approach from their peers. Those who return from abroad wanting nothing so much as the comfort of a McDonald's hamburger nonetheless may return to the memories of their experiences and find in them the data for more mature decisions and choices in later life.

It must also be recognized that the guest speakers and their issues are not, finally, so remote from my students. An increasing percentage of students in California is *not* white; many at Santa Clara and at similar schools are no longer practicing Catholics; gay and lesbian students have traditionally been discouraged by subtle means from making their presence known on campuses (and this has been especially true at schools with a religious affiliation), but as their civil rights are increasingly recognized this is enabling some students to identify themselves more publically; physically disabled students still have a rough time in gaining access to the "normalcy" that should be available to them, but are no longer allowing themselves to be overlooked or merely patronized. All these individuals need a voice in the student body and in the classroom. In bringing them all together in one classroom, if you will, the point that may become clear is that "difference" is not different anymore. I have seen the enemy, and. . . . Increasingly, the class cannot presume to speak in universal terms; instead, it learns to expect someone "different" to be present, and speaking as an individual. As Henry Giroux puts it, "essential to a critical pedagogy is the need to affirm the lived reality of difference as the ground on which to pose questions of theory and practice" (102).

The choice of reading material supports this idea, as well. Some of the novels I have used over the years have been devoted to the world of children, others to the elderly. Disabilities shape the themes in such books as Dalton Trumbo's *Johnny Got His Gun,* with its strong anti-war statement (itself a disability in some students' views); in Oliver Sacks's *Seeing Voices,* which introduces students to the deaf, a world most would never encounter; in Christopher Nolan's *Under the Eye of the Clock,* which many students compare to Stephen Hawking's works as a revelation. Gay issues dominate David Leavitt's fiction, especially *The Lost Language of Cranes,* where the question of honesty and self-definition, of finding a "language," moves beyond questions of sexual orientation; a lesbian view is presented to students in Jeanette Winterson's hilarious *Oranges Are Not the Only Fruit,* which is as much an attack on religious fundamentalism as it is an attack on other forms of potential intolerance. Bruce Jay Friedman's *Stern* and Edward Said's *After the Last Sky* show students a degree of alienation that many find quite foreign and uncomfortable to their sense of what "should" be—at least as it has been known on the West Coast of the United States. But Carlos Fuentes's *Burnt Water,* Amy Tan's *The Joy Luck Club,* Rigoberta Menchu's autobiography, and Bharati Mukherjee's *Jasmine* bring the questions much closer to home and lead to rather spirited debates over the role of immigration in the definition of the country, and the role of commercial restrictions in maintaining the strength of the American economy.

This may all sound like a class in sociology rather than composition, but students have never made that complaint. They find, if anything, that there is an *abundance* of writing. The individual conferences deal not only with ideas but with questions of grammar and style. And the examinations, after all, are further essays that demand coherent analyses of the reading, comparative discussion of the issues, and a well-supported argument for their own response to the questions at hand. There is never enough time to complete the exams to their full satisfaction, and that leads to a recognition that none of these questions is "answerable." Dialogue ensues, and spills over into class.

In the three or so films that students view each term, the same points ramify. Ken Russell's imaginative *Altered States* addresses the Faustian myth that remains central to the Western canon, but does so in the context of merging cultures—drugs, Harvard, Aztecs, romance literature, science fiction—and ultimately asks traditional philosophical questions about the definition of the individual and what choices one makes to maintain an ethical position in the world. A similar merging of cultures shapes *My Beautiful Laundrette*, which focuses on class conflict, gender questions, and race relations, all in the traditional framework of a Horatio Alger story. *My Left Foot* presents Christy Brown as a brilliant and not totally sympathetic man whose struggles with his body echo those in his soul.

El Norte graphically demonstrates the unconscious assumptions of North American culture, and the impact unscrupulous economic practices on *both* sides of the border have on likeable people with *no* options. This film led to an argument between those students who had taken classes in economics: some felt that market conditions demanded the maintenance of strict borders, and others reasoned that the current market depended upon this unfair exploitation of peasant labor. Students in the humanities listened with interest, and then jumped in on one side of the argument or the other, vehemently arguing the comparative ethics of both positions.

I agree with, and worry about, Giroux's reminder to the teacher that "this is a pedagogy that rejects detachment, though it does not silence in the name of its own ideological fervor or correctness" (101). The variety of input is designed to touch each student, but most often in unknown ways. Not too surprisingly, I agree with an older student who wrote that the course would be one that "will affect students' lives later on, whether they realize it now or not." It is very gratifying when students indicate that the course "deals with ideas and concepts that are central and critical to life as a human," but it is even better when they go out on a limb in front of their peers and express an unpopular opinion of the material. As the class progresses, this happens with greater regularity. I do not, therefore, necessarily "win over" the recalcitrant, but am satisfied to provide a forum for meaningful debate: that is, a debate of *meaning*.

As the makeup of the student body slowly changes, so does the atmosphere in these discussions. As more Vietnamese, African Americans, and Chicanos enter the classroom and a critical mass of non-Europeans begins to sense that they share a common cause, a bit more anger begins to show around the edges, a bit more personal expression of having been badly treated begins to be heard. In such circumstances, it is not surprising to note rumblings among the fading majority against all this "bitching" from minorities. I have never felt the need to intervene when this becomes heated. With Giroux, I would suggest that "the pedagogical practice at work here is not meant to romanticize these subjugated knowledges and 'dangerous memories' as much as to critically appropriate and renew them as part of the reconstruction of a public philosophy that legitimates a politics and pedagogy of difference" (101).

It is against just such difference, at least so the story goes, that the Jesuits were founded: a Counter Reformation to halt the rebellion. Yet we all must inevitably function according to the "structure of perception" that we nurture in ourselves—and in our students. As a Father Gerard, S.J., told participants at an Educational Conference of 1884: "Teaching is an art amongst arts. To be worthy of the name it must be the work of an individual upon individuals. The true teacher must understand, appreciate, and sympathize with those who are committed to him. He must be daily discovering what there is (and undoubtedly there is something in each of them) capable of fruitful development, and contriving how better to get at them and to evoke whatever possibilities there are in them for good" (qtd. in Quick 57–58).

This is not far from Giroux's advocacy of "a pedagogy that replaces the authoritative language of recitation with an approach that allows students to speak from their own histories, collective memories, and voices while simultaneously challenging the grounds on which knowledge and power are constructed and legitimated" (105). Where Giroux and educators like him may differ from early Jesuits and educators like them, perhaps, is in their desire to "expand the range of social identities that students may become" (105). To a great extent, this is not so much a question of becoming but of allowing the shell to crack and fall away, revealing the unique and beautiful creation that need not be sat upon any longer.

As the President of the University stated in his most recent annual report, "a Santa Clara education means inspiring students and graduates to make a difference in the world. . . . We hope our mission of fashioning a better world spreads to corporations, courtrooms, Congress, and beyond. And we believe some of that is happening now as it has throughout the university's 140-year history." To be honest, it must be said that this is not a belief shared by all the faculty; it is not one to which all students aspire. Nonetheless, if there is some historical truth in the charge that Jesuit schools in the past produced clever casuists who invested little of themselves in their arguments, it is clear in today's multicultural world, a world of conflicting hermeneutic structures, that making debating points will not equip a graduate for *anyone's* reality. The spiritual thrust that underlies Jesuit education is Ignatius's stated desire to help others become men and women *for others*. But the "others" must first be acknowledged and valued as different, or the embrace will be no more than a new confinement.

PART VI
Rereading, Rethinking, Responding

19

Empty Pedagogical Space and Silent Students

Gary Tate _____

Almost forty years ago, in an *AAUP Bulletin* essay entitled "How to Escape Teaching Composition," John Sherwood listed six ways in which writing teachers avoided teaching writing: teaching literature; teaching grammar; practicing "stimulation" (that is, presenting students with provocative, controversial ideas to write about); teaching logic/ semantics; shifting the emphasis from writing to reading; and, finally, by constructing "communications" courses that involved not just writing but speaking, listening, and reading.

I was reminded of Sherwood's piece as I read the essays in *Left Margins,* especially his discussion of the origins of the stimulation approach during the Depression, when "young English teachers . . . boiling with social consciousness . . . thought that the greatest service they could do humanity was to unsettle the middle-class prejudices of their students" (286). Although I find the tone of portions of Sherwood's essay offensive, he is correct, I believe, in identifying a tendency that seems to have existed since the beginnings of composition as a college course: the tendency for writing teachers to teach something other than writing.

For many teachers, the composition course is an empty pedagogical space that needs to be filled with "content." Anyone who has been around the teaching of college composition for more than a semester or two could easily add to Sherwood's list. I have seen poured into the course literature of all kinds, religion, feminism, anthropology, and so on and so forth. I myself have done some of this pouring. So I am not surprised to see cultural studies used to fill the seemingly empty space that is college composition, even though we have learned in the last thirty years that if we are serious about teaching *writing* rather than literature or politics or religion, we can—should—make the writing of our students the focus (content) of the course. Only one or two of the authors in this book even hint that they are interested in such a focus. (I am speaking here and elsewhere about those writers who claim to be describing composition courses, not about the several who describe courses of different kinds that *use* writing. It is a troublesome feature of these essays that this distinction is sometimes difficult for the reader to make.)

Reading this book, I was reminded of a brief exchange I had a few years ago with a leading proponent of cultural studies. After listening to him read a paper describing a freshman composition class he had taught the previous year, a paper that made no mention of the writing of his students, I asked him how they wrote in the course. "Like freshmen always write," he sneered, as he walked away, obviously bored by the thought of student writing. Whether the authors of the essays in this book share the same lack of interest in the writing of their students, I have no way of telling for certain, but the evidence in most of their essays suggests that other matters take priority over writing, in their minds and in their classrooms. Here is some evidence.

Although there is much talk in most of these essays about student attitudes and beliefs, student resistance, and so on, the reader hears only the words of the various authors. The students themselves are silent. Their writing is invisible. In only one or two essays is student writing displayed, and even then the purpose of quoting the students is always to make a point about attitudes or beliefs, never to demonstrate the quality of their prose or the nature of their development *as writers.* Ironically, Mary Beth Hines, one of the few authors who show us examples of student writing, is not the teacher of the students she is quoting—and the students she quotes are in a literature class, not a composition class.

I very much wanted to read what students had written in response to the many assignments and topics that are discussed in these essays. What happened to their prose as they struggled with new ideas? How did their resistance manifest itself in their writing? How did they respond in writing to the large amount of reading they often were asked to do? (Some teachers, indeed, seem far more interested in what their students are reading than in what they are writing, an attitude that harks back to the fifties, when many of us weren't quite certain how to focus on student writing.) What happened to their writing during the course of the semester? Did it change? How? The authors in this collection are silent—as are their students—about these matters.

This silence seems not so strange when one looks at the various assignment and course goals that appear in these essays. Here are two—I would argue representative—examples:

> . . . the goal of this assignment is to alert students to their own ideological subjectivity, especially as "gendered" subjects (Wise 129).

> By the end of the semester, most of my students had come to a much broader understanding of how language (and everything that might augment it, such as color, music, or graphics) functions rhetorically to shape our views of reality (Caulfield 170).

What interests me about these statements is that they completely ignore student *writing*. Even Caulfield's statement about rhetoric says nothing about the writing of his students. One would think that the goals of a composition course would say something about composition.

Whether teachers of composition focus on the writing of students or on other issues depends, I believe, on how they construct students. Every teacher "creates" her students, constructs them in her mind, and then teaches those creations, those constructions. When I began teaching in the late fifties, it was not uncommon to construct students as unworthy, unprepared, untalented individuals. Only a very few really "had what it took" for a true college education. The rest should not have been admitted and needed to be weeded out. And my grades reflected that construction. During one two-year period, 1958–60, in five sections of freshman composition, I gave two *A*s. No one—not even the students!—complained about my grading. Today, we construct students in a variety of ways: as troubled adolescents who need the therapy of personal writing, as representatives of academic disciplines (a history major, an engineering student, a biologist) who need to be taught the discourse of those disciplines, and so forth. Although the authors in *Left Margins* do not employ the terminology I have been using, it is quite clear that many of them construct students as victims of the "dominant culture"—and possibly as potential allies in the fight against hegemony. Adam Katz writes:

> This means, with regard to teaching within the capitalist university, at least the following: students cannot be regarded as possessing a "good" democratic kernel which needs to be released from external restraints and permitted to flourish, nor as free and rational subjects who can simply "choose" from among a variety of intellectual

options . . . ; rather they must be understood as contradictory sites constituted by the enormous investment of the dominant culture in producing "authoritarian individuals," that is, by their resistance to "democracy" in the sense of any social and material forces which advance democracy in a consistent way (211).

Interestingly, although this portrait of students sounds harsh (they are neither "free" nor "rational"—and certainly not humane—they are "sites" and "subjects," not people) almost all the writers in this book write in caring ways about the individuals in their classes. In other words, when they abandon the jargon of cultural studies and write about real people in ordinary prose, they show a genuine concern for their students. This apparent disjunction is yet another important topic ignored in these essays.

The problem with constructing students as victims, or as potential allies, or in any number of other ways, is that it ignores them *as writers*. If the revolution in the teaching of college composition that took place in this country beginning in the early sixties did anything, it showed us how to construct (and teach) our students as writers. These students will, of course, be history majors and chemistry majors; they may well be victims in all sorts of ways, some far more significant than those highlighted in this book, but in a composition class they *deserve* to be seen as writers. If the authors in *Left Margins* view their students primarily as writers, if their courses are primarily writing courses, it is not apparent in their essays.

Also missing from these discussions is any serious consideration of how exactly to avoid "imposing" one's ideas on students. Apparently aware of the popular fear that teachers with obvious political agendas will impose their ideas on their students, several of these authors say that they wish not to do this, but hardly any do much more than mention their desire to avoid imposition. One of the exceptions is Donald Lazere:

> I am firmly opposed, however, to instructors imposing socialist (or feminist, or Third-World, or gay) ideology on students as the one true faith—just as much as I am opposed to the present, generally unquestioned (and even unconscious) imposition of capitalist, white-male, heterosexual ideology that pervades American education and every other aspect of our culture (189–90).

Lazere continues by describing his grading practices:

> My grading, then, is not based on whether the students' views agree with mine, but on how skillfully they have located and articulated

opposing lines of argument and analyzed the rhetorical strengths and weaknesses of each source's arguments (190).

These are admirable statements, although as any student will tell you, "strengths" and "weaknesses" in arguments often seem not unrelated to the beliefs of the teacher. I wish other authors had been as forthcoming about their evaluation practices as Lazere because it is in evaluation that teachers impose, no matter how much they try to avoid it. But in almost every essay, evaluation and grading go unmentioned. No easy talk about "not imposing my views on students" can substitute for serious discussion of evaluation/grading and the relationship between these activities and the imposition of ideas and beliefs. Anyone who thinks they are not related should again talk to students.

I regret having to say all I have said in this response because, in spite of my strong reservations, many of these essays are intellectually and pedagogically stimulating. I suspect that even at this late date my teaching will change because I have read them. Their strength lies in their attempts to make the college writing course a site of inquiry, a scene of intellectual struggle. It is obvious that reading is an important part of these courses. I applaud that. It is obvious that serious discussions of important matters take place. I applaud that. What I cannot applaud is the apparent lack of focus on the actual writing of students.

Adam Katz raises the right questions:

> Is the kind of writing they expect to master in this very course perhaps designed to make such questions invisible, and if so how? How can we reassess such "mainstream" writing and thinking in this context? And what would a type of writing interested in placing such questions on the public agenda look like, what would criteria regarding its quality be, and how would it be evaluated by the dominant culture? (218).

Unfortunately, these important questions about writing, and a host of others, are never answered in *Left Margins*.

20

The Dilemma of Oppositional Pedagogy: A Response

Gerald Graff _____

In reading a partial selection of the essays in this collection, I am struck by the reappearance in them of a classic double bind that, it seems to me, has plagued radical pedagogy since its emergence in the late 1960s. On the one hand, the oppositional teacher declares an aggressive political agenda that supposedly goes far beyond mere liberal pluralism and with its ideologically suspect defense of "open debate" and a "free marketplace of ideas." On the other hand, in order to avoid the authoritarianism entailed by enforcing any such agenda without open debate, the oppositional teacher inevitably has to reinstate the very pluralism that has supposedly been repudiated. It seems the only way oppositional pedagogy can avoid being authoritarian is by ceasing to be oppositional.

I have my doubts that this double bind can be overcome as long as pedagogical thinking remains fixated at the level of the individual *course* at the expense of the *organization* and *interrelation* of courses in the curriculum—that is, as long as teaching is assumed to be an activity that is just naturally performed by a lone teacher in a classroom without any dialogical relation to other courses and classrooms. However unconventional the present group of essayists may be in their political outlooks, they remain quite conventional in their acceptance of the assumption that teaching is by nature a solo performance. Nor with one exception do these writers see a connection between the atomized course and the depoliticized, individualistic ethos of the curriculum.

The Oppositional Double Bind

Theorists of oppositional pedagogy argue that it is necessary to go beyond the ideologically deceptive ideal of the free marketplace of ideas that is so dear to the vision of liberal pluralism. As James R. Bennett puts it in a 1989 essay in *College English*, "the conditions of free and equal competition of ideas have already been nullified by the prior, enormous distortion in favor of one side" (810). The point of the oppositional course, then, as Adam Katz puts it (citing Giroux, Ben Agger, and others), must be not merely to "open a space for a more ethical discourse," but to "engage in incessant struggle against the dominant culture." Like Paulo Freire's "pedagogy of the oppressed," Katz's teaching will present students with "sustained critiques of the hegemony exercised throughout everyday life" by that dominant culture (210–11).

Transcending merely "pluralistic ideals of neutrality and fair play," the oppositional teacher, in Bennett's words, must "create the critical knowledge and stance necessary for critical engagement with the U.S. corporate-military-CIA-FBI national security state" (809). Indeed, according to Bennett, "the scrutiny of the U.S. system of power in defense of a democratic political system" should be not simply the project of an oppositional minority of teachers. It should be "a broad goal of *all humanistic disciplines and courses . . .* " (807; emphasis added).

But what follows from these arguments for pedagogical practice? How does Bennett propose to make his political critique of corporate America a "goal of *all* humanistic disciplines and courses" when many teachers and students in those disciplines clearly do not identify with such a critique? And what follows for Bennett if, as he says, "the conditions of free and equal competition of ideas have already been nullified," so that the liberal model of open debate is only a myth that papers over the perpetuation of coercive orthodoxies?

Does this mean, for example, that oppositional teachers are licensed to counteract the official forms of indoctrination with their own counterindoctrination? Does one form of authoritarian behavior justify another? Even if it were true that conservatives already monopolize virtually all discourse outside the campus—and I would not be alone on the Left in questioning whether they do—would it still follow that it is all right for oppositional teachers to suppress student conservatives?

Bennett *seems* to accept the legitimacy of such suppression when he argues, at the end of his essay, that "we can affirm the freedom to dissent radically in the classroom by refusing equal time to ruling powers" (816). On the other hand, Bennett may not mean that teachers are justified in refusing "equal time" to students who agree with the "ruling powers." In practice I suspect that few oppositional teachers actually do suppress dissent in their classrooms. And few theorists of oppositional pedagogy go so far as to unequivocally endorse such a brutal practice, even if their logic often seems to leave them with no good reason not to.

On the contrary, in order to avoid acceding to such an obviously undemocratic position, oppositional theorists tend to dilute or abandon their avowed antipluralism without acknowledging it. Quietly and without acknowledgment they shift to a pedagogical strategy that is indistinguishable from the despised model of the classroom as a forum for open debate. Thus oppositional theorists vacillate by turns between strong and weak versions of the oppositional position, denouncing mere pluralism in order to certify their radical credentials and then unobtrusively reverting to pluralism in order to avoid the totalitarian trap.

Mary Beth Hines succinctly sums up the oppositional teacher's dilemma in her account of Richard, a Marxist instructor who seeks "to 'expose' students to 'alternative ways of seeing' without 'imposing' his particular perspectives on students" (231). Though Hines here identifies the problem—that oppositional pedagogy can easily become authoritarian—she fails to follow the logic of her analysis far enough to take it really seriously. The problem is, if students do not enter the class already acquainted with the "alternative ways of seeing" that the teacher is encouraging, then these ways of seeing can only come from the teacher. Not that the teacher would necessarily have to "impose" his or her alternative ways of seeing by force on his students, but such coercion could be avoided only through some process resembling open discussion, however problematic such a concept may be in the absence of a level playing field in the larger society.

So Hines's Richard, whose ambition is " 'to disturb,' to challenge the dominant powers" (232), and who professes to reject the idea of the classroom as "kind of like a free market" (233) nevertheless ends up "creating a debate" (233) in his class just like any liberal pluralist. Richard turns his classroom into the very "free market" of ideas that he purports to reject. He respects "the beliefs of his students," even those who reject his alternative ways of seeing and who defend the social status quo that he wants to transform (234). Richard—to his credit in my view—cannot bring himself to suppress conservative students even though he evidently thinks their dominant position in the culture makes it legitimate to suppress them.

To be sure, Richard in his class, according to Hines, candidly acknowledges the "interested" nature of his own views—he concedes that he does have "a particular ideology and a particular agenda, and that's okay." But nothing in such a disclaimer differentiates Richard's classroom practice from that of any liberal pluralist. Nor does the political aim of Richard's class seem particularly radical, judging by the comment of the student "Greg," who credits his teacher with having "got me thinking about things I probably wouldn't have thought about, like with the advertisements . . . " (244).

In a similar fashion, Adam Katz opens with a bang by scornfully rejecting the idea of the classroom as a space of free and rational choice between positions and then ends with an anticlimactic whimper in his account of his own class. In his class, Katz tells us, the focus is on "opposing positions, and the arguments supporting such positions, which circulate within culture at large with regard to specific sites of contestation: what are the consequences of following through the 'logic' of one argument as opposed to another?" (214). John Stuart Mill would hardly have raised an eyebrow.

To be sure, Katz claims that he refuses to treat his students as "free and rational subjects who can simply 'choose' from among a variety of intellectual options" (211; Katz disparagingly identifies this assumption with my own theory of "teaching the conflicts"[1]). But why does Katz present his students with "opposing positions" unless he takes them to be capable of a degree of rational choice? Either Katz bullies his students into accepting *his* account of the social determinants of their thinking or else he grants them a degree of rational agency and freedom of choice.

It is hard to tell which is the case: Katz vacillates between a picture of his classroom as a scene of engagement with ideas and as a scene of indoctrination. "The point here," he writes, "is not to 'silence' students by 'condemning' their 'opinions,' but to enable them to see their 'opinions' as historical and social products (and not as their own private property), which can be critiqued and transformed" (214). But Katz evades all the hard questions by hiding behind wiggle-words like "*enable* them to see" and "*can* be critiqued and transformed," words that conveniently obscure the extent to which Katz's students have to accede to his explanation of their behavior or not.

What if some of Katz's students were to reject Katz's story about their "opinions" (or decline to accept what is implied in the derogatory scare-quotes Katz places around the word *opinion*, as if we all agree that agency is illusory)? What if they prefer instead to go on thinking of their ideas as "private property?" Does Katz accord these students' dissenting view a legitimate place in his classroom—in which case he reverts to liberal pluralism—or does he treat that view as an error to be corrected from a position of superior political insight? Katz avoids facing up to this crucial question.

Bennett seems more willing than Katz to commit himself to a thoroughgoing rejection of pluralism, or would be if one took him to be defending the silencing of views that are sufficiently dominant outside the class. Not only does Bennett leave the question unclear, however (as we saw), but he appears subsequently to have reconsidered his position. In an essay published two years after the *College English* essay to which I have referred, Bennett argues that the classroom should become an arena of "competing theories" in which "all have their place in the debate." He argues that "students who grapple simultaneously with the struggle for truth exemplified in the writings of Cleanth Brooks, Terry Eagleton, Gayatri Spivak, Roland Barthes, and Norman Holland will earn the spirit of the Bill of Rights, defender of a 'polyphony of voices contending for truth' in self-government" (189). Though Bennett does not mention it, such an argument seems to reject his earlier view that we do not enjoy "the conditions of free and equal competition of ideas" that would make possible the sort of debate that he now advocates.

Beyond the Course Fetish

It will come as no surprise, then, that to these ambiguous and equivocal defenses of oppositional pedagogy I much prefer the strategy expounded by Donald Lazere in "Teaching the Conflicts." On the one hand, Lazere's essay refutes Katz's assumption that "teaching the conflicts" can mean only a rarefied academic debate, not an engagement of "contradictory sites" constituted by investments in material power (211). Lazere makes clear that teaching the conflicts is a thoroughly *political* pedagogy. On the other hand, Lazere recognizes that political pedagogy requires the creation of a larger political debate. After all, "left" positions can hardly make sense to students unless presented in relation to other positions.

More significantly for our purposes, Lazere's unashamed acceptance of debate as a classroom model safeguards his approach from the authoritarian danger that oppositional pedagogy is always courting and then having to retreat from. Lazere, that is, takes seriously the concern of conservative and liberal critics that oppositional courses, as he puts it, "can all too easily be turned into an indoctrination into the instructor's particular ideology." He takes seriously the problem posed by "some leftist teachers and theorists" who "assume that all students and colleagues agree—or *should* agree with—their views" (189). He recognizes that oppositional teachers need to take "respectful account of opposing views," if only because we cannot hope to change the minds of others unless we respect their resistances to our views, and even risk having our own minds changed by them.

Lazere's strategy of teaching political conflicts—in this case about Reaganomics[2]—can be called "liberal pluralist" inasmuch as it recognizes that the perspectives of conservative and liberal students have to be respected. But it goes an important step beyond the conventional pluralistic glorification of "diversity," since it insists that different positions *engage* one another instead of coexisting side by side, as if all positions were equal. Unlike Freirean pedagogy of the oppressed and other current critical pedagogies, teaching the political conflicts does not claim to teach the true, authentic politics of opposition. This, however, is precisely what figures to make it more effective in getting students not already converted to left perspectives to take political issues—and left perspectives—seriously.

For Lazere recognizes that resistant students are more likely to give a sympathetic hearing to oppositional ideas if these ideas are presented not as a privileged standpoint but as one option among several. Lazere knows as well as anyone that such options are always socially constrained, never simply a matter of neutral rationality or of choices made on a level playing field. He is as critical as anyone of "the convention that teachers and textbooks are expected to be blandly neutral" (191). But Lazere also sees that to reject neutrality is not to reject rational persuasion. In fact, I suspect he would say that the only means by which oppositional viewpoints can hope to gain support in the United States is through *persuasion*, if only because these viewpoints by definition have little material power.

For Lazere, in other words, the fact that we do not have a level playing field, that the conditions of debate may be stacked in favor of the status quo, is an argument *for* open classroom debate, not against it. Instead of seeing the inequalities of power as an argument against classroom debate, Lazere's tactic is to make that condition of inequality part of the agenda of classroom debate.

To put it another way, Lazere, I think, would argue that even if we agree with James R. Bennett that "the conditions of free and equal competition of ideas have already been nullified by the prior, enormous distortion in favor of one side," teachers have no choice but to act *as if* these conditions existed, or at least as if it is possible to create them in our classrooms if not everywhere else. Again, to deny such a claim is to excuse the bullying of our students on the cynical grounds that the dominant culture will bully them anyway.

I noted at the outset that, whatever the radicalism of current oppositional pedagogies, they take for granted the conventional picture of "the classroom" as an autonomous entity, a "course" taught by a single teacher with no regular or functional contact with other courses and teachers. Among the essayists here only Lazere looks up from the confined space of his own class to the larger curriculum. In doing so he draws an important connection between American education's avoidance of politics and political controversy and "a departmentalized curriculum of unrelated courses . . . broken up into discontinuous units corresponding to television's blips of information" (191). Lazere's point is that the very disconnection of the curriculum enforces an apolitical ideology quite independently of the content of the courses that comprise it, and probably more powerful in shaping the attitudes of students.

Though Lazere, too, is concerned with his particular course, his argument points beyond it to a larger vision of a curriculum that conceives itself as a scene of political conflicts, or that at least is willing to bring into the foreground the debate over the extent to which education is or is not inevitably political. Such a vision may seem naive or improbable when one considers the depth of hostilities in today's culture war. We teachers tend, however, to get so caught up in these hostilities that we overlook the fact that students are often so alienated from the culture of political discourse that in their eyes *all* political positions—left, right, and center—seem about equally remote, mysterious, and uninteresting. Given a student body alienated from political discourse as such, partisans of the Left and the Right are in some respects in the same boat.

In this sense, Lazere is not being naive, I think, in arguing that "the left agenda of prompting students to question the subjectivity underlying socially constructed modes of thinking can be reconciled with the conservative agenda of objectivity and nonpartisanship" (190). What Lazere is saying, I think, is that the left and conservative agendas are "reconcilable" not in their content as political philosophies (though important areas of overlap exist), but in their shared *pedagogical* relation to a student body that often lacks any strong investment in either agenda.

What Lazere seems to be saying—but if not I will simply speak for myself—is that, ethical considerations aside, it is foolish to seek to radicalize students until we have first created a political debate in the university that enables political positions to make sense to them. In a depoliticized academic environment, instead of seeking to radicalize students directly, radicals should try to create a political debate that engages their interest to begin with. The culture war over multiculturalism, feminism, gender, and sexuality has begun to create that debate and to engage a portion of the student body, if still only to a limited and uneven degree. The task of politically committed teachers should be to make that debate a central issue for the whole curriculum, trusting to students to choose intelligently when the competing arguments are presented to them.

For it is only within a structure in which the assumptions of teachers of all persuasions are contested by equally powerful peers that the double bind of oppositional pedagogy can be overcome. In a curriculum in which clashing views did not simply coexist side by side but directly engaged one another, teachers could become *more* aggressive in expressing political beliefs with less fear of coercing their students. Since students would experience the authority of any position against the counterauthority of other positions, professors of all perspectives could take stronger positions with less danger of authoritarianism.

Instead of expecting students to join a debate that they never see— or that they see only in disconnected and disjunctive glimpses—the university would be presenting students with a real intellectual community and a real political debate. This in my view would constitute a more "radical" break from business as usual than counterindoctrination projects conducted in the privacy of the single course.

I recognize that untenured instructors, to say nothing of part-timers and adjuncts, will not necessarily have the luxury to think about the whole curriculum, much less anything more grandiose than next Monday's class. "Intellectual community" must seem a matter of secondary concern to those who are marginal members of the community. Yet it is the absence of such a community that deepens the isolation of such marginal or disempowered instructors and leaves them without a public sphere forum in which to dramatize their situation. The kind of public community that I wish to see constructed at the center of the curriculum would not in itself redress the grievances of marginalized and exploited instructors, but it could create the kind of discussion that might produce change. And even if it did not, students would learn something in the process.

Counterstatements

A Response to Gary Tate and Gerald Graff

Colleen M. Tremonte _____

"When *I* use a word," Humpty Dumpty said in rather a
scornful tone, "it means just what I choose it to mean—
neither more nor less."
    "The question is," said Alice, "whether you *can* make
words mean so many different things."
    "The question is," said Humpty Dumpty, "which is
to be master—that's all."
              —Lewis Carroll, *Through the Looking Glass*

. . . a gentle chill, an ambiguity, begins to creep in among
the words. Heretofore the naming of names has gone on
either literally or as metaphor. But now . . . a new mode
of expression takes over. It can only be called a kind of
ritual reluctance.
              —Thomas Pynchon, *The Crying of Lot 49*

Disparate thoughts for desperate times—as I reconsider Gerald Graff's
and Gary Tate's responses to *Left Margins*. Do we, the contributors,
merely deceive ourselves and trick our students (and colleagues), intentionally or unintentionally, by mistaking *liberal pluralism* for *radical
pedagogy*? Do we forget the need to teach students how to "master"
words—so as to hold power—through effective and logical writing?
Perhaps we do. More likely, though, we challenge the latter at the risk
of the former in our attempts to make visible the symbiotic relationship between language, culture, and identity.

    Tate's concern for "empty pedagogical space" (269) is well taken,
as much of composition theory fails to critically inform classroom
practices. So too is Graff's observation that to avoid playing the very
demagogues we seek to rout, "oppositional theorists tend to dilute or

abandon their avowed antipluralism without acknowledging it" (277). Certainly between the land of radical pedagogy and the shores of indoctrination many a beast lies in wait, as any practitioner soon discovers. However, the classroom that purposely embraces oppositional praxis does not necessarily equal an *absence* of writing instruction—it merely demands a reconfiguration of *writing*. And the teacher who creates space for "competing theories" so as not to "impose" a political perspective on students does not necessarily lapse into *liberal pluralism*—she subverts this very possibility by demonstrating language as political in-total and not in-kind.

Graff also comments that it "is foolish to seek to radicalize students until we have first created a political debate in the university that enables political positions to make sense to them" (281–82). I would agree; we do need to help students see larger curriculum connections to our individual courses to be successful cultural critics. But I also suspect that most of the contributors in this collection speak to issues of multiculturalism, feminism, and gender—how can we not? Many of us, no doubt, invite our students to challenge selected "readings" and "writings"—both in our own courses and in others. And some of us even confront openly our institutionalized positions of authority as bestowers of the grade.

Teaching has taught me not to define writing or radical pedagogy in *either/or* terms. To do so is to reject the possibilities as well as the problems of language and discourse. It is to long for an ideal classroom—for a different mode of communication, one that avoids the pitfalls of the literal and the metaphorical by emptying a classroom of concerns beyond students' "words" or by objectifying and thus equalizing all political positions.

Counterstatement to Ohmann

by Paul Gutjahr

Not that it makes me proud, but my first reaction to criticism is often defensiveness. Frequently when I read a critique of my work, I immediately begin formulating my counterattack. To this, I will say that. To that, I will say this. Instead of looking for a critique's truth, my tendency is to hone in on its weaknesses.

In reading—and rereading—Richard Ohmann's Afterword, I confess that I was already beginning to formulate my defensive position before I paused long enough to think about why he had struck such a nerve in me. Ohmann ends his essay by thinking about the question of what is next for students once they complete our courses. In saying, "Are they to live on as sad sophisticates, pessimists, smartasses, cynics?" Ohmann captured in a few words what has troubled me for years. I am not interested in only showing my students that the world is a hopelessly complex place, riddled with subjectivity and problems that can only be analyzed but never answered.

Ohmann pushed me once again to consider what I have long wanted to incorporate into my writing class, namely, avenues of action which force my students out of their sophisticated complacency and into a world desperately in need of people who want to do more than moan and theorize. If I truly want my students to come to terms with just how much power words have, there is no better way for them to realize this than to get them into arenas where such power can be clearly seen. Thus, in the semesters ahead I am planning to give a portion of my class over to writing assignments tied to activities that happen outside the classroom. Most specifically, I would like to give my students hands-on experience with the importance of reading and writing skills through getting them involved in programs such as teaching illiterate adults how to read, writing letters for legal services who serve the poor, reading books for the blind, or helping out in primary or secondary school reading labs.

I am not expecting to change the world overnight through these activities, but I do want my students to experience in as many ways as possible just how important the skills of reading and writing are. More than this, however, I want them to know that the problems we have talked about in my class, such as inequities in material and educational distribution, are not problems from which they are disconnected, or problems beyond their ability to help.

Some may question whether I can really accomplish anything through this enforced volunteerism. To be honest, I do not know; I have not tried this plan yet. I do know that cultural studies demands that we pay attention to the ways we are socially connected, dependent, destructive. I also know that the teaching of writing demands that students realize that the words they use, and how they use them, are inexplicably tied to social relationships. Thus, I believe that any attempt to address this social connection is best done through helping students see their role in culture not as something predetermined by culture's sheer complexity but as something they can help determine in small, if not large, ways.

As I read over this, I realize that this is not really a "counterstatement" to Ohmann's Afterword. If anything, it is an agreement. I agree with Ohmann that we as teachers have opportunities in our classes to move our students beyond the paralysis of analysis into creative avenues of cultural change. What these avenues may be will take myriad forms, guided by myriad ideologies, but in the end they need to be avenues of practice, not just theory. It is here where my heart beats with Ohmann's in saying that it is truly questionable whether teaching that does not reach outside the classroom should be in the classroom in the first place.

A Letter from Kathleen Dixon

Jan. 4, 1994
Grand Forks, North Dakota

Dear Al and Karen:

Thanks for the opportunity to read and respond to the articles slated for *Left Margins*.

I curled up on my couch at the end of a cold and tiring day (35-below with the wind chill) to read the pieces on composition/cultural studies pedagogy written by my peer teachers; and yes, they rekindled my inner furnace. None of the commentators (Giroux, Kennedy, Tate, Graff, Ohmann) mention how taxing this kind of teaching—the joining of composition and cultural studies—can be. We're tackling enormous social problems; the work can be frustrating for us as well as our students. I appreciate knowing that there are others out there doing this difficult work, and that these folks are such sophisticated practitioners *and* theorists of writing pedagogy. The isolation of teaching Graff notes is partly mitigated for me in reading this volume: my colleagues are out there!

I must say that I was similarly impressed with your preface and postface. Finally, someone to articulate cultural studies theory in a readable style, able to make the appropriate connections to writing pedagogy. Your argument in response to Tate and Graff is first-rate. I can't add anything there.

With the notable exception of Richard Ohmann's, the theory/commentary pieces were disappointing. Did they read our pieces before they wrote, or were they responding primarily to the title of the manuscript, *Left Margins*? It seems odd that anyone who read our pieces would accuse us of indoctrination. Most of these courses seem to be built upon the notion of self-reflexivity: both students and teachers are made hyper-aware of the social and political contexts within which thinking and writing transpires. How could that be indoctrination (Kennedy)? And how could that be some kind of avoidance of teaching writing (Tate)?

The self-reflexive nature of the articles on teaching can sometimes be seen in the forms themselves. The persona I use in my narrative, "Making and Taking Apart Culture in the (Writing) Classroom," is deliberately intended to evoke hero narratives of our culture (note the ending, "change *can* come"). I, and my students, are intended to be figured as heroes. This choice doesn't proceed out of naivete or easy triumphalism. After rigorous deconstruction, what? More and more now, I am asking students to consider hero models, and other myths, as ways to think about the possibilities of agency, commitment, and responsibility. I believe this is a partial antidote to the serious side-effect of radical teaching Richard Ohmann posits in his commentary: What happens to our students once they begin to question radically? Do they become cynics?

I would say that many already come to our classes steeped in the cynicism spread by the mass media and by my own generation of baby boomers. Benjamin R. Barber writes in *Harper's* that the U.S. underfunds education because "we have given up on the future" (46). And I think that's true. One might consider this a kind of generational hatred; thus the emergence of "Generation X." Hear the voice of "Generation X," a largely white male voice, I would conjecture, in the person of one of my students, a farm boy from a state where our much-vaunted work ethic is often said to snare more jobs for North Dakotans than for inner city kids: "Why ask why? Don't ask why anymore. In the world of today, it does not matter how hard you try, what you do for a living, where you live, how you treat people, or how much money you have, there will always be somebody who is unhappy. You might as well get used to fending for yourself and living with the unhappy people around you. I say if you're not sure what to do, do what you first thought right and then if it doesn't work you don't have anybody or anything to blame for the failure." I believe that bell hooks is right, that the time is ripe for many more of us to work together, alienation having spread so widely: "The overall impact of postmodernism is that many other groups now share with black folks a sense of deep alienation, despair, uncertainty, and loss of a sense of grounding even if it is not informed by shared circumstance. Radical postmodernism calls attention to those shared sensibilities which cross the boundaries of class, gender, race, etc., that could be fertile ground for the construction of empathy—ties that would promote recognition of common commitments, and serve as a base for solidarity and coalition" (27).

The young generation still faces problems of race, gender, and class so deeply embedded in our psyches as to resist discovery even, much less examination and refiguration. In addition, young people face the problems of rapid technological change, deterioration of the planet, and increasing concentration of money and power in the hands of fewer multinational corporations. These are huge problems that would daunt any sane person. In the face of this, how can anyone carry on business as usual? *Topoi, memoria, logos* itself—all have changed. I can find no ethical alternative to teaching in such a way as to address these problems and to try to find, together with my students, some methods for tackling them. I say "together with my students" because I admit to not knowing the answers to the problems we face. Since I am (usually) older and trained as a thinker, I can lead the way, though, at least for the length of a semester.

We are now critically lacking in our public life what used to be supplied in private by women: maternal nurturing. This Ohmann does not acknowledge, but I think it bears the mention. Before students or anyone can even want to become involved in political work, and while one is so involved, one needs the foundation of a basic belief in one's own worth and in the worth of work-in-the-world. Skepticism is absolutely necessary, but cynicism wounds. Our students—and more broadly, the people of the present youthful generation—need to know that we, the older generations, love them and believe in their ability to carry out the work that needs to be done. Someone needs to say this, and to act upon it. It may be that we no longer wish to name these sustaining activities "maternal nurturance," but we'd better figure out how to achieve the effect of feeling worthy and able. Women should be credited with their historic and continuing contributions to this vital work; skilled nurturers of both sexes must be recognized for their expertise in any refiguring of the public sphere.

Judging from the pieces on pedagogy I've read in this volume, there are many fine teachers in composition programs demonstrating such skill and concern for their students. Would that the phenomenon were more widespread. And not just in a thousand isolated classrooms, but in transformed curricula taught by transformed professors and instructors who know how to act jointly with their students in pursuit of the best thinking and writing of which they are capable, on matters of great moment to us and to them. Perhaps this book can play a part in that scenario.

Yours,
Kathleen Dixon

Counterstatement on Gerald Graff's "The Dilemma of Oppositional Pedagogy: A Response" and Gary Tate's "Empty Pedagogical Space and Silent Students"

*Christopher Wise*_____

In his essay "The Dilemma of Oppositional Pedagogy: A Response," Gerald Graff argues that he sees in this volume "the reappearance of a classical double bind that . . . has plagued radical pedagogy since its emergence in the late sixties." Graff characterizes this "double bind" in terms of a conflict between the oppositional teacher's commitment to a critique of liberal pluralism (or a "free marketplace of ideas") and his/her desire to avoid assuming an authoritarian (i.e., Stalinist) posture: "[T]he only way oppositional pedagogy can avoid being authoritarian," Graff states, "is by ceasing to be oppositional" (275). Graff's argument in this regard is essentially a rehash of his earlier thesis from "Co-optation" in *The New Historicism*, where he explored a remarkably similar "double-bind" (173), largely by critiquing the role of the "Uncompromising Cultural Radical [*sic*]" (168). In Graff's latest essay, he also seems committed to revealing for us the "silliness" of the various radicals' views in these pages (174), perhaps because they, like the "young instructor" from the Midwest in his "Co-optation" essay (168), are not yet seasoned enough to understand that being a subversive today means "little more than a plus-mark [or] a gold star" on one's curriculum vitae (173), and that shop-worn "terms like 'radical' and 'left' may be on their way out" (180).

To this end, Graff summarizes for us the "contradictory" pedagogical theories of James R. Bennett, who once wrote an essay for *College English* which apparently typifies the error of contemporary radical teachers Graff sees in these pages. However, Bennett's views, at least in my opinion, are not particularly representative of the majority of essays printed in this book: They certainly are not representative of my own. Bennett's essay seems rather to be a convenient vehicle for Graff to air his own already well-known views and to avoid dealing with the writers in this volume on their own merits.

The chief problem with Gary Tate's otherwise valuable essay is that he inadvertently maintains the traditional hermeneutic distinction between thought and language, or, borrowing from Wilhelm von Humboldt, between *energeia* ("intentional meaning") and *ergon* ("articulated system") (see Jameson 108–9). Obviously, such a view might be successfully defended, but only if Tate could articulate more precisely what he means by *"writing"* (270; Tate's emphasis) in opposition to the wholly different definition of this term that is advanced by most contributors to this volume. For Tate, *writing* seems to mean merely "prose" or "style," the assumption being that instructors can somehow improve their students' "writing styles" as a pedagogical practice distinct from engaging their thought processes. The Derridean view, of course, suggests the opposite, and most advocates of postmodern theory would reject this division as erroneous. While I personally respect this traditional distinction, I hope my own position involves considerable more deliberation than Tate's.

What he might have said, by way of strengthening his argument, is that he wished writing instructors were more concerned with the formal articulation, or even reification, of their students' thoughts *on paper*, rather than being satisfied with "merely" altering their perceptions of reality. I myself find it difficult to separate these spheres in practice, though I insist that such a distinction retains a theoretical value, especially as a necessary ruse against the hegemony of deconstructive ideology. The justification for such an approach could also lie in that it would offer students valuable survival skills, both outside and inside the academy, or Tate might have defended what he calls "writing" in terms of rhetoric, or the quasi-objective "rules" of social discourse. In any case, this is the position taken in my own essay, where, incidentally, my "silenced" students are quoted nearly a dozen times.

Talk, Thought, Writing and Politics

Peter J. Caulfield _____

Where does talk end and writing begin? Where does thought end and writing begin? Where do talk, thought, and writing end and politics begin? Where does education begin and politics end, or vice versa? What's the relationship between a liberal and a useful education? When does writing become part of a historical "conversation"? What's the connection between a writing class, even a politically oriented one, and real politics? What is real politics anyway?

As I reflect on the various critiques by Tate, Graff, and Ohmann of the essays in this anthology, these and more questions spin through my (socially constructed) mind. Bakhtin says, in effect, minds without signs are vacant spaces, mere potentialities (930). Vygotsky says, "A thought embodied in words remains a shadow" (153). Tip O'Neil says (or liked to say often), "All politics is local."

What can *I* say in response to these thoughtful critiques of the essays in this volume? Let me begin with the personal. Gary Tate says, "Even Caulfield's statement about rhetoric says nothing about the writing of his students. One would think that the goals of a composition course would say something about composition" (271). A final question, a big one: What is composition or writing?

On one level, of course, it's what Hemingway once said of it: "Getting the words right." So one goal of a composition or writing course, including mine, ought to be helping students to get their words right. So some of my goals ought to, and do, involve helping my students understand things like subject-verb agreement, parallelism, and paragraph development.

Yet we all know that words are just signs for other things, primarily thoughts or concepts (including thoughts or concepts about elements of material reality). So it seems to me that another legitimate goal of a composition or writing course is helping students to "get their thoughts *right*." Yet what might that really mean? It could mean helping them to get their thoughts to be "politically correct," but that's not what I mean by it. Though I can't speak for the other authors in this text, what I mean by it has more to do with getting students to a more sophisticated understanding of the origins, development, and ramifications of their existing thoughts about a host of critically important historical, political, social, and economic issues.

Moreover, I am convinced that our thoughts originate and develop primarily through rhetoric: through listening, reading, speaking, and writing, through the dizzyingly complex permutations of these language experiences throughout our lives. I maintain, therefore, that it is a wholly legitimate goal of a composition course to encourage students to think about their thoughts, beliefs, and values, and where those came from—before, during, and after writing. Neither we teachers, nor our students, can ever get the words right until we get the thoughts right.

As to Graff's concerns on the relationship between politics and education, and between the politics of an individual classroom and other political sites, I agree with Tip O'Neil. All politics *is* local, and one local political site is my classroom. I also believe in the axiom, "Everything is political," including the most ostensibly apolitical classroom. Having said that, though, I hasten to add that I am not a politician, let alone a revolutionary. What I am is a politically and socially concerned writing teacher trying, among other things, to influence those I teach to become somewhat more politically and socially concerned human beings.

Obviously, I am also trying to help those students become better writers. Given my understanding of the relationship between thought and language, however, I am convinced that they cannot become better writers until and unless they also become better, more sophisticated, less solipsistic thinkers.

Thoreau says, "A man [sic] has not everything to do, but something; and because he cannot do *everything*, it is not necessary that he should do *something* wrong" (133). Writing teachers cannot do everything, but we can do something, and we have to trust our own senses of morality and responsibility to insure ourselves that the something we are doing is right for ourselves, for our students, and for our society. Regarding the class I describe in this volume, as well as my other classes, I feel reasonably comfortable with what I'm doing.

Reply to Gary Tate

Raymond A. Mazurek _____

One day when I was in graduate school, an elderly man who lived across the street asked me about my work. I explained that I was a graduate student in American literature, but what I did for a living was teach courses in writing. He asked me what sort of writing I taught: Was it literature? Was it journalism? I tried to explain that it was neither of these, but a more general introduction to writing applicable to any and all circumstances. To my neighbor, however, this seemed to be another example of the strangeness of university folks, analogous to the physics professor he had once rented an apartment to who had trouble with the simplest electrical work. How, he asked, could one teach a general course in writing, rather than something more specific?

I was reminded of this incident, with its suggestion that there is nothing natural about the way universities divide writing from content, when reading Gary Tate's "Empty Pedagogical Space and Silent Students." There is much that Tate says that I sympathize with. It is probably true that many of the essays in this volume, including my own, might be improved by more focus on student writing. However, I find much more questionable his acceptance of the naturalness of the "writing/content" opposition. If we look at this opposition historically, then it seems far from accidental that the intellectual seriousness Tate applauds in our practice is something that has been so hard to achieve in the college writing course. Composition developed as a nonfield taught by nonfaculty, and at most institutions across the United States that description is still more or less accurate, despite the progress made by composition as a research field. The apparent naturalness of the theoretical opposition between "writing" and "content" rests on the hierarchical division of labor within colleges and universities.

Practically, Tate's call for more focus on student writing has some merit. Given the place of writing courses in the curriculum—as almost the only courses many students will have where a significant amount of writing takes place—I feel a responsibility to focus a sufficient amount of time and energy on student writing, using many traditional methods: reading examples of student essays, suggesting strategies for successful papers, conferencing and workshop sessions, written comments on basic literacy issues as well as content, and so on. It is difficult to juggle all this while also trying to avoid the trivialization of content that frequently takes place in composition courses. Most of the writing courses I teach focus on the tensions between the public discourses students are immersed in and the academic discourses (the strange ways of the university, which we are always part of whether we want to admit it or not) which students are being initiated into. I continue to think of these courses within the terms Paulo Freire set forth: How can I select materials which will lead to an exploration of the ideological tensions and social conflicts within public life? How can I create a "safe space" where students will speak honestly and where I can also bring to them my own analysis of the issues? However, part of my political commitment to the students is providing them the means to learn to write in ways that will be acceptable in the various contexts in which they wish to succeed. Recently, with the increased number of African-American students at my campus, I have (for almost the first time) students that might be located to my "left" politically; some of these students are also from very underprivileged backgrounds. I am myself from the lower levels of the white working class, and I can sympathize with the needs of all my students to survive economically; I would not want the kind of writing instruction I provide to become unconventional in ways that threatened my students' employability. (This goal may sound a bit conventional to some of my colleagues on the Left, but I have not noticed, having recently attended the annual conference of the Modern Language Association, that academics, radical or otherwise, are themselves unconcerned about finding jobs.)

The job crisis is hardly the only aspect of contemporary culture that students and teachers share in common. Tate suggests that many of the contributors implicitly construct students as "victims of the 'dominant culture' " (271). Thinking about it, I have to admit that I see my students and myself as both victims of dominant culture and as participants in other complex cultural tendencies from which a more truly democratic culture might emerge. The major difference between my students and myself is not our "victimization" (I don't live on another planet from them, or in a purified "liberated" zone); it is that I am more at home within the codes and conventions of the university, with all its contradictory possibilities.

Tate recognizes the difficulty of initiating students into those codes, raising another issue that has been very important in my writing classes: What happens to student writing when students respond to difficult reading? I have on file many essays from the "Media, Self, and Culture" classes, which I plan to reexamine in the future in order to better understand something that happened in those sections: the course was most successful, both in the sophistication of the writing and the critical thinking about culture, for about one-third of the students, many of whom were nontraditional students (some only a few years older than 18), and least successful for another third, many of whom had been basic writers who had been in the developmental course the previous semester. The upper third appeared to do better because they had a broader acquaintance with a range of culture and thought and a greater self-confidence in expressing their views; the lower third had a greater difficulty integrating complicated prose into their work and found some of the assignments too difficult. They were often struggling with basic issues, such as how to organize an essay or avoid sentences that sprawled into incoherence, which grew more intense when the assignments became more difficult. This experience has led me to teach basic writing again, for the first time since 1987, in order to get a better understanding of what is happening.

A detailed examination of the student writing produced when students encounter assignments that are both intellectually and ideologically challenging might lead to a better essay than the one I wrote for this volume. However, something else is also at work here, for what happens in composition courses is related to the historical conditions in which composition is taught. When I taught my two sections of "Media, Self, and Culture," I was also teaching a course in popular culture for the first time and an honors section of contemporary literature. I also wrote most of my essay for this volume and did a considerable amount of advising and committee work. I recognize that part of the problem my more basic students had was that I did not shift quickly enough to deal with the local problems of one of the two sections. A few of the more basic students made breakthroughs, mostly by coming in for lots of individual help. The others needed more one-on-one coaching than I gave, or felt able to give. Tate talks about his grades during a two-year period when he taught five sections of freshman composition. I don't know what his course load has been, but in fourteen years teaching full-time at three universities, I have taught sixty-six sections of composition (mostly first-year writing) and twenty-one sections of other areas (literature, humanities, American studies). I also taught five sections of writing during the summer, and had a one-semester sabbatical thrown in. I can't find a two-year period where I taught fewer than eight or nine sections of freshmen and sophomore writing, even given the sabbatical year. And yet I am not really a member of the underclass that teaches composition. I have tenure, and the freedom to experiment. Most composition in the United States, I suspect, is taught by part-time instructors, full-time adjuncts with positions that cannot lead to tenure, and teaching assistants (though a cursory glance at the statistics regarding student enrollments nationally suggests that TAs do not teach most composition courses in the United States, because so much of the student enrollment is at universities without graduate programs—yet one still hears prominent academics in composition studies refer to composition as something primarily taught by TAs).

When Tate wishes to define a space for composition studies that is not completely dominated by other concerns, one of my responses is to applaud—I have spent most of my career teaching composition and have seen too many instances of the way professors of literature (and others who hold sway within English departments) treat composition as a despised and third-rate field not to at least partially agree. There have been real gains from the years of serious intellectual reflection on composition—including the reaffirmation of pedagogy as a worthwhile concern and the questioning of elitist notions of literacy such as those Tate attacks. However, not very much of the scholarship on composition (radical or otherwise) filters down to the classroom. The writing class has always been taught primarily by an academic underclass, and the composition/literature, writing/content split is dependent on the historical reproduction of this class.

Composition pedagogy is often so unimaginative because composition is conceived as a noncourse taught by nonfaculty. Course outlines, syllabi, and lists of required texts are distributed partly because of concerns for control of these nonfaculty. (I do agree that there should be *some* continuity, as well as academic freedom, in course offerings, and have even been shocked to remember hearing myself sound like Gary Tate when I talk to new adjunct faculty at my campus, but I believe that there should be much more democracy in curricular planning). I would guess that Tate, like myself, is outraged at the class inequities in our profession; perhaps it is partly to defend writing programs against yet another encroachment from powerful outsiders, this time "cultural theory," that has moved him to respond in the way he has. However, I think that such a defense is mistaken: first, because new ideas in cultural studies and rhetoric (including some that are discussed in this volume) provide the intellectual potential to overcome, at least intellectually, the composition/literature split that has plagued English departments; and second, because the split between writing/content has always depended on the existence of an underclass that taught writing.

As Robert Connors, Jim Berlin, and others have pointed out, courses in composition developed in the late nineteenth and early twentieth centuries, when the German research university was grafted onto the American college. Professors of rhetoric, who held respectable academic posts, left rhetoric for literature as courses in rhetoric were redefined as courses in writing, not speaking, with grading loads that even today's academic underclass can hardly imagine. The production of a trivialized composition course was based in a historical reality where some instructors tried to respond to frequent (even daily) "themes" by a hundred or so students, and others lectured about the "higher concerns" of literary study. As Berlin notes, a positivist epistemology which contrasted literal and symbolic language also undergirded the rhetoric/literature split. The existence of an underclass of composition instructors (graduate students and permanent instructors, many of the latter women, some of them men) helped to free the professor of literature from the more dreary and labor intensive work of writing instruction; it also provided a continual reminder of the unexamined, "literal" language to which the literary could be contrasted.

Much has changed in the past hundred years; however, at many colleges and universities, students still do most of their writing in composition courses taught by marginal faculty, supplemented by a few courses in writing-across-the-curriculum. I sometimes feel that my project, which includes initiating students into academic writing, is rendered absurd by the fact that students do so little writing of any kind in their other courses. Looking at my students as *writers* is, therefore, only one of the ways which I need to see my students. To reify the writing/content split is only to perpetuate the historical inequalities that have structured the profession. I want more "content" in writing courses and more writing in "content" courses. I want to see all writing instructors begin to challenge their students in more imaginative ways. Controls are best exercised by bringing everyone into dialogue, by treating all teachers as faculty—yet even as I write this, I know that it is very unlikely to happen because "our profession, as it is now practiced in this country, rests on, *is based on*, a foundation of despicable inequality" (Slevin 2).

I have no wish to lay these inequalities at Tate's door, for I see him as an ally more than an opponent, although I would go further than he would in reconstructing the English department around areas such as cultural studies. However, such curricular reforms are probably not the most important changes we can make. I suspect that attempts to reform the internal politics of colleges and universities—particularly the class divisions that separate teachers from researchers, marginal from "real" faculty—would have more lasting impact on the politics of composition courses than experiments in radical pedagogy.

In Reply to Gerald Graff

Adam Katz _____

Before responding to Gerald Graff's criticisms of my essay and his attack on oppositional pedagogy in general, I consider it necessary to pose the following question: Why is a confirmed centrist (actually reactionary, as we shall see) like Graff invited to "oversee" (and from what "vantage point") a collection of essays intended, at least originally, to represent "critical margins" within the academy? Why, that is, is Graff permitted to occupy the academic "Panopticon" (or guard tower) from which he can "survey" opposition, while the other contributors to the volume were told explicitly that their submissions were to deal with the "nuts and bolts" of classroom practices (which, among other things, allows Graff to use these "narrow" concerns as a point against opposition and in favor of his "broader" outlook)? Why does the dominant assumption—that radical pedagogy can only maintain its credibility (its right to existence) by answering, time and time again, the objections of the Right and Center, however reactionary or simplistic—go unquestioned here, at least in practice? (For example, in relation to the theoretical yield in terms of advancing inquiries into the possibilities of oppositional pedagogy, I would have preferred, in this response, to address some of the questions raised by Ohmann; however, such is the political economy of knowledges that it is more urgent that I address the way in which the presence of Graff, as a guarantee of institutional legitimacy, functions to repress oppositional knowledges.)

I should make it clear that I am not asking a question about the editors' intentions; rather, I want to inquire into the objective function served by Graff's "overseeing." We can see very clearly what this function is by turning to Graff's article (written with Gregory Jay) in the fall 1993 issue of *Democratic Culture*, the literary organ of Teachers for a Democratic Culture ("Some Questions About Critical Pedagogy"). This article represents the overt transformation of TDC into a policing force on behalf of the institutional center, with an eye toward an alliance with forces on the right. (Graff's and Jay's disclaimer that this essay "represents our personal view" can be discounted, since this move was implicit in TDC's agenda from the beginning, as can be seen from the complaint in its "Statement of Principles" that right-wing critics "make no distinction between extremists among their opposition and those who are raising legitimate questions about the relations of society and culture"—that is, the goal of TDC from the beginning has been to make this distinction absolutely clear, and Graff and Jay are consistent with TDC "Principles" in insisting upon this point with sycophantic repetitiveness.)

Graff and Jay announce that "the time has come when some serious efforts at Left self-criticism have to be ventured, even if they give some aid and comfort to the enemy. The risk is necessary, for it is only such self-criticism that can save the movement for the democratic transformation of the academy from being undermined by its own advocates" (1). Not surprisingly, these "democratic transformations" need to be saved from the work of oppositional pedagogues, who are guilty, above all, of treating questions (like those regarding the necessity to oppose inequality—which one might consider a part of "democratic transformations") as "settled" (1). Like all centrists, Graff and Jay prefer not draw the actual conclusions of their argument; they are content to place "hints" which will be understood by the initiated. So Graff and Jay claim that, despite their criticisms, "[w]e grant that critical pedagogy has its place at the level of individual teaching practices [although, as we shall see, Graff also opportunistically uses this limitation to criticize the "narrowness" of oppositional pedagogy—AK], *at least when it is willing to respect the resistance of students*" (16; italics added).

Let's reverse this democratic claim: if oppositional pedagogy does not respect the resistance of students, it does not have a place, even at the level of individual practices. And according to Graff's and Jay's "dialogic" theory of truth, how would we know when sufficient "disrespect" has been displayed? Since the teacher, the other faculty members, and the students each represent "just one among a number of possible conclusions" (16) ("this class wasn't any fun," "we don't do things that way," "this is a composition class, not a class in political science," "the professor did not respect my opinions," being some "possible conclusions"), "some" student complaints (expressed, say, through student evaluation forms) along with "some" faculty disapproval (how much? one of course would not want to get too precise and tie one's hands, but it would probably be best to err on the side of "respect," whatever this is taken to mean in any pragmatically defined instance, i.e., whatever it is convenient to take it to mean) would have to be enough "proof," subject, of course, to the "discretion" of those who actually possess institutional power (dialogue, according to Graff and Jay, should not come to end in the classroom, but, as they well know—as do others, albeit from the barrel's end—someone ultimately decides in practice who gets to continue to "dialogue" and who is excluded). In other words, this "acceptance" of oppositional pedagogy as an individual practice is in fact a *general* rejection of it which can be applied at *any time*, since oppositional pedagogues will always, by definition, according to the understandings of Graff, Jay, and others, be unwilling to respect the resistance of students (they will always insist that certain questions are "settled"; they teach from a position).

As usual, then, contained within the velvet glove of "dialogue" is the iron fist of the threat of institutional banishment, for which Graff and Jay provide an acceptably liberal legitimation. To translate Graff's and Jay's idealist ruminations into institutional practices: if the oppositional pedagogues do not "cooperate" with their "ideological opponents" (16), they will be excluded (fired, denied tenure, blacklisted . . .). The insistence on cooperation is key here, because Graff speaks from the standpoint of institutional stability, that is, of stabilizing the crisis in academic knowledges and practices, which involves accepting what has already been "changed" (this "realism" distinguishes Graff and Jay from the right), while adamantly opposing any other changes (this requires an attempt to forge alliances with the right).

I must assume that, since Graff's aims in no way coincide with the declared ones of the volume (where has Graff openly supported "left" goals, and aligned his own pedagogy and intellectual work with those goals, such as, at a minimum, substantial wealth redistribution—on the contrary, Graff explicitly opposes those who teach from these "premises," meaning that his claim to criticize the left from "within" is a fraud), the inclusion of his essay (or that of an equivalent "overseer") was an implied or actual precondition for the acceptance of this volume for publication by a "mainstream" publisher. In other words, for the Left to mainstream itself, it must internalize the policing function of the dominant culture (i.e., Graff's "dialogue").

This, in other words, is the "pluralism" supported by Graff, and which he chides the Left for rejecting: the pluralism of the powerful, based upon unchallenged "axioms" (e.g., that "education is an institution in an overlapping system of democratic processes," so "the school should not enforce a program that commits everyone to a predetermined worldview, however just we may believe it is" [16]—of course, the logically rigorous Graff and Jay do not note the internally contradictory status of this statement), while the powerless must do little more, it seems, than endlessly question their own premises ("[t]he premise that the classroom, like society, is constituted by a readily identifiable hierarchy of the disenfranchised and the dominant is not unreasonable or indefensible, but it *is* a premise and one that should be as open to criticism as any traditional axiom . . . " [16]). The powerless and marginal can be included insofar as they are careful not to "impose" anything—including the reality of powerlessness itself—that is, as long as they are prepared to "cooperate" (to recognize existing reality as democratic) and do no more than "persuade" the dominant to make a place for them (in this way, the changes which are actually imposed by the struggles of the oppressed can be exploited by opportunities like Graff and Jay). Bourgeois pluralism, that is, is nothing but the incorporation of the subordinated on the terms which reproduce the rule of the dominant—the subordinated are entitled to plead for a different type of rule, and the dominant allows for (and even benefits from) the criticism of certain aspects of its rule, all on the condition that the terms of domination—that the Left show "balance" (i.e., that despite the widely disproportionate share of resources controlled by the different "sides," the Left cannot make a move without showing that it "respects" every hackneyed "objection" that can be posed, with the Right and Center of course subjected to no similar obligation)—are not challenged (in which case force is explicitly introduced, not least for its "pedagogical" effect on those with some questions about which "premises" are off limits).

Now we can move on to Graff's criticisms of oppositional pedagogy, and my own essay in particular. I already mentioned Graff's exploitation of a condition imposed by the structure of the volume itself, that the submissions focus on specific classroom practices: so, Graff remarks that none of the essays point to "a connection between the atomized course and the depoliticized, individualistic ethos of the curriculum" (275). It is now possible to demonstrate the significance of this criticism, which is to delegitimate any pedagogical practices which are not aimed at "dialogue," or, more accurately, "cooperation." Graff's liberal complacency is such an unquestioned presupposition of his practices that he doesn't think to ask why acceptable centrist pedagogues like himself, who cooperate with institutional aims and even provide more sophisticated strategies for policing dissent, are able to take a "broader" viewpoint—for example, that of determining the structure and content of curricula—while those who struggle against the institution have little more than their individual classrooms (and often not even that).

That is, contrary to the fantastic nightmares of the Right (which Graff, who apparently finds it necessary—in the passage cited above—to warn against constructing the educational system from a radical viewpoint, seems to share), "radicals" have not taken control of the American university. Rather, it is the Graffs who are asked to stabilize social conflicts within a formalized curriculum which reduces these conflicts to different "ideas," and to decide which conflicts are properly dialogic and which are not. This is no reason for revolutionary intellectuals not to "generalize," that is, to theorize the conditions of transformation beyond their own classroom practices (when they are not explicitly precluded from doing so on pain of exclusion or expulsion); however, it does mean that the purpose of such work is not to provide raw material for academic entrepreneurial crisis managers like Graff ("workable programs"), but rather to posit transformations which are "impossible" on existing terms, and therefore really challenge those terms.

Graff's entire distinction between "pluralism" and "authoritarianism" (I know that Graff must have questioned these premises somewhere) can therefore be understood as a logic of inclusion and exclusion. Thus, the effectivity of his "carrot and stick" method of criticizing oppositional pedagogues—the real problem with opposition, according to Graff, is that it is "inconsistent." In my own case, "Katz vacillates between a picture of his classroom as a scene of engagement with ideas and a scene of indoctrination" (278). The usefulness of Graff's method here is to combine "consent" with "force": you are not quite acceptable, but you might yet be, given a few modifications, a different emphasis, etc. That these "inconsistencies" are in fact effects of the regime of pluralism (its systematic "impositions"), supported by Graff's criticisms, is obviously a possibility beyond the purview of Graff's "premises."

According to Graff, *if* students' "opinions" are subjected to systemic materialist critique (and if the classroom is constructed for this very purpose), *then* these "opinions" are not being given a "legitimate place in the classroom" (279). Graff can't find this apparently logical construct in my essay, so he must assume that my argument is "inconsistent." Since Graff must see the classroom as a purely ahistorical, idealist space ("logical" and not material), he cannot understand that the "legitimacy" of students' "opinions" as a historical fact, supported by the dominant culture, can be "recognized" by the oppositional classroom, precisely as a way of questioning the production of that "legitimacy" itself. What is excluded, in this case, is that the students "go on thinking of their ideas as 'private property' " (278) without offering an explanation for this in relation to the premises of the class which have advanced an argument for the political and intellectual untenability of this position. Again, the hypocritical and reactionary character of Graff's position is evident in the fact that he condemns oppositional pedagogy for doing what any classroom does: include some knowledge-positions and exclude others, and use standards for determining the value of students' contributions to the class. In other words, any classroom evaluates the "legitimacy" of students' knowledge-positions: the difference in the oppositional classroom is that it openly posits and explains its criteria (the ability to "follow through," to theorize "consequences"—and not merely rehearse the present "standoff"/division of labor between liberal and conservative forces), rather than allowing them to be based on the oppressive pluralist commonsense of the institution.

So, Graff and his allies never have to justify their premise that the institution really is pluralist and democratic (even on their terms): the acceptance of this claim is simply a condition of entering into institutionally sanctioned "dialogue." In quoting a (good, pluralist) passage from my essay, Graff notes that "John Stuart Mill would hardly have raised an eyebrow" (278). I don't wish to speak in the name of the spirit of John Stuart Mill (this is Graff's desire), but if Graff is right about this he only demonstrates the degeneration of liberal pluralism in our time: let us keep in mind that Mill did not propose conditioning the institutional protection of minority positions upon the degree of their "respect" for their public's resistance to their positions, explicitly noting that this would disqualify minority positions from the start. Graff does, indeed, "raise an eyebrow" about a pedagogy which insists upon following through the "logic" of one argument as opposed to another and which can only be undertaken on the basis of strongly held, consistent "premises" that can "follow through" the consequences of positions, a pedagogy which assumes that there are necessary connections between ideas and practices and does not simply leave them as cognitive differences or "hypotheses" which are primarily concerned with insisting upon their merely hypothetical character. After all, if students, like pragmatists such as Graff, deny that positions have consequences (that "something follows"), then Graff would have to acknowledge that even my Millian formulation is an "imposition" upon students, who, as Graff recognizes, might want to "resist" the teacher's insistence that she/he account for the connection between the notion that "opinions" are "private property" and oppressive social relations. According to Graff, the insistence that the connection or lack of connection be argued for would be oppressive to the student who is of the opinion that his/her opinion is not connected to anything else, or that opinions are sacred ground not to be trampled upon by vandalistic teachers, or that writing is about "form" not "content" (i.e., all the constituencies of a tuition-payers' revolt whom, like Clinton's "Reagan Democrats," TDC would probably like to wrest away from their more "natural" alliance with the National Association of Scholars). In other words, for Graff, the only democratic position is to accept that opinions are indeed private property (leaving the inquiry into the social and collective consequences of opinions as the inevitable "totalitarian" opposite, and defining public discourse as negotiations over the most effective way to protect one's property, to avoid having one's premises violated—the "consequences" of which I have already noted). Finally, in order to address the "hard questions" (278) that, according to Graff, I "evade" (even while recognizing that Graff's posing of these "hard questions" is akin to the "provocations" of secret police agencies), it should be made clear that of course oppositional pedagogy represents an "imposition" upon students, since "culture" is nothing other than the totality of such impositions by unequally situated economic, political, and ideological agents: so, while the dominant pedagogy imposes upon students the understanding that they are seekers after universal value or social reconciliation, oppositional pedagogy imposes upon them the understanding that their discourses and practices are sites of irreconcilable social contestation.

There is, as Graff notes, an "inconsistency" in opposing dominant institutions from within in the name of an "external" principle, one not recognized by the institution: collective and democratic control over economic and cultural institutions (that such control does not characterize existing institutions I consider a "not unreasonable or indefensible premise"). This inconsistency consists in the requirement that oppositional pedagogues challenge the rules, conventions, and assumptions of academic practices, and therefore that they critique their everyday, commonsensical operation, even while these operations are imposed upon them (even more forcefully than upon those who have so internalized the dominant assumptions that they don't need to pay much attention to them, do not need to be reminded of them, are not under the constant watchful eye of those charged with enforcing them, and even experience them as "freedom"). It is this "inconsistency," or, rather, historical contradiction and material antagonism (which oppositional pedagogues propose transforming into a site of pedagogy), which allows reactionary ideologues like Gerald Graff to present the following "choice" to oppositional intellectuals: play by the rules or get out! (Graff needs to support a notion of free and rational individual agency, so exclusions can be understood as results of individual behavior and not social economic and power relations—thus, his impositions are naturalized as the protection of the freedom of individuals from authoritarian teachers, while oppositional pedagogues theorize their impositions in relation to the warring social forces which they locate in the student's discourses). The purpose of oppositional pedagogy, of course, is not to produce simulations of this choice for our students by formalizing it as "for or against dialogue." Rather, oppositional pedagogy is interested in undermining the existing social and economic relations by attacking their ideological and institutional supports. This involves exploiting social contradictions, like that between an apparent pluralism and a fundamentally exploitative social system, or between an institution which claims to support rational discourse and that institution's actual ground in systemic material irrationalities which it is unable to question, in order to show that "differences" are really "inequalities" and "contradictions," that is, sites of struggle—and not only in ideas, but in places like the classroom.

Presumably, we can now expect the resources of Teachers for a Democratic Culture to be deployed against teachers who work from this "undemocratic" "premise," and from the further premise that theoretical positions have practical political consequences. Graff, that is, is not against compulsion as such, he is only against compulsion that refuses the mask of "dialogue," that is tied to a pedagogy which does not pretend to be outside of power and authority but rather demystifies them and explains their uses, and which uncovers the global economic compulsion underlying the claims of pluralism: "democracy," for Graff and his allies, is nothing more than unconditional defense of systematic institutional duplicity, cynicism, and repression. The open recognition of this fact will serve a useful purpose if it teaches oppositional pedagogues not to rely upon the paternalistic protection of those who can accept radical ideas once they have become established institutional realities (i.e., once they are no longer radical), but to depend only upon the strengths of their critiques, the power of exposures of contradictions between expressed principles (public relations) and institutional practices, and the effectivity of organized practices grounded in firm and coherent theoretical principles.

Beyond the Binary: The Plenitude of "This Subject Which Is Not One"

*Mary Beth Hines*_____

As the contributors to this collection suggest, cultural studies is at this moment a contested term, always politically charged, always interdisciplinary and, as Giroux argues, always oblivious to pedagogical theory. Yet, as the chapters in this book also demonstrate, the classroom is the site from which rhetorical cultural studies issues are constructed and contested; therefore, pedagogical theory and research can provide texture to our sketches of rhetorical cultural studies classrooms.

But it is not the "subordination" of cultural studies to pedagogy or the "supplementation" of composition with cultural studies that I wish to emphasize here. Echoing North, I fear that the "addition" of cultural studies to composition pedagogy simply threatens to add yet another room to the rambling "House of Lore" (27). That is, instead of adding on, we need to reconceptualize, exploring the ways in which the principles of composition and rhetoric work both in tandem and at odds with those of cultural studies in educational settings.

However, in order to understand how classroom subjects produce diverse knowledges, write new versions of culture, and promote social justice, we might move our analyses beyond the binaries that Graff and Tate suggest. These include Graff's formulation of (invisible) pedagogical theory vs. (visible) cultural studies theory as well as the tension between "good" teacher and "bad" teacher/citizen. The politically correct oppositional teacher ostensibly engages students while the liberal pluralist instructors ostensibly (and merely) elicit conflicting positions. Tate, likewise, advances the polemic that writing pedagogy can service either clear communication or cultural critique. Underlying his endorsement of composition as a service course is an assumption that language offers a transparent window onto reality, a view counterpoised to the belief that language mediates and shapes our understanding of reality. While the turn to dualisms may clarify (read: simplify) the issues at stake in the culture wars, it does not facilitate the exploration of nuance or the development of fine-grained analysis. Just as Irigaray rejects the man/woman binary in order to foreground the multiplicity within and among women, so too might we reject the binaries that threaten to constrain our views of this subject "which is not one." Like woman, rhetorical cultural studies invites as it renders a multiplicity that "resists all adequate definition" (Irigaray 26).

In moving beyond the binary, we can calibrate the contestations and confirmations that occur as teachers and students together analyze language and culture. We can chart those complications and equivocations that unfold as teachers and students work both within rhetorical cultural studies contexts and against larger systems of domination. We can then generate analyses that take into account cultural complexities and pedagogical specificities. In naming the interdisciplinary and material forces acting within, on, and against the cultural subject, we can thereby enrich as we complicate our analyses of practices issuing from classrooms, universities, curricula, and cultures.

And as I suggest that we avoid the binary, I nonetheless resort to it, casting Richard's dilemma as a tension between "imposing" or "exposing" before inviting readers to either abandon reductionist notions or abandon binaries. While I wish to acknowledge that I am implicated in this debate, operating within as I argue against a binary mode, I also contend that these contradictions signal a larger, more compelling issue. That is, despite our collective efforts to "contain" rhetorical cultural studies, its multiplicity of disciplinary articulations and pedagogical orientations suggests a subject that refuses to subordinate its elements into a neatly coherent whole, one whose synergistic effect is more than the sum of equal parts of rhetoric, composition, cultural studies, and pedagogy.

Let us, then, move our discussion beyond the binary and begin to name the implicit and explicit assumptions, goals, conflicts, and contradictions that animate the rhetorical cultural studies classroom. Let us begin to account for the contradictory and competing forces of pedagogy and cultural politics, cultural studies, and rhetoric, just as we begin to acknowledge the material conditions of actual teachers and students. It is, in short, a *transformation* rather than a *supplementation* of composition and cultural studies, a metamorphosis staged within and against the educational state apparatus (Althusser) that this book marks. The rhetorical cultural studies classroom is the site of a plenitude of multiple (inter)disciplinary discourses, practices, and subjects, provocatively exceeding the binaries that threaten to bind it. It is from this vantage point that I measure the comments made by Tate and Graff, marking our collective efforts as indexes to the nascent status of this interdisciplinary subject.

A Response to Gary Tate and Gerald Graff

John C. Hawley, S.J. _____

Without a drop of blood the long roads would be
featureless.
                              —Mahmud Darwish

Gary Tate is concerned because he finds little evidence in this volume to support the conclusion that these various teachers are dedi-
cated to "the quality of [students'] prose." He sees little discussion
of "the nature of their development *as writers*" (270). He seems to
reduce the definition of the word to its least common denominator:
the pure mechanics of prose. His implication is that in exposing "the
tendency for writing teachers to teach something other than writing"
(269) he strikes a blow for justice, implicitly reminding the erring
that *that*, after all, is what they are there to do—not, God help us, to
focus their attention on encouraging the students to have something
to express in the first place. Yet the lack of content and passion are,
in most cases, the paralyzing problem that plagues most students—
writer's block.

Tate asserts that "every teacher . . . constructs [students] . . . and then
teaches those creations" (271). Fair enough, and an explicit recognition
of that fact by teachers should, in my view, be included in a writing
course's content. But one must wonder whether or not Tate admits he
is inescapably "constructing" the teachers he is criticizing. Teaching
"writing" obviously involves attention to grammar, but by the time
one reaches college the real emphasis is more significantly put on
rhetoric. Clarity of thought is the necessary precondition to clarity of
expression; passion prompts one to do whatever is necessary to communicate. Even using a spellcheck and rewriting a clumsy first draft.
Perhaps that dull fact should have been more clearly indicated in the

volume's essays—but to suggest that this is the heart of "writing" is to miss the point of language.

Gerald Graff more compellingly argues that the "oppositional" pedagogue would do well to "try to create [on campus] a political debate that engages [student's] interest to begin with," rather than laying too heavy a burden for such interchange in any single writing course (282). That would certainly help obviate the criticism that the politically committed teacher, in a position of power, feels compelled by justice and truth, as he or she sees it, to engineer "a thoroughgoing rejection of pluralism" in the classroom (279). But debate in the larger forum of the campus (let alone "the world") will not truly engage a student until his or her view of truth is personally challenged. This, I believe, is most effectively encouraged not by the teacher's preaching or psychological intimidation, but by confusing the student. By this I mean the decentering of the student's *Weltanschauung*, a challenge that the student will either accept or avoid. The consideration of a broader view of "reality," offered by the syllabus almost without comment and without clear valorization, can lead to anger and boredom; it can also lead to a *metanoia,* a change of heart that the student *him/herself* brings about.

POST/FACE

*Karen Fitts and Alan W. France*_____

The responses of Gary Tate and Gerald Graff serve not only to increase the dialectical rigor of the book but also to locate the contributors politically in the current national debates over university curricula. Tate raises for examination what he sees as a central tenet of the essays in this collection: a perception that "the composition course is an empty pedagogical space that needs to be filled with 'content' " (269). He argues that, whether the imported "content" be from cultural studies or other subject areas, it is misguided to remove the focus from "the quality of [students'] prose or the nature of their development *as writers*" (270). In describing the act of teaching writing as one in which prose is crafted, rather than as one in which students and teachers confront the more basic issue (in our assessment) of the roles and powers of language, Tate draws attention to a question often heatedly debated in our field: Can we, and if so should we, distinguish between composition courses, which teach writing, and content courses, which use writing? Tate is certainly right to insist that in a composition class the referential substance of writing not be isolated from the student's struggle to give verbal and syntactic shape to it on the page or screen. We think, though, that contributors to this volume manifest their concern with the personal meanings written discourse assumes for the individual writer: the writer's sense of self-awareness conferred by the process of bringing his or her experience into language, of making it meaningful. *Left Margins* is a call to practitioners not to lose sight of the public and social substance (most often misfigured, as we would argue, as "content") that inevitably forms the referent of language. For there must always be content: the question is how will it be validated? What discursive rules will apply to shape it? Who will decide what "quality" should be cultivated, what discouraged, which experiences explored, and which formulations will be recognized as creativity?

Graff, as cofounder of Teachers for a Democratic Society, has been instrumental in mounting the liberal defense against neoconservative critics like George Will, Lynn Cheney, and Dinesh D'Souza. His advocacy of "teaching the conflicts" offers one important resolution of the "culture wars," a resolution which foregrounds the centrality of rhetoric in the classical sense.

Yet Graff's concern to avoid "imposing" a political viewpoint on students and his judgment that most teachers represented in *Left Margins* are, in practice, "denouncing mere pluralism in order to certify their radical credentials, then quietly reverting to pluralism in order to avoid the totalitarian trap" (277) should themselves be thoroughly examined. It is his view that instruction must be democratic in that instructors must *persuade* students to adopt different political perspectives. But we think many contributors to this volume do not understand "persuasion" in the classically rational sense that he seems to intend. That is, in fact, the central question implied by this collection of essays on teaching rhetoric and writing: what does it mean to teach, or learn, or practice the "available means of persuasion?"

While we wrote the paragraph above (on a sticky table in a fast-food restaurant), we overheard an expectant couple at the next table lament to friends that, not having had amniocentesis performed, "we don't know what colors to buy." It is in the context of this remark that we want to provide the "counterface" between persuasion in the classical rational sense and persuasion of the kind already at work on the unborn child of our anecdote. We believe that it is this difference in understanding the relationship between individual and culture that distinguishes the left center from the left margins.

All parties to the communication (including the unintended) understood the meaning of color, although we did not all understand it in the same way. The intended parties were thinking of nursery decor and baby clothes; the unintended, of engendering a subject. The unborn child had already begun its subjection to an overdetermined regime of gender-typing, which will render "unavailable" most of the means by which he or she might be persuaded, say, that men belong at home with small children. This is to say that the conviction of naturalness accorded gendered characteristics will already have been *imposed* by our common culture on the unborn child long before he or she enters a college composition course. These characteristics are inaccessible to logical, ethical, or emotional suasion in the Aristotelian sense. The subject will always already know the right colors.

However, many of the essays in this book suggest ways to teach the rhetorical analysis of our cultural "footprints" (to use Brantlinger's metaphor). In these pages, the classical rhetorical situation of the individual (masculine) deploying the tool/weapon of language to "have his way with" an audience (feminine) is more likely to be understood as a historically specific model of communication. For language as a vehicle of culture is not a tool/weapon "out there" in reality; it is epistemic, shaping the self-identity of the writer or speaker and the reality she or he perceives. By ex- or implicit application of this "cultural-epistemic" model of rhetoric, the contributors to *Left Margins* make available to us and to their students "extra-rational" means of persuasion that have gone on behind our backs or beneath the threshold of our conscious determination. Inquiry into cultural subjectivity makes the historical source of self-identity—both students' and teachers'—the object of investigation. This inquiry forms the *topoi* of the essays in this volume.

The master-trope (of course, *sic*) by which contributors extend the available means of persuasion is, of course, "culture." The experience or opinion or politics of "the student" or "the writer" is displaced rhetorically by this trope indicating ascription to diverse social groups, each with a cumulative historical experience. Once we think of composition itself as cultural studies—as a transpersonal inquiry into the historical source of meanings (that is, as ascription)—the danger that writing instructors might impose their politics on students is largely circumvented—except to the degree that all education is an imposition of authorized knowledge. While teachers can no doubt shout down, ridicule, and out-argue their students, few would imagine that they had thereby "imposed" a viewpoint on a student. Most would agree that such stridency would merely discredit the instructor's point of view. (Elsewhere, we have attempted to classify the rhetorical means by which students subvert challenges to their ideological commitments.)

It would be a mistake, nevertheless, to represent the writing class as an unproblematic forum for writing. Gary Tate makes the point that the hand that holds the grade book is never just another interlocutor. The institutional requirement that we evaluate writing guarantees that the instructor impose authorized topics on students. Nevertheless, Tate seems to imply that there is some kind of writing that can escape its cultural overdetermination, just as Graff appears to believe that students rely primarily on conscious choice in adopting or altering their convictions.

An incident related by Christopher Wise brings into sharp focus the issue of "imposition" in the transmission of knowledge. His student was "informed" by a psychology professor that "Freud's work on infantile sexuality had been thoroughly discredited by contemporary American psychologists" (132). Such a view represents an undemocratic imposition of authority (a failure, as Graff would say, of teaching the conflicting interpretive "schools" in favor of a supposed monolithic disciplinarity). While Wise democratically allowed his student to dissent from Freud's position on childhood sexuality, he insisted that all students in the class learn the argument. This insistence recognizes that the cultural formation of childhood innocence will very likely be fomenting the students' resistance to it beneath the level of rational persuasion, thus defeating in advance any real conflict. The student, the psychology professor, the writing instructor, all presumptively "normal" members of our culture, share, at some level of unconsciousness, a "natural" abhorrence of infantile sexuality. The means of persuasion, though, are not available *except* as we inquire into the cultural formation of our own consciousness.

Mas'ud Zavarzadeh makes this point most thoroughly in his "apologia" to his student. Self-knowledge cannot be had except in the context of one's cultural subjectivity. The very historical formation according the student a bourgeois self (the "me-in-crisis") also shapes the student's "determination" (in both senses) to refuse or resist understanding it. It is certainly possible that the hypersensitivity to imposing political discomfort on students is also part of the complex process that we call late-capitalist subject formation.

It might be revealing to historicize this conflict over instruction in rhetoric and writing. The millennial decade in which we write is engrossed in an epistemic revolution governed by an ensemble of discursive resources that John Bender and David Wellbery have named "rhetoricality." By this term, they refer to "a transdisciplinary field of practice and intellectual concern . . . a generalized rhetoric that penetrates to the deepest levels of human experience" (25). We believe that rhetoricality is a global phenomenon in contemporary Western societies, which in its local manifestation (that is, in English studies) is radically altering what is meant by reading and writing. While indeterminate relations between reader and text have already to a large extent been codified into literary study, as indicated by the now-obligatory chapter in anthologies outlining critical reading theories, composition theory has largely preserved a Cartesian indifference to the problematics of rhetoric.

In their historical overview of rhetoric, Bender and Wellbery locate the death of the classical rhetorical tradition in the epistemic

changes of the Enlightenment and Romanticism. The former univer-
salized the discursive positions of writer, reader, and referent, postu-
lating an ideal of "objectivity" and "neutrality" (22). The latter
particularized the originary power of language in "a specific epiphanic
moment in the history of a single speaking subject" (20). Across the
curriculum, however, this culturally ascribed model of communication is giving way to one or another version of rhetoricality: in the
sciences, "observation sentences" and the "paradigms" that generate
them are now seen as rhetorical; in the humanities, post-Freudian theory
has decentered and "de-neutered" the subject; and in linguistics, post-
Saussurean theory reduced language from neutral medium of communication to a mystifyingly complex web of signification, understood
systemically rather than individually.

We think that the pedagogical work of contributors to this volume
exemplifies, in varying ways and to varying degrees, the entry of
rhetoricality into the composition classroom (now that it has begun to
pervade theorizing about writing instruction). Teaching composition in
an age of rhetoricality means transcending both objectivist and subjectivist presuppositions as well as the fixed social and intellectual order
on which they rest. Instead, we believe, to write must be reconceived as
the critical ability (1) to articulate the conventions of a wide range of
discursive positions—including those that are *politically uncomfortable*—
and (2) to understand how these positions are related in a larger
cultural constellation. Alan Kennedy has named this complex literate
competence as "positionality" (37–38). Teaching students to write posi-
tionally links composition studies to the theoretical revolution of the
last generation, which is beginning to coalesce as "cultural studies."

The objections of Graff and Tate seem to us to impede the
transdisciplinary work of composition studies. Graff's concern that
politically implicated positions be articulated as conflicting arguments
appears to rest on an "objectivist" notion of conflict in which competing positions become *topoi* in the classical sense. Because we believe
knowledge is shaped by cultural subjectivity, we think students learn
much more about their fundamental commitments from the practice
of articulating *uncongenial* positions than from the process of selecting
a preferred articulation from among conflicting positions. Tate, on the
other hand, seems to want to preserve a "subjectivist" understanding
of "writing" by restricting it to the process of encoding the "epiphanic
moment," which in our experience is most often insulated both from
the sources of its own determination and from the public world of
conflicts that Graff wants students to enter.

The contributors to *Left Margins* seem to speak with one voice on this issue: composing written discourse is inevitably an expression of the writer's cultural subjectivity. In other words, it has never been possible to isolate anything like "writing" in general, distinct somehow from the realization of highly determined cultural formations. Yet that is what has repeatedly been attempted by composition theorists. The belief that a "process" can be abstracted from the substantive content of social life dies hard. But the contributors to this volume are also unanimous in rejecting the view that writing can be limited to self-expression. To be sure, conservative critics in our field argue that we have no "expertise" and therefore are not qualified to assign students writing on substantive topics. This was also Plato's view. But to the extent that we are all subjects of culture, we are all (potentially) "experts" in researching the formative sources of our own subjectivity.

While Graff is certainly right to maintain that the pedagogies described in *Left Margins* are "democratic" in their insistence on granting freedom of expression, they do seem to us to move beyond the rationalist paradigm of persuasion suggested by his primarily forensic approach to cultural politics. And while Tate is clearly wise to insist on the centrality of student writing in composition courses, a cultural studies approach to composition (as enunciated by the authors of these essays) suggests a new synthesis, the *Aufhebung* of "writing" and "subjectivity" into new dialectical compounds: critical consciousness, cultural critique, even ideological transformation.

AFTERWORD

Richard Ohmann _____

These essays either claim or take for granted that the ways we teach have political consequences, or (a stronger version) enact a politics. There is no neutral pedagogy, any more than there can be politically neutral content. Those who profess to teach in the standard or natural way—to teach transparently—simply conceal from themselves and perhaps from their students the social relations (usually hierarchical) of their pedagogies; just as those who profess to teach objectively about economics or art mask the politics of their courses and of economics and art. It follows that one may denaturalize either pedagogy *or* content and not the other. Further, pedagogy may contradict content. Henry Giroux realized at a particular moment that he was "politically enlightened in my theorizing and pedagogically wrong in my organization of concrete class relations" (11). This reminded me of an MLA session about 1970: some of the radicals who had challenged the claims of the organization to professional neutrality and won some influence within it received authorization to organize a prominent session. A big moment—the first major hearing for Marxism at MLA in several decades, perhaps ever. The planners out-MLAed MLA: four prominent, white, male scholars gave long, formal, Marxist papers to the assembled crowd, which quickly dwindled to a handful who presumably felt no dissonance between the content and the pedagogy.

Meanwhile, other academic radicals of the 1960s had been experimenting vigorously with the politics of teaching, putting issues on the agenda that remain there for the writers of these essays. The subtitle of *Left Margins* announces its subject as "cultural studies and composition pedagogy," and indeed the strong growth of cultural studies in the past decade creates a new context for those efforts stemming from the 1960s, along with fresh opportunities for radical pedagogy. Giroux poses a tantalizing question: "what is it about pedagogy that allows cultural studies theorists to ignore it?" (6) (Or maybe *forget* it, as his brief historical discussion suggests; certainly cultural studies at Birmingham in the 1970s was driven by one pedagogical revolution after another.) But the essays in this book are not about this question, nor do they take as a given something called "cultural studies" and search for the pedagogy that will best realize "its" political project.

Many of them do propose working with mass culture and some take on cultural studies language and problematics. But unless I'm missing the point, most of the authors start in a different place and with a different question: what pedagogies for teaching composition will advance radical politics? "Radical" is my attempt at a catch-all word, to signal but not supplant other words that are used or might be used in this collection: "feminist," "socialist," "contestatory," "resistant," "subversive," "counter-hegemonic," "liberatory," and so on. We are all talking, I think, about pedagogies that challenge, from one or another radical democratic standpoint, the dominations and injustices of the present social order, and do so in connection with the teaching of writing.

How? Well, for one thing, by disrupting the social order where students inhabit it daily, in their activities *as* students; by breaking classroom rules; by refusing the normal relations of instruction. I don't want to make this practice seem central, by treating it first, but it is striking. Take course beginnings. Tremonte tells a story about a colleague who identified herself in the first class as a Marxist and a feminist, asks students what they heard, then answers her own question: "That I'm a commie and a bitch!" Tremonte uses the anecdote to initiate discussion at the outset on "the power of language to create identity" (53). Bodziock and Ferry wear funny hats to the first class, raise questions about why students sit and instructors stand, invite students to move about and speak without raising hands. Gutjahr withholds a syllabus for several classes, asks students to meet in small groups and build their own syllabi reflecting their goals for the course, and presses them toward candor about "why they are in the classroom at all" (73). Giroux begins by talking about power and authority in the classroom, not about the subject of the course. His students form groups to articulate how they would like the course to proceed. They help choose texts, teach about them in pairs, do collaborative papers, take part in the evaluation of work. Rosenthal's students join in deciding on the number of papers, the topics, and the weighing of various activities in determining grades.

Many of the authors defy students' expectations about that which can be studied: what counts as a text? Those who teach about Monday night football, *Pee-Wee's Playhouse*, advertisements, and rap build on the perceived dissonance between academic seriousness and the popular. Some depart more sharply from expectations: Gutjahr initiates a study of swear words and taboos; Katz brings in institutional documents such as memoranda on merit pay raises for instructors in the writing program. If the texts are more conventional, approaches to them may not be. Miller, de los Santos, and Witherspoon subvert the autonomy of King's "I have a dream" speech and the authority of the textbooks that reprint it by probing the conditions of its production and reproduction. Tremonte gives her students "license to 'assault' the text," and so "challenge how society composes and interprets the world through the word" (54). Of course the real target of these raids and infiltrations is the student's relation to the texts that construct his or her subjectivity.

Do such practices cause discomfort? That's what many of these instructors want. Gutjahr presses his students' common sense with what he calls the "relentless why" (73). Tremonte promotes "confrontation and conflict" (53). In working with rap, Dixon insists on keeping in focus just what her students "want to forget"—female rappers—and she will not allow discussion to end with the liberal tolerance of "there's good and bad in both" (male and female rappers) (104). Students wearing glasses in Bodziock and Ferry's class find themselves stigmatized and rounded up like Jews in the Third Reich, as they and the others learn about social practices of exclusion. A student in Nowlan's class objects to the hurtful, racist things other students are allowed to say; Nowlan responds courteously but firmly (in writing) that the only way to unseat racism is to force students really to own theirs, or to face the contradiction between their easy liberalism and their acceptance of white privilege. A student in Zavarzadeh's class offers him a conventional excuse for not having an assignment done on time; Zavarzadeh responds at length, not all that courteously, that the student may not take personal crisis as unexamined first cause of failure, but must ruthlessly historicize personal experience itself. Often, these pedagogies withdraw the comforts, along with the rigors, of classroom conventions and of familiar assumptions about what a course is, what a teacher is, what learning is, what a student is.

Not always: there is some talk about creating a safe space in the classroom or about empowering students to take democratic control of their learning. And by and large the pedagogues of shock and disruption do not entirely reject, along with Zavarzadeh, the "pedagogy of pleasure." Still, what strikes me about the essays as a whole, when I compare them to similar efforts of the late sixties, is how peripheral now, how qualified, is the ideal of the democratic classroom. Then, many assumed that canceling the normal, dominative relations of pedagogy would release authentic motives for learning along with liberatory politics. We believed, as Katz well puts it, "that 'democracy' is already 'in' the 'people,' in their inherent diversity and plurality, and simply needs to be released from attempts to restrain its emergence through the proliferation of democratic sites and practices" (210). Rarely do I see that assumption at work in the present volume. Rather, many of its contributors assume or argue that there is something deeply *wrong* with our students that disables them as subjects of democracy.

Not their fault, of course; and in no way should these writers be confused with the sort of teacher we all know who sees students as ruined human material or as the enemies of culture. On the contrary, what's wrong with them *is* culture, culture in them, culture as it speaks them, themselves as constructed by our culture. Hence the choice of culture as material for study in many of these writing courses. Their project is to re-view with students the culture that saturates our lives, from popular music to family, home, the masculine and the feminine, the habitual language of class and race and gender, all that seems most ordinary or natural or transparent. Look at it critically, ask the relentless why, assault the texts of our daily lives, see our categories of understanding as constructed, expose the myths we live by, make ideology visible. Show that there are other cultures than the white, middle-class, heterosexual one that seems inevitable to most of the students; show that there are other politics and political vocabularies. For some, this is enough. To demystify the natural is to free up students from false consciousness (an antique term that does not, I believe, appear in this volume, but that describes the contributors' quarry well enough), and allow them real choices, "empower them to make their own autonomous judgments' (Lazere 190).

For other contributors that is far from enough: the autonomous judgment and the individual choice are themselves ideological effects. Hines, Nowlan, Katz, and others want to dynamite the bedrock of "my opinion" by showing that opinions come from somewhere, are socially produced, conceal deep contradictions. Those who adopt this goal tend to see individuality, the private, the personal, as ideological constructs and illusory refuges from social process. Ditto for the liberal platitudes that accompany the idea of the personal opinion: "there's good on both sides," "everyone has a right to his own opinion," and so on. Such tolerance might be welcome in many classrooms, but for some of the writers in *Left Margins* it shores up liberal pluralism, hides real conflict, and prevents students from grasping their relation to the dominant ideology.

What is that relation? It varies across the range of students we teach, needless to say, and it is not fixed or stable in any given student. But the toughest premise for a radical pedagogy to work from is that most of our students most of the time have been enlisted through their "common sense" into the "party of the ruling class" (Gramsci's terms). Katz articulates such a position most fully. I wonder how many of the other contributors—quite a few, I imagine—would assent to something like his position, that "the enormous investment of the dominant culture in producing 'authoritarian individuals' " (211) has situated our students as its agents. If that is the case, the disruptions and refusals practiced by these teachers are certainly to the point, but can they do more than make students nervously acknowledge their implication in the hegemonic process, before proceeding to make the best of it? What incentive do they have to make "social needs and possibilities" their own, and become "different" in the way that Katz envisions at the end of his essay? What incentive to give up the "pedagogy of pleasure" in favor of "knowledges that are effective in transforming the existing society" into a just and equal one (Zavarzadeh 225)?

That's a hard question that should be asked more often and more explicitly by people like the authors and likely readers of this book. Because, as is noted a few times in these essays, students came to college to gain social advantage, not to defect; to elaborate their individuality, not discard it; to learn the ropes, not see who's at the other end. Of course many students come to college, *also*, and without feeling any contradiction, to escape or test the bromides of home and high school. Insight into the ways they have been constructed by the dominant culture may answer to this wish for enlightenment, though not as anticipated. As Zavarzadeh notes, the tough pedagogy of critique offers its own kind of pleasure, that of "emancipation from established views" (225). A number of the contributors assume the efficacy of such an incentive, and have seen their students' pleasure.

But what next, for those students—for the ones who say they will never see the world the same way again? Are they to live on as sad sophisticates, pessimists, smartasses, cynics? All too likely, unless they find to their taste the other pleasure identified by Zavarzadeh in the pedagogy of critique: that of "participation in the construction of a new world, free from class, gender, race exploitation" (225). Without

that possibility, radical pedagogy terminates in the individual consciousness it has tried to deconstruct. But how might students imagine
joining with others to change the world? Hines speaks of trying to
connect "classroom discussions and activities to larger movements for
social justice" (231), but there is scarcely a mention of such movements
in this collection. Why?

To ask for it may be a little much. After all, these essays are mainly
about writing classes; not all the instructors are tenured; a few are (or
were) graduate students. How specifically political can one be, or *should*
one be, in this situation? Or maybe the writers do talk with students
about political movements; maybe the possibility of activism is alive
throughout their courses, and taken for granted in what are after all
essays on pedagogy. I know some of the authors, and know them to
be activists. Still, this is the one point on which *Left Margins* leaves me
dissatisfied, the point at which radical enlightenment and critique
connect with activity outside the classroom.

I don't have in mind signing students up for the progressive organization of one's choice after the last paper is in. But I wish I saw
more evidence here of *some* social and political connections beyond
those of the one (private?) classroom and its utopian possibilities. There
is little mention of progressive colleagues, of networks, of working
together so that individual pedagogies reinforce one another. Nobody
talks about the political culture of his or her campus—about how
urgencies push into the classroom from it, or how energies from the
politicized classroom might flow out into it. This is particularly surprising in that these essays were written during the moment when,
according to the National Association of Scholars and its many friends
in the media, campuses have been seething with political correctness,
and when millions of students have been sensitized (by the media if
not by events at their own colleges) to battles over identity politics.

I'd like to have heard more about how these interesting pedagogies
play into and against the political forces at work in this historical
conjecture (Lazere, Mazurek, and a few others do engage this question). Is one radical pedagogy right for all historical situations? Clearly
no contributor thinks so, yet there is little discussion of what openings
are especially promising now. The explosive reconsideration of sexuality? The fight over "family values?" The ever-increasing mobility of
capital, which will surely threaten the prospects of educated workers
like our students? The space opened up by the collapse of the Second
World for rethinking alternatives to capitalism? What could be the last
good chance to contend for the future of the biosphere? The intensi-

fication of inequality, especially along racial lines, in the United States and globally?

Well, maybe that's for another collection. The essays in this one are ambitious enough in their educational and political aims. And practical. Credit and thanks to all, for taking pedagogy this seriously. We're in your debt.

CONTRIBUTORS

JOSEPH CHRISTOPHER BODZIOCK and **CHRISTOPHER JOSEPH FERRY** were born in the same hospital, lived in adjoining North Philadelphia neighborhoods, attended rival Big Five colleges, but did not meet until they came to Clarion University in 1991. Joe teaches writing and African-American literature; Chris teaches writing and rhetorical theory. When they're not thinking deep thoughts or plotting to overthrow the English department, Joe and Chris usually sit around.

PETER CAULFIELD is Associate Professor in the Literature and Language Department of the University of North Carolina Asheville, where he co-coordinates the writing across the curriculum program and teaches composition, humanities, and the teaching of writing. He has published work on Paulo Freire, tagmemic invention, and writing across the curriculum. His current research interests are epistemic rhetoric and pragmatism.

GERARDO DE LOS SANTOS is a Ph.D. candidate in educational administration at the University of Texas at Austin. At Arizona State University, he wrote a master's thesis on Martin Luther King Jr.'s "I Have a Dream."

KATHLEEN DIXON is Assistant Professor of English at the University of North Dakota, where she teaches composition, composition theory, cultural studies, and women's studies courses. Her essays have appeared in *College Composition and Communication* and the *Journal of Basic Writing* (the *JBW* article earned the 1991 Mina Shaughnessy Writing Award). She is currently writing a book on gender, class, and academic community.

KAREN FITTS, Assistant Professor in the Writing and Media Department of Loyola College in Maryland, teaches writing and rhetoric. In a current project, she is examining the discourse of breast cancer treatment and survivorship.

ALAN W. FRANCE is Associate Professor of English and Director of Composition at West Chester University, where he teaches composition and basic writing. His study of the politics of writing instruction,

Composition as a Cultural Practice, was recently published by Bergin and Garvey.

HENRY A. GIROUX is the Waterbury Chair Professor of Education at Penn State University. His current research interests focus on the intersection of cultural studies, pedagogy, and radical democracy. His most recent books include *Border Crossings: Cultural Workers and the Politics of Education* and *Disturbing Pleasures: Learning Popular Culture.*

GERALD GRAFF is George M. Pullman Professor of English and Education at the University of Chicago. His recent books include *Professing Literature* (1987) and *Beyond the Culture Wars* (1992).

PAUL GUTJAHR is working toward the Ph.D. in American studies at the University of Iowa. His dissertation examines various transformations the Bible underwent between the Revolution and the Civil War. His research interests include early American publishing, American frontier religion, and American Studies pedagogy. His work has appeared in various journals including *Mosaic, The Palimpsest,* and *The Explicator.*

JOHN C. HAWLEY is Associate Professor of English at Santa Clara University. He is the editor of *Reform and Counterreform: Dialectics of the Word in Western Christianity since Luther* (Mouton de Gruyter, 1994) and *Cross-Addressing: Discourse on the Border* (forthcoming SUNY, 1995). He has written on Victorian religious aestheticism and postcolonial fiction for such journals as *Victorian Literature and Culture, Ariel,* and *Research in African Literatures.*

MARY BETH HINES, Assistant Professor in the School of Education at Indiana University, teaches courses in English education. A former secondary and college composition instructor, she received a Ph.D. from the University of Iowa. She is currently exploring the ways in which teachers develop pedagogical frameworks with feminist, Marxist, and reader response theories.

ADAM KATZ recently completed the Ph.D. in English literature at Syracuse University. His dissertation, "Postmodernism and the Politics of 'Culture,' " is a Marxist critique of contemporary cultural studies. His work also addresses questions of pedagogy, Holocaust discourses, and postcoloniality.

ALAN KENNEDY is Professor of English at Carnegie Mellon. He was Chair of the English Department at Dalhousie University in Canada and then Head of the English Department at CMU until 1994. He is the author of several books, most recently *Reading Resistance Value: Deconstructive Practice and the Politics of Literary Critical Encounters* (St. Martin's Press). Recently he has published "Committing the Curriculum and Other Misdemeanors" in *Cultural Studies in the English Classroom* (eds. James Berlin and Michael Vivion, Boynton/Cook Heinemann); and (with Christine M. Neuwirth, Kris Straub, David Kaufer) "The Role of Rhetorical Theory, Cultural Theory, and Creative Writing in Developing a First-Year Curriculum in English" (ed. David B. Downing, NCTE).

DONALD LAZERE is Professor of English at Cal Poly, San Luis Obispo. He is the author of *The Unique Creation of Albert Camus* (Yale University Press) and editor of *American Media and Mass Culture: Left Perspectives* (University of California Press). His journalistic and scholarly articles have appeared in periodicals including *The Chronicle of Higher Education*, the *New York Times* and *Los Angeles Times* book reviews, *The Nation*, *The Village Voice*, *In These Times*, *Radical Teacher*, *New Literary History*, *College English*, *College Composition and Communication*, and *The Journal of Basic writing*, as well as in many collections.

RAYMOND A. MAZUREK is Associate Professor of English at the Berks campus of Penn State University. He has published articles on contemporary literature and nineteenth-century American literature and has a forthcoming essay on "Class, Composition, and Reform in Departments of English" which will appear in *This Fine Place so Far From Home*, a book on working-class academics.

KEITH D. MILLER has written *Voice of Deliverance: The Language of Martin Luther King, Jr., and Its Sources* (Free Press, 1992) and numerous scholarly essays about King's rhetoric. He is currently Associate Professor of English and Director of Composition at Arizona State University.

ROBERT ANDREW NOWLAN is Assistant Professor of Contemporary Critical Theory with the Department of English at Arizona State University. He has presented numerous papers and published many articles in the areas of critical theory, cultural studies, film studies, queer theory, and theory of sexuality. His forthcoming book—*Queer Theory, Cultural Studies, Marxism*—is a historical materialist critique of contemporary queer theory.

RICHARD OHMANN teaches English and American Studies at Wesleyan University and is on the editorial board of *Radical Teacher*. His last book is *Politics of Letters*.

RAE ROSENTHAL is Associate Professor of English and Coordinator of the College Honors Program at Essex Community College. She has written essays on D. H. Lawrence, Elizabeth Gaskell, and feminist composition theory. She is currently at work on a study of Gaskell's letters.

TODD SFORMO, Adult Basic Education Instructor at Arctic Sivunmun Ilisagvik College in Barrow, Alaska, received the MFA (1994) in poetry and nonfiction from the University of Alaska at Fairbanks and the MA (1993) in art history from SUNY Buffalo. He has taught English and humanities courses in diverse institutions ranging from the University of Alaska at Fairbanks to Attica Prison. His interests include the study of Dada, Cubism, and Arctic survival.

GARY TATE is Professor of English at Texas Christian University. With three colleagues, he is preparing a book-length study of the language of the discipline, *Key Words in Composition Studies.*

COLLEEN M. TREMONTE is Assistant Professor in James Madison College at Michigan State University. Her research interests include composition pedagogy, rhetorical theory and literature, and film studies; her previously published works include essays on the feminine in Walker Percy's fiction and on visual metaphors in contemporary action/adventure films.

BARBARA J. TUDOR is a member of the adjunct faculty in art history at the University of Alaska at Anchorage. Her MA in art history was earned at SUNY Buffalo. She has research interests in feminist and cultural studies.

CHRISTOPHER WISE is Assistant Professor of English at West Georgia College in Carrollton. Articles by Wise have appeared in *Religion and Literature, Rethinking Marxism, M.E.L.U.S.,* and other journals. Currently, Wise is coauthoring a book with Georg M. Gugelberger on postcolonial studies and literature of the Third World.

ONDRA WITHERSPOON is a graduate student in English at Arizona State University. She is writing a master's thesis on Anne Moody's civil rights autobiography, *Coming of Age in Mississippi.*

MAS'UD ZAVARZADEH's most recent book, *Pun(k)deconstruction, Posttheory and Ludic Political Imaginary* will be published in 1995. He is an editor (with Teresa Ebert and Donald Morton) of a new journal, *Transformation: Marxist Boundary Work in Theory, Economics, Politics and Culture,* and is writing a book on the theory of class and class analysis.

NOTES AND REFERENCES

Preface

Notes

1. For a compelling instance of race and gender narratives as "story fields" in the emergence of a science, see Haraway, especially 186–88.

2. A phrase we since regret using because a number of contributors and reviewers have objected to its elitist implications. Originally, we intended the phrase as an ironic reference to the title of a 1973 *College English* special issue on composition pedagogy.

Works Cited

Bauer, Dale. "The Other 'F' Word: The Feminist in the Classroom." *College English* 52 (1990): 385–96.

Berlin, James A. "Rhetoric and Ideology in the Writing Class." *College English* 50 (1988): 477–94.

Berlin, James A., and Michael J. Vivion, eds. *Cultural Studies in the English Classroom*. Portsmouth, NH: Boynton/Cook, 1992.

Bizzell, Patricia. "Arguing about Literacy." *College English* 50 (1988): 141–53.

Brantlinger, Patrick. *Crusoe's Footprints: Cultural Studies in Britain and America*. New York: Routledge, 1990.

Bullock, Richard, and John Trimbur, eds. *The Politics of Writing Instruction: Postsecondary*. Portsmouth, NH: Boynton/Cook, 1991.

Easthope, Antony. *Literary into Cultural Studies*. New York: Routledge, 1991.

Edsforth, Ronald, and Larry Bennett, eds. *Popular Culture and Political Change in Modern America*. Albany: State University of New York Press, 1991.

Giroux, Henry. *Border Crossings: Cultural Workers and the Politics of Education*. New York: Routledge, 1992.

Grossberg, Lawrence, Cary Nelson, and Paula Treichler, eds. *Cultural Studies*. New York: Routledge, 1992.

Hairston, Maxine. "Required Writing Courses Should Not Focus on Politically Charged Social Issues." *Chronicle of Higher Education* 23 Jan. 1991, sec. 2: 1+.

Haraway, Donna. *Primate Visions: Gender, Race, and Nature in the World of Modern Science.* New York: Routledge, 1989.

Harkin, Patricia, and John Schilb, eds. *Contending with Words: Composition and Rhetoric in a Postmodern Age.* New York: MLA, 1991.

Hurlbert, C. Mark, and Michael Blitz, eds. *Composition and Resistance.* Portsmouth, NH: Boynton/Cook, 1991.

Jameson, Fredric. "On 'Cultural Studies.' " *Social Text* 34 (1993): 17–52.

Jarratt, Susan C. "Feminism and Composition: The Case for Conflict." Harkin and Schilb 105–123.

Johnson, Richard. "What Is Cultural Studies Anyway?" *Social Text* 6 (1987): 38–80.

Miller, Susan. "The Feminization of Composition." Bullock and Trimbur 39–53.

Murphy, Peter F. "Cultural Studies as Praxis: A Working Paper." *College Literature* 19 (1992): 31–43.

Phelps, Louise Wetherbee. "A Constrained Vision of the Writing Classroom." *Profession 93.* New York: MLA, 1993. 46–54.

Ross, Andrew, ed. *Universal Abandon? The Politics of Postmodernism.* Minneapolis: U of Minnesota P, 1988.

Schilb, John. "Cultural Studies, Postmodernism, and Composition." Harkin and Schilb 173–88.

Stotsky, Sandra. "Conceptualizing Writing as Moral and Civic Thinking." *College English* 54 (1992): 794–808.

Trimbur, John. "Cultural Studies and Teaching Writing." *Focuses* 1 (1988): 5–18.

Chapter 1. Who Writes in a Cultural Studies Class? or, Where Is the Pedagogy?

Notes

1. One of the most important critiques of Cultural Studies treating this issue of purpose and meaning has been made by Meaghan Morris.

2. This issue is taken up in Franklin, Lury, and Stacey; see also Clarke, esp. ch. 2; Parry; and Hall, "Cultural Studies and its Theoretical Legacies."

3. See, for example, Nelson, "Always Already"; Nelson et al., "Cultural Studies: An Introduction"; and Bennett.

4. For expressions of this position see Grossberg, *We Gotta Get Out;* Hall, "Cultural Studies and its Theoretical Legacies"; and Grossberg, "The Formation."

5. A number of writers in the Grossberg et al. anthology take this position.

6. As a representative of this type of critique, see any of the major theoretical sources of Cultural Studies, especially the Centre for Contemporary Cultural Studies in Birmingham. See Hall, "Cultural Studies: Two Paradigms" and "Cultural Studies and the Centre"; Richard Johnson; and Morris.

7. See Grossberg et al. for examples; also, various issues of *College Literature* under the editorship of Kostas Myrsiades. It is quite revealing to look into some of the latest books on Cultural Studies and see no serious engagement of pedagogy as a site of theoretical and practical struggle. For example see Brantlinger; Turner; Clarke; Franklin et al. In Punter there is one chapter on identifying racism in textbooks.

8. While there are too many sources to cite here, see Connell et al.; Henriques et al.; Sears; Fine; Simon; and Donald.

9. For instance, while theorists such as Jane Tompkins, Gerald Graff, Gregory Ulmer, and others address pedagogical issues, they do it solely within the referenced terrain of literary studies. Moreover, even those theorists in literary studies who insist on the political nature of pedagogy generally ignore, with few exceptions, the work that has gone on in the field for twenty years. See, for example, Felman and Lamb; Henricksen and Morgan; Donahue and Quahndahl; Ulmer; and Barbara Johnson.

10. One interesting example of this occurred when Gary Olson, the editor of the *Journal of Advanced Composition,* interviewed Jacques Derrida. He asked Derrida, in the context of a discussion about pedagogy and teaching, if he knew of the work of Paulo Freire. Derrida responded, "This is the first time I've heard his name" (Olson 133). It is hard to imagine that a figure of Freire's international stature would not be known to someone in literary studies who is one of the major proponents of deconstruction. So much for crossing boundaries. Clearly, Derrida does not read the radical literature in composition studies, because if he did he could not miss the numerous references to the work of Freire and other critical educators. See, for instance, Atkins and Johnson; Brodkey; and Hurlbert and Blitz.

11. The two considerations and quotation come from Morris (20).

Works Cited

Aronowitz, Stanley. *Roll Over Beethoven: Return of Cultural Strife.* Hanover: UP of New England, 1993.

Atkins, C. Douglas, and Michael L. Johnson. *Writing and Reading Differently: Deconstruction and the Teaching of Composition and Literature*. Lawrence: U of Kansas P, 1985.

Bennett, Tony. "Putting Policy into Cultural Studies." Grossberg, Nelson, and Treichler, *Cultural Studies* 23–34.

Brantlinger, Patrick. *Crusoe's Footprints: Cultural Studies in Britain and America*. New York: Routledge, 1990.

Brodkey, Linda. *Academic Writing as a Social Practice*. Philadelphia: Temple UP, 1987.

Butler, Judith. "Contingent Foundations: Feminism and the Question of Postmodernism." *Feminists Theorizing the Political*. Ed. Judith Butler and Joan Scott. New York: Routledge, 1992.

Clarke, John. *New Times and Old Enemies: Essays on Cultural Studies and America*. London: Harper Collins, 1991.

Connell, R. W., D. J. Ashenden, S. Kessler, and G. W. Dowsett. *Making the Difference*. Boston: Allen and Unwin, 1982.

Donahue, Patricia, and Ellen Quahndahl, eds. *Reclaiming Pedagogy: The Rhetoric of the Classroom*. Carbondale: Southern Illinois UP, 1989.

Donald, James. *Sentimental Education*. London: Verso, 1992.

Felman, Shoshana, and Dori Lamb. *Testimony: Crisis of Witnessing in Literature, Psychoanalysis, and History*. New York: Routledge, 1992.

Fine, Michelle. *Framing Dropouts*. Albany: SU of New York P, 1991.

Franklin, Sarah, Celia Lury, and Jackie Stacey. "Feminism and Cultural Studies: Pasts, Presents, Futures." *Off-Centre: Feminism and Cultural Studies*. Ed. Sarah Franklin, et al. London: Harper Collins, 1991. 1–19.

Grossberg, Lawrence. "The Formation of Cultural Studies: An American in Birmingham." *Strategies* 2 (1989): 114–49.

———. *We Gotta Get Out of This Place*. New York: Routledge, 1992.

Grossberg, Lawrence, Cary Nelson, and Paula A. Treichler, eds. *Cultural Studies*. New York: Routledge, 1992.

Hall, Stuart. "Cultural Studies and its Theoretical Legacies." Grossberg, Nelson, and Treichler, *Cultural Studies* 277–86.

———. "Cultural Studies and the Centre: Some Problematics and Problems." *Culture, Media, Language: Working Papers in Cultural Studies*. Ed. Stuart Hall, et al. London: Hutchinson, 1980.

———. "Cultural Studies: Two Paradigms." *Media, Culture, and Society* 2 (1980): 57–72.

Henrickson, Bruce, and Thais E. Morgan. *Reorientations: Critical Theories and Pedagogies*. Urbana: U of Illinois P, 1990.

Henriques, Julian, Wendy Hollway, Cathy Unwin, Couze Venn, and Valerie Walkerdine. *Changing the Subject*. London: Methuen, 1984.

Hurlbert, C. Mark, and Michael Blitz, eds. *Composition and Resistance*. Portsmouth: Heinemann, 1991.

Johnson, Barbara, ed. *The Pedagogical Imperative: Teaching as a Literary Genre*. New Haven: Yale UP, 1983.

Johnson, Richard. "What is Cultural Studies, Anyway?" *Social Text* 6.1 (1987): 38–80.

Morris, Meaghan. "Banality in Cultural Studies." *Discourse* 10.2 (1988): 3–29.

Nelson, Cary. "Always Already Cultural Studies: Two Conferences and a Manifesto." *Journal of Midwest Modern Language Association* 24.1 (Spring 1991): 24–38.

Nelson, Cary, Paula A. Treichler, and Lawrence Grossberg. "Cultural Studies: An Introduction." Grossberg, Nelson, and Treichler, *Cultural Studies* 1–22.

Olson, Gary. "Jacques Derrida on Rhetoric and Composition: A Conversation." *(Inter)views: Cross-Disciplinary Perspectives on Rhetoric and Literacy*. Ed. Gary Olson and Irene Gale. Carbondale: Southern Illinois UP, 1991.

Parry, Benita. "The Contradictions of Cultural Studies." *Transitions* 53 (1991): 37–45.

Punter, David, ed. *Introduction to Contemporary Cultural Studies*. New York: Longman, 1986.

Sears, James T. *Growing Up Gay in the South: Race, Gender, and Journeys of the Spirit*. New York: Harrington Park, 1991.

Simon, Roger I. *Teaching against the Grain*. New York: Bergin and Garvey, 1992.

Turner, Graeme. *British Cultural Studies*. London: Unwin Hyman, 1990.

Ulmer, Gregory. *Applied Grammatology*. Baltimore: Johns Hopkins UP, 1985.

Williams, Raymond. "Adult Education and Social Change." *What I Came to Say*. London: Hutchinson-Radus, 1989. 157–66.

———. "The Future of Cultural Studies." *The Politics of Modernism*. London: Verso, 1989. 151–62.

Chapter 2. Politics, Writing, Writing Instruction, Public Space, and the English Language

Notes

1. One could add Bakhtin's dialogic theories, and Volosinov's (the same person it seems) *Marxism and the Philosophy of Language.*

2. Mark Poster reiterates the point for us in a recent essay in *Diacritics.* In differentiating cultural studies from poststructuralism, Poster focuses on *resistance* as the key term. He argues that de Certeau's work reflects and draws on the central poststructural themes, "but has a unique direction that also brings him close to cultural studies. Whereas poststructuralists generally shied away from the problem of resistance as a result of their hesitance theoretically to define the subject, de Certeau had no such inhibitions" (95).

3. I have dealt with this issue in *Reading Resistance Value.*

4. One would need to enter into a full analysis of the writings of both Richard Lanham and Greg Ulmer *(Teletheory)* to elaborate this point properly.

5. See "The Role of Rhetorical and Cultural Theory in Developing a Curriculum in English," by Kennedy, Neuwirth, Straub, and Kaufer.

Works Cited

Barthes, Roland. *Mythologies.* New York: Noonday Press, 1972.

Bolter, Jay David. *Writing Space: The Computer, Hypertext, and the History of Writing.* New Jersey: LEA, 1991.

Bromwich, David. *Politics by Other Means: Higher Education and Group Thinking.* New Haven: Yale UP, 1993.

Burke, Kenneth. *A Rhetoric of Motives.* Berkeley and Los Angeles: U of California P, 1969.

Kean, Patricia. "Building a Better Beowulf: The New Assault on the Liberal Arts." *Lingua Franca* 3.4 (May/June 1993): 22.

Kennedy, Alan, Chris Neuwirth, Kris Straub, and David S. Kaufer. "The Role of Rhetorical and Cultural Theory in Developing a Curriculum in English." *Changing Classroom Practices: Resources for Literary and Cultural Studies.* Ed. David B. Downing. Urbana, IL: NCTE, 1994. 235–262.

Kennedy, Alan. *Reading Resistance Value: Deconstructive Practice and the Policy of Literary Critical Encounters.* NY: St. Martin's, 1990.

Ohmann, Richard. *Politics of Letters.* Middletown, CT: Wesleyan UP.

Poster, Mark. "The Question of Agency: Michel de Certeau and the History of Consumerism." *Diacritics* 22.2 (1992): 94–107.

Ulmer, Greg. *Teletheory: Grammatology in the Age of Video.* NY: Routledge, 1989.

Volosinov, V. N. *Marxism and the Philosophy of Language.* Trans. Ladislav Matejka and I. R. Titunik. NY: Seminar Press, 1973.

Chapter 3. Teaching "Myth, Difference, and Popular Culture"

Works Cited

Berthoff, Ann E. *The Making of Meaning: Metaphors, Models, and Maxims for Writing Teachers.* Upper Montclair, NJ: Boynton/Cook, 1981.

Doty, William G. *Mythography: The Study of Myths and Rituals.* University, AL: U of Alabama P, 1986.

Freire, Paulo. *Cultural Action for Freedom.* Monograph Series 1. Cambridge: *Harvard Educational Review* and Center for the Study of Development and Social Change, 1970.

———. *Pedagogy of the Oppressed.* Trans. Myra Bergman Ramos. New York: Continuum, 1971.

Giroux, Henry A. *Theory and Resistance in Education: A Pedagogy for the Opposition.* New York: Bergin, 1983.

Gould, Eric. *Mythical Intentions in Modern Literature.* Princeton: Princeton U P, 1981.

Lasch, Christopher. *The Culture of Narcissism.* New York: Norton, 1978.

Tompkins, Jane. "Pedagogy of the Distressed." *College English* 52 (1990): 653–60.

Chapter 4. *Gravedigging: Excavating Cultural Myths*

Notes

1. My thanks to Lisa Jordan of the University of Notre Dame for sharing her experience with me.

2. In "The Other 'F' Word: The Feminist in the Classroom," Dale Bauer proposes a similar strategy for dislocating restrictive boundaries that narrowly define acceptable discourse in "identification narratives."

3. "Individual and Community in American Society" is the first-semester, "content-based" writing course at James Madison; sections, though thematically linked, draw on various pedagogies and approaches.

4. Though I have not yet worked with it, *kairos*, another principle often associated with pre-Socratic philosophy and rhetoric, holds much promise for radical pedagogy. See Michael Carter's "*Stasis* and *Kairos*: Principles of Social Construction in Classical Rhetoric" and Susan C. Jarratt's "Feminism and Composition: The Case for Conflict."

5. For further discussion of pedagogical value of stasis see Kathryn Rosser Raign's "Stasis Theory: A Techne For Teaching Critical Thinking."

6. I am thinking here of the distinction drawn by James Berlin between cognitive rhetoric and social-epistemic rhetoric. See Berlin's "Rhetoric and Ideology in the Writing Class."

7. Here I accept Jean MacGregor's definition of social constructionism as "an expanding web of epistemological perspective in several disciplines, spring[ing] from the assumption that knowledge is socially, rather than individually, constructed by communities of individuals. Knowledge is shaped, over time, by successive conversations and by ever-changing social and political environments" (23).

8. In "Popular Culture as a Pedagogy of Pleasure and Meaning," Henry Giroux and Roger Simon argue: "The basis for a critical pedagogy [that] cannot be developed merely around the inclusion of particular forms of knowledge that have been suppressed or ignored by the dominant culture, . . . must attend to ways in which students . . . regulate and give meaning to their lives. . . . The value of including popular culture offers the possibility of understanding how students make investments in particular social forms and practices . . . " (3).

9. I borrow this term from James Baumlin, who adapted it from Aristotelian rhetoric for classroom practice.

10. Appropriate readings for this section are Toni Cade Bambara's "The Lesson" and any number of essays on culture and class in *Rereading America*. For a general economic perspective, see the introduction to Teresa L. Amott and Julie A. Matthaei's *Race, Gender and Work: A Multicultural Economic History of Women in the United States*.

11. An alternate search and seizure model (adapted from social relations) has students scrutinize a concrete product rather than advertisement that constructs and promotes identity, such as clothing, CDs, tapes, cars, artwork, etc. Working in groups, students first select a product, define its appeal to individualism, and assess whether its promotion excludes an Other. Students then spend time in a public place, such as a shopping mall, observing how people appropriate or use the commodity differently. This "field observation" moves from objective observation to subjective judgment. Though students are usu-

ally uncomfortable with this assignment, as they do not like to play voyeur, it does forcefully illustrate the manner in which we make assumptions about people on the basis of our own values.

12. Readings might include Gina Marchetti's "Action-Adventure as Ideology" and Frederick Jackson Turner's "The Significance of the Frontier in American History" in *Rereading America*, and Susan Faludi's "The Media and the Backlash" and "The Backlash on TV" in *Backlash: The Undeclared War Against American Women*.

Works Cited

Amott, Teresa L., and Julie A. Matthaei. *Race, Gender, and Work: A Multicultural Economic History of Women in the United States.* Boston: South End, 1991.

Bauer, Dale M. "The Other 'F' Word: The Feminist in the Classroom." *College English* 52 (1990): 385–96.

Berlin, James. "Rhetoric and Ideology in the Writing Class." *College English* 50 (1988): 477–94.

Carter, Michael. "*Stasis* and *Kairos:* Principles of Social Construction in Classical Rhetoric." *Rhetoric Review* 7 (Fall 1988): 96–111.

Colombo, Gary, Robert Cullen, and Bonnie Lisle, eds. *Rereading America.* New York: St. Martin's, 1992.

Faludi, Susan. *Backlash: The Undeclared War Against American Women.* New York: Crown, 1991.

Gage, John T. "An Adequate Epistemology for Composition: Classical and Modern Perspectives." *Essays on Classical Rhetoric and Modern Discourse.* Ed. Robert Connors, Lisa Ede, and Andrea Lunsford. Carbondale: Southern Illinois UP, 1983. 152–69.

Gitlin, Todd. "Television's Screens: Hegemony in Transition." *American Media and Mass Culture: Left Perspectives.* Ed. Donald Lazere. Berkeley and Los Angeles: U of California P, 1987. 240–65.

Giroux, Henry A. *Theory and Resistance in Education: A Pedagogy for the Opposition.* S. Hadley, MA: Edward Arnold, 1978.

Giroux, Henry A., and Roger I. Simon. "Popular Culture as a Pedogogy of Pleasure and Meaning." *Popular Culture, Schooling, and Everyday Life.* Ed. Henry A. Giroux and Roger I. Simon. South Hadley, MA: Bergin and Garvey, 1989. 1–30.

———. "Schooling, Popular Culture, and a Pedagogy of Possibility." *Journal of Education* 170.1 (1988): 9–26.

Jarratt, Susan C. "Feminism and Composition: The Case for Conflict." *Contending With Words: Composition and Rhetoric in a Postmodern Age.* Ed. Patricia Harkin and John Schilb. New York: MLA, 1991. 105–23.

MacGregor, Jean. "Collaborative Learning: Shared Inquiry as a Process of Reform." *New Directions for Teaching and Learning* 42 (Summer 1990): 19–30.

Ozersky, Josh. "TV's Anti-Families: Married . . . with Malaise." *Popular Writing in America.* 5th ed. Ed. Donald McQuade and Robert Atwan. New York: Oxford UP, 1993. 342–46.

Raign, Kathryn Rosser. "Stasis Theory: A Techne For Teaching Critical Thinking." *Focuses: A Journal of Writing Lab Theory and Practice* 1 (1989): 19–26.

Chapter 5. Constructing Art&Facts: The Art of Composition, the Facts of (Material) Culture

Notes

1. See the Appendix for a brief sampling of some of the writing assignments students have constructed for this class.

2. A good beginning to the topic of the constructed nature of grammar is Geoffrey Nunberg's "The Decline of Grammar: An Argument for a Middle Way between Permissiveness and Tradition."

3. An excellent study on cultural linguistics in general, and some of the changes in biblical language in particular, is Kenneth Cmiel's *Democratic Eloquence.*

4. Our discussions on the power of words provides one of the most helpful avenues I have found to explain why learning to write well is important. Much of our lives depends on how we choose and arrange words. I pound away at the fact that what a person is able, and not able, to build with words is a matter of no little consequence.

5. A helpful treatment of this perspective on the American Dream is Jay MacLeod's *Ain't No Makin' It.*

6. The best article I have found on teaching practical approaches to examining material artifacts is James Farrell's "Introducing American Studies: The Moral Ecology of Everyday Life."

Works Cited

Beecher, Catharine. *A Treatise on Domestic Economy.* New York: Source Book Press, 1970.

Berry, Wendell. "What Are People For?" and "Why I Am Not Going to Buy a Computer." *What Are People For?* San Francisco: North Point, 1990.

Cmiel, Kenneth. *Democratic Eloquence.* New York: Morrow, 1990.

Farrell, James. "Introducing American Studies: The Moral Ecology of Everyday Life." *American Studies* 33.1 (Spring 1992): 83–102.

Havrilesky, Thomas. "A Compassionate Solution to the Distributional Conflict." *Challenge* 32 (Mar./Apr. 1989): 54–56.

Hayden, Dolores. *Redesigning the American Dream: The Future of Housing, Work, and Family Life.* New York: W. W. Norton, 1984.

hooks, bell. "Homeplace: A Site of Resistance." *Yearning, Race, Gender, and Cultural Politics.* Boston: South End, 1990. 41–51.

Isaac, Rhys. *The Transformation of Virginia, 1740–1790.* Chapel Hill: U of North Carolina P, 1982.

Katlowitz, Alex. *There Are No Children Here: The Story of Two Boys Growing Up in the Other America.* New York: Doubleday, 1991.

Kidder, Tracy. *House.* New York: Avon, 1985.

MacLeod, Jay. *Ain't No Makin' It.* Boulder, CO: Westview, 1987.

Nunberg, Geoffrey. "The Decline of Grammar: An Argument for a Middle Ways between Permissiveness and Tradition." *Atlantic Monthly* Dec. 1983: 31–46.

Thoreau, Henry David. *Walden and "Civil Disobedience."* Ed. Sherman Paul. Boston: Houghton Mifflin, 1960.

Walker, Alice. *The Color Purple.* New York: Pocket Books, 1983.

Williams, Raymond. *The Sociology of Culture.* New York: Schocken, 1981.

West, Cornel. "Marxist Theory and the Specificity of Afro-American Oppression." *Marxism and the Interpretation of Culture.* Ed. Cary Nelson and Lawrence Grassberg. Urbana: U of Illinois P, 1988.

Chapter 6. Recovering "I Have a Dream"

Notes

1. Listen to "I Have a Dream" in *The Great;* "I Have a Dream," in *Martin Luther King, Jr.;* "I Have a Dream" in *Montgomery; I Have a Dream;* "I Have a Dream" in *The Speeches;* and "I Have a Dream" in *We Shall Overcome.*

2. See Day and McMahan; Guth and Hausmann; Laguardia and Guth; McQuade and Atwan; G. Miller; Raphael; Rottenberg; Seyler; Shrodes, et al.; Taylor; and Wyrick. We do not pretend that this list is exhaustive.

3. Listen to "I Have a Dream" in *The Great;* "I Have a Dream" in *Martin Luther King, Jr.;* "I Have a Dream" in *Montgomery; I Have a Dream;* "I Have a Dream" in *The Speeches;* and "I Have a Dream" in *We Shall Overcome.*

4. See Day and McMahan; Guth and Hausmann; LaGuardia and Guth; Levy; McQuade and Atwan; G. Miller; Raphael; Rottenberg; Seylor; Shrodes, et al.; Taylor; and Wyrick.

5. Listen to "I Have a Dream" in *The Great;* "I Have a Dream" in *Martin Luther King, Jr.;* "I Have a Dream" in *Montgomery; I Have a Dream;* "I Have a Dream" in *The Speeches;* and "I Have a Dream" in *We Shall Overcome.*

6. See Day and McMahan; Guth and Hausmann; Laguardia and Guth; Levy; McQuade and Atwan; G. Miller; Raphael; Rottenberg; Seylor; Shrodes, et al.; Taylor; and Wyrick.

7. For other collections with significant errors, see Annas and Rosen; Hennings; and McCuen and Winkler. For anthologies whose texts of the speech are fully or virtually accurate, see Klaus, et al.; Muller; Murray; Reinking and Hart; Rivers; and Smith. We do not pretend that these lists are exhaustive.

8. See Annas and Rosen; and Hennings.

9. Alvarez is the only editor to print the speech with audience reactions, but her edition appeared in a scholarly journal and unfortunately is not widely read.

10. For a further explanation, see de los Santos. De los Santos's argument rests partly on the analysis of everyday metaphors offered by Lakoff and Johnson.

Textbooks Cited

Annas, Pamela and Robert Rosen. *Literature and Society: An Introduction to Fiction, Poetry, Drama, Non-Fiction.* Englewood Cliffs, NJ: Prentice-Hill, 1990. 1384–1388.

Day, Susan and Elizabeth McMahan. *The Writer's Source: Readings for Composition.* Second edition. New York: McGraw-Hill, 1988. 429–433.

Guth, Hans and Shea Renee Hausmann. *Reading with the Writer's Eye.* Belmont, CA: Wadsworth, 1987. 345–348.

Hennings, Dorothy. *Reading with Meaning: Strategies for College Reading.* Englewood Cliffs, NJ: Prentice-Hall, 1990. 220–223.

Klaus, Carl H., Chris Anderson, and Rebecca Blevins Faery. *In Depth: Essayists for Our Time.* Second edition. Fort Worth, TX: Harcourt, 1993. 332–335.

LaGuardia, Dolores and Hans Guth. *American Voices: Multi-Cultural Literacy and Critical Thinking.* Mountain View, CA: Mayfield. 1993. 389–392.

Levy, Peter. *Let Freedom Ring: A Documentary History of the Modern Civil Rights Movement.* New York: Praeger, 1992. 122–125.

McCuen, Jo Ray and Anthony Winkler. *Readings for Writers.* Sixth edition. San Diego: Harcourt, 1989. 26–29.

McQuade, Donald and Robert Atwan. *Popular Writing in America: The Interaction of Style and Audience.* New York: Oxford UP, 1988. 631–633.

Miller, George, ed. *The Prentice-Hall Reader.* Englewood Cliffs, NJ: Prentice-Hall. 450–451.

Muller, Gilbert. *McGraw-Hill Reader.* Fourth edition. New York: McGraw-Hill, 1991. 267–269.

Murray, Donald. *Read to Write: A Writing Process Reader.* New York: Holt, Rinehart, 1986. 241–245.

Raphael, Carolyn. *The Writing Reader: Short Essays for Composition.* New York: MacMillan, 1986. 93–97.

Reinking, James and Andrew Hart. *Strategies for Successful Writing: A Rhetoric, Reader, and Handbook.* Second edition. Englewood Cliffs, NJ: Prentice-Hall, 1991. 519–523.

Rivers, William. *Issues and Images: An Argument Reader.* Fort Worth, TX: Harcourt, 1993. 414–417.

Rottenberg, Annette. *Elements of Argument: A Text and Reader.* Third edition. Boston: St. Martin's, 1989. 626–629.

Seyler, Dorothy. *Read, Reason, Write.* Third edition. New York: McGraw-Hill, 1991. 361–363.

Shrodes, Caroline, and Harry Finestone. *The Conscious Reader.* Fifth edition. New York: MacMillan, 1992. 752–755.

Smith, Wendell. *The Belmont Reader: Essays for Writers.* Belmont, CA: Wadsworth, 1986. 383–386.

Taylor, Sally. *The Critical Eye: Thematic Readings for Writers.* Fort Worth, TX: Holt, Rinehart, 1990. 386–389.

Wyrick, Jean. *Discovering Ideas: An Anthology for Writers.* Second edition. New York: Holt, Rinehart, 1987. 285–289.

Other Works Cited

Alvarez, Alexandra. "Martin Luther King's 'I Have a Dream': The Speech Event as Metaphor." *Journal of Black Studies* 18 (1988): 337–357.

Ansbro, John. *Martin Luther King, Jr.: The Making of a Mind.* Maryknoll, NY: Orbis, 1982.

Bakhtin, Mikhail. "Response to a Question from *Novy Mir.*" *Speech Genres and Other Late Essays.* Trans. Vern W. McGee. Ed. Caryl Emerson and Michael Holquist. Austin: U of Texas P, 1986.

Bosmajian, Haig. "The Inaccuracies in the Reprinting of Martin Luther King's 'I Have a Dream' Speech." *Communication Education* 31 (1982): 107–114.

Branch, Taylor. *Parting the Waters: America in the King Years, 1954–1963.* New York: Simon and Schuster, 1988.

Burke, Kenneth. *Attitudes toward History.* 1937. Berkeley: U of California P, 1984.

Carey, Archibald. "Address to the Republican National Convention." *Rhetoric of Racial Revolt.* Ed. Roy Hill. Denver: Golden Bell, 1964. 149–154.

Cone, James. *Martin and Malcolm and America.* Maryknoll, NY: Orbis, 1991.

de los Santos, Gerardo. "The Metaphorical Systems of the Language of Martin Luther King, Jr." Master's Thesis, Arizona State University, 1993.

Fairclough, Adam. *To Redeem the Soul of America: The Southern Christian Leadership Conference and Martin Luther King, Jr.* Athens: U of Georgia P, 1987.

Garrow, David. *Bearing the Cross: Martin Luther King, Jr., and the Southern Christian Leadership Conference.* New York: Morrow, 1986.

Hariman, Robert. "Time and the Reconstitution of Gradualism in King's Address: A Response to Cox." *Texts in Context: Critical Dialogues on Significant Episodes in American Political Rhetoric.* Ed. Michael Jeff and Fred Kauffeld. Davis, CA: Hermagoras, 1989. 205–218.

King, Martin Luther, Jr. "Address at the Holt Street Baptist Church." Montgomery, AL. 5 Dec. 1955. King Center Archives. Atlanta.

———. "Annual Report to the Montgomery Improvement Association." Montgomery, AL. 3 Dec. 1956. King Center Archives. Atlanta.

———. "Birth of a New Nation." Montgomery, AL. April 1957. King Center Archives. Atlanta.

———. "Desegregation and the Future." 1 Dec. 1956. King Center Archives. Atlanta.

———. "Facing the Challenge of a New Age." In Washington. 135–144.

———. "Fragment." 5 Dec. 1957. King Center Archives. Atlanta.

———. "I Have a Dream." In *The Great March on Washington.* Gordy Records. 908. 1963.

———. "I Have a Dream." In *Martin Luther King, Jr.: His Great Speeches.* Motown Records. 6022. n.d.

———. "I Have a Dream." In *Montgomery to Memphis.* King Center Archives. Atlanta. Videotape. n.d.

———. *I Have a Dream.* Pro Arte 566. Compact Disc. 1991.

———. "I Have a Dream." In *The Speeches of Martin Luther King, Jr.* The Speeches Collection. MPI Home Video. MP 1410. 1990.

———. "I Have a Dream." In Washington 217–220.

———. "I Have a Dream." In *We Shall Overcome: Documentary of the March on Washington.* Folkways Records. FD 5592. 1964.

————. *Strength to Love.* New York: Harper, 1963.

————. "Who Is Their God?" *The Nation* 195 (Dec. 1962): 209–213.

Lakoff, George and Mark Johnson. *Metaphors We Live By.* Chicago: U of Chicago P, 1980.

Meier, August. "The Conservative Militant." *Martin Luther King, Jr.: A Profile.* Ed. C. Eric Lincoln. New York, Hill and Wang, 1984. 144–156.

Miller, Keith D. *Voice of Deliverance: The Language of Martin Luther King, Jr., and Its Sources.* New York: Free Press, 1992.

Oates, Stephen. *Let the Trumpet Sound: The Life of Martin Luther King, Jr.* New York: Harper, 1982.

Toulmin, Stephen. *Cosmopolis: The Hidden Agenda of Modernity.* New York: Free Press, 1990.

Trimbur, John. "Essayist Literacy and the Rhetoric of Deproduction." *Rhetoric Review* 9 (Fall 1990): 72–86.

Washington, James, ed. *A Testament of Hope: The Essential Writings of Martin Luther King, Jr.* New York: Harper, 1986.

Chapter 7. Making and Taking Apart "Culture" in the (Writing) Classroom

Works Cited

Bartholomae, David. "Inventing the University." *When a Writer Can't Write: Studies in Writer's Block and Other Composing Problems.* Ed. Mke Rose. New York: Guilford, 1985. 134–165.

Bizzell, Patricia. "Marxist Ideas in Composition Studies." Harkin and Schilb 52–68.

Bruffee, Kenneth A. "Collaborative Learning and the 'Conversation of Mankind.' " *College English* 46 (1984): 635–52.

George, Diana, and John Trimbur. *Reading Culture: Contexts for Critical Reading and Writing.* New York: HarperCollins, 1992.

Harkin, Patricia, and John Schilb, eds. *Contending with Words: Composition and Rhetoric in a Postmodern Age.* New York: MLA, 1991.

Jarratt, Susan C. "Feminism and Composition: The Case for Conflict." Harkin and Schilb 105–23.

Schilb, John. "Cultural Studies, Postmodernism, and Composition." Harkin and Schilb 173–88.

Sosnoski, James J. "Postmodern Teachers in Their Postmodern Classrooms: Socrates Begone!" Harkin and Schilb 198–219.

Stock, Patricia L. and Jay Robinson, "Literacy as Conversation: Classroom Talk as Text Building." *Conversations on the Written Word.* Ed. Patricia L. Stock and Jay Robinson. Portsmouth, NH: Boynton/Cook, 1990.

Wallace, Michele. "When Black Feminism Faces the Music, and the Music is Rap." George and Trimbur 25–28.

Will, George. "America's Slide into the Sewer." George and Trimbur 29–31.

Chapter 8. *Monday Night Football:* Entertainment or Indoctrination?

Works Cited

Connell, R. W. "Curriculum Politics, Hegemony, and Strategies of Social Change." Giroux and Simon 117–130.

Giroux, Henry A., Roger I. Simon. "Popular Culture as Pedagogy of Pleasure and Meaning." *Popular Culture, Schooling, and Everyday Life.* South Hadley, MA: Bergin and Garvey, 1989: 1–30.

———. "Schooling, Popular culture, and a Pedagogy of Possibility." Giroux and Simon 219–236.

Morris, Barbara S., and Joel Nydahl. "Sports Spectacle as Drama: Image, Language, and Technology." *Journal of Popular Culture* 18.4 (Spring 1985): 101–10.

Ortner, Sherry. "Is Female to Male as Nature Is to Culture?" *Woman, Culture, and Society.* Ed. Michelle Zimbalist Rosaldo and Louise Lamphere. Stanford: Stanford UP, 1974. 67–87.

Chapter 9. Pee-Wee, Penley, and Pedagogy, or, Hands-On Feminism in the Writing Classroom

Notes

1. I recommend *Pee-Wee's Playhouse,* Episode 9 ("Monster in the Playhouse"), which is most central to Penley's argument and is widely available at video stores. In this episode the theme of the show is overcoming fear of difference, best symbolized by a phallic, one-eyed monster named Roger.

Works Cited

Freud, Sigmund. "Infantile Sexuality" *A World of Ideas.* 3rd ed. Ed. Lee A. Jacobus. New York: St. Martin's, 1990. 271–91.

Penley, Constance. "The Cabinet of Doctor Pee-Wee: Consumerism and Sexual Terror." *The Future of an Illusion: Film, Feminism, and Psychoanalysis.* Minneapolis: U of Minnesota P, 1989. 141–62.

Chapter 10. Feminists in Action: How to Practice What We Teach

Notes

1. Mary Rose O'Reilley makes a similar point in her thought-provoking confessional "Exterminate ... the Brutes," where she states, quite rightfully, "you can't just put your chairs in a circle and forget about the human condition" (146).

2. Joy S. Ritchie reports that in a women's literature class taught by her colleague, Barbara DiBernard, DiBernard began the semester by assigning an article on feminist teaching which she had written. Ritchie explains that "Barbara believed that sharing her philosophy of teaching from the outset of the class was consistent with her desire to help them see 'teaching as a political act' " (252). This strikes me as an excellent idea, one with which I would like to experiment.

3. Jerry Farber tells an apt tale of his officemate, Jackie, who "walked into Intro to Lit and said, 'OK, people, it's your class. What do you want to do with it?' But, of course, they didn't want to do anything with it. They didn't even want to be there. It was a GE class, for God's sake. Was she kidding?" (135).

4. I once had a graduate professor who compiled the reading list for the course on the first day of class. The course was Comparative Fiction, and he distributed a list of approximately one hundred novels from which we could choose, and the twelve earning the most votes were then the texts for the semester.

5. I have often thought that one of the most interesting aspects of Jane Tompkins's widely discussed essay, "Pedagogy of the Distressed," was the aftermath—the number of sharp, bitter, aggressive attacks made in reply. The antagonistic spirit of the ensuing conversation was exactly what Tompkins has been trying, in that essay and in "Me and My Shadow" and "Fighting Words: Unlearning to Write the Critical Essay," to expose.

6. Unfortunately, women all too often respond to cultural training which encourages female selflessness. We tend to put our own needs last and assume that, somehow, what is not good for us must be good for those around us. More and more, I have begun to take into the classroom the motto which I have adopted at home: "The best mother (teacher) is a happy mother (teacher)." If I overextend myself, I cannot possibly meet the needs of my children or my students, so I am not really doing them any favor.

7. Coincidentally, Linda Peterson offers basically the same suggestion; she says, "For insight and originality, try 'cross-dressing'—that is, use the

writerly strategy of viewing experience through the eyes of someone of the opposite sex or from a different racial or ethnic background" (178).

8. Another unexpected side benefit to these groups is the frequency with which they spill over into nonclass time; I am told that students within a group often call one another for advice and support during the writing process. (At the beginning of every semester, I distribute a sheet which has each student's name, address, and phone number.) This type of intellectual connection is particularly important at a commuter school, like mine, where a sense of community can be difficult to build, and I suspect that nonconstant peer-editing groups are less likely to have the same result.

9. The idea for this checklist came from Richard Bucher, a colleague at Baltimore City Community College.

10. In imitation of bell hooks, I deliberately refer not to "the" feminist movement but to feminist movement, a term preferable in its inclusivity: hooks says, "I drop the definite article rather than speaking of 'the' feminist movement. When we do not have a definite article, we are saying that feminist movement can be located in multiple places, in multiple languages and experiences" ("Conversation" 68).

Works Cited

Alcoff, Linda. "Cultural Feminism versus Post-Structuralism: The Identity Crisis in Feminist Theory." *Signs: A Journal of Women in Culture and Society* 13 (1988): 405–36.

Annas, Pamela J. "Style as Politics: A Feminist Approach to the Teaching of Writing." *College English* 47 (1985): 360–71.

Bauer, Dale M. "The Meanings and Metaphors of Student Resistance." Conference on College Composition and Communication. Cincinnati, March 1992.

———. "The Other 'F' Word: The Feminist in the Classroom." *College English* 52 (1990): 385–96.

Belenky, Mary Field, Blythe McVicker Clinchy, Nancy Rule Goldberger, and Jill Mattuck Tarule. *Women's Ways of Knowing: The Development of Self, Voice, and Mind.* New York: Basic, 1986.

Bolker, Joan. "Teaching Griselda to Write." *College English* 40 (1979): 906–08.

Caywood, Cynthia L., and Lillian R. Overing, eds. *Teaching Writing: Pedagogy, Gender and Equity.* Albany: State U of New York P, 1987.

Chodorow, Nancy. *The Reproduction of Mothering: Psychoanalysis and the Sociology of Gender.* Berkeley and Los Angeles: U of California P, 1978.

Cixous, Helene. "The Laugh of the Medusa." Trans. Keith Cohen and Paula Cohen. *The Signs Reader: Women, Gender, and Scholarship.* Ed. Elizabeth Abel. Chicago: U of Chicago P, 1982. 279–97.

de Lauretis, Teresa. "The Essence of the Triangle or, Taking the Risk of Essentialism Seriously: Feminist Theory in Italy, the U.S., and Britain." *differences* 1 (1988): 3–37.

Farber, Jerry. "Learning How to Teach: A Progress Report." *College English* 52 (1990): 135–41.

Farrell, Thomas J. "The Female and Male Modes of Rhetoric." *College English* 40 (1979): 909–21.

Flynn, Elizabeth A. "Composing as a Woman." *College Composition and Communication* 39 (1988): 423–35.

———. "Composing 'Composing as a Woman': A Perspective on Research." *College Composition and Communication* 41 (1990): 83–89.

Frey, Olivia. "Beyond Literary Darwinism: Women's Voices and Critical Discourse." *College English* 52 (1990): 507–26.

Fuss, Diana. *Essentially Speaking: Feminism, Nature, and Difference.* New York: Routledge, 1989.

Gilligan, Carol. *In a Different Voice: Psychological Theory and Women's Development.* Cambridge: Harvard UP, 1982.

Hairston, Maxine. "Diversity, Ideology, and Teaching Writing." *College Composition and Communication* 43 (1992): 179–93.

hooks, bell. "A Conversation about Race and Class." *Conflicts in Feminism.* Ed. Marianne Hirsch and Evelyn Fox Keller. New York: Routledge, 1990. 60–81.

———. "Essentialism and Experience." *American Literary History* 3 (1991): 172–83.

Juncker, Clara. "Writing (with) Cixous." *College English* 50 (1988): 424–36.

Lakoff, Robin. *Language and Woman's Place.* New York: Harper, 1973.

Lamb, Catherine E. "Beyond Argument in Feminist Composition." *College Composition and Communication* 42 (1991): 11–24.

Lerner, Gerda. *The Creation of Patriarchy.* New York: Oxford UP, 1986.

Nelson, Dana D. "Being a Woman Academic, or, The Importance of 'Me Mates.' " *Concerns* 22.3 (1992): 32–37.

O'Reilley, Mary Rose. " 'Exterminate . . . the Brutes'—And Other Things That Go Wrong in Student-Centered Teaching." *College English* 51 (1989): 142–46.

Peterson, Linda H. "Gender and the Autobiographical Essay: Research Perspectives, Pedagogical Practices." *College Composition and Communication* 42 (1991): 170–83.

Pigott, Margaret B. "Sexist Roadblocks in Inventing, Focusing, and Writing." *College English* 40 (1979): 922–27.

Ritchie, Joy S. "Confronting the 'Essential' Problem: Reconnecting Feminist Theory and Pedagogy." *Journal of Advanced Composition* 10 (1990): 249–73.

Rosenthal, Rae. "Male and Female Discourse: A Bilingual Approach to English 101." *Focuses* 3 (1990): 99–113.

Sadker, Myra, and David Sadker. "Confronting Sexism in the College Class-room." *Gender in the Classroom: Power and Pedagogy.* Ed. Susan L. Gabriel and Isaiah Smithson. Chicago: U of Illinois P, 1990. 176–87.

Spender, Dale. "Disappearing Tricks." *Learning to Lose: Sexism and Education.* Ed. Dale Spender and Elizabeth Sarah. London: The Women's P, 1980. 165–73.

———. "Talking in Class." *Learning to Lose: Sexism and Education.* Ed. Dale Spender and Elizabeth Sarah. London: The Women's P, 1980. 148–54.

Tompkins, Jane. "Fighting Words: Unlearning to Write the Critical Essay." *Georgia Review* 42 (1988): 585–90.

———. "Me and My Shadow." *New Literary History* 19 (1987): 169–78.

———. "Pedagogy of the Distressed." *College English* 52 (1990): 653–60.

Weedon, Chris. *Feminist Practice and Poststructuralist Theory.* Oxford: Basil Blackwell, 1987.

Zawacki, Terry Myers. "Recomposing as a Woman—An Essay in Different Voices." *College Composition and Communication* 43 (1992): 32–38.

Chapter 11. Teaching Rhetoric as a Way of Knowing

Works Cited

Bakhtin, Mikhail. *Marxism and the Philosophy of Language. The Rhetorical Tradition: Readings from Classical Times to the Present.* Ed. Patricia Bizzell and Bruce Herzberg. Boston: Bedford Books, 1990.

Baldwin, James. "My Dungeon Shook: Letter to My Nephew on the One Hundredth Anniversary of the Emancipation." *The Fire Next Time.* New York: Dell, 1963.

Berlin, James A. *Rhetoric and Reality: Writing Instruction in American Colleges, 1900–1985.* Carbondale: Southern Illinois UP, 1987.

Bruffee, Kenneth A. "Collaborative Learning and the 'Conversation of Mankind.' " *College English* 46 (1984): 635–52.

Burns, Ken. *The Civil War.* Florentine Films and WETA-TV, 1989.

"Conversations." Host David Hurand. Natl. Public Radio. WCQS. Asheville, NC. 17 June 1992.

Cooper, Marilyn. "The Ecology of Writing." *College English.* 48 (April 1986): 364–75.

Helms for Senate Committee. "Quotas." October 1990.

Knoblauch, C. H., and Lil Brannon. "Writing as Learning Through the Curriculum." *College English.* 5 (September 1983): 465–74.

King, Martin Luther Jr. "Letter From Birmingham Jail." *Critical Reading and Writing Across the Disciplines.* Ed. Cyndia Susan Clegg. New York: Holt, Rinehart, and Winston, 1988. 291–304.

Leff, Michael. "In Search of Ariadne's Thread: A Review of the Recent Literature on Rhetorical Theory." *Central States Speech Journal* 29 (Summer 1978): 73–91.

Moyers, Bill. *Listening to America.* Corporation for Public Broadcasting. April, 1992.

Muller, Herbert J. "The Premises of Inquiry." *Critical Reading and Writing Across the Disciplines.* Ed. Cyndia Susan Clegg. New York: Holt, Rinehart, and Winston, 1988. 326–28.

Riggs, Marlin. *Color Adjustment. Point of View.* Corporation for Public Broadcasting and WUNF-TV, 1992.

Scott, Robert L. "On Viewing Rhetoric As Epistemic: Ten Years Later." *Central States Speech Journal* 27 (Winter 1976): 258–66.

Chapter 12. Freirean Pedagogy, Cultural Studies, and the Initiation of Students into Academic Discourse

Notes

Note: I wish to acknowledge the help and influence of several friends and colleagues who have had a considerable influence on my thinking about composition pedagogy: Regina Rinderer of Delta College, who first introduced me to the work of Paulo Freire when we both taught at Southern Illinois University in Carbondale; Mike Riley, my colleague in the hinterlands of English Studies at the Berks Campus of Penn State, who has developed his own somewhat different cultural studies composition approach, centered on Bill Moyers's *The Public Mind;* and Jim Berlin of Purdue University, who generously gave of his time to discuss his ideas on composition and cultural studies when I visited Purdue during my sabbatical in the fall of 1990.

Works Cited

Bauer, Dale. "The Other 'F' Word: The Feminist in the Classroom." *College English* 52 (1990): 385–96.

Berlin, James. "Composition and Cultural Studies." *Composition and Resistance.* Ed. C. Mark Hulbert and Michael Blitz. Portsmouth, NH: Boynton/Cook, 1991. 47–55.

———. "Rhetoric and Ideology in the Writing Classroom." *College English* 50 (1988): 477–93.

———. *Rhetoric and Reality: Writing Instruction in American Colleges 1900–1985.* Carbondale: Southern Illinois UP, 1987.

———. "Rhetoric, Poetic, and Culture: Contested Boundaries in English Studies." *The Politics of Writing Instruction.* Ed. Richard Bullock and John Trimbur. Portsmouth, NH: Boynton/Cook, 1991. 23–38.

Bizzell, Patricia. *Academic Discourse and Critical Consciousness.* Pittsburgh: U of Pittsburgh P, 1992.

———. "Argument, Community, and Knowledge." *Diversity: A Journal of Multicultural Issues* 1 (1992): 9–23.

Blanchard, Bob, and Susan Watrous. "An Interview with Frances Moore Lappe." *The Progressive* (February 1990): 34–37.

Bloom, Lynn. "Teaching College English as a Woman." *College English* 54 (1992): 818–25.

Elbow, Peter. *Writing with Power.* New York: Oxford UP, 1981.

Finlay, Linda Shaw, and Valerie Faith. "Illiteracy and Alienation in American Colleges: Is Paulo Freire's Pedagogy Relevant?" *Freire for the Classroom.* Ed. Ira Shor. Portsmouth, NH: Boynton/Cook, 1987. 63–86.

Freire, Paulo. *Education for Critical Consciousness.* Trans. Myra Bergman Ramos. New York: Continuum, 1973.

———. *Pedagogy of the Oppressed.* Trans. Myra Bergman Ramos. New York: Continuum, 1989.

Freire, Paulo, and Ira Shor. *A Pedagogy for Liberation: Dialogues for Transforming Education.* South Hadley, MA: Bergin and Garvey, 1987.

Friedman, Sharon, and Stephen Steinberg. *Writing and Thinking in the Social Sciences.* Englewood Cliffs, NJ: Prentice-Hall, 1989.

George, Diana, and John Trimbur, eds. *Reading Culture.* New York: Harper-Collins, 1992.

Gitlin, Todd. *The Sixties: Years of Hope, Days of Rage.* New York: Bantam, 1987.

Lazere, Donald. "Back to Basics: A Force for Oppression or Liberation?" *College English* 54 (1992): 7–21.

Macrorie, Ken. *Uptaught.* New York: Hayden, 1970.

Moyers, Bill. *The Public Mind: Image and Reality in America.* Directed by Gail Pellett. Alexandria, VA: PBS Video, 1989.

North, Stephen. *The Making of Knowledge in Composition: Portrait of an Emerging Field.* Portsmouth, NH: Boynton/Cook, 1987.

Ohmann, Richard. *English in America: A Radical View of the Profession.* New York: Oxford UP, 1976.

———. *Politics of Letters.* Middletown, CT: Wesleyan UP, 1987.

Rose, Mike. *Lives on the Boundary: The Struggles and Achievements of America's Underprepared.* New York: Macmillan, 1989.

Shor, Ira. *Critical Teaching and Everyday Life.* Boston: South End, 1980.

Tompkins, Jane. "Pedagogy of the Distressed." *College English* 52 (1990): 653–62.

Trimbur, John. "Cultural Studies and Teaching Writing." *Focuses* 1.2 (1988): 5–18.

Williams, Raymond. *Marxism and Literature.* New York: Oxford UP, 1977.

Wilson, William Julius. *The Truly Disadvantaged: The Inner City, the Underclass, and Public Policy.* Chicago: U of Chicago P, 1987.

Chapter 13. Teaching the Conflicts about Wealth and Property

Works Cited

Lazere, Donald. *American Media and Mass Culture: Left Perspectives.* Berkeley: U of California P, 1987. iv–xii, 1–26, 555–58.

———. "Teaching the Political Conflicts: A Rhetorical Schema." *College Composition and Communication* 43.2 (1992): 194–213.

Chapter 14. Pedagogy, Resistance, and Critique in the Composition Class

Works Cited

Agger, Ben. *The Decline of Discourse: Reading, Writing and Resistance in Postmodern Capitalism.* New York: Falmer, 1990.

Giroux, Henry. "Resisting Difference: Cultural Studies and the Discourse of Critical Pedagogy." *Cultural Studies.* Ed. Lawrence Grossberg, Cary Nelson, and Paula A. Treichler. New York and London: Routledge, 1991. 199–212.

Graff, Gerald. "Teach the Conflicts." *South Atlantic Quarterly* 89 (1989): 51–67.

Chapter 15. The Pedagogy of Pleasure 2: The Me-in-Crisis

Works Cited

Marx, Karl. *Capital*. Vol. 1. Trans. Ben Fowkes. New York: Vintage, 1976.

———. *Early Writings*. Trans. Rodney Livingston and Gregor Benton. New York: Vintage, 1975.

Zizek, Slovoj. *The Sublime Object of Ideology*. New York: Verso, 1989.

Chapter 16. Contested Terms, Competing Practices: Language Education and Social Change

Works Cited

Althusser, Louise. "Ideology and Ideological State Apparatuses." *Lenin and Philosophy and Other Essays*. Trans. B. Brewster. London: New Left Books, 1977. 127–86.

Aronowitz, Stanley, and Giroux, Henry. *Postmodern Education: Politics, Culture, and Social Criticism*. Minneapolis: U of Minnesota P, 1991.

Barrett, Michele. (1988). Introduction. *Women's Oppression Today*. 2nd ed. London: Verso, 1988. v–xxxiv.

Bennett, Tony. *Formalism and Marxism*. London: Methuen, 1979.

———. *Outside Literature*. London: Routledge, 1990.

———. "Texts, Readers, Reading Formations." *Midwestern Modern Language Association Bulletin*, 16 (1983): 3–17.

Davies, Kath, Julienne Dickey, Teresa Stratford, eds. *Out of Focus: Writings on Women and the Media*. London: Women's Press, 1987.

Giroux, Henry. *Theory and Resistance in Education*. South Hadley, MA: Bergin & Garvey, 1983.

Hartsock, Nancy. "Foucault on Power: A Theory for Women?" *Feminism/ Postmodernism*. Ed. Linda J. Nicholson. New York: Routledge, 1990. 157–75.

Lather, Patti. *Getting Smart: Feminist Research and Pedagogy Within the Postmodern*. New York: Routledge, 1991.

Chapter 17. Teaching Against Racism in the Radical College Composition Classroom: A Reply to a Student

Works Cited

Baldwin, James. "If Black English Isn't a Language, Then Tell Me What Is?" *The Price of the Ticket: Collected Non-Fiction 1948–1985*. New York: St. Martin's, 1985. 649–52.

Chapter 18. A *Ratio Studiorum* for the Postcolonialist's Classroom

Works Cited

Altered States. Dir. Ken Russell. 1980.

Bailey, Charles R. "French Secondary Education, 1763–1790: The Secularization of Ex-Jesuit Colleges." *Transactions of the American Philosophical Society* 68.6 (1978): 3–124.

Bonachea, Rolando E., ed. *Jesuit Higher Education: Essays on an American Tradition of Excellence.* Pittsburgh: Duquesne UP, 1989.

Dainville, Francois de, S.J. *Les Jesuites et l'education de la societe francaise. La naissance de l'humanisme moderne.* Paris: Beauchesne & fils, 1940.

El Norte. Dir. Gregory Nava. Farmington Hills, Mich.: CBS/Fox Video, 1984.

Friedman, Bruce Jay. *Stern.* New York: Arbor House, 1983.

Fuentes, Carlos. *Burnt Water: Stories.* Trans. Margaret Sayers Peden. New York: Farrar, Straus, & Giroux, 1980.

Ganss, George E., S.J. *Saint Ignatius' Idea of a Jesuit University.* Milwaukee: Marquette UP, 1954.

Giroux, Henry. *Border Crossings: Cultural Workers and the Politics of Education.* New York: Routledge, 1992.

Joseph Campbell and the Power of Myth. Mystic Fire Video: 1988.

Leavitt, David. *The Lost Language of Cranes.* New York: Knopf, 1986.

Menchu, Rigoberta. *I, Rigoberta Menchu: An Indian Woman in Guatemala.* Ed. Elisabeth Burgos-Debray. Trans. Ann Wright. London: Verso, 1984.

Mukherjee, Bharati. *Jasmine.* New York: Grove P, 1989.

My Beautiful Laundrette. Dir. Stephen Frears. Irvine, CA: Karl Lorimar Home Video, 1986.

My Left Foot. Dir. Jim Sheridan. New York: HBO Video, 1990.

Nolan, Christopher. *Under the Eye of the Clock: The Life Story of Christopher Nolan.* NY: St. Martin's Press, 1987.

O'Brien, William J., ed. *Splendor and Wonder: Jesuit Character, Georgetown Spirit, and Liberal Education.* Washington, D.C.: Georgetown UP, 1988.

Ong, Walter J., S.J. *Frontiers in American Catholicism.* New York: Macmillan, 1957.

Quick, Robert H. *Essays on Educational Reformers.* London: Longmans, Green, 1904.

Sacks, Oliver. *Seeing Voices: A Journey into the World of the Deaf.* Berkeley: U of California P, 1989.

Said, Edward. *After the Last Sky: Palestinian Lives.* New York: Pantheon, 1986.

Scaglione, Aldo. *The Liberal Arts and the Jesuit College System.* Amsterdam: John Benjamins, 1986.

Tan, Amy. *The Joy Luck Club.* New York: Putnam's, 1989.

Trumbo, Dalton. *Johnny Got His Gun.* New York: Bantam, 1984.

Winterson, Jeanette. *Oranges Are Not the Only Fruit.* NP: Grove-Atlantic, 1987.

Chapter 19. Empty Pedagogical Space and Silent Students

Works Cited

Sherwood, John. "How to Escape Teaching Composition." *AAUP Bulletin* 41 (Summer 1954): 282–90.

Chapter 20. The Dilemma of Oppositional Pedagogy: A Response

Notes

1. This charge that "teaching the conflicts" would amount to replacing real politics with a polite debating society for real politics has become the official "line" in some radical circles. Stanley Aronowitz and Henry Giroux, for example, suggest that I would reduce pedagogy to an apolitical and there-fore "lifeless methodological imperative of teaching conflicting interpretations of what counts as knowledge" (82).

2. Lazere has developed a broader statement of his program in "Teaching the Political Conflicts: A Rhetorical Schema."

Works Cited

Aronowitz, Stanley, and Henry A. Giroux. *Postmodern Education: Politics, Culture, and Social Criticism.* Minneapolis: U of Minnesota P, 1991.

Bennett, James R. "Literary Theory and the Bill of Rights." *Arkansas Quarterly* 1.3 (1992): 187–96.

———. "National Power and Objectivity in the Classroom." *College English* 51 (1989): 805–24.

Lazere, Donald. "Teaching the Political Conflicts: A Rhetorical Schema." *College Composition and Communication* 43.2 (1992): 194–213.

Counterstatements

Dixon—Works Cited

Barber, Benjamin R. "America Cuts School." *Harper's Magazine* 287 (Nov. 1993): 39–46.

hooks, bell. *Yearning: Race, Gender, and Cultural Politics.* Boston: South End, 1990.

Wise—Works Cited

Jameson, Fredric. *The Political Unconscious: Narrative as a Socially Symbolic Act.* Ithaca: Cornell UP, 1981.

Caulfield—Works Cited

Bakhtin, Mikhail. *Marxism and the Philosophy of Language. The Rhetorical Traditions: Readings from Classical Times to the Present.* Ed. Patricia Bizzell and Bruce Herzberg. Boston: Bedford, 1990.

Thoreau, Henry David. "Civil Disobedience." *A World of Ideas: Essential Readings for College Writers.* 3rd ed. Ed. Lee A. Jacobus. Boston: Bedford, 1990.

Vygotsky, L. S. *Thought and Language.* Ed. and trans. Eugenia Hanfmann and Gertrude Vakar. Cambridge: M.I.T. P, 1962.

Mazurek—Works Cited

Berlin, James. *Rhetoric and Reality: Writing Instruction in American Colleges, 1900–1985.* Carbondale: Southern Illinois UP, 1987.

Connors, Robert. "Rhetoric in the Modern University: The Creation of an Underclass." *The Politics of Writing Instruction: Postsecondary.* Ed. Richard Bullock and John Trimbur. Portsmouth, NH: Boynton/Cook, 1991. 23–38.

Slevin, James F. "Depoliticizing and Politicizing Composition Studies." *The Politics of Writing Instruction: Postsecondary.* Ed. Richard Bullock and John Trimbur. Portsmouth, NH: Boynton/Cook, 1991. 1–22.

Katz—Works Cited

Graff, Gerald, and Gregory Jay. "Some Questions about Critical Pedagogy." *Democratic Culture* 2 (1993): 3–7.

Hines—Author's Note

I wish to acknowledge my debt to Janice Norton, whose reading of Irigaray's *This Sex Which Is Not One* made this argument possible.

Hines—Works Cited

Althusser, Louis. "Ideology and Ideological State Apparatuses. *Lenin and Philosophy and Other Essays.* Trans. B. Brewster. London: New Left Books, 1977. 127–86.

Irigaray, Luce. *This Sex Which Is Not One.* Ithaca, NY: Cornell UP, 1985.

North, Steven. *The Making of Knowledge in Composition: Portrait of an Emerging Field.* Portsmouth, NH: Boynton Cook/Heinemann, 1987.

Post/face

Works Cited

Bender, John, and David E. Wellbery. "Rhetoricality: On the Modernist Return of Rhetoric." *The Ends of Rhetoric: History, Theory, Practice.* Ed. John Bender and David E. Wellbery. Stanford: Stanford UP, 1990. 3–39.

Brantlinger, Patrick. *Crusoe's Footprints: Cultural Studies in Britain and America.* New York: Routledge, 1990.

Fitts, Karen, and Alan W. France. "Advocacy and Resistance in the Writing Class: The Discovery of Stasis." *Pedagogy in the Age of Politics: Reading and Writing (in) the Academy.* Ed. Patricia Sullivan and Donna Qualley. Urbana: NCTE, 1994. 13–24.

Kennedy, Alan. "Committing the Curriculum and Other Misdemeanors." *Cultural Studies in the English Classroom.* Ed. James A. Berlin and Michael J. Vivion. Portsmouth, NH: Boynton/Cook, 1992. 24–45.

Afterword

Works Cited

Gramsci, Antonio. *An Antonio Gramsci Reader: Selected Writings, 1916–1935.* Trans. Quintin Hoare, Geoffrey Nowell-Smith, John Matthews, and William Boelhower. Ed. David Forgacs. New York: Schocken, 1988.

INDEX

Agger, Ben, 210, 211, 359
Alcoff, Linda, 144, 145, 354
Altered States, 263, 361,
Althusser, Louis, xiii, xv, 232, 233, 238, 314–15, 360, 363
Alvarez, Alexandra, 349
Amott, Teresa L., 344, 345
Anderson, Vivienne, xvi
Anderson, Chris, 348
Annas, Pamela, 140, 143, 348, 354
Ansbro, John, 349
Aronowitz, Stanley, 6, 234, 339, 360, 362
Atkins, C. Douglas, 339, 340
Atwan, Robert, 347, 348

Bailey, Charles, 255, 361
Bakhtin, Mikhail, 83, 158, 295, 349, 356, 363
Baldwin, James, 162, 163, 164, 165, 251–52, 356, 360
Barber, Benjamin R., 290, 363
Barrett, Michele, 235, 360
Barthes, Roland, 17, 18, 34, 342
Bartholomae, David, 99, 351
Bauer, Dale, ix, xvi, 139, 150, 153, 177, 183, 337, 343, 344, 354, 357
Baumlin, James, 344
Beecher, Catharine, 76-77, 346
Belenky, Mary Field, 143, 354
Bender, John, 322-23, 364,
Bennett, James R., 276-77, 279, 280-81, 293–94, 362
Bennett, Larry, xi, 337
Bennett, Tony, 232, 235, 339, 340, 360

Berlin, James A., x, xvi, 60, 157, 161, 164, 177, 182, 219, 301, 337, 344, 345, 356, 357, 358, 363, 364
Berry, Wendell, 80, 346
Berthoff, Ann E., 40, 101, 343
Birmingham Centre for Cultural Studies, 7, 339
Bizzell, Patricia, 99, 174–75, 337, 351, 358
Blanchard, Bob, 179, 358
Blitz, Michael, x, 338, 339, 341
Bloom, Lynn Z., 177, 358
Bodziock, Joseph C., xiv, 39, 326, 327
Boelhower, William, 364
Bolker, Joan, 140, 143, 145, 149–50, 354
Bolter, Jay, 29–32, 342
Bonachea, Rolando E., 255, 361
Bosmajian, Haig, 84, 349
Bourdieu, Pierre, xiii
Branch, Taylor, 87, 90, 349
Brannon, Lil, 157, 357
Brantlinger, Patrick, xiii, 321, 337, 339, 364
Brodkey, Linda, 339, 340
Bromwich, David, 23–24, 342
Bruffee, Kenneth A., 99, 164, 351, 356
Bullock, Richard, x, 337, 358
Burke, Kenneth, 18, 22, 23, 36, 91, 342, 350
Burns, Ken, 161, 162, 163, 164, 356
Bush, George, 197–200
Butler, Judith, 11, 340

Campbell, Joseph, 261, 361
Carey, Archibald, 88, 350

365